Strategic Financial and Investor Communication

C000045429

In today's aggressive marketplace, listed companies can no longer rely on their numbers to do the talking. If companies can't communicate their achievements and strategy, mounting research evidence suggests, they will be overlooked, their cost of capital will increase and stock price will suffer.

In *Strategic Financial and Investor Communication: the stock price story* Ian Westbrook, Principal of Australia's leading independent financial communications firm, argues just this: stock price is more a story than a number. Moreover, the book will teach you how to tell your own story by guiding you through the fast-paced world of financial corporate communication with a professional's pragmatism as well as academic rigour.

Whether you're a student or a professional of PR, investor relations or corporate communications, this much-needed guide will teach you how to tell a compelling story about your company that the stockbroker, fund manager and corporate media cannot ignore.

Ian Westbrook is Principal of Westbrook Financial Communications, Australia, and a part-time lecturer at the University of Sydney, having established the Financial and Investor Communication unit of study for postgraduate students in the Department of Media and Communications.

In this new work on the vital linkage between communication and stock market price Ian Westbrook challenges a number of old assumptions and provides clear evidence that the future for corporate investment lies in the vertical integration of communication throughout the firm.

It is at once a good read and a significant contribution to the theory and practice of financial communication. Mr Westbrook has taken a considered approach to the vexed issue of how, why and when CEOs should engage with stakeholders: he provides timely advice on dealing with provocateurs such as news media, citizen journalists and activist investors.

His description of "proxy fights" in which corporations allow others, particularly media, to become leading actors is engaging while the case studies he has chosen provide a well-balanced complement to the processes and theories set out in a highly readable narrative. This book should be a "must read" for everyone in the corporate world, or as Mr Westbrook argues, engaged in the corporate "stakeholder" world rather than the "shareholder" world.

Richard Stanton, Department of Media and Communications,
the University of Sydney, Australia

Westbrook is most instructive and current with best practice and thinking as regards navigating the capital markets. He stresses an understanding of both non-financial and basic elements of the value mosaic and is realistic in his theses, which are well resourced in academic study. Westbrook recognizes that factual information and comparative metrics only tell part of the story ... colour counts. He underscores the importance of communicating with one voice and in a timely manner. This text is for the serious student of capital and value formation. Westbrook digs deep into the underlayment of the art and presents a strong case for his conclusions. This book is a standard-setter for IROs, with valuable lessons.

Robert D. Ferris, Chair, Capital Markets Practice, RF Binder Partners

This outstanding book will be a great resource for students, scholars and practitioners as it combines solid theoretical background with very practical and current examples from the world of financial communications and investor relations.

Alexander V. Laskin, PhD, Associate Professor and Director of Graduate Studies,
Department of Public Relations, Quinnipiac University, USA

Strategic Financial and Investor Communication

The stock price story

Ian Westbrook

Routledge
Taylor & Francis Group

LONDON AND NEW YORK

First published 2014
by Routledge
2 Park Square, Milton Park, Abingdon, Oxon OX14 4RN

and by Routledge
711 Third Avenue, New York, NY 10017

Routledge is an imprint of the Taylor & Francis Group, an informa business

British Library Cataloguing in Publication Data
A catalogue record for this book is available from the British Library

Library of Congress Cataloguing in Publication data
Westbrook, Ian.
  Strategic financial and investor communication: the stock price story / Ian Westbrook.
    pages   cm
  Includes bibliographical references and index.
  1. Corporations–Public relations.   2. Corporations–Investor relations.
  3. Stocks–Prices.   4. Business communication.   5. Public relations–
  Management.   I. Title.
  HD59.W43 2014
  659.2′85–dc23
  2013037909

ISBN: 978-0-415-81205-4 (hbk)
ISBN: 978-0-415-81206-1 (pbk)
ISBN: 978-0-203-06951-6 (ebk)

Typeset in Times New Roman
by Out of House Publishing

To Owen

Contents

Illustrations

Figures

Tables

Preface

The theme of this book is that, for stock exchange listed companies, communication counts.

Over the past few decades in the area of media and investor relations, there has been a revolution in communications technology and yet it is striking that one thing has not changed.

That issue is an ongoing debate among stock market participants and listed companies about the value of communication and whether it has any direct effect on stock price. One critical view is summed up in the expression that the "numbers speak for themselves", effectively meaning that all investors need do is analyse financial information, making any other communication virtually superfluous.

At the opposite extreme is a view from those with a vested interest in communication, who have long claimed it has substantial value. As evidence they point to media clips, stockbroker reports, increasing numbers of shareholders in a company and a buoyant stock price. As part of their salesmanship they say – well, of course – all this has come about because of a successful communications programme.

There are four things wrong with this argument. First, is a confusion of linking outcomes with effort with no substantiation of a causal link. Second, is a preparedness to see communication as a total answer, without due recognition of other influences on stock price. Third, is lack of appreciation from the presenters of this "evidence" that the market and those paying for the outcomes are not totally convinced by their claims. Fourth, despite a growing body of academic research and development of theoretical work on the communication of information, and its value in the marketplace, there is little attempt by practitioners to link with this theory in substantiating their efforts.

Despite varying views about the value of communication, many large companies invest in it and have departments devoted to it. In fact, it would seem unusual if they did not, they would be the odd ones out. They have large numbers of shareholders and contend with a powerful investment community and media that take an interest in what they are doing. The importance and vocal nature of these stakeholders demand that companies be prepared to respond to them. For companies that are not so large, the extent of investment in communication can be variable and in some cases for smaller companies, non-existent.

Irrespective of the size of a company, there remains an equivocation among many about whether communication does genuinely deliver what its proponents claim. While this question has not been satisfied to a widely appreciated extent, there have been many books that have covered the areas of media and investor relations. There are "how to" books that lay out the tools and mechanics of helping listed companies communicate, there are books on the theory of communication and there is much work in applied finance about the impact of information on market prices.

This book seeks to bring these strands together in substantiating the value of corporate communication in the marketplace. A unifying idea to achieve this is that of story, the way in which corporations communicate to their stakeholders and have them understand what drives their endeavours. The structure of the book and sequence of its argument parallels a course developed by the author for postgraduate students at the University of Sydney. The course is titled Financial and Investor Communication.

One writer, in discussing the idea of rhetoric, used the phrase that "truths do not have legs", since they need people to take them to people, in the form of communication. In applying this to financial and investor communication, the extension of this is that facts and numbers might be self-evident truths but, without a narrative to make sense of them, they are isolated, historic and open to varying interpretations. The intention behind this book is to show how to give legs to the facts and figures of listed company information by linking them to the persuasive power of story. The book brings together elements of theory from communication, public relations and applied finance as well as research evidence of communication being a powerful influence on stock price. The outcome, as indicated by the book's subtitle, is the stock price story, in which the basis for a company's stock price is seen to be more of a story than a number.

Acknowledgements

Some of the case studies in this book include illustrations, which have been reproduced with kind permission from Berkshire Hathaway, Brambles Limited, Fairfax Media Limited, QBE Insurance Group Limited and Stockland Limited. The case study on Enron relies on excellent research by DM Boje, CL Gardner and WL Smith.

The CAM Commerce case study was written by Geoff Knapp, with this version abbreviated from a longer article he wrote, and is reproduced with his permission. The original case study was helpfully supplied by John Mattio of New York headquartered investor relations firm, MZ Group.

James Hall, senior director, investor relations and corporate affairs, Brambles Limited, kindly agreed to be interviewed for the book, with the interview appearing as a case study. James was also generous with his time in contributing a guest lecture on his role in investor relations as part of the University of Sydney course that derives its content from this book.

In representing a crossover between finance and communication, the content of the book reflects aspects of my career path over the years, with its many mentors along the way. In investment banking, mentors included the late David Clarke, Mark Johnson, Tony Berg, Peter McGovern, the late Will Buttrose and the late Ken Gourlay. My friend and colleague from those days, David Waghorn, provided a suggestion that became the book's sub-title. The late Don Wilson, a talented writer, financial analyst and co-founder of Australia's first financial public relations firm, taught me a vast amount about financial communication. Along the way there have been many generous clients who have helped refine my thinking about corporate stories. My long-time friend from the world of journalism, senior Fairfax writer and author in his own right, Brian Robins, provided generous encouragement. Rod Gillespie, from Gillespie Advertising, kindly contributed an artwork suggestion that became the cover for the book.

When I explored an interest in teaching at university, Dr Richard Stanton, Senior Lecturer in the Media and Communications Department at the University of Sydney, provided an opportunity. He also encouraged me in the establishment of the unit of study, Financial and Investor Communication, an elective course in the Master of Strategic Public Relations degree. Richard helped with gaining approval for the subject, encouraged me to write a book for the course and assisted in finding a publisher. I greatly appreciated the enthusiasm of my first batch of students who provided a positive reaction to the course content.

I have appreciated the support provided by my publisher, Routledge, and the assistance of Amy Laurens, Rosemary Baron and Nicola Cupit.

The writing and finalization of the manuscript could not have taken place without the generosity of spirit of my wonderful family, especially my wife Heather, who took time to read and provide comment on the content. My friend, former investment banker and now art business entrepreneur, Raj Nanda, also contributed valuable feedback on the manuscript. My colleague, Marcha van den Heuvel, not only took time to read the manuscript but also took care of business when I was diverted on writing, teaching and marking tasks.

During the writing of the book, I was inspired by the brave fight my nephew, Owen Denoon, waged against a deadly form of cancer. His stamina, courage and positive attitude were something I will always admire and I dedicate the book to him.

Introduction

As the stock exchange listed company has evolved, so too has the amount of legislation and regulation governing the way companies provide information. Information is how investors and many other stakeholders form a view about a company, its prospects and progress. These stakeholders can be many, from employees to customers, shareholders, the investment community, media and bankers. For companies listed on stock exchanges, information provided is often referred to as "disclosure", since it may have an impact on a company's stock price. Information also takes many forms, from accounting numbers to announcements about achievements and descriptions of activities and various corporate endeavours.

One of the themes of this book will be to explore the extent to which information equates with communication, since there is a difference between the two terms. Each day across stock exchanges around the world, huge volumes of information are released by companies, with a lot of it just absorbed into databases that record companies simply meeting their reporting obligations, and only a fraction of it being picked up by the media or focused on by investors. Does this matter and is it really relevant to a corporation's stakeholders?

There are a number of strands to answering this question which demonstrate that it does matter and that communication is vital in a company progressing. This book will bring together various elements of those strands.

Communication theory

A starting point is to consider aspects of communication theory. There is not a unified body of work that spells out communication theory, especially as it applies to corporate communication. However, there are many influences. Some trace the origins of the importance of communication to the ideals of discourse presented by the ancient Greek philosophers Plato and Aristotle. For them, the art of discourse had three components, logic, grammar and, in particular, rhetoric. Rhetoric was the basis for developing argument and persuasion. In a corporate communications context, rhetoric forms a link between information and how it is communicated. Rhetorical argument brings together three components to be successful, termed by the Greeks as logos, pathos and ethos, meaning a reliance on the logic and reason of an argument, an appeal to the emotions of the audience and a connection with the authority and honesty of the presenter. In the language of corporate communication, equivalents of these components could be considered as content, style of presentation and reputation. Simply providing corporate information to the marketplace quite often does not match these ancient ideals that lead to persuasion to a point of view or communication of an impression of how a company might perform in the future.

While it is a long distance in an overview of communications theory to leap from the ancient Greek Lyceum to our current electronic era, it is during the twentieth century that we have seen corporations add public relations departments and academics look back on the influences that have formed the development of communication. In a sense, the discipline of public relations has always been with us. As one writer, Sheehan, has put it:

> It is difficult when dealing with something as pervasive as public relations to find a commencing date. If we extrapolate the interpretative notion based on something as fundamental as persuasion it could be argued, as some authors have, that: the Epistles of St Paul were a successful public relations campaign; the image making methods of Phillip II of Macedonia, juxtaposing his statue with those of the gods, was a foray into image management and that the "Monuments and other art forms of the ancient world ... Pyramids, statues, temples, tombs, painting, announce the early divinity of rulers" means public relations is as old as civilisation itself.[1]

In the corporate world, public relations theorist James Grunig, in the 1980s traced the evolution of the discipline from an early twentieth-century focus on achieving publicity, to a more sophisticated two-way engagement with stakeholders today. Analysis of the processes of implementing communications strategy by Vincent Hazleton has shown how the characteristics of stakeholder groups also influence the form of engagement between them and corporations. Another development in communications theory has been analysis by sociologist Leon Mayhew, who has described the evolution of spin in the political and corporate worlds, seeing it as a corruption of the ideals of discourse laid down by the Greek philosophers. In the post-modern era, communication theory links language and the competition for capital.

While the world of corporate communication is hardly immune from the processes of spin, its effectiveness would be questioned by a number of theorists in the area of applied finance. A prominent theory of the past few decades has been the efficient market hypothesis, developed by Nobel Prize-winning economist Eugene Fama in the 1970s. While there are a number of assumptions around the theory, it essentially asserts that markets are efficient, reacting quickly to any new information about listed companies, with this being reflected in stock prices. Active investors have challenged this theory, arguing that fundamental analysis of company numbers can unearth stocks where appreciation of the value of a company's public information has not been widespread.

Despite where one's sympathies might lie with these arguments, there is agreement in the financial marketplace that information has value. From the perspective of communication theory, there are also strongly held views that how information is communicated is also influential, bearing out the value of the corporate equivalent of logos, pathos and ethos.

The information age

In the current era, it is often said we live in an information age. Information is everywhere, increasingly evident as traditional media is facing challenges from a myriad of online sources. In this competitive environment, information released by stock exchange-listed companies that is simply in conformity with regulation, and not seeking to communicate a perspective of its relevance, will be overlooked, the tenets of the efficient market hypothesis notwithstanding. In this respect, communication has to be distinguished from spin and marketing information at one extreme and, at another extreme, accounting numbers released with minimal accompanying explanatory context.

This is where the concept of the corporate story becomes relevant. When applied effectively, the corporate story is an outcome of the principles of theory in communication and applied finance. It reflects a process of converting information into relevant communication, by giving it a context and purpose as well as enhancing understanding for receivers of the communication.

The research that validates this assertion actually highlights the distinction between going through the motions of regulated corporate disclosure, that is simply providing information, and making an added effort at communication, by providing explanation and context. The research also shows that dissemination of that communication, beyond the regulated exchange to relevant stakeholders, which is the function of investor relations, actually produces tangible benefits. The research is the outcome of work in several countries by a number of academics who have analysed the connection between stock price and communication. Where this communication includes effort at engaging with stakeholders and achieving media coverage around disclosure, there are notable results that contribute positively to stock price growth. As a general conclusion, there is the idea that familiarity breeds investment.[2] As the media, investors and the investment community come to know a company better, and understand its operations and direction, they are more likely to invest. Other research points to increased analyst coverage, higher turnover, closer buy-sell spreads and increases in shareholder numbers as outcomes of going beyond information disclosure by making added communication effort.

These research outcomes tend to confirm the strategies larger corporations have implemented over some decades. The function of corporate public relations has become established and part of management, with the function itself moving on from, to use Grunig's description, "press agentry", to a more widespread engagement with stakeholders. From the stock market perspective, there has been a broader understanding of the range of stakeholders relevant to a listed company. Shareholders are actually in two categories, retail and wholesale, requiring different forms of engagement, and there are also analysts, journalists and market commentators, all representing differing stakeholder interests. As management strategy has evolved as a discipline, so too has communication. Most companies that take the communications process seriously have strategies for engagement with stakeholders and generally work towards these stakeholders acquiring a better understanding of what companies are trying to achieve.

The crossover

While process is important, accompanied by a wider appreciation of the value of communication, the three components of the Greek ideals of discourse remain critical to corporate communication being effective. In corporate terms, content, style and reputation are ultimately the determinants of whether communication is deemed credible by stakeholders on the receiving end. A relevant distinction in corporate and investor communication is that stakeholders may be well-informed to begin with, so content, style and reputation are not straightforward issues. Communication in this sphere means appreciating the differences between the languages of marketing and spin while at the same time making disclosure information educational. Thus begins the process of developing a corporate story that encompasses facts, numbers and narrative.

Another distinction from other forms of communication in developing a corporate story is that its content is not entirely derived from being inward-looking, as, for example, marketing communication tends to be. Just as the ideals of discourse are oriented towards persuasion, the corporate story is more persuasive if it develops an outward perspective, placing a company in the context of its marketplace. Stakeholder perspectives also influence the content of the story. As investors are increasingly concerned about the role in society corporations are prepared to play, they have developed criteria about companies that influence their investment decisions and consequently they expect to hear from companies about these issues. These criteria go by varying initials and include corporate social responsibility (CSR) and environment, social and governance (ESG), reflecting the extent to which companies are pursuing these goals in addition to providing financial returns to shareholders.

Sometimes these issues impinge on a company's reputation, an area that has become a growing concern in the field of public relations. Reputation is relevant to all a company's stakeholders, not just those with a financial perspective. A reputation is something that is earned, whether good or bad, but it comes about not just from a company's actions but also from communication about those actions.

The three elements of ideal discourse in the corporate sphere – content, style and reputation – are not achieved from a minimalist meeting of the statutory obligations of disclosing information. That approach reflects an increasingly out-of-date cliché of the stock market, that "the numbers speak for themselves", reflecting the view that financial performance can be a substitute for needing to engage with stakeholders. That approach cannot survive in the more competitive communication age, especially in financial markets where investors every day are being informed about market events and their implications for listed companies. A step towards more effective communication in the current era is for companies to weave together facts, numbers and narrative as they convey their own story in a way that stakeholders find credible. The subtleties of developing this corporate story, shaped for differing groups of stakeholders in the context of financial markets, is the theme of this book.

The first two chapters explore the theoretical framework. Chapter 1 covers aspects of theory that relate to communication and public relations, focusing on corporate communication. In Chapter 2, we encapsulate relevant aspects of theory around management and financial markets as they connect with corporate communication. Chapter 3 embarks on the idea of storytelling and how this relates to corporations. Chapter 4 brings together the links between corporate strategy and communication strategy, with the notion that the corporate story is the ultimate expression of corporate strategy. In this chapter we also look at research evidence which substantiates that communication has an impact on stock price. Chapter 5 adopts the vantage point of investment perspectives on building a corporate story and how this relates to information about a corporation as well as examining the elements that key stakeholders want to hear. Chapter 6 illustrates how words and numbers combine in a corporate story, highlighting key numbers that are relevant in this process. In Chapter 7 we consider aspects of disclosure and the communications context around information that is given to financial markets and key stakeholders. Chapter 8 explains the broader financial market context in which corporate communication takes place. Chapters 9, 10 and 11 cover communication with the three key stakeholders in financial and investor communication – the investment community, the media and shareholders. Chapter 12 looks at the main transactions and issues in which corporate communication and telling the corporate story have a significant influence, traversing mergers and acquisitions, the initial public offer of shares to the public and listing on a stock exchange, and crisis. Chapter 13 examines the role and responsibilities of a chief communications officer or investor relations officer. In the concluding Chapter 14, we bring together six key arguments that link theory and practice for financial and investor communication.

The theme

In his 2012 report on UK equity markets, Professor John Kay highlighted the problem of short-termism and argued that a major culprit was an exaggerated faith in the efficient-market hypothesis. In his view, this had led to undue reliance on information disclosure as a response to divergences in knowledge, producing large quantities of data, much of which was of little value. To turn this around, Kay argued for companies to disengage from managing short-term earnings expectations and to institute high quality, succinct narrative reporting.[3]

This book takes up that theme of giving importance to narrative, with it being a vehicle for converting disclosure into communication and for companies to develop a longer-term perspective for investors.

Notes

1 Sheehan, M, "Australian Public Relations Campaigns: A Select Historical Perspective 1899–1950", Conference Paper, Australian Media Traditions, 2007, www.csu.edu.au/special/amt/publication/sheehan.pdf
2 Huberman, G, "Familiarity Breeds Investment", November 1999, http://ssrn.com/abstract=199314 or http://dx.doi.org/10.2139/ssrn.199314
3 Kay J, *The Kay Review of UK Equity Markets and Long-Term Decision-Making, Final Report*, July 2012, pp 9–10

1 Applying theory from communication

A longstanding question in many disciplines is why there is a need to cover theory when it is really the practice and practicalities that people want to know about. Surely whether one is a surgeon, pilot or listed company managing director, it is how to perform those jobs that counts rather than some theory that might relate to abstract elements of the task. While that view has many proponents, it is theory that allows a reflection on the ideals of tasks and effectiveness in undertaking them, enabling a considered application of established thought from a variety of disciplines over many years from researchers, writers and academics.

In the area of corporate communication, especially financial communication, there are many sources of theory that have relevance for the practical. Without an appreciation of them, there is no structure or template for implementing ideal processes that become a guide to action.

While there are many sources of theoretical background, the purpose here is to summarize key influences in the one place and draw from them their relevance to corporate communication. In bringing together theoretical underpinnings from the areas of communication, public relations and applied finance, there is the establishment of a bridge that guides corporations in reaching out to the influences on their stakeholders. If corporations are to form a view about how to communicate ideally, there is supporting strength from underlying theory and research that substantiates the value of following these ideals. The sequence of the theoretical influences covered is to look at the processes of rhetoric as they apply in corporate communication, how the theory of public relations developed, aspects of applied finance theory that relate to the value of information in the marketplace and various models and influences on the processes of corporate communication. Following a survey of theory from communication we examine theoretical influences on communication from a financial perspective

Evolution of rhetoric

The origins of rhetoric can be traced back to Greece in the fifth century BC and the public, philosophical discussions of Socrates, Plato and Aristotle. A contemporary of these three, Isocrates, is also noteworthy and has been the subject of recent examination because of a closer connection between his ideals of rhetoric and their application to today's modern version of public relations.[1] These philosophers have had a permanent influence, not only on the development of philosophy over the centuries but also on providing organized thought about public presentation of information. It was Cicero, the Roman orator in the first century BC, who said of Socrates that he "first called philosophy down from heaven, set her into the cities, introduced her into men's homes, and compelled her to investigate life and customs, good and evil".[2] By this he was meaning that philosophy and the rhetorical way in which it was presented had ethical and practical applications for how people should relate to each other. From this broader perspective of making philosophy and rhetoric applicable to daily life, there are influences on how corporate communication has developed. Socrates was renowned not only for applying rhetorical principles in developing philosophical points of view but also for what has become known as the Socratic Method. The Socratic Method describes a form of discussion between individuals with differing views based on asking and answering questions to stimulate critical thinking. By laying out a thesis and then considering an antithesis, a path was established towards achieving a synthesis of ideas. The Socratic Method has many applications today in modern management practices. While the idea that "knowledge is power" has become a common expression, the Socratic Method in corporations can become a way of sharing knowledge, learning through dialogue and reaching consensus.[3]

For the Greek philosophers, where discussion took place in public forums, the three ideals of public discourse that evolved were grammar, logic and rhetoric. It was rhetoric that became the art which has guided public speaking over the centuries and, just as in ancient times, there have been differing views since then about the way rhetoric is used. While Plato was critical of elements of rhetoric, especially when it involved deceit in persuading the ignorant to a point of view,[4] it was his student Aristotle who gave structure to a more scientific application of rhetoric in discourse. He defined rhetoric as having three components that guided a persuasive appeal to audiences – logos, pathos and ethos. Establishment of these three aspects of rhetoric – which translate as reason, emotion and character – have been a guide to education and public speaking ever since. In a sense, individuals engage in the process of rhetoric any time they speak or seek to impart meaning to their words. A philosophical argument that has continued over the years essentially perpetuates the differences between Plato and Aristotle, which is the relationship between rhetoric and truth, or the extent to which rhetoric reflects knowledge across the subjects it covers or merely shapes an argument intended to persuade.

Plato believed that rhetoric and persuasion should only be used "in the service of absolute truth".[5] An exception he made was for rulers, for whom he believed it was acceptable to lie if it was for the benefit of the state and its subjects.[6] For Aristotle, rhetoric was the available means of persuasion, with one critic describing this as subordinating truth to victory, since it involved using persuasive techniques to hide the weaknesses of one's own argument, while diverting the audience's attention away from the strength of an opponent's argument.[7] Representing an alternative to both these perspectives is Isocrates, whom Cicero described as "the father of eloquence" and "the Master of all rhetoricians".[8] For Isocrates, rhetoric was the discourse of responsible citizenship, built on a combination of core values of justice and moderation. Far from relying totally on persuasion or absolute truth, Isocrates saw rhetoric as "a community-building discipline in a world that didn't always offer Platonic certainty".[9] In this sense, Isocrates was prepared to assume a moral responsibility as well as ethics in the art of persuasion.

There are a number of links between these ancient practitioners of rhetoric and the modern practice of corporate communication. Logos refers to the use of reasoning to construct an argument. It is strengthened by the addition of statistics, facts and logic.

While pathos refers to emotional appeals to affect an audience's judgement, in business it is more effectively applied through the processes of metaphor and storytelling, so that arguments are constructed to evoke a connection with the speaker's perspective. Ethos refers to character and credibility, with authority coming from a speaker's title, qualifications and expert references used to support the speaker's point of view. All these characteristics have relevance in financial and investor communication when the terms are given a corporate translation, with logos becoming content, pathos becoming style of presentation, recognizing what an audience wants, and ethos being reputation, of speaker and corporation. In this way, development of a corporate story, with narrative binding together facts and numbers, becomes a corporate equivalent of rhetorical persuasion.

While rhetoric has been part of education over many centuries, it is revived in the modern era through language and persuasion being increasing features of our current media-centric consumption of information. There are also other classical influences that are relevant. The Roman orator, Cicero, argued that successful orators should know not only the specifics of their own argument, which he termed the hypothesis, but also the more general principles from which the argument is derived, the thesis. In a corporate sense, the industry and market context around a corporate story is an important factor in adding independent objectivity to its explanation and, in the process, making it more compelling.

Common to the Greeks and Romans was the importance of the structure of a rhetorical argument. It was Cicero in the mid-first century BC who set out what has become known as the five canons of an effective rhetorical argument and these principles have not only remained influential over the centuries but apply equally today to corporate communication. The first canon is that of invention, involving not only an investigation of the topic itself but also the needs and beliefs of the audience. This leads to the second canon in which an argument is developed, structured and supported by evidence to provide proof of the argument, with these combined in a way considered to achieve the greatest effect. Next for consideration is the style of presentation to be given, relating to words and sentences and also what is most likely to be effective for the audience that will be listening or reading. The fourth canon was called memory, recognizing that most speeches in that earlier era were not read, with effectiveness enhanced by the process of memory, as the speaker recalls and implements a persuasive argument. Similarly today, the most effective corporate presentations today are those that are not overly reliant on PowerPoint slides. The final step in presenting a rhetorical argument is actual delivery, requiring consideration of voice, intonation and volume as the presentation traverses its various phases.[10] While these five canons of rhetoric may have been developed many centuries ago, there are many corporate presentations today, as well as written annual reports and news releases, that would benefit from a reminder about whether these key persuasive elements are present.

Over the years as rhetoric has gone in and out of favour as an area of study, there have been warnings from many writers not to let style overcome substance. Francis Bacon, a literary and scientific scholar in the sixteenth century, became concerned that scientific discovery had become too reliant on Aristotle's observations from many centuries before. He was wary of conclusions reached by rhetorical argument rather than closer observations of nature, facts and simpler descriptions of these things.[11] The evolution of writers pursuing plain speech and the vernacular has followed trends in literature, from Chaucer to the modern day, but it has not necessarily dislodged the place of rhetoric.

Modern applications of rhetoric

In the modern era, the concept of rhetoric has been extended to cover the visual, which is prevalent in advertising, especially in the area of behavioural research that guides the presentation and style of products to meet the subconscious needs of consumers. Another modern application of rhetorical concepts sprang from Marshall McLuhan whose dictum, "the medium is the message", highlighted the idea that content was less important than the medium that carried the content. A common illustration of his view is that the message of a news broadcast about an unpleasant crime was less about the story itself, than the effect on public attitudes as this sort of story was watched on television in the family home. McLuhan argued that since humans are essentially communicative animals, it is the technologies of communication that influence how people think and form views and are subject to persuasion. He pointed to three eras of communication technology – from the phonetic alphabet to the printing press and then twentieth century communication technology – which connected communication with all human senses.[12] Another twentieth century writer who revisited the place of rhetoric in society was Lloyd Bitzer who coined the term "rhetorical situation", referring to a public issue arising, such as health care, in which the government of the day needed to apply rhetoric to influence public opinion towards change. Bitzer contends that it is the situation that defines how rhetoric is applied, rather than principles defining a rhetorical argument.[13] One of Bitzer's critics several decades later, Richard Vatz, described this form of public rhetoric more as competitive persuasion, which was open to manipulation through agenda-setting and framing issues with spin.[14]

Another modern writer who applies rhetoric to corporate communication and sees it as a theoretical basis for public relations is Robert Heath. He describes rhetoric in a few forms – at one end of a spectrum is rhetoric as an ideal search for truth through discourse while at the other end is rhetoric as a manipulative process. The best form of rhetoric, he says, in sharp contrast to those two extremes, is to use "discourse to seek the best available truth and set of value priorities to help the community of interested parties to make sound and principled decisions".[15] He highlights the value of rhetoric when corporations are faced with a "legitimacy gap between what they do and what their markets and publics expect".[16] In these circumstances there can be competing narratives, with the corporate perspective challenged by outsiders, leading to a corporation needing to communicate its stewardship effectively to achieve concurrence with its standards of corporate social responsibility. Heath sees a parallel here with the first century Roman rhetorician Quintilian, who described the effective citizen as the good person who could speak well, with this being reflected in the idea of a corporate citizen.[17] Simple explanations of the corporate perspective are informative but can be made more persuasive by encompassing strategic positions, such as differentiation, association with the general ideas of stakeholders or identifying with independent experts. While facts might substantiate a corporate perspective, rhetoric allows advocacy around the facts: "Truths cannot walk on their own legs. They must be carried by people to other people. They must be explained, defended, and spread through language, argument, and appeal."[18]

Heath also notes the link between corporate rhetoric and the corporate narrative, with the organization as storyteller:

> Stories are the eternal and compelling substance of human communication. They
> help people to achieve shared knowledge, identity, and practices that allow for a

workable society. People not only tell stories, but also frame their actions, opinions, and lives in narrative form or substance. They frame one set of stories in terms of other stories. Those stories either agree with and complement or compete with and challenge one another.[19]

From a corporate perspective, stories need to be faithful to facts and represent real-life experience if they are to be persuasive. They also need to be consistent on several levels, from the corporation connecting with external society and internally, especially for managers who actually become the storytellers. Only by displaying these characteristics will the rhetoric of corporate storytelling reach resolution with varying stakeholder perspectives.[20]

In applying these concepts from rhetoric over the years to corporate communication by listed companies, there are a number of signposts towards effective communication. The three basic concepts of Aristotelian rhetoric – logos, pathos and ethos – are present in their corporate equivalents of content, style and reputation. The ongoing shadow cast over rhetoric, that it can be associated with a deceitful form of persuasion, can also be seen in the caution exercised by the investment community that has seen many corporate failures over the years and become wary of attempts at having glossy style overtake substance. However, applying rhetoric with a corporate definition of pathos, which recognizes those audience attitudes by presenting a story in appropriate ways, can be influential in having investors understand businesses and gain a broader appreciation of a company's value.

An effective investment presentation, including numbers and statistics, strengthens the objectivity or logos of the rhetoric. The ethos of presentations can be reinforced if presenters of this numerical component are chief financial officers, with their title adding credibility to the explanation of content. Providing a broader context beyond a company, covering its industry, markets, competitors and external influences on its business, highlights corporate reputation objectively, adding further to the logos of information and making it more convincing than a presentation totally focused on an individual company.

Mayhew and his tokens of rhetoric

One critique of how the principles of rhetoric and other aspects of communication have been corrupted in the modern era has been made by the American sociologist Leon Mayhew. His argument also has relevance for corporate communication. In his book *The New Public*[21] and other writings, Mayhew is critical of political communication in the latter part of the twentieth century, seeing the manipulation of public opinion as a betrayal of the ideals of democracy and how communication should be conducted in the public sphere. His criticism is of the shallowness of many political views, a number of which are not grounded in what might be considered widespread opinion, and the use of market research and spin to develop and promote these views for personal political advancement. His critique of these trends is based on comparing them with the ideals of rhetoric and the views of twentieth century writers Jürgen Habermas and Talcott Parsons, both of whom, while analysing society differently, developed principles of democratic structure. Mayhew's critique is worth summarizing since it also contributes to a theoretical basis for developing a model of effective corporate communication.

Mayhew's views originated when he was watching progress of a United States presidential campaign and wondering how what he was witnessing fitted with notions of how a democratic society should work. He felt it was reasonable to believe that in today's mass society, the public was not really open to manipulation by elites, that the public was quite capable of reinterpreting the views of elites, and that there was an equal and reverse flow of communication between the public and leaders.[22]

What Mayhew really decided he was witnessing in the campaign was the domination of public persuasion by professional communicators who were actually eroding a more genuine and widespread public opinion. Supporting the persuaders was market research that was providing information about what was likely to prove persuasive. From this perspective, genuine public opinion was losing its social moorings. In its place grew a new version of public opinion, one not representative of the masses but a product manufactured from market research, which had demonstrated it would be politically persuasive.[23]

For Mayhew, the traditions of democratic theory rest on properly organized public life, with a public capable of discussing issues and forming a collective will. In the ancient society of Aristotle and Plato, rhetoric was the inescapable medium of public discussion, being the available means of persuasion through which the public was influenced. Public rhetoric was seen as necessary because, while reason could produce conviction, it was persuasion that led to action. For Aristotle and Plato, rhetoric was practiced by people of character who spoke the truth and pursued the right ends. Similarly, in our current Western cultural tradition, a genuine notion of persuasion implies that persuaders must provide good reasons and not simply rely on authority or force. Ideally, we have come to expect reasonable rhetoric, even though this is not often what we observe in the era of political spin.[24]

In arguing public rhetoric was not living up to its ideals, Mayhew brings in the views of Habermas and Parsons to complete his critique. For Habermas, the ideals of public discussion were in forums where views were exchanged reasonably and decisions were the outcome of ethical discourse. This represented a two-way communication, with leaders needing to take into account the views of audiences. To apply this forum model to society today, Mayhew adopts the concept of influence developed by Talcott Parsons. Parsons developed systems theory and for him the medium through which society worked effectively was that of influence, with it having an institutional function. Parsons perceived influence as providing an authority to persuade people in the public sphere, taking him a step beyond Habermas, who relied on pure reason. Parsons identifies stratification in society, with certain people achieving a status based on trust, which gives them authority to persuade public opinion. This public position of trust implies a respect, which in turn reinforces a legitimation of a position of influence, with a position of status conferring prestige.[25]

Mayhew brings together these three concepts of ideal public discussion – rhetoric (Aristotle), reasoned argument in the public sphere (Habermas) and influence (Parsons) as a tool for social analysis. In doing so he forms a template of how society should work, in contrast to the outcomes of research manufactured public opinion. The link between the concepts is the way rhetoric builds solidarity behind an argument presented eloquently in the public sphere. This in turn builds a following behind the person presenting the argument, allowing this person to build and wield influence. Of course this position is stronger if the argument is backed by reason, but in the "new public" this is not always the case. Mayhew quotes Socrates who criticized teachers of rhetoric who sought to win rather than bring enlightenment. Mayhew traces the beginnings of this process entering public life to the advent of market research, initially in advertising and then to the creation of support for political viewpoints.[26]

In advertising, Mayhew identifies the first use of market research in the United States in the 1870s, when an advertising campaign for threshing machines began with research to identify likely purchasers.[27] By the 1930s the technique was entering politics, with it being used to locate likely supporters for points of view, to establish special interest grassroots groups and to use these processes to build campaign funding. Focus groups have become the more modern extension of these research techniques, as they allow pre-testing of opinion on issues and the development of side issues that can categorize opposing candidates and polarize opinion about them. The creation of interest groups adds sophistication to lobbying efforts, moving them away from the older style of who you know to what you know, as information and support for a point of view is built. One outcome of this has been astroturfing, an artificial form of grassroots campaigning since it is the outcome of market research creating an interest group. As techniques become further developed, they pay lip service to aspects of genuine rhetoric, seeking to enhance credibility, not by a genuine influence, but with endorsements and independent corroboration of viewpoints by experts discovered for the purpose.[28]

While Mayhew sees legitimacy in the use of rhetoric in presenting reasoned argument and building support for it to achieve influence, he is critical of the way these ideals have been corrupted in the modern political process. He argues that it leads to a lack of meaningful policy issues on the public agenda, that promoted attitudes do not reflect a widespread solidarity for effective responses to some social issues, that public discourse is too often one-sided, and that challenges to points of view tend to result in spin rather than straightforward answers. Among Mayhew's solutions for this is a return to more widespread public forums, which would allow more genuine challenges to market-researched policy views.[29]

There are a number of parallels with corporate communication in the analysis that Mayhew has developed. Essentially he confirms the value in communication of the principles of rhetoric, reason and influence. This value is enhanced if it is based in genuineness, rather than being the outcome of spin and manufactured opinion. In emphasizing these principles, he is also outlining the process in which rhetoric builds solidarity and influence, a contrast with the perspective of companies letting financial results speak for themselves. A concept developed by Mayhew is that of the tokens of rhetoric, in which symbols can carry meaning. Having accounts audited by an accounting firm with a reliable reputation provides an objective touchstone for trust. The actions of chief executives that reflect integrity are factors in building corporate reputation on which investors can rely. The ability of CEOs to build trust with investors and hold a position of leadership is an outcome of being able to fulfil promises. A position in the media, for performance, achievements and points of view, adds to authority and influence. Companies where a story is easily identified can be simply understood and are more likely to be supported by investors. A preparedness to provide disclosure and be open about corporate performance in forums with which investors can connect is influential in producing an informed market and garnering long-term support. Conversely, reputations built on spin will only have a short time frame as events overtake unfulfilled promises.

As a platform for identifying an effective communications process for listed companies, the concepts developed by Mayhew offer a powerful template.

Evolution of public relations

There are many definitions of public relations, some of them ambitiously lengthy. The Public Relations Society of America has recently settled on a brief encapsulation, giving emphasis to relationships between an organization and its stakeholders:

> Public relations is a strategic communication process that builds mutually beneficial relationships between organisations and their publics.[30]

The Public Relations Institute of Australia tends to focus more on what might be expected as an outcome of public relations in its definition:

> The deliberate, planned and sustained effort to establish and maintain mutual understanding between an organisation (or individual) and its (or their) publics.[31]

One view of public relations in recent decades is that it has evolved into a management discipline, reflecting the importance corporations attach to communication of their worldview. It has also become an academic discipline, leading to the development of various theories around public relations processes and how they are best implemented.

In adopting a broad view of what public relations represents, its origins can be seen as going back centuries, especially if the term is applied retrospectively to successful use of the media to promote personal publicity and implement campaigns. One writer[32] has identified St Paul as one of history's first practitioners of public relations, linking his messianic message with rhetorical training and strategic campaigning, leading another commentator to describe him as "Christendom's first PR agent".[33]

There are a number of competing explanations around when modern public relations began as a profession. One researcher has found the first use of the term by the Association of American Railroads in 1897,[34] while another traced the origins of the first public relations agency established to generate publicity to 1900 in Boston.[35] Issuing the first press release has been attributed to Ivy Lee after the Atlanta train wreck in 1906, and Edward Bernays is often described as the first modern public relations practitioner. This was due to his involvement with President Woodrow Wilson in establishing the Committee on Public Information, which sought to unite public opinion to support American involvement in the First World War. This led to the implementation of a campaign to target audiences with specific messages – techniques that have become the basis of much subsequent public relations work.

The initial advantages of modern public relations at work are often illustrated by the efforts of PT Barnum in the US in the 1870s when he "created a wave of publicity stunts and coverage that made his circus 'The Greatest Show on Earth'".[36] The impetus for public relations being taken up by corporations is attributed to the rapid growth of capitalism in the 1890s, dubbed the age of the "robber barons", when some of their tough attitudes towards employees were shown up in the media by so-called "muckrakers". This led to corporations learning to see the value of cultivating the media through the application of professional public relations techniques, as a way of publicizing the corporate view to counter these accusations. This era of business is often characterized by a quote from businessman William Vanderbilt, who, when asked why he would not build a railroad for public interest instead of profit, responded with "the public be damned".

Case study

LTCM – when Nobel Prize-winners broke the bank

A case of the symbols of rhetoric overcoming investment judgement

> In 1998, Long Term Capital Management (LTCM) had around 200 employees with IQs in the 150s. The employees of LTCM had some of the highest IQs in the US. They each had 15–20 years of experience, worked with their own money, and were good people. However, they almost took down the whole financial system. They became too comfortable and their models did not predict a hiccup like the East Asian currency crisis. Leverage got them into trouble. Stay away from emotions, the crowd, and borrowed money.
>
> Warren Buffett[37]

When Long-Term Capital Management (LTCM) began as an investment fund in 1994 it was on the premise that if you brought together the best and brightest you could beat the market. It was a formula that worked incredibly well for four years, delivering such high returns that it created an aura of invincibility. But when markets turned in 1998, the size of LTCM was so great and its tentacles of liability so all-encompassing, that its potential downfall threatened not only its existence but the whole surrounding financial system.

While the financial story is fascinating, spawning a book (*When Genius Failed*) and a movie (*Trillionaires*), it also has communication implications. It shows the mesmerizing influence of image and the way tokens of rhetoric (a term from Mayhew[38]) added power to reputation and a story of invincibility that made it easy for a company to raise funds for investment and to play down the risks involved. Adding to the power of the story was that LTCM was only available to professional investors, seasoned judges of the risks and rewards of investment markets, who were in awe of the qualifications and reputations of the LTCM team. When the dream unravelled after four years, many lessons were learned, not the least being that perceptions for a time overcame reality.

LTCM was established by John Meriwether, a renowned Wall Street trader who spent the 1980s with investment bank Salomon Brothers. He brought together a team, most with PhDs, to start a new hedge fund intended to be different from anything Wall Street had seen before. The stars of the team were Robert Merton and Myron Scholes, who were co-inventors along with the late Fischer Black of the options pricing model and who in 1997 were jointly awarded the Nobel Prize for Economics. They and their colleagues developed mathematical models intended to point the way towards earning high returns with minimal risk, not based on betting on the direction of markets but on developing ingenious arbitrage plays. Along with the mystique LTCM created from its star-studded team was the novelty of locating its headquarters in Greenwich, Connecticut, distant from the noise of Wall Street.[39]

The fund's initial focus was on convergence arbitrage. A simplified example of this is buying two bonds that would be expected to track each other in the market, betting that the cheaper bond would go up and that the other would go down. Money would be made as the spread narrowed so in theory an investor was protected from changing prices as long as the two varied in the same way. To magnify returns from this type of trade, LTCM took these positions in markets around the world and used large amounts of leverage. It achieved high borrowings against its positions at low cost because it avoided the "haircut", which was extra collateral banks would have commanded, had they not been blinded by the LTCM cast and been investors in the fund themselves.[40] Returns in the first three years were phenomenal, with investors having tripled their money. By this stage, LTCM had raised capital of US$7 billion, against which it had wagered around US$125 billion with an off-balance sheet notional principal commitment through derivatives of more than US$1 trillion.[41]

Towards the end of 1997, convergence arbitrage opportunities began drying up so LTCM turned its focus to stocks, adding several layers of risk in search of higher returns. Its new direction took the fund away from its original area of expertise in bonds. Stocks are less amenable to mathematical analysis than bonds and to achieve high levels of leverage the positions were taken through derivatives that simulated stock movements. Nevertheless, LTCM maintained its model, wagering large amounts on small market movements, with its mass of data reflecting the way assets had moved historically over decades.

In August 1998, markets changed in a dramatic way, with many negative influences happening at once. It was triggered by Russia devaluing the rouble and partially defaulting on rouble denominated debt. The surprise and ramifications for world markets were immense since the Russian economy was not in such bad shape but instead of printing money, the default and temporary blocking of some foreign exchange trades by some Russian banks caused significant losses for many Western banks. This lead to a "flight to quality" around the world, to a greater extent than predicted by LTCM models, as investors panicked and banks wanted more collateral for their exposures. The crisis spread to Asian economies and world stock markets dived. Interest rates moved up, stock and bond prices that were supposed to converge diverged, liquidity dried up and credit spreads rose. By the end of August, LTCM's fund had lost 52 per cent of its 31 December value, its equity level had dropped faster than its assets and its leverage ratio had increased from 27 to 50 to 1. It had taken LTCM four years to reach the pinnacle of respectability and invincibility but in a space of five weeks it all unravelled.[42]

The banks' exposure to LTCM was so large that the US Federal Reserve called them together to develop a rescue plan for LTCM. Liquidation of the fund would have caused billions of dollars of losses and destabilized the financial system. As a rescue plan was being developed, Warren Buffet broke into his holiday on Bill Gates' yacht[43] to make an offer but time was so scarce to get approval for it from counter parties that there was no alternative but for a syndicate of 14 banks with large exposures at stake to step in and take control, allowing LTCM commitments to be met.

Markets recovered by December 1998 and so too did the LTCM portfolio but the idea that genius, and a reputation for it, could beat the market was in ruins.

In contrast to this attitude, when former Wall Street reporter Ivy Lee began his public relations business in 1904, his publicity policy was "the public be informed".[44]

As Edward Bernays expanded his client base in the 1920s and 1930s, he built a following for his view that public relations was an "art applied to science". However, revisionist views of his work in the 1990s described him more as the father of spin, focused on "the art of intentionally manipulating public opinion in support of ... products, services, ideas, or issues without regard for truth or reality".[45]

Another influential figure in public relations who emerged in the 1920s was Arthur W Page who joined AT&T in 1927 with the intention, not of being a publicist but to be involved in communications policy. His philosophy was:

> All business in a democratic society begins with public permission and exists by public approval. If that be true, it follows that business should be cheerfully willing to tell the public what its policies are, what it is doing and what it hopes to do. This seems practically a duty.[46]

Page developed principles for corporate public relations based on frankness between a company and the public, its employees who were required to deal with the public, and the media. Any questioning and criticism from outside the company was to be brought to the attention of management. These became guiding principles in succeeding decades and formed the basis for development of ethics as the public relations profession grew and became organized through codes of practice.

This professional evolution was mirrored in the United Kingdom and other Western economies. In Australia, the origins of public relations activity were similarly identified in the First World War, with information campaigns being used to encourage recruitment and to assist referendum campaigns aimed at achieving compulsory conscription for military service. In the Second World War, General Douglas MacArthur visited Australia with a large public relations entourage, focused not only on publicity, but also the influencing of public opinion for the war effort.[47]

These developments and Page's views coincided with public relations and communication being accepted as part of the senior management of corporations. The importance of this was also highlighted as prominent corporate crises arose, showing the value of communication in contributing to crisis resolution and salvaging reputation. The growth of successful corporations in turn led to a greater appreciation of how communication contributed to a broader understanding that companies also were part of surrounding communities. The disastrous oil spill in Alaska by an Exxon tanker, and Exxon's slow movement towards taking responsibility, is often cited as an example of how things can go wrong if communication is not given a priority. Conversely, the rise and rise of McDonald's around the world is often attributed to the excellence of its public relations efforts in making its golden arches a prominent part of family life

Evolution of public relations theory

The growth of the idea of public relations as a management function has been accompanied by the development of theory around the discipline. In the evolving history of public relations there has been a progression from a singular focus on media relations towards a broader activity of providing information and encouraging discussion with those for whom the information was intended to reach and influence. It is these issues that have inspired the development of public relations theory.

The theorist who has been prominent in the early development of public relations theory is US academic Professor James Grunig through his description of four models of public relations and excellence theory. In their survey of public relations theory, Botan and Hazleton describe the development of theory around the discipline of public relations as having come from a desert in the 1950s to a verdant landscape in the 1980s, with Grunig's work representing a substantial tree that has inspired other growth.[48] In recent years there has been a flowering of other perspectives, leading to one critic classifying Grunig as a representative of a once dominant paradigm now subject to many challenges.[49]

During the 1950s and 1960s, public relations research began as an offshoot of mass communications research. The prevailing view was that the media was all powerful in influencing opinion but subsequent research has led to the conclusion that the media has more powerful effects on what people think rather than what they do.[50] Today's perspective is that the media is not the solution to every public relations problem.

To the emergence of public relations as a management function in the 1950s, Grunig applied organization theory and introduced the idea of symmetrical communication, merging disciplines of management and communication. By way of leading up to this,

Grunig developed four models of public relations and "used the four models both to describe the historical development of public relations in the United States and as a set of ideal types that described typical ways in which contemporary public relations is practiced".[51] Of the four models reflecting this historical progression, the first two represented what Grunig described as one-way communication, since they reflected a corporation disseminating its own views to stakeholders, with the other two being two-way communication, in which stakeholders became more involved in the communications process. The first model he described as press agentry, in which communication was focused principally on the media with a view to gaining publicity for a corporate point of view. The second was the public information model, reflected in corporations issuing press releases and other organizational information. The third model he called two-way asymmetrical communication since it described organizations trying to persuade stakeholders to a corporate point of view. The fourth model, which he viewed as ideal, was two-way symmetrical communication, in which communication with stakeholders was more of a negotiation and conflict resolution process with a view to arriving at mutual understanding.[52]

In 1984, Grunig began a research project to find out how public relations might make an organization more effective and given this, how public relations should be organized and managed to achieve excellence in implementation. The research was across the United States, Canada and the United Kingdom and led to establishment of a theoretical benchmark of what represented excellence in public relations. The study across 5,000 people and more than 300 organizations looked at public relations implementation from the perspectives of individual programmes, the functions performed, how these programmes and functions affected an organization, and how they contributed to the way organizations related to society. It took into account the goals of the programmes, the way they related to surrounding environments and constituencies and the way values were exchanged with those constituencies.[53]

Among conclusions from the research was that public relations contributed most to an organization when it achieved four things. These were: when it reconciled corporate goals with the expectations of strategic constituencies; when it built long-term relationships with those constituencies; when it could be seen to have monetary value; and when people leading the public relations function were senior executives involved in organization goal-setting and in determining who represented strategic constituencies.[54] Grunig believed that his extensive research project determined that the link between effectiveness and excellence in public relations was represented by his fourth model of two-way symmetrical communication.

Grunig concluded that public relations was a unique management function in being able to help an organization interact with social and political components of its environment, especially publics critical to its success. He argued that the value of public relations came from relationships that organizations developed and maintained with strategic constituencies, with the quality of those relationships enhanced more from the behaviour of an organization than from the messages communicators disseminated. It was the value of information that communicators brought in from engagement with stakeholder groups that made relationships more effective from symmetrical communication. As an example, Grunig argued that while some organizations might see activists opposed to them as a threat, organizations that found an effective way of engaging with them were actually developing a competitive advantage.[55]

Two propositions underlying Grunig's original theory have relevance for the practice of financial and investor communication. One is that Grunig believed persuasion was not an ideal characteristic of effective public relations. The other was his view that, in line with his definition of two-way symmetrical communication, there was a fundamental equality of relationship between a corporation and key stakeholders.

Among some of the challenges listed corporations face in developing business strategies that have a long-term perspective is that the value of these strategies needs to be communicated in an environment of short-term fluctuations in economic and stock market conditions. Corporations also confront investors who have short-term perspectives in making investment decisions. In these circumstances, companies need to adopt asymmetrical as well as symmetrical communications strategies. Additionally, they need to apply them with persuasion and education as part of the process of seeking understanding of the corporate perspective. The difficulty of this task can be all the harder if a longer-term perspective needs to be imposed on top of a company's varying financial performance and market fluctuations that influence short-term investment community views. In these circumstances, companies cannot be left without the armoury of persuasion and education, seemingly in contravention of Grunig's original outline of his theory of public relations.

In a subsequent revision of his theory, Grunig recognized a need for reconciling these issues and resolving "the criticism that the symmetrical model forces the organisation to sacrifice its interests for those of the public".[56] His new model, called "Mixed Motive", allowed for a "win-win" zone between organization and stakeholder, which made it acceptable for organizations to pursue enlightened self-interest supported by persuasion.[57]

One critique of Grunig's original model that has relevance for financial and investor communication was from Page and Hazleton[58]. They argued that Grunig was too focused on the corporation's perspective and on how communication should be implemented, a normative view, rather than how communications strategies are actually developed, a positive view. From this perspective, communications strategies should not be fixed, such as in always applying Grunig's fourth model of two-way symmetric communication, but flexible, since it was the situation and stakeholder characteristics that were determinants of the type of communications strategy a corporation might select at a point in time. Too close a reading of Page and Hazleton does not apply comprehensively to financial and investor communication since the corporate perspective is critical. However, their research conclusion, that the characteristics of stakeholder groups are key determinants of the type of communications strategy that corporations might select in relating to that stakeholder group, does apply to a number of corporate issues. Page and Hazleton brought together in their research two aspects of theory around corporate communication, by looking at the functions corporations expect their messages to perform and also the way in which some functions would work better than others, depending on the characteristics of the receivers of those messages.

In relation to receivers of messages, Page and Hazleton discerned four attributes of publics or stakeholders, with these attributes varying according to the extent a stakeholder group was informed or engaged with issues. The four attributes they described as:

- problem recognition;
- level of involvement;
- the extent to which a stakeholder might experience barriers to taking certain actions;
- goal compatibility between corporation and stakeholder group.[59]

In looking at the functions of messages, which they equated with public relations goals or strategies, they identified six differing purposes for messages – to facilitate, inform, persuade, coerce, bargain and solve problems.[60]

The value of the Page and Hazleton research is that it was based on survey responses from public relations practitioners in the United States and showed strong correlations between communications strategy selection being varied and applied according to situation and the attributes of publics. While these correlations seem to work on a general level to inform decision-making in corporate public relations, they are not always applicable to actual issues that might arise in the area of financial and investor communication. The key stakeholders in this area – the investment community, business media and shareholders – are often very well-informed, have a high level of involvement in observing corporate news and information, have similar goals to corporations when it comes to seeing profit growth and do not have any barriers to actions they might take as active stakeholders. Consequently, for corporate communications decision-makers, a number of strategies are needed in relating to these stakeholder groups. At times they need to inform them with objective information, sometimes they need to persuade them and from time to time they might also need to bargain and solve problems together. The Page and Hazleton research is helpful in delineating the idea of the connection between stakeholder attributes and communications strategy selection. In investor relations, where stakeholder attributes tend to be more stable since investors are generally well-informed, good communication requires a higher degree of strategy variability.

Relationships and public relations theory

Aspects of public relations theory covered so far relate in a general sense to various aspects of the message and structure of the sender and receiver process. However, an alternative theory around this process was introduced in the late 1990s and early 2000s by US academic John Ledingham.[61] His theory was based on the nature of the relationship between an organization and its stakeholders. His work evolved from the notion of public relations being a management function and so his view was that an organization with effective public relations is one that attains positive public relationships.[62] By focusing on relationship management, the central function of public relations moves away from communicating specific messages to relationships, with communication being one of the tools by which relationship-building is achieved. This also meant a change in the way public relations outcomes are measured, with communications outputs, such as press clips, being an inappropriate measure and less important than relational or behavioural outcomes.

Among the concepts Ledingham introduced were that relationships between an organization and its publics were important when the actions of either affected the wellbeing of the other and that relationships were effective when there was mutual benefit. Ledingham developed five dimensions to measure the quality of relationships:[63]

- trust, where an organization does what it says it will do;
- openness, where an organization shares its plans for the future;
- involvement, where an organization is involved in the welfare of a community;
- investment, such as in a public's welfare; and
- commitment, where an organization shows concern for the ongoing welfare of a community.

Ledingham's research provided evidence of these five factors being important in an organization achieving consumer satisfaction, and they are equally relevant concepts for corporations in dealing with investors.

Ledingham's work noted that relationships involved interpersonal as well as professional connections and that models of relationships needed to account for how the relationship came into being, how it evolved subsequently and the consequences of this progression. There are also degrees of formalization and complexity of relationships, with a flow of information and resources between an organization and publics being determinants of how relationships progress. Ledingham developed models of how public relations could work, involving research into the characteristics of publics, implementing and evaluating campaigns of engagement with them and adjusting communication to achieve better relationships.[64] His work led to this definition of his relationship theory of public relations:

> Effectively managing organisational relationships around common interests and shared goals, over time, results in mutual understanding and benefit for interacting organisations and publics.[65]

Ledingham's views also describe much of the way investor relations works. For listed companies, dealings with key stakeholders such as the investment community and the media do not involve huge numbers of people, so personal and business relationships can be developed easily. Conversely, shareholder numbers are usually so large that the relationship veers more towards information sharing, except with the larger institutional shareholders where connections can also have a personal dimension.

Contemporary public relations theory and a framework for investor relations

Much of the work around public relations theory that sees public relations as a management discipline, with its focus on symmetrical communication and how corporations can be more effective from their excellence in communication, is part of what Jacquie L'Etang[66] describes as the dominant paradigm. Ledingham, with his focus on relationships, both interpersonal and organizational, and rhetorical approaches are among the newer directions in public relations theory but there are also a number of others.

Postmodern critics have drawn attention to the political component inherent in public relations activity, in that there is a choice of siding with a prevailing political or cultural view or being opposed to it, with public relations practitioners portrayed as the conscience of an organization.[67] Growth of the Internet and social media has also led to a widespread lateral form of communication between targeted publics and others, making symmetrical communication seem redundant. The advent of new media also challenges traditional sender-receiver models as well as concepts such as opinion leaders, third-party endorsement by traditional media, agenda-setting through sponsorship and events and other public relations tactics.[68]

An interesting development of public relations theory has been to place it in the area of sociology. One of the leading writers in this area of linking social theory to public relations is Ihlen, who says that to understand the role of public relations "in building trust or creating mistrust and in developing – or destroying – a company's licence to operate, public relations also needs to be studied as a social phenomenon".[69] Ihlen develops the link between capital and public relations, relying on the work of twentieth century sociologist Pierre Bourdieu, who described three forms of capital in society – economic (relating to money and property), cultural (knowledge, skills, qualifications) and social (connections and membership of groups). From Bourdieu's perspective, capital in society is scarce, in demand and creates differences. So there is competition for it and the extent to which it is possessed is a way of describing power relationships in society. As organizations seek to develop competitive positions and build capital, in its three forms, communication and language are important aspects for Bourdieu in this process. This is the basis for Ihlen seeing public relations as a component in organizations being competitive and explaining the interrelation between the three types of capital and how organizations use and apply them. He does not make the extra link with investor relations but there are strong parallels as communication is a factor in the raising of economic capital and also in explaining to stakeholders how organizations use it, share returns from it and show a social responsibility in how listed corporations act as social citizens.

There are a number of developments and signposts from a selective choice of contributions from public relations and communications theory that have relevance for financial and investor relations. Rhetoric in its pure form of relying on ethos, pathos and logos can be applicable to company CEOs building credibility in the investment marketplace. A descent from these ideals to rhetoric that declines into spin will not build solidarity of support that is critical to providing stock price momentum. While Grunig's original ideal of two-way symmetrical communication may represent excellence in recognizing an equality between corporations and stakeholders in some circumstances, there also needs to be a flexibility in allowing for the attributes of stakeholders and the way situations can require variations in communications strategy. For example, stock analysts have a variety of perspectives on investment analysis, some journalists are closer followers of a sector than others and some retail shareholders are better informed than others, with some being prepared to be activists in opposition to corporations from social and environmental perspectives. In all these circumstances, communication strategies will need to differ, rather than having a uniform corporation worldview. Lateral communication with stakeholders through social media is also an increasingly used component of investor relations, warranting another perspective on communications strategy.

While developments in public relations theory are influential in listed corporations communicating to relevant stakeholders, of equal importance are the influences of management theory, theory from investment markets and applied finance and portfolio theory, which we will explore in the next chapter. These too have an influence in shaping the corporate story.

Notes

1   Marsh, C, *Classical Rhetoric and Modern Public Relations: An Isocratean Model* (Routledge, New York: 2013)
2   Cicero MT, Tusculan Disputations, V, IV, also in Shields, C (ed.), The Blackwell Guide to Ancient Philosophy (Blackwell, Oxford: 2002), www.blackwellreference.com/public/tocnode?id=g9780631222156_chunk_g97806312221566
3   Remenyi, D and Griffiths, P, "The Socratic Dialogue in the Work Place: Theory and Practice", *The Electronic Journal of Knowledge Management* 7 (1), 2009, p 155
4   Marsh (2013), p 6
5   Marsh (2013), p 5
6   Marsh (2013), p 6

7   Marsh (2013), p 7

8   Marsh (2013), p2

9   Marsh (2013), p 8

10 Cicero MT, De Inventione, Book I, VII (CD Yonge translation at http://classicpersuasion.org/
    pw/cicero/dnv1-1.htm) and Cicero MT, De Oratore, Book I, XXI, 142–143 (JS Watson trans-
    lation at http://pages.pomona.edu/~cmc24747/sources/cic_web/de_or_1.htm)

11 Klein, J, "Francis Bacon", in EN Zalta (ed.) The Stanford Encyclopedia of Philosophy
    (Winter 2012 edition), http://plato.stanford.edu/archives/win2012/entries/francis-bacon and
    Wheeler H, "The Semiosis of Francis Bacon's Scientific Empiricism" at www.constitution.
    org/hwheeler/baconsemiosis.htm

12 www.theglobeandmail.com/news/national/the-return-of-marshall-mcluhan/article587143/?
    page=all

13 Bitzer, L, paper presented at Cornell University (1966), www.cwrl.utexas.edu/~davis/crs/
    E398t/Bitzer--Rhetorical%20Situation.pdf

14 Vatz, R, "The Myth of the Rhetorical Situation", *Philosophy & Rhetoric* 6 (3), 1973, pp 154–
    161, www.public.iastate.edu/~drrussel/www548/vatz.pdf

15 Heath, R, "A Rhetorical Approach to Issues Management", in CH Botan and V Hazleton
    (eds), *Public Relations Theory II* (Lawrence Erlbaum Associates, New York: 2006), p 80

16 Heath (2006), p 66

17 Heath (2006), pp 69–70

18 KK Campbell quoted in Heath (2006), p 85

19 Heath (2006), p 89

20 Heath (2006), p 89–90

21 Mayhew, L, *The New Public* (Cambridge University Press, Cambridge: 1997)

22 Mayhew (1997), p ix

23 Mayhew (1997), p ix

24 Mayhew (1997), Ch 2

25 Mayhew (1997), Chs 3 and 4

26 Mayhew (1997), Ch 5

27 Mayhew (1997), Ch 7

28 Mayhew (1997), Ch 8

29 Mayhew (1997), Ch 9

30 PRSA (2011/12), www.prsa.org/AboutPRSA/PublicRelationsDefined

31 PRIA (2012), www.pria.com.au/aboutus/what-is-public-relations

32 Brown, RE, "St. Paul as a Public Relations Practitioner: A Metatheoretical Speculation on
    Messianic Communication and Symmetry", *Public Relations Review* 29, 2003, p 1

33 Vos, TP, "Explaining the Origins of Public Relations: Logics of Historical Explanation",
    Journal of Public Relations Research 23 (2), 2011, p 125

34 Quoted in Sheehan (2007)

35 Vos (2011), p 121

36 Bates, D, "'Mini-Me' History: Public Relations from the Dawn of History", Conference
    Paper, Institute for Public Relations (2006), p 8

37 Tinkle, PA and Buller, PF, "Wisdom from Warren Buffett", *Research in Higher Education
    Journal*, 2011, www.aabri.com/manuscripts/111062.pdf

38 Mayhew, L, *The New Public* (Cambridge University Press, Cambridge: 1997)

39 Lowenstein, R, *When Genius Failed: The Rise and Fall of Long Term Capital Management*
    (Random House, New York: 2001)

40 Editorial review of Lowenstein (2001), www.amazon.com/When-Genius-Failed-Long-Term-
    Management/dp/0375758259/ref=sr_1_4?ie=UTF8&qid=1359697384&sr=8-4&keywords=
    roger+lowenstein#_

41 Jorion, P, "The Story of Long Term Capital Management", *Canadian Investment Review*,
    1999, www.investmentreview.com/print-archives/winter-1999/the-story-of-long-term-capital-
    management-752

42 Jorion (1999)

43 Editorial review of Lowenstein (2001)

44 Bates (2006), p 11

45 Bates (2006) p 13

46 Bates (2006), p 14

47 Sheehan (2007)

48 Botan, CH and Hazleton, V, *Public Relations Theory II* (Lawrence Erlbaum Associates, New York, 2006)

49 L'Etang, J, *Public Relations: Concepts, Practice and Critique* (Sage, London: 2011), pp 250–261

50 Grunig, JE, Grunig, LA and Dozier, DM, "The Excellence Theory", in Botan and Hazleton (2006), p 22

51 Grunig, JE, "Two Way Symmetrical Public Relations: Past Present and Future", in RL Heath (ed.), *Handbook of Public Relations* (Sage, Thousand Oaks, CA: 2001), p 11

52 Grunig et al (2006), pp 46–47

53 Grunig et al (2006), pp 21–28

54 Grunig et al (2006), pp 32–34

55 Grunig et al (2006), pp 54–56

56 Grunig (2001), p 25

57 Grunig (2001), p 27

58 Page, K and Hazleton, V, "An Empirical Analysis of Factors Influencing Public Relations Strategy Selection and Effectiveness", paper presented at the annual meeting of the International Communication Association, San Francisco, May 1999

59 Page and Hazleton (1999), p 8

60 Page and Hazleton (1999), p 6

61 Ledingham, J, "Relationship Management: A General Theory of Public Relations", in Botan and Hazleton (2006), pp 465–483

62 Ledingham (2006), p 466

63 Ledingham (2006), pp 470–1

64 Ledingham (2006), pp 473–5

65 Ledingham (2006), p 476

66 L'Etang, J, *Public Relations: Concepts, Practice and Critique* (Sage, London: 2011) pp 251–253

67 D Holtzhausen, quoted in Mackey, S, "Changing Vistas in Public Relations Theory", *PRism* 1 (1), 2003

68 Mackey (2003), pp 7–8

69 Ihlen, O and van Ruler, B, "Applying Social Theory to Public Relations", in O Ihlen, B van Ruler and M Fredriksson, *Public Relations and Social Theory* (Routledge, New York: 2009), p 1

2 Applying theory from management and markets

Considering theory from communication and public relations establishes an enhanced capability to explain how corporations actually go about relating to their stakeholders. Theory provides a guide to content and the manner in which information is conveyed so there can be a level of confidence that it is having the impact, and achieving the value, intended. Since financial and investor communication relates not only to a corporation but also to the financial marketplace, there are a number of aspects of theory from a financial perspective that have relevance for the practice of communicating business and financial information. A considerable amount of theory has been developed around how companies are managed and implement strategy for growth in their markets. Since we are concerned with companies listed on stock exchanges, there is economic theory that gives financial markets a context and role in society. There are also aspects of theory about how financial markets react to information and the way in which investment portfolios are put together. These aspects of theory coalesce around a concept like "shareholder value", which not only has implications for management and accounting but also the communication perspective of singling out a particular stakeholder group. Increasingly as corporations occupy a larger role in society, so their social role is an important consideration, which brings in other stakeholders such as employees and the wider environment, making them additional priorities in corporate communication. These issues highlight the value of understanding a link between the practice of financial and investor communication and theory from a communications and financial perspective. An interesting starting point for this is to look at how the listed corporation came into being, since this sets up considerations about who owns these corporations, the separation over time of the concepts of ownership and management and the way management thinking has evolved to give communication a critical role in the execution of strategy.

Rise of listed corporations, evolution of management theory

Some of the things we take for granted today in the world of financial markets are that investors can easily buy stock in a variety of listed entities and that there is credible financial information to be assessed as part of making investment decisions. This set of circumstances has actually taken several centuries to evolve. The origins of the listed corporation can be traced back to the seventeenth century in England and Holland when businessmen realized that if they wanted their international trading ventures to grow, they needed to raise more capital than they as individuals could provide. This meant bringing in new shareholders with whom they would share the risk, and the reward. By establishing a corporation, they also limited the liability of individuals since it was a separate legal entity, the corporation itself, which owned assets and bore liabilities. It was formation of the Dutch East India Company as a joint stock company in 1602 that also marked the beginnings of the stock market. When the company opened its books to new shareholders, 1,143 investors subscribed capital on the basis that share trading would begin instantly, which also led to the establishment at the same time of the world's first stock exchange, the Amsterdam Stock Exchange.[1] While risk management might have been an initial motivation for introducing new investors, shareholders were also well rewarded, receiving annual dividends, although there were significant fluctuations in stock prices. With Amsterdam being the early focus of listed company share trading, it also led to the first book about this arcane art. Joseph de la Vega, in 1688 wrote *Confusion of Confusions*, which explained the workings of the city's stock market, taking the form of a dialogue between "an erudite shareholder, a cautious merchant, who gradually becomes aware of a new way of making money, and a quick witted philosopher".[2] The book has been described as the first precursor of modern behavioural finance,[3] with its descriptions of investor decision-making still reflected in the way some investors operate today, and in 2001 was still rated by the *Financial Times* as one of the ten best investment books ever written.[4] De la Vega noted how the establishment of a stock exchange had a significant influence on the life of the city:

> If one were to lead a stranger through the streets of Amsterdam and ask him where he was he would answer, "Among Speculators", for there is no corner in the city where one does not talk of shares.[5]

He also colourfully described how market manipulation took place:

> The greatest comedy is played at the Exchange. There, the speculators excel in tricks, they do business and find excuses wherein hiding places, concealment of facts, quarrels, provocations, mockery, idle talk, violent desires, collusion, artful deceptions, betrayals, cheatings, and even tragic end are to be found.[6]

With similar characteristics observable on some chat room websites today, it would seem the only thing technology has changed from de la Vega's day is that rumours are spread more quickly, with stock prices showing a faster response.[7] While this might reflect how communication has continued to have an effect on stock prices over a period of 300 years, it should also be noted that regulators' market supervision capabilities are far more sophisticated today in cracking down on market manipulation than they were in bygone eras.

The growing connection between Amsterdam and London as financial centres led to the establishment of the London Stock Exchange in 1698. The lively coffee house trading atmosphere contributed to growing interest in owning shares, leading inevitably to the over-exuberance of the 1720s and the subsequent South Sea Bubble crash. Despite this, the market survived and prospered and, nearly 100 years after it began, 24 stockbrokers gathered under a buttonwood tree in Wall Street, New York, in 1792 to agree rules for buying and selling bonds and shares, leading to establishment of the New York Stock Exchange.[8]

One development that precedes the establishment of stock exchanges but that has had lasting repercussions was the codifying of double entry bookkeeping in the fifteenth century in Venice. This established the system of debits and credits, enabling the separation of capital and income and clear discernment of the profitability of a business. The system was devised in 1494 by Luca Bartolomeo de Pacioli, "Renaissance mathematician, monk, magician, constant companion of Leonardo da Vinci".[9] A recent analysis of the value of Pacioli's work described double entry bookkeeping as "one of the greatest advances in the history of business and commerce"[10] and observed that accounting was actually our first communication technology. It was Pacioli who was able to show that accounts were a way of making conclusions about the health of a company and, from discerning the profits of a company's products and components, to assess information for making decisions about a company's direction. From the perspective of financial and investor communication, the numbers from accounts are a critical component of developing a company's story, with the origins of this emerging some 500 years ago.

Another issue from the history of the corporation that has had an impact on communication is that of the gradual separation of ownership and control as corporations grew in size. The crux of this was the transfer of power to managers from the successful entrepreneurs of the late nineteenth and early twentieth centuries in the United States. These businessmen had built extremely large corporations from a position of majority ownership but maintaining growth meant raising more capital and diluting ownership as more shareholders joined in the pursuit of return on investment. Another consequence was managers taking over the running of these large organizations, giving way to the phenomenon known as managerialism. The prominent writers who described this process were Berle and Means in 1932. Their concern about manager power was that it was undemocratic, concentrating too much power in the hands of a few whose interests were not necessarily aligned with those of shareholders. While owners might prefer to pay out profits as dividends, Berle and Means believed managers would prefer to reinvest profits and further their own privileges in the form of higher salaries, contrary to the interests of shareholders and in the process creating an unaccountable oligarchy.[11] While concerns about managerial salaries have become a subject of shareholder activism in the post-global financial crisis era, the general fears expressed by Berle and Means have not come to pass and many scholars since then have seen the advent of managerialism as actually bringing in more democracy. Analysis of profit rates have shown no difference from the early twentieth century entrepreneurs compared with the managerialism era and also, Berle and Means did not account for the checks and balances provided by boards of directors.[12] Other countervailing powers to that of managers have also emerged, with institutional shareholders increasingly having an influence on corporate decision-making, and also the power of the stock market overall delivering an ultimate determination through stock price. Sharing of ownership has resulted in increasing numbers of investors becoming shareholders. At the same time, because the way corporations are governed has become an influence on investment decisions and a concern for regulators, managers have had to ensure the highest standards of accountability. While there is little doubt that managers have significant power in the running of corporations, they have also acquired obligations to communicate about how they are exercising their managerial capability, since this has a capacity to influence the judgements investors make through the mechanism of the stock market. Underlining the relevance and importance of managerial power is the fact that of the world's largest 100 economies in 2011, 51 were corporations and only 49 were countries.[13]

Along with the rise in power of managers of corporations, as well as the more powerful positioning of corporations in the economy, came the establishment of management as an academic discipline and the development of theory around how corporations should be managed and strategy implemented. The first description of management as a science is attributed to the American Frederick Winslow Taylor, who in the late nineteenth century developed principles around the division of labour and training workers and managers for individual components of work. He believed it was better to separate the planning from execution, with planning being the responsibility of management.[14] Taylor's views about the rationality of management were adopted by Henry Ford in implementing a moving assembly line, involving 84 discrete steps to produce the Model T Ford. When this new assembly line was introduced in 1913, it reduced time for manufacturing the Model T Ford from 12.5 hours to 93 minutes[15] and by 1925, a new car was rolling off the assembly line every ten seconds.[16] Principles of management were further developed by Taylor's contemporary Henri Fayol, who was concerned with the personal duties of management, while Max Weber looked at management from a sociological perspective and developed a theory of authority based on an ideal type of organization.[17] Furthering the study of management, the first Master of Business Administration degree was established at Dartmouth College in New Hampshire in 1902.[18]

A focus on achieving greater efficiency led to a progression from scientific management to a realization that human relations were also important, with a study in the 1920s by Harvard professor Elton Mayo showing that encouraging a positive mental attitude by workers and a team culture had positive effects on productivity. Mayo highlighted that the human aspects of an organization were as important as the rational.[19] A contemporary, Chester Barnard, developed further the idea of the organization having a social dimension, requiring it to relate to stakeholders like investors and customers, as well as managers needing to develop the morale of workers.[20]

The introduction of the human element of management was extended further in the 1950s by behaviourists such as Douglas McGregor, who identified two categories of managers, those with an authoritative approach and others who were prepared to empower workers with more responsibility, with this latter approach leading management thought for decades afterwards. Following this line of thought and by noting the success of Japanese corporations in the 1980s, William Ouchi added that an important aspect of management was to promote a stable environment so there was an element of trust between a corporation and its employees.[21]

There have been many subsequent developments in management thought, encompassing the structure of organizations, description of them as learning organizations and the orientation of their strategy towards the pursuit of excellence. One of the leading contemporary influences on management strategy has been the contribution of Harvard professor Michael Porter. Porter's original work in 1979 – which led to him becoming influential for subsequent decades – was a *Harvard Business Review* article, titled, "How Competitive Forces Shape Strategy".[22] In this he described five forces that determine the competitive intensity and attractiveness of a market. In an attractive market, firms could apply their skills and business model to earn profits above an industry average, while in an unattractive market where there were many competitors, profitability would be driven down. Porter's five forces that describe a company's position in an industry are: the threat of substitute services or products; the threat of increased competition from rivals in the market; the threat of new entrants to the market; the bargaining power of suppliers; and the bargaining power of customers.

How a company is able to respond to these threats becomes a determinant of current and future profitability and the key influence on business strategy. Assessment of a company's competitive forces enables a corporate strategist to consider strengths and weaknesses and identify a strategy through them. For Porter, this was not just a strategy for growth but also survival. It led to serious consideration of terms that have become commonplace in management strategy, such as "barriers to entry", "competitive advantage" and "product differentiation". Strategists also had to consider relationships with suppliers and customers, taking into account the extent to which they exercised a form of control over a company's destiny. Given that all companies face these five competitive forces, Porter argued that there were really only three alternative strategies they could adopt – achieve the lowest costs, differentiate its products and services, or dominate a niche. Trying to do some of each was not viable since it would mean losing to competitors who adopted just one of those strategies.[23] An interesting extension to Porter's work suggested by former Intel CEO Andrew Grove was to consider adding a sixth force, "the power, vigour and competence of complementors".[24] These are companies that sell products which add value to another company's products, such as software to run on computer hardware.

The influential nature of Porter's work has meant that from a communications perspective, there is explanatory power in using the competitive forces concepts in developing descriptions of businesses, strategy and progress, especially since external analysts also use these concepts. Adopting these concepts provides a more objective presentation of a company's performance since it takes into account a company's operating environment beyond individual company performance. Using a Porter template to go beyond the company to describe the forces of the wider market can be a more compelling explanation of a strategy offering returns for the longer term.

When *Harvard Business Review* asked Porter in 2008 to revisit his competitive forces ideas, he concluded his article by bringing in the investment perspective. He argued that understanding industry structure from the five forces perspective was as important for investors as managers. If both investors and managers looked at competition from this perspective, he believed that the capital markets could be a far more effective force for company success and economic prosperity. This would come from companies and investors being focused on the same fundamentals that drove sustained profitability, leading to greater emphasis on industry structure rather than short-term events. He asks us to imagine the benefits – for company performance and the wider economy – that might come if all the energy companies expended on trying to please Wall Street was instead redirected to the factors that created true economic value.[25]

Another twentieth century American writer on management to mention is Peter Drucker. Among his many contributions was to see marketing as a crucial component of the success of a corporation, a proposition that also has implications for financial and investor communication. While Drucker has written many books, it was one of his earliest, *The Practice of Management*, which contains his most often cited quotations:

> There is only one valid definition of business purpose: *to create a customer*. Markets are not created by God, nature or economic forces but by business men. The want they satisfy may have been felt by the customer before he was offered the means of satisfying it … But it was a theoretical want before; only when the action of business men makes it an effective demand is there a customer, a market … What the business thinks it produces is not of first importance – especially not to the future of the business and to its success. What the customer thinks he is buying, what he considers "value" is decisive – it determines what a business is, what it produces and

whether it will prosper ... Because it is its purpose to create a customer, any business enterprise has two – and only these two – basic functions: marketing and innovation ... Marketing is the distinguishing, the unique function of business.[26]

As Drucker highlights, the aim of marketing is to know the customer so well that products would effectively sell themselves, almost making selling unnecessary. An implication of this line of thinking for investor relations is that if – in line with the view of investment guru, Warren Buffett – investors should invest only in companies they understand, then companies seeking to market themselves as an investment need to make their businesses easily understood. From this corporate marketing perspective, investors are customers and if the product, the company as a listed stock, is to be so appealing as to sell itself, then communication about it is a critical factor.

Growth in world equities markets, competing for capital

While the evolution of corporations and management theory governs one strand of influence on listed company communication, it is the increasing competition to attract capital in world equities markets that is an equally important driver. Availability of finance, both capital and debt, is a key factor in economic, and corporate, growth. It has been an economic argument over the years as to which comes first – the initiation of growth by companies and economies, or the availability of finance or capital that makes this possible in the first place. The first economist to argue that an efficiently functioning capital market had a positive effect on growth was Joseph Schumpeter. Born in Austria and later a US citizen, Schumpeter published two influential works, the first in 1911 and the second in 1942. His initial argument was that small entrepreneurial ventures were seedbeds of technological discovery and later he recognized that large firms with market power to accelerate the rate of innovation could enter and come to dominate an industry, a process he described as "creative destruction".[27] Then Citibank economist and subsequent international banking figure Stanley Fischer, in a speech in 2003, highlighted the importance of Schumpeter's contribution in describing the primacy of finance in influencing economics on corporate growth:

Schumpeter contended that financial development causes economic development – that financial markets promote economic growth by funding entrepreneurs and in particular by channelling capital to the entrepreneurs with high return projects. He developed his case in vivid language: "the banker ... is not so much primarily a middleman in the community 'purchasing power' as a *producer* of this commodity ... he stands between those who wish to form new combinations and the possessors of productive means. He is essentially a phenomenon of development, though only when no central authority directs the social process. He makes possible the carrying out of new combinations, authorises people, in the name of society as it were, to form them. He is the ephor (overseer) of the exchange economy."[28]

While the views of Schumpeter and Fischer do not anticipate the demonization of bankers following the ongoing global financial crisis since 2008, these events tend in a sense to underline their view about the highly influential role of finance in economic events. Finance, in the form of too easily available debt for governments, institutions, companies and households, was the cause of the global financial crisis and yet ensuring its ongoing availability is the position policymakers have taken to stave off collapse and provide a stimulus for recovery.

Accepting that finance in the form of debt and capital is the fuel of economic and corporate growth, then a prime corporate objective is obtaining that funding at the best price. There are a number of factors that influence this – corporations' balance sheets, their credit rating and market views on their business prospects. Stock market prices of listed securities are a dual reflection of how companies fare in the competition for finance – they are indicators of competitiveness for obtaining finance at attractive pricing and also a reflection of success, or lack of it, in raising capital and debt. An objective guide to pricing in the battle for finance is the state of companies' audited accounts. Additionally, there are subjective influences, such as varying views about interpreting numbers in those accounts and differing conclusions about future prospects. A factor that has a considerable weight on these subjective views, and ultimately how corporations rank in the battle for capital, is how companies communicate about their businesses and prospects. Decision-makers who provide capital and debt are bankers and investors, comprising wholesale and retail investors. Each of these is subject to a range of individual influences, all with different weightings in their decision-making processes. Since companies in the crucial competition for capital and debt seek to influence these decisions, it is useful to look at the body of theory that has evolved around investment decision-making. Theory in this field takes account of varying views about risk and return and how investment markets work and this in turn has led to a range of investment styles. If companies are to communicate effectively with these decision-makers as they compete for finance, then it is important to understand not only how they think but the influences on their thinking and how these have evolved.

Modern portfolio theory

A starting point for looking at the development of theory around investment decision-making is the 1950s with what became known as modern portfolio theory. The leading light was Harry Markowitz, with his work extended in subsequent years by William Sharpe. Both shared a Nobel Prize for their efforts in 1990. Modern portfolio theory is based on the idea that investors generally want to avoid risk and so demand a reward for undertaking risky investments. In the terminology of the theory, the reward is taken as a risk premium, an expected rate of return higher than available on alternative risk-free investments. The theory was an attempt to establish a mathematical basis for modelling investment returns to derive a portfolio of equities investments that maximized returns for a given amount of portfolio risk. From modern portfolio theory comes a mathematical formulation that substantiates the idea of diversification in investment, with the intention of selecting a collection of assets that together would have lower risk than if the portfolio were invested in just one asset. If the choice of investments were from a group that has differing returns, there are basically three factors that guide making the best choice. One is the return of an individual asset, second is the risk of achieving that return and third is selecting assets non-identical in nature, that is they will not have perfectly correlated returns.[29]

The return on an individual asset is a combination of income and capital gain. In looking at a group of individual assets, there will be an average return for the group and individual assets will show a distance from that average. The average distance from the mean for the group is known by the statistical term "standard deviation". Another way of expressing the distance from the average return is that it represents a risk of achieving the average, making standard deviation a measure of risk. Consequently, the best assets to include in a portfolio are those with the highest return in relation to the risk of achieving that return. Using these measures of risk and return, it is possible to weight combinations of assets in a portfolio that will give the best risk-adjusted return. The measure that gives its name to an asset or portfolio achieving an expected return, adjusted for risk, is known as the "Sharpe ratio". It is calculated by dividing the expected return of that portfolio, less what might have been earned from a risk-free investment, by the standard deviation from that portfolio's average return. The higher the Sharpe ratio, the more investors are compensated for the risk taken on. This is a common concept in portfolio management and is a theoretical guide to investment decision-making since it involves rational thinking about return in relation to risk.[30]

Another important mathematical concept within modern portfolio theory is the capital asset pricing model. This model helps with investment decision-making around the components of a portfolio. It guides how much in a portfolio should be allocated to risk-free assets and the proportions given to riskier assets, on the basis of assessing risk and return for adding new assets to the portfolio. The mathematical formula (provided on page 129) underlying the model calculates the expected return from an asset, recognizing the basic return from a risk-free asset, as well as the impact of the return from just investing in the overall market. If the expected return of an asset derived from the formula does not exceed the risk-free rate plus a premium for taking on additional risk, then it indicates the new investment should not be taken on. The expected return derived by the formula also provides a rate at which the asset's future cash flows can be discounted, giving a value that establishes an intrinsic value for the asset, which can be compared with its market price. The capital asset pricing model provides a guide for purchasing individual assets and supports the underlying principle of modern portfolio theory, that firm-specific risk can be overcome through portfolio diversification.[31]

Like many mathematical tools applied to the real world, modern portfolio theory is based on certain assumptions to achieve a degree of simplification. While these assumptions add a level of abstraction, they have not detracted from the power of the tools and their common usage to guide investment decision-making. Among the assumptions are that there are no transaction costs, there is an efficient market with all investors having access to information at the same time, that investors are rational and that historic returns are a guide to expected returns. The idea that there is such a thing as an efficient market with all information available to investors at the one time and being instantly reflected in stock prices has been challenged, especially since the global financial crisis. There are strongly held alternative theories on how markets work and how investment decisions should be made but these challenges have not undermined the widespread usage of the mathematical tools within modern portfolio theory.

There are several implications for corporate communication from modern portfolio theory. While corporations need to focus on producing returns to make their securities attractive to investors, there is also a need to recognize that returns alone are not the sole factors in investment decisions about adding another asset to a portfolio. Individual companies may be too closely correlated with other companies in a portfolio. Recognizing the principle of diversification can guide company investor relations efforts towards fund manager portfolios into which their securities and their characteristics represent an appropriate fit for investment managers. The strength of belief in the notion of efficient markets, which underlies modern portfolio theory, is at the heart of

Case study

Chainsaw Al and the end of shareholder value

"Chainsaw" was the nickname earned by US businessman Al Dunlap as he downsized companies where he was chief executive in the interests of the principle of shareholder value. It worked for a while. His stint at Scott Paper, over two years beginning in 1994, involved a corporate restructuring that reduced the workforce by 35 per cent, putting 11,000 people out of work, while achieving a rise in share value of 225 per cent.[32] However, it was his move in 1996 to Sunbeam, a household name in business that had produced toasters, mixers and blenders for generations of Americans but wasn't performing well financially, that led ultimately to his downfall and extensive questioning of the concept of shareholder value.

Dunlap's reputation for delivering stock price increases was such that the mere announcement of him joining Sunbeam as chief executive resulted in the stock surging 50 per cent.[33] He described himself at the time as "Rambo in Pinstripes".[34] On his first day in the job he called together the Sunbeam management team and, without wasting time on introductions, delivered his credo:

> This is the best day of your life if you're good at what you do and are willing to accept change. And it's the worst day of your life if you're not.[35]

Shortly afterward he had teams of accountants roaming the operations and four months later produced a restructuring plan that turned Sunbeam upside down, eliminating half of the company's workforce, getting rid of 6,000 people, and 87 per cent of its products while shutting down 18 plants. The market was ecstatic, with Sunbeam's stock price jumping further. It reached US$53 at its height, up fivefold from the time of Dunlap joining the company. This reflected Dunlap's philosophy – "stockholders are the only constituency I am concerned about"[36] – indicating his priorities, rather than worrying about people losing their jobs.

This enthusiastic stock market reaction actually foiled Dunlap's initial strategy, which was to sell the company but it was now too highly priced, forcing him to consider a new acquisition strategy, with three companies being bought in a short space of time. From then on, the pressure was on the management team to deliver the sales the growth strategy demanded. It resulted in Sunbeam negotiating forward sales with large customers, at a discount, with stock stored in warehouses to be delivered when sales were concluded. The accounting effects of this were to bring forward sales from a future period into current periods and along with other measures – such as scaling back R&D, postponing maintenance spending and relying on reserves – began to create suspicion in the market of whether the momentum could be maintained.[37]

By early 1998 one stock analyst who had noted the spike in inventories began closer questioning and found out that a respected senior executive had been fired. He then called the investor relations chief, only to find out that he had just resigned. The analyst concluded that his accounting concerns and these personnel changes were not good signs and he advised his clients to sell, leading to a stock price fall of 25 per cent and the start of the Dunlap era coming to an end.[38]

Sunbeam's financial position deteriorated as the aggressive push on forward sales could not be sustained and as the public glare on accounting policies led to reversals, Dunlap was sacked by the board two years after his fanfare-filled arrival. Stock price fell to around US$6, below the level where the adventure had begun. The episode did not end happily. The Securities and Exchange Commission launched a civil action in 2001 and Dunlap settled by paying a US$500,000 fine and agreeing he would never again be an executive of a public company. Sunbeam sought bankruptcy protection in February 2001, citing US$3.2 billion in debt, some of it linked to Dunlap's acquisitions.[39]

Dunlap had not made himself popular from his tough policies but, undaunted, he travelled to Australia not long after he lost his job to participate in a series of leadership lectures with Norman Schwarzkopf and Mikhail Gorbachev, purportedly for a fee of US$500,000. Among his one-liners at the time was to dismiss any need to win popularity contests in business: "If you want a friend, buy a dog. I've got two."[40]

The Sunbeam example has become a focus for criticisms of the shareholder value philosophy, with its too narrow focus on just one stakeholder group. UK critic, John Kay, believes the focus should be more on business building, not creating shareholder value:

> The price of a company's stock depends not on the value of a company but on the market's perception of that value, which is often easier to change than value itself. Mr Dunlap's relentless self-promotion and his purported emphasis on the primacy of shareholder value achieved this ... But judging the quality of a manager by his effect on the stock price is exactly equivalent to judging a weather forecaster on whether you like what they tell you ... Where business judgement and market judgement differ, managers' responsibility is to implement their business judgement ... Managers who focus closely on the stock price, whether by inclination or because they have incentives to do so, will often fail to serve the best interests even of their stockholders.[41]

Today, for most companies, their communication strategy is based on the view that they face a stakeholder, not just a shareholder, world.

two main attitudes about investing, active and passive. Understanding these investment perspectives influences how corporations shape their corporate stories in different ways to connect with how investment decision-makers view market behaviour. The notion of expected return, from the capital asset pricing model, which influences corporate decision-makers on whether they should invest in new projects or initiate merger and acquisition strategies, underlie ideas of shareholder value, another factor that has held sway over the implementation of investor communication.

Efficient market hypothesis and its critics

There are a number of views around how stock prices and markets work but a common feature of all of them is that information is critical, underlining the value of communicating information to the marketplace.

One of the most prolonged ideas about stock market prices is that they move randomly. An early analysis of this proposition was by French mathematician Louis Bachelier, with this quote from his PhD thesis published in 1900 summing up the random prices view:

> It seems that the market, the aggregate of speculators, at a given instant can believe in neither a market rise or a market fall, since, for each quoted price, there are as many buyers as sellers.[42]

While a number of analysts over the years had developed ideas around patterns of movements in stock prices, it was the need for extensive data to establish a sound basis for theory that began the process of statistical analysis of stock price movements. This database was established in 1960 at the University of Chicago and has become the world's biggest database of stock prices, forming the basis for much subsequent development of empirical financial economics. There is an interesting anecdote around its beginnings:

> It all began with a phone call, from a banker at Merrill Lynch who wanted to know how investors in shares had performed relative to investors in other assets. I don't know, but if you gave me $50,000 I could find out, replied Jim Lorie, a dean at the University of Chicago's business school, in so many words. The banker, Louis Engel, soon agreed to stump up the cash, and more. The result, in 1960, was the launch of the university's Centre for Research in Security Prices. Half a century later CRSP (pronounced "crisp") data are everywhere. They provide the foundation of at least one-third of all empirical research in finance over the past 40 years.[43]

Among the better-known items of research from the early days of CRSP were those published between 1965 and 1970 by Eugene Fama who confirmed the random walks view of stock prices, which he believed was based on markets being efficient. For him this meant that intrinsic values of stocks, calculated by financial analysis, and actual prices were the same, presenting challenges for chartists and fundamental analysts who argue that individual stock analysis can beat the market. Unless an analyst had a particular insight or information not generally available to the market, Fama believed the analyst "may as well forget about fundamental analysis and choose securities by some random selection procedure".[44] Or, as a contemporary of Fama's, Burton Malkiel, writing in support of the random walks view of stock prices, said, "a chimpanzee throwing darts at the *Wall Street Journal* could select a portfolio that would do as well as the experts".[45]

Fama's work on efficient markets became known as the efficient market hypothesis (EMH). Essentially EMH states that the price of a financial asset reflects all available information that is relevant to its value. Fama developed three forms of EMH: the weak form, with prices reflecting all historically available information; the semi-strong form, with prices reflecting all publicly available information; and the strong form, with prices reflecting insider information as well. Underlying EMH is the idea that stock prices are unpredictable but far from this being an indicator of irrationality, it was taken as a rational reflection of intelligent investors competing to discover relevant information on which to buy or sell stocks before the rest of the market became aware of that information.[46]

EMH holds that markets are informationally efficient. This means that it is only information that can move a stock price, whether it is good news or bad, and that this information is available to all investors at the one time. This is achieved by companies announcing information that is relevant to stock prices through a stock exchange platform and so it becomes immediately reflected in stock pricing. Informational efficiency means that investors cannot achieve returns in excess of average market returns on a risk-adjusted basis over time, given the information available to everyone at the time of investing. When information becomes available in the market, individual investors may react in different ways but the overall effect is that investors' reactions are random.

Fama's view is that the best investment strategy is to be passive, following a buy and hold model, preferably of a broad-based market index. In this way, investors avoid costs of research and trading. If all the available information is factored into stock prices, then investors can't beat the market. One economist, Michael Jensen in 1978, went so far as to declare "there is no other proposition in economics which has more solid empirical evidence supporting it than the efficient markets hypothesis".[47]

Despite the sweeping nature of this view, there has been an increasing divergence of opinion about EMH in recent decades. From one perspective, there are active investors who base their views on individual stock analysis. From another direction, the school of behavioural finance has emerged, developing an alternative theoretical view to EMH based on a broader social science perspective, including psychology and sociology. Empirical analysis of stock data has also sought to discover anomalies that reveal market inefficiencies. A number have been uncovered, such as the small firm in January effect, post-earnings announcement price drift and the book-to-market effect to name a few, but since they have not proven to be permanent, there is still debate about whether they represent widespread inefficiency.

While EMH still has many supporters, it has come under fire in recent years as representing one of the causes of markets turmoil in the lead-up to the financial crisis of 2008. In the preceding years there was significant expansion of financial engineering and securitization, with the development of instruments such as credit default swaps and collateralized debt obligations. Behind these creations was the view that markets were correctly pricing underlying securities despite the growing bubble nature of credit markets. Fama has come out strongly in defence of his EMH and in one interview he was asked: if markets are efficiently priced, why did they crash? He answered:

> Efficient market theory can't cause a recession (laughter). It gets blamed for everything. In a period of high uncertainty, it's very difficult to figure out what the right prices are for stocks. For example, how do you value all these toxic mortgages and other stuff sitting on banks' balance sheets? This is basically a general market crash. If you want to take a message to investors, this is a period where diversification is more important than ever, because not only has the volatility of the market as a whole gone up, but individual stock volatility has gone up. There's much more dispersion of returns now than there was when the stock market volatility was lower.[48]

Critics of EMH have been led largely by the school of behavioural economics. It is their view that it is emotion that leads to stock market fluctuations, not rationality. A leading light of this school is Yale University economics professor Robert Shiller. Shiller argues that in a rational stock market, investors would base stock prices on the expectation of future dividends, discounted to a present value. He examined the performance of the US stock market between the 1920s and 1980 and considered the kinds of expectations of future dividends and discount rates that could justify the wide range of variation experienced in the stock market. Shiller concluded that the volatility of the stock market was greater than could plausibly be explained by any rational view of the future. In place of an efficient market, he saw a range of emotions behind investment decisions, such as overconfidence, limited investor attention to information in the market and overreaction generally to market trends. A term he gave to it was "irrational exuberance", which became the title of his bestselling book published, as he says, with some luck at the peak of the stock market bubble in 2000.[49] For Shiller, it was the occurrence of stock market bubbles that undermined the idea that markets could be efficient since continually rising prices could not be established as rational decision-making.

The severity of the global financial crisis has led to something of a fusion of the two views, of rationality and emotion, in what has been termed the "adaptive markets hypothesis". This proposes that in relation to investing in the stock market, humans are neither fully rational nor psychologically unhinged. Instead, they work by making best guesses and by trial and error. If one investment strategy fails, they try another and if that works they stick with it, in a form of evolution.[50] The evolutionary world of the adaptable markets hypothesis operates on the basis of "survival of the richest", with only successful investors surviving and the unsuccessful being eliminated.[51] The creator of the adaptive markets hypothesis, Professor Andrew Lo, believes his observations of how markets work have five implications. One is that the relation between risk and reward actually exists and is unlikely to be stable over time, that contrary to the EMH, arbitrage opportunities exist from time to time, that investment strategies wax and wane based on success, that innovation of investment strategy is the key to survival and that survival in investment markets is the only objective that matters.[52]

Information is all pervasive in these views of how markets work. Whichever theory of stock market prices analysts follow, it is information that moves stock prices, whether in a rational or irrational way. What companies say about themselves, how they say it and the financial information they release is going to be analysed carefully by investors and become the basis not only for influencing stock prices but also for investment decision-making.

Shareholder value

The information that has an effect on stock prices is a combination of facts, numbers and narrative. One particularly powerful influence for several decades on financial and investor communication was the shareholder value movement since it not only brought together numerical information in guiding communication messages but also sought to single out the importance of one particular stakeholder group. The leading proponents of shareholder value as it gained interest in the 1980s were, on the academic side, accounting professor Alfred Rappaport and, from a business perspective, General Electric CEO Jack Welch. Their view was that the primary goal for companies should be to improve the wealth of shareholders, which was presented as a different concept from simply increasing profit. The accounting interpretation of this was that profit was not only a short-term measure but also one that did not allow for the time value of money nor dividends or risk. A better measure, which ensured the value of the firm was being increased, was to discount future cash flows at a benchmark rate like a company's cost of capital, arriving at a value per stock unit of a company, its intrinsic value, which could be compared with stock price on the market. A company's stock price, multiplied by the number of stock units on issue, is its market capitalization, the measure the shareholder value concept seeks to maximize since stock price itself is based on expectations of future cash flows rather than traditional accounting measures of corporate performance. Rappaport's argument also linked with Professor Michael Porter's identification of the five competitive forces that companies face in their markets, with Rappaport arguing that, in line with his shareholder value concept, competitive advantage was achieved through cost leadership and differentiation.

Rappaport believed these concepts were not contrary to the idea of an efficient market because the concept of what management considers to be shareholder value is not always communicated to the market. That is, it is not part of the information that the market assimilates in forming a consensus view of stock price.

Rappaport argued it was the role of investor communication to close the gap between what management believed was an appropriate stock price compared with the market's view.

> The fundamental purpose of investor communication is to provide information, within competitive limits, that enables security analysts and investors to make soundly based forecasts of the value drivers.[53]

Rappaport noted several areas of focus for the role of investor communication in trying to educate the market about a company's business. While in Rappaport's mind these aspects are rooted in the concept of shareholder value, they also have wider applicability beyond this idea. Among these areas of focus were:

- Explaining the business and the environment in which the business operates so that the market does not discount the stock for something it does not understand
- Emphasizing future prospects rather than historical performance. The past is relevant only to the extent it helps an investor assess future prospects
- Focusing on strategies and opportunities for long term value enhancement rather than the outlook for the near term. Long-term values usually carry more weight than short-term performance
- Avoiding the creation of over-expectations, because when actual results fall short of expectations the reaction usually more than offsets any benefit that may have been gained by a temporary run up of market values
- Facing bad news openly so that investors are not left with the impression that management does not understand their problems.[54]

While the concept of shareholder value has increasing numbers of critics today, a number of its concepts continue as a way companies explain their businesses. Many use the term "business drivers", cost of capital remains the basis for discounting cash flows and business-specific metrics for judging the performance of individual operations have been developed and perpetuated. The importance of cash flow as a basis for analysing corporate performance continues as an influential measure. However, the main basis for criticism of shareholder value has been its narrow focus on that one group, shareholders. This realization has even come from one of its architects, Jack Welch, who in 2009 sought to revise some of his original concepts.

Shareholder value in the 1980s and subsequent decades became allied with a view about management, known as value management, based on determining the drivers of value within the various operating units of a business so that winners could be supported while underperformers could be cut off since they were not adding to shareholder value. This in fact led to many people losing their jobs. Welch's view when he was General Electric CEO was that each of the group's businesses had to be either number one or two in their markets or they should be closed down or sold. This led to a significant reduction in the GE workforce in pursuit of shareholder value, with the company's bureaucracy also being slashed as "underperforming" and Welch described as one of America's toughest bosses.[55] Welch had a very successful 20-year tenure as CEO of GE, beginning in 1981, and during that time value for shareholders increased 21.3 per cent a year compared with the S&P 500 average of 14.3 per cent a year over the same period.[56] However, Welch's revisionist views in 2009 were that a longer-term perspective was needed and that employees were important stakeholders too. He was quoted on the front page of the *Financial Times*:

> On the face of it, shareholder value is the dumbest idea in the world ... Shareholder value is a result, not a strategy ... Your main constituencies are your employees, your customers and your products.[57]

By this time, however, many observers had agreed that shareholder value had to transform into a broader stakeholder value concept in which social issues were also included. One recent critic has sought to expose shareholder value as a myth since, from her analysis, putting shareholders first actually harms investors, corporations and the public. Professor Lynn Stout's starting point is that conventional shareholder value thinking is a big mistake since it encourages management to focus on the short term at the expense of longer-term performance.[58] An example she cites to prove this point is the 2010 Gulf oil spill disaster, when BP's offshore rig exploded and led to large amounts of oil spilling onto the ocean for several months before it was capped. Stout puts a lot of the blame for this down to a blind pursuit of shareholder value: "In trying to save $1 million by skimping on safety procedures at Macondo well, BP cost its shareholders alone a hundred thousand times more, nearly $100 *billion*."[59] Among other points of criticism Stout makes are that shareholders are not homogeneous and have many competing objectives, making the concept of maximizing shareholder value logically weak since it is not easy to define a common cause. Supporting her argument that shareholder value is a myth, Stout finds no solid grounding for it in corporate law, economics or from empirical evidence. In her view, it is only by taking a longer-term and broader view of the best interests of shareholders and the corporation that the overall welfare of shareholders and other stakeholders is served as well.

CSR and ESG

The development of concepts such as corporate social responsibility (CSR) and environment, social and governance (ESG) has come about as groups of stakeholders have come to expect corporations to recognize that their activities have a broad impact on many levels of society. Some investors want to see social issues intrude on the management of corporations and they take these factors into account in their investment analysis. These trends have also had an effect on corporate communication. The term CSR began to be used in management strategy in the late 1960s as corporations took on a wider stakeholder view of the influences on them implementing longer-term growth strategies.[60] An early critic of the term was economist Milton Friedman who believed that too much emphasis on CSR rather than maximizing returns for shareholders would be detrimental to corporate performance. The title of his celebrated article in *Time* magazine in 1970 expressing this view was "The Social Responsibility of Business is to Increase its Profits".[61] While concerns have also been expressed about corporations having insincere motives for adopting CSR because they wanted to be seen to be doing good, in current times there has been a considerable turnaround in attributing importance to companies adopting the principles of CSR and ESG.

Some early examples of the effects of ethical concerns on investment were decisions by some companies not to invest in South Africa during its apartheid regime in the 1970s, and the establishment of an investment pressure group called the Ceres Coalition in 1989 in response to the environmental damage caused by the oil spill on the Alaskan coast from the sinking of the *Exxon Valdez*. Today the Ceres investor network has 100 institutional investor members with US$11 trillion under management who give priority to ESG concerns in investment decisions.[62] A recent report from Ceres links ESG concerns with modern portfolio theory, portraying sustainable investing as a logical way of accounting for risk in investment decision-making.[63] Triple bottom line reporting, taking into account financial, social and environmental factors also became influential by the start of the twenty-first century and the establishment of Principles for Responsible Investment (PRI) with United Nations backing in 2005 has become a global initiative with around 1,200 signatories, including the world's largest investing institutions.[64]

While for some years the Friedman view about there being a trade-off between return and responsible investing prevailed, a demand for investing in companies that demonstrate social responsibility has increased in recent years, along with evidence that the Friedman view is no longer valid. As institutions have established funds devoted to responsible investing, in response to the market seeking out this sort of product, they have implemented techniques such as positive selection of companies meeting ESG criteria. These activities include being activist in using voting power to influence corporate governance decisions, excluding from their investment universe companies that do not follow ESG guidelines, and including ESG in portfolio risk assessment. Supporting the value of these trends, some Harvard University research over a large sample of firms for the 16-year period to 2008 has shown that CSR strategies have a positive effect on value creation in public equity markets. Among the outcomes of this research was that socially responsible firms, especially those with a higher visibility of their CSR activities, received more favourable recommendations by stock analysts, and that as there are increasingly more analysts with CSR awareness, they are also more likely to perceive the value of CSR more favourably.[65]

Another group that brings together concerns about communication, investing and ESG principles, is the International Integrated Reporting Council (IIRC). It is a global coalition – of regulators, investors, companies, standard-setters, the accounting profession and NGOs – which shares the view that communication about businesses' value creation should be the next step in the evolution of corporate reporting.[66] The IIRC wants to move corporate thinking away from just a bottom line accounting view of performance towards a longer-term perspective that has three components. These are: linking reporting to longer-term strategic planning; accounting for the various forms of capital, in addition to financial capital, that play a role in creating value; and the way in which working with a broad range of stakeholders, such as workers, customers, local communities and regulators, encourages managers and boards to think more broadly about long-term drivers of value creation.[67] A framework adopted in December 2013 is being used to accelerate the adoption of integrated reporting across the world, where it is currently being trialled in over 25 countries, 16 of which are members of the G20 (the group of nations focused on strengthening the global economy).[68]

The implications for corporate communication of this are, not only that there is value in pursuing CSR and ESG strategies in themselves, but there is also value from communicating about them and describing the extent of commitment and importance companies give to them.

Shared value

An attempt to combine social issues with management strategy has been receiving high-profile support in recent years, especially since the push has been led by Michael Porter with his concept of "shared value". Porter's starting point for the concept is that, despite the term "corporate social responsibility" being in vogue for decades, there is ongoing distrust of business, especially since the global financial crisis. Porter believes that companies have brought this on themselves because they have been "trapped in an outdated approach to value creation"[69] with a focus on short-term financial success rather than achieving longer-term objectives. From this confusion of priorities about the short and long term, Porter points to companies not seeing what customers really want, the damage that comes from depleting natural resources and how communities can deteriorate from unemployment as companies seek cheaper labour offshore. He argues for companies to reconnect company success with social progress, developing in the process a shared value that moves away from a narrow conception of capitalism. Porter's ideas have picked up some big name followers – Novartis, GE and Nestlé among them – and, along with their adoption of the concept, is a pursuit of measurement of value in a way that links social and business results. Establishing widespread agreement around measurement may take some time, so supporters of the concept argue that, for investors who can see the need for companies to adopt a longer-term perspective, it is just a matter of asking some simple questions, such as: what are the demographics and locations that support revenue growth? How will new products reach these markets? How will access to and efficiency of resources be guaranteed? How stable is the supply chain across those locations?[70] These questions and the seeming growing support for shared value among larger companies also point to communication issues and the role of shared value in corporate stories.

Signposts from the theoretical framework

In preceding pages, we have traversed a number of theoretical influences on corporate communication, spanning a few thousand years as we have progressed from the Greek Lyceum to today's electronic dealing room. There are many more influences that might have been included. However, the main purpose is to show that by combining influences from the areas of public relations and finance, there are signposts for the way corporate communication should be structured and implemented. From the principles of rhetoric all the way through to ESG, there is a connection with ethos, covering not only the character of the presenter of argument but also the ethics of a corporation. Persuasion and rational argument, presented to groups of influence, such as the media and investment community, can shape perceptions more powerfully than spin. Building relationships with the receivers of corporate messages, or the stakeholders in corporations, not only becomes an influence on communication strategy but also the content of the messages. Embracing a larger group of stakeholders than just the owners of a corporation reflects the evolution of a concept such as shareholder value into stakeholder value. The actual content of corporate messages is also more powerful if it goes beyond the internal focus of a corporation and recognizes, as Michael Porter does, that a corporation does not operate in a vacuum but in a market with powerful forces that need to be recognized in demonstrating competitive advantage and differentiation. This touches on the idea of corporate story, which is the next subject of our analysis.

The combination of these influences on corporate communication, when disclosed to the investment marketplace in the form of market information, is what influences stock prices, whether or not one sees rationality or irrational exuberance as the influential force in equities markets.

In modern portfolio theory, diversification is the principle that maximizes risk-adjusted return. In applying this to financial and investor communication, there is room for companies to communicate that their story may have merits for consideration in any diversified investment portfolio but the content of that story – combining facts, numbers and narrative – needs to be presented in an appropriate way. It is that idea of story that now needs to be added to the theoretical framework.

Notes

1 Petram, LO, *The World's First Stock Exchange: How the Amsterdam Market for Dutch East India Company Shares Became a Modern Securities Market, 1602–1700*, Thesis, University of Amsterdam (2011), pp 17–18
2 Corzo, MT, Prat, M and Vaquero Lafuente, ME, "Behavioral Finance in Joseph De La Vega's Confusion De Confusiones" (2012), SSRN: http://ssrn.com/abstract=2145343, p 5
3 Corzo et al (2012), p 1
4 Quoted in Leinweber, DJ and Madhavan, AN, "Three Hundred Years of Stock Market Manipulation", *The Journal of Investing*, Summer 2001
5 Quoted in Held, P, "*The Confusion of Confusions*: Between Speculation and Eschatology", *Concentric: Literary and Cultural Studies* 32 (2), 2006, p 112
6 Quoted in Leinweber and Madhavan (2001), p 2
7 Leinweber and Madhavan (2011)
8 NYSE, History, www.nyx.com/who-we-are/history/new-york
9 Gleeson-White, J, *Double Entry: How the Merchants of Venice Created Modern Finance* (Allen & Unwin, London: 2012), p 27
10 Gleeson-White quoted in *The Economist*, 25 August 2012
11 Mizruchi, MS, "Berle and Means Revisited: The Governance and Power of Large US Corporations", *Theory and Society*, 33 (5), 2004, p 581
12 Mizruchi (2004), pp 584 and 591
13 www.unesco.org/education/tlsf/mods/theme_c/popups/mod18t04s01.html
14 Kamal, KK, "A Brief History of Management Thought", *Social Science Research Network* (2009), www.researchgate.net/publication/228177541_A_Brief_History_of_Management_Thought, p 2
15 www.thenewamerican.com/culture/history/item/12226-model-t-ford-%E2%80%94-the-freedom-machine
16 www.americanheritage.com/content/citizen-ford
17 Kamal (2009), p 3
18 Kamal (2009), p 1
19 Kamal (2009), p 4
20 Kamal (2009), p 6
21 Kamal (2009), pp 5 and 8
22 Porter, ME, "How Competitive Forces Shape Strategy", *Harvard Business Review*, March–April 1979
23 Colvin, G, "There's No Quit in Michael Porter", *Fortune*, 29 October 2012
24 Grove as quoted in Hill, C and Jones, GR, *Strategic Management Theory: An Integrated Approach* (Cengage Learning, Mason, OH: 2009), p 54
25 Porter M, "The Five Competitive Forces that Shape Strategy", *Harvard Business Review*, January 2008, p 40
26 Drucker, PF, *The Practice of Management* (Elsevier, Oxford: first edn 1955, this edn 2007), pp 31–32
27 Nicholas, T, "Why Schumpeter was Right: Innovation, Market Power, and Creative Destruction in 1920s America", *The Journal of Economic History* 63 (4), 2003

28 Fischer, S, "The Importance of Financial Markets in Economic Growth", paper presented to International Derivatives and Financial Market Conference, Brazil, 2003

29 Bodie, Z, Kane, A and Marcus, AJ, *Investments* (McGraw-Hill, Boston MA: 1999), p 148

30 Bodie et al (1999), Chapter 6

31 Bodie et al (1999), Chapters 7 and 8

32 Fastenberg, D, "Al Dunlap", *Time*, 18 October 2010, www.time.com/time/specials/packages/article/0,28804,2025898_2025900_2026107,00.html

33 Byrne, JA, "How Al Dunlap Self Destructed", *BusinessWeek*, 7 June 1998

34 Byrne JA, Chainsaw*: The Notorious Career of Al Dunlap in the Era of Profit-at-any Price* (HarperBusiness Books, New York: 2003), book excerpt at www.businessweek.com/stories/1999-10-17/chainsaw-al

35 Byrne (2003)

36 Quoted in Kay, J, "A Misleading Obsession with Share Prices", *Financial Times*, 7 June 2005, www.johnkay.com/2005/06/07/a-misleading-obsession-with-share-prices

37 Byrne (1998)

38 Byrne (2003)

39 Cooper, J, "Financial Statement Fraud – Corporate Crime of the 21st Century", *AICD Directors Briefing*, 8 June 2005, www.asic.gov.au/asic/pdflib.nsf/LookupByFileName/AICD_speech_080605.pdf/$file/AICD_speech_080605.pdf, p 5

40 Byrne (2003)

41 Kay (2005)

42 Quoted in Bernstein, PL, *Capital Ideas* (John Wiley & Sons, Hoboken, NJ: 2005)

43 *The Economist*, 18 November 2010

44 Fama, EF, "Random Walks in Stock Market Prices", Paper 16, Selected Papers, Graduate School of Business, University of Chicago, *Financial Analysts Journal*, September–October, 1965, p 59

45 Malkiel, BG, "The Efficient Markets Hypothesis and its Critics", *Journal of Economic Perspectives* 17 (1), 2003, p 60

46 Bodie et al (1999), p 329

47 Quoted in "Efficiency and Beyond", *The Economist*, 16 July 2009

48 CBS News interview, 9 March 2009, www.cbsnews.com/8301-505123_162-51277142/eugene-fama-why-you-cant-time-the-market

49 Shiller, RJ, "From Efficient Markets Theory to Behavioural Finance", *Journal of Economic Perspectives* 17 (1), 2003, p 93

50 *The Economist*, 16 July 2009

51 Lo, A, "The Adaptive Markets Hypothesis: Market Efficiency from an Evolutionary Perspective", *Journal of Portfolio Management*, August 2004

52 Lo (2004)

53 Rappaport, A, *Creating Shareholder Value: The New Standard for Business Performance* (Macmillan, New York: 1986), p 167

54 Rappaport (1986), pp 167–168

55 Froud, J, Sukhdev, J, Leaver, A and Williams, K, "General Electric: The Conditions of Success", CRESC Working Paper 5, September 2005

56 Cohan, P, "Jack Welch: Pot Calling Kettle Black", *Forbes*, 10 October 2012, www.forbes.com/sites/petercohan/2012/10/10/jack-welch-pot-calling-kettle-black

57 Quoted in Guerrera, F, "Welch Condemns Share Price Focus", *Financial Times*, 12 March 2009, www.ft.com/intl/cms/s/0/294ff1f2-0f27-11de-ba10-0000779fd2ac.html#axzz2GgLoyZ31

58 Stout, L, *The Shareholder Value Myth: How Putting Shareholders First Harms Investors, Corporations, and the Public* (Berrett-Koehler Publishers, San Francisco, CA: 2012)

59 Stout (2012), p 2 (emphasis in original)

60 Blowfield, M and Murray, A, *Corporate Responsibility: A Critical Introduction* (Oxford University Press, Oxford: 2008), p 57

61 Friedman, M, "The Social Responsibility of Business is to Increase its Profits", *Time*, 13 September 1970, www.umich.edu/~thecore/doc/Friedman.pdf

62 www.ceres.org/about-us/who-we-are

63 Burr, BB, "Ceres urges institutional investors to promote sustainability", *Pensions & Investments*, www.pionline.com/article/20130626/REG/130629914

64 www.unpri.org/about-pri/about-pri

65 Ioannis, I and Serafeim, G, "The Impact of Corporate Social Responsibility on Investment Recommendations", Harvard Business School, Working Paper 11–017, 2010

66 www.theiirc.org

67 Adams, C, "Integrated Reporting to Walk More than the Bottom Line", *The Conversation*, 21 June 2013

68 Alembakis, R, "IIRC CEO Favours Market-led Adoption of Integrated Reporting", *The Sustainability Report*, 31 May 2013

69 Porter, ME and Kramer, MR, "Creating Shared Value", *Harvard Business Review*, January 2011, http://hbr.org/2011/01/the-big-idea-creating-shared-value

70 Bockstette, V, "Shared Value: The Questions Investors Need to Ask Companies", *The Guardian*, 16 August 2012, www.guardian.co.uk/sustainable-business/shared-value-questions-investors-need-to-ask-companies

3 Storytelling and application to corporate communication

Among the reasons for looking at a theoretical framework from the perspectives of public relations and applied finance are that it provides a palette of influences for financial and investor communication, helping to establish priorities and guide implementation. Within this framework is a conception of corporations as they relate to stakeholders, a connection between messages, senders and receivers and signposts towards what makes communication effective. This establishes a further topic for consideration, which is the actual content of those messages. When companies listed on stock exchanges consider sending messages to their key stakeholders, they are subject to certain rules surrounding the compulsory disclosure of information. On any one day, thousands of these pieces of information are released, sometimes just technical details, at other times accounting figures or collections of facts or descriptions of company performance. These pieces of information in isolation do not necessarily contain a mechanism that can release the complexity they contain or one that can create a ripple effect of reverberations through a market that helps to make sense of information that has been released. If we adopt an analogy from rhetoric, facts and numbers are fundamental truths that on their own do not have legs. If they are to be more influential they need to be carried by people to people in the form of communication. We already know, from considering the efficient market hypothesis and the views of behavioural economists, that information has an influence on stock prices. Additionally, there is a growing body of evidence, reviewed in the next chapter, which shows that how information is communicated is a further influence on stock price. One notion that binds together the facts and figures of information, and provides a context, is narrative or story. Story is a device for converting information into communication. It is a powerful concept in interpersonal communication and has historical connections in myth. Story is used by historians and in fiction, in its many genres there are common narrative plots. Politicians rely on story to combine a reduction of complexity with a motivational platform and in business and management there is increasing use of narrative to bring about change and inspiration for new directions. Increasingly there are instances of company CEOs describing themselves as the chief storyteller. The corporate story can be a compelling mechanism for creating a structure around the communication of information and, to appreciate its role in the corporate sector, it is instructive to examine the pervasiveness of story in many aspects of our lives.

Story in our daily lives

There is a sense in which stories are the threads that hold our lives together in our communities. They are such a large part of our daily conversations with people, the books we read and television programmes we watch that we do not realize we are involved in a daily storytelling ritual that has been passed down over centuries.

Stories are not just for fiction, they are how we relate daily events. As we talk about things that happen to us, we do not present them as a series of facts. Without thinking, we want the hearer of what we are talking about to be interested in what we are telling them. So we put some context around the facts we relate and we have a beginning, a middle and an end, to meet the classic definition of a story that Aristotle laid out in his *Poetics*. Aristotle went further by putting story into the context of drama that should have six components – plot, character, diction, thought, spectacle and song[1] – and, in the public presentation of stories by politicians and business people, these characteristics are often enacted. In the media, journalists have long since referred to their output as stories and in newspapers journalists usually have to write several stories a day to meet their quota of news coverage for online and print editions.

It has become commonplace in the business world for executives to talk about their companies to varying groups, such as employees, customers, bankers and investors. The accepted way of doing this has become the PowerPoint presentation, with its dot point summaries of words and numbers, lists of facts and occasional diagrams and tables. While some of these can be effective, there are also many examples where a story or context is not put around the information provided, ignoring what happens in interpersonal conversation and despite the characteristics for presentation laid out by Aristotle. As corporate presentations have become more pervasive there has been a growing emergence of self-help literature, which plays up the showmanship aspects of giving presentations to win over audiences. The performance orientation may well suit some personalities but not others and can also run the risk of not taking into account what an audience is expecting to hear and see. For example, in the investment environment, showmanship runs the risk of appearing trite and can decrease the extent to which an audience might take chief executives seriously, causing questioning about whether to entrust investment funds to their care. The issue this raises is that it is not just any story that can be applied in the corporate sector. It needs to be appropriate, not shallow, and illustrate conviction, not showmanship, so it is relevant to look at the history of stories and their structure as a guide towards what is the most effective form of storytelling in the corporate environment.

Theory and history of narrative

A term that came into being in the mid-twentieth century was the word "narratology" to describe the theory and study of narrative and narrative structure. While creation of the term might be relatively recent, the discipline has classical origins in the work of Aristotle and his descriptions of narrative structure. A leading writer on narratology breaks narrative down to three components – fabula, story and text.[2] Fabula is the raw material of content, story is the ordering of this material to provide a narrative sequence and text is the medium by which it is delivered, whether by physical storyteller, in writing, graphically or in film. This structure can be applied to a range of narrative, going as far back as myth, which has been identified as an early part of civilization, relating to many aspects of cultural and religious development.

Myths are part of an oral storytelling tradition, with one of the earliest examples identified among Australia's indigenous people whose stories, or songlines, have a widespread influence on their culture. Twentieth century British writer Bruce Chatwin, in his book *Songlines*, which explores the existence of order in nomadic cultures, gave this description to songlines:

> the labyrinth of invisible pathways which meander all over Australia and are known to Europeans as "Dreaming tracks" or "Songlines"; to the Aboriginals as the "footprints of the Ancestors" or the "Way of the Law".
>
> Aboriginal Creation myths tell of the legendary totemic beings who had wandered over the continent in the Dreamtime, singing out the name of everything that crossed their path – birds, animals, plants, rocks, waterholes – and so singing the world into existence.[3]

In a culture that had no written works given from one generation to another, Australia's indigenous people passed on their lore through oral storytelling, which gave the elders with this knowledge of the past a revered position in their communities. Stories explained how the land came to be shaped and how people should behave and so stories became how adults gave their children an education about not only their ancestors but around how they should lead their lives. One Aboriginal elder described songlines this way:

> The Songlines are such an important part of our mental and spiritual structure. They are lines of energy that run between places, animals and people. We know at times where the Songlines are and we like to follow them for the energy, not only because we can send a message to other neighbouring tribes but so we can keep in touch with animal and bird life. We follow the Songlines of the animals to know where they are and to see if they have moved on. If they have moved on then we can start a burn-off to create more life without hurting the animals.[4]

In many cultures the oral tradition gave way to written stories, with Homer's *Iliad* and *The Odyssey* among the earliest examples. Also part of this transition are the tales of *One Thousand and One Nights* in which the power of story is so great it becomes the device for Scheherazade saving her own life as she keeps telling stories to prevent her execution by a tyrant Persian king:

> But morning overtook Shahrazad, and she lapsed into silence. Then Dinarzad said, "What a strange and entertaining story!" Shahrazad replied, "What is this compared with what I shall tell you tomorrow night if the king spares me and lets me live!" The following night Shahrazad said...[5]

The study of narrative and story has become a diverse field across many disciplines. Study has progressed across the structures of narrative and the way narrative is used to represent reality. Since narrative is a way we organize our memories and experiences of events, it becomes a representation of reality which is not subject to empirical verification but more a judgement about whether the information is transferred in a way that follows a logical narrative structure in making it easier to communicate knowledge.[6] An influential component of narrative structure is "narrative accrual" in which – unlike in science, where knowledge is based on fundamental principles – narratives over time accrue understanding so that they create culture, history and tradition.[7]

One development in the study of narrative worth highlighting for its relevance in financial and investor communication is reader-response criticism. This had its origins in the

1920s in looking at emotional responses to literature and has since itself become a wider tool of analysis in assessing how people can react in various ways to what they read. Reader-response criticism looks at how differences can arise in the meaning readers might give to a work, which can contrast with what the writer intended and also may vary from reader to reader. The idea that it is the reader who actively participates in giving meaning is a powerful one, even though it may be the originator of the text who begins the understanding process.[8] This can be a powerful analytical tool in investment markets where investors can react in quite differing ways to information companies release publicly.

This brief survey of narrative concepts provides several indicators of applicability to corporate communication, from narrative structure to the way a songline through a landscape becomes part of a story, the connection between narrative and reality, and the inextricable link between presenter and audience in creating meaning and understanding. The way story is applied to history and fiction also has implications for corporate communication.

Story as history

How history is written has long been a battleground, with many of the arguments crystallized in EH Carr's 1961 Cambridge lectures, *What is History?* For Carr, there were two heresies to be avoided: "scissors and paste history without meaning or significance" and "propaganda or historical fiction [which] merely use facts of the past to embroider a kind of writing that has nothing to do with history".[9] For Carr, writing history was an ongoing process and inevitably involved an historian in interpreting facts and developing a story to convey understanding while also making it interesting to read. Many examples might be given of this but some differences in story and interpretation can be given from several Australian historians.

It was only in the mid-twentieth century that Australian history became established as an academic discipline. Before then the emphasis had been on British and European history. A prominent figure in this transition was historian Manning Clark, who moved beyond the facts of history to take on the role of storyteller. In a sense, he became a player, a moralist who cast history's actors into the roles of goodies, or enlargers, and baddies, or conservatives.

One of Clark's critics, Paul Carter, in his *The Road to Botany Bay*,[10] describes Clark as history's secretary who colludes with history's wish to see chaos yield to order. Carter's interpretation of the Australian story is that it was shaped by a sense of place and journey as discovery of the continent unfolded. Carter describes Clark as drawing Nature's painted curtains to reveal historic man at his epic labour on the stage of history. What is shown is a kind of imperial history, or story, in which there is no search for the choices people at the time might have made but rather a legitimization of their decisions, such as why the governor decided to erect a tent here rather than there or why soldiers blazed a trail in one direction rather than another.[11]

Another prominent Australian historian and storyteller is Geoffrey Blainey who does not escape Carter's criticism either, with Carter seeing his version of historic storytelling as looking through a telescope onto a sublime working model of events. Blainey, too, has a selective blindness about the aborigines, Carter says, with them appearing physically but not culturally is his diorama model of the colonizer's history.[12] What Carter believes this diorama model overlooks is the spatial history he advocates, which is not to treat landscape as something which is "objectively" or "passively" there, but to look at the influence it had on the imaginations of people at the time. For them, history was not a destiny they were following for a future storyteller but a story they were unfolding for themselves at the time.[13]

From a different perspective, Australian historian Alan Frost, in his *Botany Bay Mirages*, shows how limited documents available to historians at a point in time can allow myths to develop and become part of generally accepted belief, even though subsequent examination of newly found documents and their context can explode those myths. Some of these myths surround supposed poor planning of the Australian colony triggered because of overcrowded prison hulks in Britain leading to a new antipodean colony, which was left to its own devices to survive. Frost's research shows the opposite to these and many other myths, from examining more documents and taking on a wider historical perspective.[14]

To add a broader international view to some of these perspectives, English historian Simon Schama shows how landscape itself can be interpreted in differing ways. In his book *Landscape and Memory*, Schama writes that, even though we are accustomed to separating nature and human perception into two realms, they are, in his opinion, indivisible. In many powerful examples, he illustrates that the landscape around us influences us in ways that are really only possible because of man's interaction with that landscape. One of these examples is wilderness, which is not just untouched landscape but nature that we can only imagine fully since man has infiltrated and created images and stories from it.

> The founding fathers of modern environmentalism, Henry David Thoreau and John Muir, promised that "in wildness is the preservation of the world". The presumption was that the wilderness was out there, somewhere, in the western heart of America, awaiting discovery, and that it would be the antidote for the poisons of industrial society. But of course the healing wilderness was as much the product of the culture's craving and culture's framing as any other imagined garden. Take the first and most famous American Eden: Yosemite. Though the parking is almost as big as the park and there are bears rooting around the McDonald's cartons, we still imagine Yosemite the way Albert Bierstadt painted it or Carleton Watkins and Ansel Adams photographed it: with no trace of human presence. But of course the very act of identifying (not to mention photographing) the place presupposes our presence, and along with us in all the heavy cultural backpacks that we lug with us on the trail.[15]

While Yosemite was obviously there since the beginning of time, Schama's argument is that it only came into being in our current Western minds by an Act of Congress in 1864 and so it did not name itself or locate itself but needed human assistance for this. This is Schama's inseparability of landscape and memory.

There are interesting parallels of varying historical perspectives with corporate information. Story overlaid on facts can alter meaning in many ways and it is open to corporate storytellers to guide interpretation for audiences to help with their understanding of the corporate landscape, which is not separate from the corporation itself.

Parallels with fiction

While in business, there certainly needs to be a distinction between fact and fiction, there is a contribution to corporate storytelling that comes from the fictional genre. One aspect that relates to corporate communication is the way in which there are common themes across myth and works of fiction that delineate stereotypes of stories. Two writers who have contributed to seeing patterns in this way are Joseph Campbell, the American scholar and mythologist and perhaps best known for his connection with *Star Wars*, and English writer Christopher Booker, who early in his career was one of the founding editors of *Private Eye* magazine.

Campbell's research across myths and religion led to his view that myths have four functions that have contributed to the evolution of modern society. These functions are: mystical, involving a sense of awe at the mystery of the universe; cosmological, providing an explanation of the universe; sociological, which explains the existing social order; and pedagogical, providing a guide to how to live a life in any circumstances.[16] Campbell saw these common threads through ancient myths as not only being tools that guided the progress of ancient societies to more advanced levels but also lessons for the modern world. One of the most celebrated applications of Campbell's ideas is in the film *Star Wars*, in which filmmaker George Lucas credits Campbell with helping him connect the theme of his film to ancient myth. One of Campbell's concepts was that of the "monomyth", which he saw as common to many myths:

> The standard path of the mythological adventure of the hero is a magnification of the formula represented in the rites of passage: separation – initiation – return: which might be named the nuclear unit of the monomyth.
> A hero ventures forth from the world of common day into a region of supernatural wonder: fabulous forces are there encountered and a decisive victory is won: the hero comes back from this mysterious adventure with the power to bestow boons on his fellow man.[17]

George Lucas was already involved in drafting the *Star Wars* script when he encountered Campbell's work and found in it an inspiration for the adventures of Luke Skywalker.

Christopher Booker's *The Seven Basic Plots* discerns common themes across many works of fiction, applying to novels and film. He draws some striking parallels, showing the similarity between the story lines of the first work of fiction in English, *Beowulf*, and the film *Jaws*, common comedic traits between the plays of Shakespeare and films by the Marx brothers and similarities between the quest undertaken in Tolkien's *Lord of the Rings* and Spielberg's film *Raiders of the Lost Ark*. The seven common plots Booker sees repeated in works of fiction are overcoming the monster, rags to riches, the quest, voyage and return, rebirth, comedy and tragedy.

A point in highlighting these common themes in myth and fiction is that it shows ways in which the presentation of story can have a familiar connection with audiences. While business leaders may not want to make such obvious connections in presenting their own corporate stories, it is not uncommon for companies, in their own corporate language, to describe the world they know and explain their quest to take on new markets with a strategy intended to bring back rewards for shareholders. When they do embark on this form of explanation, it is not too distant from a path followed by storytellers over the centuries.

Story and communication

An influential twentieth century writer who proposed that narrative is the basis for all human communication and relationships is Walter Fisher who developed the "narrative paradigm". He put forward this alternative to what he saw as the reigning rational paradigm of human communication in which we are all rational beings with decision-making based on logical argument. By contrast, Fisher argues that humans are really storytelling creatures and that we are capable of making decisions based on good reason from our surrounding knowledge of situations, history, culture and judgement of character. In this sense, narrative is based in the history of rhetoric, combining persuasion and literary forms of argument.[18] The process people naturally apply when they hear a story is that of "narrative rationality", through which they determine whether the story is "trustworthy and reliable as a guide to belief and action".[19] As an example of this, Fisher shows how someone running for election will have a variety of excuses when they lose and listeners apply a process of narrative rationality as they decide whether to believe the story. This also has relevance in the business world as companies explain profit performance or disappointment, with stories sifted according to the gradations of belief prepared to be extended by key stakeholders.

Fisher elaborates on the process of narrative rationality as having two principles for judging the merits of stories – probability and fidelity. Probability relates to whether the story is free of contradictions and fidelity refers to its "truth qualities" and the soundness of its reason, covering facts, relevance and consistency. The only way to determine whether a story is a mask for ulterior motives is to test it against these two principles. The basis of Fisher's narrative paradigm is that it presents a philosophy of human communication, containing within it a way of interpreting and assessing discourse and testing its worth.

The value of Fisher's contribution to financial and investor communication is that it confirms the value of narrative as a form of communication as well as including a basis for testing the validity of narratives as they are presented in explaining corporate events.

Story and social movements

One writer who has researched the power of story in social movements is Marshall Ganz, now a Harvard professor but whose own life story has involved being an organizer with Cesar Chavez in the farm worker movement in the 1960s and more recently, mobilizing youth support for Obama's 2008 presidential campaign. In his current courses at Harvard, Ganz also applies storytelling to leadership. In relation to social movements, Ganz believes it is storytelling that distinguishes them from interest groups and other forms of collective action by achieving three things. First, stories, by being mindful of the past, give people an agency to deal with new challenges and improvise alternative futures. Second, stories construct a shared understanding of identity and third, by becoming a source of emotional learning, stories motivate people to action.[20] Ganz's attraction to the Obama campaign was the story around making "a difference between the world as it is and the world as it could one day be". His role in the campaign was to set up training camps "in which young people would be taught to tell Obama's story, to spread a message and generate the enthusiasm of a true grassroots movement".[21] As we now know, this element of the campaign was outstanding in its success.

For Ganz, stories matter, especially for leaders. He sees stories as having three components: a plot, which has to create interest; a protagonist who is presented with a challenge and has to make a choice; and an outcome that teaches a moral. In applying storytelling to leadership, "we start with the skill of relationship building, the story of self. Then we develop the skill of motivation, the story is us. Third, the skill of strategising, the story of now. And fourth, the skill of action."[22] These components form the basis of Ganz's leadership courses at Harvard.

When storytelling is successful, it can create what one researcher describes as a "storylistening trance", in which listeners believe stories are real and become totally engaged with all their senses as they take in what they are being told. It activates their own memories, which they merge with the story as they absorb it.[23]

While corporate leaders are not trying to launch social movements, there are many parallels with the storytelling guidelines Ganz develops as CEOs are engaged in financial and investor communication. As they present to investors, they are asking them to see the challenges companies face in their markets, the choices these lead to and the strategies they are implementing to build businesses and reward shareholders. The action CEOs are trying to provoke is that listeners remain or become shareholders. In recent decades, storytelling is increasingly being adopted as a management process.

Business storytelling

There is a growing body of research around how storytelling is used in the management of organizations. In positioning the relevance of storytelling in this way, two researchers have argued, from a psychological perspective, that there is a stronger connection with memory if information is conveyed by story rather than just facts or figures. In their view, stories about individuals' experiences, and those of others, are the fundamental constituents of human memory, knowledge and social communication.[24]

A commercial example of this is given by a manager at the US company 3M:

> [Organizational storytelling is] central to our identity – part of the way we see ourselves and explain ourselves to one another. Stories are a habit of mind at 3M, and it's through them – through the way they make us see ourselves and our business operations in complex, multidimensional forms – that we're able to discover opportunities for strategic change. Stories give us ways to form ideas about winning.[25]

Reinforcing this, in studying the language used by managers in business meetings, another researcher, Daphne Jameson, found it was "narrative discourse" that was a primary force in leading to management action.[26] By collectively constructing stories, "managers made sense of the past, coped with the present, and planned for the future".[27] Her research pointed to four conclusions: that managers used narrative as a way of resolving conflict; that, in building stories together, managers influenced others and achieved a unified team; that disagreements were more a result of differing perspectives on a story, with narrative preferred to overt argument in achieving agreement; and that using narrative was an important ability of management.[28] In observing how managers built stories, Jameson noticed that managers, in relating various events, developed a story together and that this in turn gave power to the story as it attained a significance beyond those events.[29] When presented with statistics, there was a reluctance to "let the numbers speak for themselves" because they felt "they didn't tell the whole story" so they used analogies and narrative to transform them into "stories that connected cause and effect, as well as the past and the future".[30]

Another writer from a management perspective who has made the connection with storytelling and business leadership is Stephen Denning. He sees storytelling as an essential component of a manager's armoury in a business world that is increasingly

Case study

Fairfax Media – facts getting in the way of a good story

For traditional media companies with print mastheads, times couldn't be tougher. Advertisers have increasingly been moving away from print to online outlets, print readership is declining while moving online without paying for anything and yet costs are rising. In this environment, taking on a job as CEO of a traditional media company would have to be one of the toughest jobs in business. Yet when Greg Hywood was appointed in February 2011 to run Australia's oldest media company, which had been operating since 1841, he saw his biggest challenge as communication and "selling the Fairfax story": "The thing I've learned in business and working in government is you have to do the job but if people don't know that you've done the job, you might as well not have done it. Basically there is a clash of ideas that we live in and everyone wants their space. If you can communicate effectively what you've done, you get the credit you deserve."[31]

Hywood came to the job with helpful credentials. He was the first Fairfax CEO to come from within the group since it had been bought out of receivership in 1990. He had been an award-winning journalist, rising to the ranks of editor and then into management roles within the business. Then, after 27 years with the company and following a difference of opinion about company direction with the then CEO, he moved on, taking a senior government position. His return to the job was preceded by appointment as a director and then taking over from his predecessor when the board felt it was time for someone new with a media background to confront a worsening business environment.[32]

The company he rejoined was certainly different. When he left in 2003, the company's two main metropolitan mastheads, *The Age* and *The Sydney Morning Herald*, with their bulging Saturday editions full of classified advertising, accounted for about 75 per cent of the business. By 2011, this had shrunk to 20 per cent, the classifieds had moved to online competitors and the business had diversified, to some online businesses but also more publications as well as a large investment in printing them. However, the story

Hywood wanted to sell was that Fairfax was a well-rounded media group. Its mastheads were strong, it had a diversified range of regional and rural publications and some of the online businesses were performing particularly well. He believed there was a bright future for media companies that could produce quality and independent journalism.[33] Even the stock market was welcoming to this approach and his appointment.

Part of the reasoning behind the market's positive view was that there was a feeling the economy could improve and, along with it, an uplift in advertising expenditure. However, this hoped-for boost did not materialize and 16 months into his tenure, Hywood was forced to take the axe heavily to costs and reorient the group more towards digital than print media. "Fairfax downsizes its future"[34] was how a rival media group described it but the main Fairfax business masthead was more positive, with its headline of "Fairfax spearheads digital future".[35]

The cuts were indeed severe – planned closure of two of its largest printing operations, its workforce of 10,000 to be cut by 20 per cent, its two main broadsheet mastheads to become tabloids and introduction of pay walls around digital editions of its publications.[26] One of the principles underlying the restructure was to avoid cross subsidization of loss-making businesses so that each business and publication had to stand on its own. Proceeds from cost-cutting and sale of equity in one online business would also contribute to reducing debt.[37]

Fairfax CEO, Greg Hywood

Again the market was welcoming, with stock price rising, but the original story had taken a dent. A commitment to quality journalism was still there but morale among the writing team sunk to low levels as many old hands took the management-encouraged redundancies. A few months later, in its financial year 2012 results, Fairfax reported a loss of A\$2.4 billion, as many of the costs of the restructure were absorbed. Advertising recovery was now nominated for 2015. These confronting facts had led to a reshaping of the Fairfax story, with it now being a "diversified publishing, radio and digital group which was positioning itself as a multi-platform operation" with a "growing digital audience" and "key growth drivers being transactional businesses".[38]

While there is market sympathy for the difficulties Fairfax faces, one influential believer in the future of newspapers is Berkshire Hathaway's Warren Buffet who has been aggressively buying newspapers over the past three years. While he says he doesn't have a "secret sauce" for making newspapers profitable in a digital age, he is confident that newspapers in certain cities and those with a local focus will survive.[39] If he's right, there might even come a time when Fairfax could revive its historical story.

challenging. He quotes these statistics in highlighting the importance of communication for chief executives:

> only 10 per cent of listed companies can sustain for more than a few years a growth trajectory that creates above average shareholder returns, less than 10 per cent of major innovations in large corporations are successful and only 15 per cent of mergers and acquisitions add value to the acquiring company.[40]

Consequently, Denning argues that it is the job of management to turn these statistics around and that, since managers spend some 75 per cent of their day talking, it is storytelling that adds a dimension of leadership to management and can make a difference. Denning sees leadership as essentially a task of persuasion, with storytelling a critical part of this process. It does not replace abstract reasoning and analysis but supplements it, he says, with storytelling being part of the performance art. He sees stories as material leaders can use to motivate others in an organization and get them to work together. Stories are also the device for building trust in leaders, their organizations and their brands. They can be used to create and share a vision and solve the problem of disruptive innovation. In this way Denning uses the device of storytelling to create a new kind of leader, one that is interactive in connecting with a team and who communicates with people on a plane of equality.[41]

Not all of Denning's views about storytelling are applicable to the area of financial and investor communication in which CEOs of stock exchange-listed corporations have to relate to the hardened audiences of business journalists and investment community analysts. One group of researchers in the UK has brought together the field of narrative and numbers in this context. On the topic of how much time UK executives of listed companies spent "talking to the City", it was found it increased from 10 per cent in 1989 to 20.5 per cent in 1998. Over this time there was also a change in the language executives used, with them increasingly adopting phrases such as "strategic focus, shareholder value and corporate governance" in the interests of connecting more closely with the concepts the City wanted to hear about. They also quote other research from 2001, which showed there was an unchanging demand from the City in terms of what it wanted to know from listed companies.

> "What fund managers want" focuses on invariant key themes which recur in almost every City analyst. These themes include the prospects going forward for earnings and growth plus the "quality of management" and the CEO, which will often be discussed in terms of delivery and shareholder friendliness. Other topics for general discussion include the business model, plan for cost recovery and any bold management moves, with much attention given to M&A (mergers and acquisitions) ... the market ideally wants a "story in a box".[42]

The work of this UK-based group of researchers highlights the bringing together of the concepts of narrative and numbers as listed companies connect with their key stakeholders of the investment community and financial media. Their research indicates that company narratives are not permanent but rather can tend to have short lives, perhaps three to five years before being discarded. This can be in contrast to industry narratives, which can last decades. A distinction their research makes is that if stories are to avoid becoming spin, then story needs to be closely connected with performance, with management initiatives becoming examples of what is being done, as well as being said, in the process of enacting strategy.[43]

Underlying the UK group research is the argument that, while there is undeniable value in the management theory of Michael Porter, who has focused on how companies are situated in an industry as a basis for devising strategy, not enough attention has been paid to the process of what they describe as "financialization". In financialization they observe two issues: the way in which management concepts such as shareholder value require companies to convert management strategies into numerical form to demonstrate they are actually delivering value; and the requirement listed companies have to explain the financial outcomes of strategy to the investment community and the financial media. This explanation process requires companies to have a narrative that articulates their strategies, with the narrative usually having three components – a grand vision, an industry narrative and a company-specific narrative. What their analysis shows, in three substantial case studies of large multinational corporations, is that there is often a gap between the rhetoric of the shareholder value oriented narrative and performance, "where financialisation sets giant company management on a utopian quest for growth and higher returns for capital whose uncertain consequences include a gap between saying and doing".[44]

In these circumstances, where there is not an exact coincidence between numbers and narrative, the narrative needs to change or be supplemented by "management initiatives", with authorship of the new narrative often being shared between company and key stakeholders:

> Various actors such as business journalists and stock market analysts can endorse, modify or challenge company narratives or conventional understandings of an industry in a world where narratives are not controlled by the corporate CEO or any one group of actors. The framing of targets, the definition of results as good news or bad news and the criteria for success and failure are a kind of collective endeavour of an unstable kind.[45]

This idea of co-authorship of a company story becomes a healthy check on the effectiveness of story as salesmanship. The numbers confront a story with a reality that requires explanation, necessitating that a corporate story must combine facts, numbers and narrative.

Warren Buffett and communication

The investment perspective on the corporate story has been influenced extensively by the world's most successful investor, Warren Buffett, who has been responsible for many quotable passages in this regard. Essentially his view is to invest only in companies you understand, run by people you admire and trust.[46] His method is to look for good businesses that will be around for the long term. One of his quotes that illustrates this is: "I never attempt to make money on the day to day change in the stock market. In fact, I purposely buy on the assumption that it'll close tomorrow and not reopen for five years."[47] For companies that do meet Buffett's criteria of being easily understood businesses that will survive for the long term, his favourite holding period is "forever".[48]

Buffett's views about investing provide sensible guidance for developing a corporate story around the type of company in which Buffett might invest. However, Buffett himself has divergent views about communication. On the one hand, he believes that acquiring communication skills is the best investment individuals can make for their advancement.[49] He also believes that companies should be open in their communication with stakeholders.[50] However, in an interview he gave on CNBC in 2011, Buffett made some critical comments about the process of investor relations. In his view, most public company CEOs, like himself, resent giving up some 15 to 20 per cent of their time to interact with Wall Street. He is not critical of those that do this but his own preference is to avoid it since his annual meeting weekend is devoted entirely to making himself available to investor questioning. In this way he feels he is treating all investors and shareholders equally, whether they have a large or small stake. As a large investor, Buffett is also on the receiving end of investor relations efforts by companies who want him to come and visit management and hear them talk about how they are running their companies. Buffett's view about this, which he realizes may annoy investor relations people, is to ignore such approaches because he would prefer management is focused on their real jobs, such as working out how to cut costs or improve sales, rather than wasting time talking to him. He does not mind companies giving a focus to helping people understand their businesses better but he sees the "schmoozing" element of this as a waste of time. As for investing in his company, Berkshire Hathaway, his preference is to focus on existing shareholders rather than travelling the country looking for new ones. He would rather have investors "that know and understand Berkshire and not look for a revolving door constituency".[51]

One investor relations observer of these comments noted that Buffett does naturally as a communicator what is essentially the task of investor relations and corporate storytelling. He has developed his investment vehicle, Berkshire Hathaway, into an easily understood company with a long-term perspective and his devices for explaining the types of companies his group invests in – his public appearances, annual report and annual meeting – are classic components of corporate communication. If you are not Warren Buffett, this critic points out, you need to adopt similar investor practices that achieve these ends:

> We need to tell our stories if we want investors to know us at all – or understand us. We need investors to see our top managers and have confidence in their ability. And we need to build relationships – with current shareholders, those who might invest in the future, and even the sell-side analysts who advise their own sets of clients.[52]

For some years, Buffett's annual report for Berkshire Hathaway has become widely respected as representing a way that companies should relate to shareholders and, in effect, tell their story to them. Two writers in the *Harvard Business Review* in 2010, Berman and Knight, analysed the 2009 letter to shareholders in that year's report, which is jointly written by Buffett and his business partner, Charlie Munger. They noted the use of conversational language and discerned four traits that contributed to effective financial communication and corporate storytelling. The four traits are indicated below with examples from the 2010 report, indicating they are an ongoing feature of the company's communication.

"Use numbers to season the points you serve – they're not the main dish"[53]

Berman and Knight point out that Buffett and Munger, through the use of simple language are able to demystify complex topics, using numbers as a tool to reinforce the language rather than having numbers do the job on their own. Examples in the 2010 report are in explanations of life insurance underwriting or the economics of a railroad investment. During the year, Berkshire Hathaway bought railroad company Burlington Northern Santa Fe, and Buffett and Munger explain the logic of their investment this way:

> Both of us are enthusiastic about BNSF's future because railroads have major cost and environmental advantages over trucking, their main competitor. Last year BNSF moved each ton of freight it carried a record 500 miles on a single gallon of diesel fuel. That's three times more fuel-efficient than trucking is, which means our railroad owns an important advantage in operating costs. Concurrently, our country gains because of reduced greenhouse emissions and a much smaller need for imported oil. When traffic travels by rail, society benefits.[54]

"Use analogies and metaphors"[55]

A number of these are spread through the letter to shareholders, which means it is colourful and easy reading and another device for explanation without jargon. This example illustrates Buffett's sceptical opinion of academic views about markets:

> John Kenneth Galbraith once slyly observed that economists were most economical with ideas: They made the ones learned in graduate school last a lifetime. University finance departments often behave similarly. Witness the tenacity with which almost all clung to the theory of efficient markets throughout the 1970s and 1980s, dismissively calling powerful facts that refuted it "anomalies." (I always love explanations of that kind: The Flat Earth Society probably views a ship's circling of the globe as an annoying, but inconsequential, anomaly.)[56]

"Be honest and transparent"[57]

Buffett is frank in relation to performance and this straightforwardness contributes to building credibility. This example relates to assessment of performance over the years:

> After 1999, the market stalled (or have you already noticed that?). Consequently, the satisfactory performance relative to the S&P that Berkshire has achieved since then has delivered only moderate absolute results. Looking forward, we hope to average several points better than the S&P – though that result is, of course, far from a sure thing. If we succeed in that aim, we will almost certainly produce better relative results in bad years for the stock market and suffer poorer results in strong markets.[58]

"Use facts to put things in realistic context"[59]

Buffett is fond of using a longer-term perspective of American history to link with his investment views, with this being an example common to several annual reports:

> Throughout my lifetime, politicians and pundits have constantly moaned about terrifying problems facing America. Yet our citizens now live an astonishing six times better than when I was born. The prophets of doom have overlooked the all-important factor that is certain: Human potential is far from exhausted, and the

American system for unleashing that potential – a system that has worked wonders for over two centuries despite frequent interruptions for recessions and even a Civil War – remains alive and effective.

We are not natively smarter than we were when our country was founded nor do we work harder. But look around you and see a world beyond the dreams of any colonial citizen. Now, as in 1776, 1861, 1932 and 1941, America's best days lie ahead.[60]

While the style of Buffett and Munger is not the only course for financial and investor communication, it does show how a combination of plain language and frank explanation can sharpen a corporate narrative.

Applications

There are many influences on the application of storytelling in business, some of which need weighing as a test of their applicability to listed company communication. Self-help literature, oriented to the performance end of the spectrum of corporate communication, needs to be treated warily. If there is a risk that tough and objective audiences such as analysts and business journalists may see this style of presentation as trite and lacking seriousness of intent then it becomes antithetical to the objectives of having people understand companies better in making an investment decision.

The challenge remains, however, in collecting information about a company in the form of facts and numbers, of how to present it in a way that achieves objectives of conveying better understanding. In a generalized sense, story is a way of making that information interesting, creating a thread that links facts and numbers, which can be termed a "narrative". The grander themes of history and literature can be equally as inappropriate as self-help literature although they do provide a link to the larger topics of corporate strategy.

Many listed companies, in connecting with their stakeholders, are wanting them to understand a reality that management faces in the present while leading them to appreciate how the corporation is striving to attain a future reality, in which it may have achieved bigger market shares, growth and higher returns. There is a journey to be made between these two points, in the face of many obstacles and across a landscape with challenging features. Within this description are links to the themes historians have taken on, the great themes of literature and recurring themes of myths. It is not that corporate leaders need to bring in these references, but they are touchstones for how a corporate story can be pieced together that will resonate with audiences.

In subsequent chapters we will refer further to the content of the story but one of the reasons story is an important part of the communications process for listed companies is the reverberation aspect of how markets work. Stories may be told in isolation in one-on-one meetings, perhaps with a journalist or analyst, but the jobs of these people is to absorb the information, digest it and then pass it on to their stakeholders, who may be stock sales teams or media audiences. An increasingly used mechanism in financial markets is chat systems among traders and across dealing rooms. Bloomberg is one of the larger purveyors of these systems, having established Bloomberg Community. Company stories are retold through these mechanisms, not just as facts or numbers, but in a story perpetuated from listening to company presentations. The quality of what they pass on is directly related to how they have heard a company story in the first place. From there it may reverberate in the form of phrases or ideas and if a company's journey and strategy has been understood then that too will become part of the communication network, initiated through a company storytelling process.

Before we look more closely at the content and putting together of a company story, there is an intermediate step: the story being told links with a company's development strategy, it is part of its branding and the investor relations strategy is part of a bigger and broader communications picture. A question to be answered is, where is the evidence that telling a corporate story actually has some value and connects with a company's stock price, which is what concerns many boards of directors? Our next chapter explores these topics.

Notes

1 Aristotle, *Poetics*, translation at http://classics.mit.edu/Aristotle/poetics.mb.txt

2 Bal, M, *Narratology: Introduction to the Theory of Narrative* (University of Toronto Press, Toronto: 2009) pp 7–9

3 Chatwin, B, *Songlines* (Jonathan Cape, London: 1987), p 2

4 Dulumunmun, M, *My People's Dreaming*, quoted on www.aboriginalsonglines.com/quotations

5 Quoted from Irwin, B, "What's in a Frame? The Medieval Textualisation of Traditional Storytelling", *Oral Tradition* 10 (1), 1995, p 27

6 Bruner, J, "The Narrative Construction of Reality", *Critical Inquiry* 18 (1), 1991, p 4

7 Bruner (1991), p 18

8 Tompkins, JP (ed.), *Reader-Response Criticism: From Formalism to Post Structuralism* (John Hopkins University Press, Baltimore, MD: 1980), pp ix–xxvi

9 Carr, EH, *What is History?* The George Macauley Trevelyan Lectures, delivered at the University of Cambridge, January-March 1961 (Random House Inc, New York NY: 1961), p 33

10 Carter, P, *The Road to Botany Bay, An Essay in Spatial History* (Faber and Faber, London: 1987), pp xiii–xxv

11 Carter (1987), pp xiv–xv

12 Carter (1987), p xx

13 Carter (1987), p xxvi

14 Frost, A, *Botany Bay Mirages* (Melbourne University Press, Melbourne: 1995)

15 Schama, S, *Landscape and Memory* (Fontana Press, London: 1996), p 7

16 Morong, C, "Mythology, Joseph Campbell and the Socio-Economic Conflict", *Journal of Socio-Economics* 23 (4), 1994

17 Campbell, J, *The Hero With a Thousand Faces* (Princeton University Press, Princeton, NJ: 2004), p 28

18 Fisher, WR, "Narration as a Human Communication Paradigm: The Case of Public Moral Argument", *Communication Monographs* 51, 1984, pp 1–22

19 Fisher, WR, "The Narrative Paradigm", *Communication Monographs* 52, 1985, p 349

20 Ganz, M, "The Power of Story in Social Movements", paper for the Annual Meeting of the American Sociological Association, August 2001

21 Abramsky, S, "A Conversation with Marshall Ganz", *The Nation*, 3 February 2011

22 Ganz, M, "Why Stories Matter", *Sojourners Magazine*, March 2009

23 Sturm, BW, "The Enchanted Imagination: Storytelling's Power to Entrance Listeners", *American Association of School Librarians* 2, 1999, www.ala.org/aasl/aaslpubsandjournals/slmrb/slmrcontents/volume21999/vol2sturm

24 Schank, RC and Abelson, RP, "Knowledge and Memory: The Real Story", in RS Wyer Jr. (ed.) *Knowledge and Memory: The Real Story* (Lawrence Erlbaum Associates, Hillsdale, NJ: 1995).

25 Shaw, G, Brown, R and Bromiley, P, "Strategic Stories: How 3M is Rewriting Business Planning", *Harvard Business Review* 76 (3), 1998, 41–48, quoted in Knudsen, SH and Jones, R, "Organisational Storytelling: Managing the Exchange of Identities", Conference Paper, 2001, http://anzmac.info/conference/2001/anzmac/AUTHORS/pdfs/Knudsen.pdf

26   Jameson, D, "Narrative Discourse and Management Action", *The Journal of Business Communication* 38 (4), 2001, p 476

27   Jameson (2001), p 476

28   Jameson (2001), pp 476–477

29   Jameson (2001), pp 493–494

30   Jameson (2001), pp 501 and 504

31   Quoted in Chessel, J, "The Hardest Story for Fairfax to Sell: Its Own", *The Australian*, 8 February 2011

32   Chessell, J, "From Cadet to CEO, Hywood Ready for Challenges of Media's Toughest Job", *The Australian*, 12–13 February 2011

33   Chessell, J, 8 February 2011

34   *The Australian*, 19 June 2011

35   *Australian Financial Review*, 19 June 2011

36   Holgate, B, "Fairfax Spearheads Digital Age", *Australian Financial Review*, 19 June 2011

37   Boyd, T, "Rinehart Ups the Ante", *Australian Financial Review*, 19 June 2011

38   Holgate, B, "Fairfax Writedowns Hurt Bottom Line", *Australian Financial Review*, 24 August 2011

39   Haughney, C, "Newspapers Work, With Warren Buffett as Boss", *New York Times*, 17 June 2012, www.nytimes.com/2012/06/18/business/media/newspaper-work-with-warren-buffett-as-the-boss.html?ref=business&pagewanted=all&_r=0

40   Denning, S, *The Leader's Guide to Storytelling: Mastering the Art and Discipline of Business Narrative* (Jossey-Bass, San Francisco, CA: 2005), p xiv

41   Denning (2005), Chapter 8

42   Froud, J, Sukhdev, J, Leaver, A and Williams, K, *Financialisation and Strategy: Narrative and Numbers* (Routledge, Oxford; 2006), p 125

43   Froud et al (2006), pp 128–129

44   Froud et al (2006), p 9

45   Froud et al (2006), p 123

46   Koch, D. and Koch, L, "Buffett's Itchy Trigger Finger", *The Daily Telegraph*, 7 March 2011

47   W Buffett, quoted at www.buffettsbooks.com/warren-buffett-quotes.html

48   W Buffett, quoted at www.buffettsbooks.com/warren-buffett-quotes.html

49   W Buffett, quoted at www.48days.net/profiles/blogs/warren-buffett-s-best-investment-advice-it-s-not-what-you-think?xg_source=activity

50   W Buffett, quoted at http://newsroom.businesswire.com/press-release/berkshire-hathaway-chairman-warren-e-buffett-suggests-open-communications-marketing-sa

51   Quoted by D Johnson at http://ircafe.com/2011/03/

52   http://ircafe.com/2011/03/

53   Berman, K and Knight, J, "Financial Communication, Warren Buffett Style", March 2010, http://blogs.hbr.org/cs/2010/03/financial_communication_warren.html

54   Berkshire Hathaway Annual Report 2010, Letter to Shareholders, www.berkshirehathaway.com/2010ar/2010ar.pdf, p 3

55   Berman and Knight (2010)

56   Berkshire Hathaway (2010), p 21

57   Berman and Knight (2010)

58   Berkshire Hathaway (2010), p 4

59   Berman and Knight (2010)

60   Berkshire Hathaway (2010), p 4

4 Linking communication with strategy, story and stock price

A corporate story, developed for stakeholders like the investment community, shareholders and business media, cannot be a story in isolation if it is to convey higher levels of understanding. The story is not distinct from a company's brand, overarching communications strategy or development strategy. Nor is it separate from the notions of reputation and relationship-building that are key components of the public relations task. It is in fact an encapsulation of all these elements. Investor relations, as an increasingly important aspect of communication, is focused on telling the larger corporate story to specialized audiences and adding facts and numbers that connect with those stakeholders. It is the corporate narrative that ties those threads together and contributes to supporting reputation. Investor relations has specific objectives and principal among them is to contribute to demand for a listed company's stock and, consequently, a company's stock price. Increasingly these days in business there is a focus on measurement of the value of corporate activities. This can be difficult with aesthetic pursuits such as communication, and investor relations is no exception in needing to demonstrate its value. While many might believe communication is value in itself, there is nevertheless increasing evidence that investor relations does add to markers that connect with stock price value.

Each of these concepts is worth looking at in greater depth. The sequence of the argument begins with the idea of a three-part connection between corporate strategy and communication strategy – corporate strategy relies on the communication function to provide the views of stakeholders as input to formulation of corporate strategy, communication is key to implementing corporate strategy and, in the financial and investor communication sphere, a large part of the content of communication is corporate strategy. These connections highlight the concept of integrated communication, involving a variety of means to communicate strategic direction. Communicating the essence of a corporation is the process of developing a corporate story and we look at two differing approaches to this, one from a reputation platform and another beginning with the idea of sustainability. Common to these approaches is developing a narrative that sums up facts, numbers and attitudes as a vehicle for engaging with stakeholders. With reputation being part of the corporate story, it is worth noting its financial effects, which include a stock market value for reputation as well as it being a factor in attracting investors. This sets up a basis for considering the many influences on stock price, including research that establishes the contribution provided by communication. What this argument seeks to show is the sequential link between corporate strategy and communication, and how this establishes a framework for the corporate story, the communication of which has a powerful influence on how investors react.

From strategy to communication

Strategy can tend to be an overworked word in business. Companies cannot be seen to be without a strategy and yet sometimes we see the word used to add importance to actions that relate more to a description of what is being done rather than to a grand plan. Communications strategy is similarly a widely used term, sometimes creating a sense that it is separate from corporate strategy, with a life of its own unconnected with the bigger picture of a company's direction. Corporate communication in its proper formulation is essentially part of a company fulfilling its strategy by giving importance to the need to communicate about it.

South African scholar Benita Steyn brought out these issues in a paper that connects corporate and communication strategy.[1] Her analysis begins with looking at the evolution of views about the role of business in society. The prevailing view in the first half of the twentieth century was the shareholder approach, stemming from the idea that managers were obliged to pursue profits to enhance the wealth of owners. In the 1960s this evolved into more of a stakeholder approach in which business was seen to be an actor in a larger environment, with several social responsibilities, from economic to legal, ethical and several discretionary categories. This led to the emergence of concepts such as corporate social responsibility and corporate social performance that, while not ignoring the need for corporate profitability, nevertheless added more considerations for managers in forming corporate strategy. This meant that stakeholders had to be recognized as groups that could hinder or enhance profitability as they have the capability to wield economic or legal power. Consequently, there was a need to account for them in strategic terms since there was also an economic rationale in building good relationships with stakeholders.[2]

This has led to what Steyn describes as a "corporate community approach",[3] in which both management and stakeholders see benefits in enhancing corporate profitability, with business creating wealth by integrating stakeholders into a productive whole. In the modern corporation, strategy involves managers acting as stewards, and leaders, in forming a political coalition that draws together resources and stakeholders to build financial and social wealth. Steyn sees this as a transformation from how management philosopher Peter Drucker saw strategy in the 1950s, namely as an indication of the organization's positioning for the future, which meant a focus on the "what" rather than the "how". For today's corporation, Steyn believes it is more important to do the right thing, which is improving effectiveness, than to do things right, reflecting Drucker's idea of improving efficiency.[4] Management strategy thus evolved to take in a broader picture of the surrounding environment, encompassing society at large, industry conditions and the internal corporate environment, including goals and strategic thinking about direction.[5] This thinking can have four determinants: what can be done, recognizing a company's competitive advantage; what might be done, accounting for the environment; what managers want to be done, in line with their aspirations; and what ought to be done, recognizing a company's wider obligations to stakeholders.[6]

For Steyn, this strategic thinking has a direct link with corporate communication, in both strategy development and strategy implementation. In formulating strategy, the communication function can contribute an understanding of stakeholders and their views as well as reconciling organizational and stakeholder interests in setting social goals alongside the financial and economic goals set by others in the management team. The coalescence of management and communications theory was reflected in the views of public relations academic James Grunig, who argued that the overall strategic management of corporations was inseparable from the strategic management of relationships with stakeholders. For Grunig, there are three stages in formulating communications strategy – identifying strategic stakeholders, engaging with stakeholders who may see problems in organizational decisions and then dealing with issues arising from this, including the media.[7]

However, Steyn identifies two bases for criticism of this Grunig model. One is a recognition that corporate communications strategy should not be entirely beholden to stakeholders, or only be a two-way communication between these groups to achieve Grunig's standard of effective communication. Companies in the real world also need to express their points of view in a combination of one-way and two-way communication. By doing so, they combine an understanding of stakeholder views and the surrounding environment along with a corporate perspective on issues. Supporting this perspective is research by van Ruler who concludes that corporate communication on a daily basis encompasses more than Grunig's ideal of two-way symmetrical communication. Corporations regularly pursue "controlled one way communication" with their communications strategies encompassing the provision of information, persuasion, consensus building and dialogue.[8] Steyn's second point of criticism of the Grunig model is to add an educational element, in which communication can be used additionally to resolve issues that impinge on implementing corporate strategy. By seeing communication in this way, Steyn is making a distinction. On the one hand there is corporate communication strategy as a fundamental component of corporate strategy, which also operates by providing direction to the function. Separately there is communication strategy focused on implementation as part of a communications plan.[9]

This higher level distinction between strategy formulation and implementation is important in considering financial and investor communication. While this field necessarily has an implementation function, its overriding purpose is the communication of corporate strategy. Consequently, corporate communication from this higher strategic conception is aimed at achieving a balance between commercial imperatives and socially acceptable corporate behaviour. In this sense it embraces several steps of the evolution of corporate purpose, from the shareholder to stakeholder models and then a corporate community approach. It deals with issues by combining these perspectives. Corporate communication contributes to helping corporations adapt to their environment and in building competitive advantage. In this process, communication establishes itself as a function that is not only relevant to strategic management but is also an important contributor to organizational effectiveness.

Strategic communication

Strategic communication, at the higher level Steyn delineates, is aimed at explaining a company's overall business strategy and contributing to enhancing its market position. To research the link between communication and corporate strategies, Professor Paul Argenti and two colleagues in 2005 spoke to 50 companies, representing a cross section of some of America's largest. Among their conclusions were:

> The research not only indicates the drivers, best practices and lessons of strategic communication but it also suggests that when companies take a strategic approach to communication, communication becomes integral to the formulation and

implementation of strategy … We found that the companies most likely to recognise the strategic communication imperative are those in which the CEO has an inherent understanding of how communication can be a differentiator for a business and thus can drive strategy … Dell chairman Michael Dell says, "I communicate to customers, groups of employees and others, while working on a strategy. A key part of strategy is communicating it. Communication is key to operations and execution and an integral part of the process." PepsiCo president and CFO Indra Nooyi puts it cogently: "You only have to go through one or two communication debacles as a senior executive to understand the importance of communication."[10]

Argenti and colleagues highlight a strategic communication framework that has many "loops, constituencies and connections".[11] The strategic elements account for the markets in which companies participate, the products and services they provide, the research that underlies them, the operations that produce them, the finance required and the culture and management that delivers performance. Argenti delineates three key drivers of this strategic communication: regulatory imperatives, organizational complexities and the need to increase credibility. The regulatory aspects, while relating to the US, reflect common Western economy jurisdictions. The principal US regulatory requirement, enacted in 2000, is Regulation Fair Disclosure, which, among other things, prohibits companies from communicating preferentially with certain outside parties, particularly stock analysts. The intention is that price-sensitive information be disclosed first to the market as a whole through established disclosure practices. In 2002, enactment of the Sarbanes-Oxley Bill made senior executives personally responsible for certifying companies' financial results and progressed the need for transparency in making management disclosures more accessible and comprehensible. As companies have grown in size, the need for a consistent communication strategy has become more critical. Corporate crises over the past decade have led to public opinion believing business does a poor job of balancing profit and the public interest, which has increased the need for a strategic approach to communication to achieve differentiation and earn higher levels of trust.[12]

The strategic management of communication that Argenti et al's research brings out is that the companies surveyed apply an integrated approach across multiple levels of communication. This incorporates communication functions that bring in the media, employees, financial stakeholders, the community, government and marketing. Each function has differing objectives, constituencies and channels and, even though they are all focused on communicating the organization's strategy, the messages are modified to break strategy into pieces so that the right pieces are presented to the right audience. As communication is implemented, obtaining feedback about it is also a determinant of its success and ongoing modification.

Argenti et al discern several lessons from the research about how communication can add to the process of translating boardroom strategy to front line execution, as well as the ability of communication to support strategy development. One lesson is that senior managers must be involved. In the companies surveyed, the CEO was in effect the senior communication officer. "When asked how much time he spends communicating, Dell's (CFO) said, 'Can you go above 100%?'"[13] Another lesson was that communication must be integrated. The strategic sense of this is that while a corporation might have a number of business units with differing functions and varying communications needs, their overall messages need to maintain the integrity of the larger corporation's messages.

Argenti et al quote a senior executive from GlaxoSmithKline: "Investor relations and corporate communications are separate functions that work very closely together but we still have one story here – one basic message."[14] Another perspective on this is given by a senior executive of the New York Times Co.: "Before investor relations and corporate communications were integrated, we didn't have problems but we failed to take advantage of opportunities."[15] Two other lessons Argenti et al bring out from the research are that communication must have a long-term orientation, despite the pervasiveness of short-term performance demands, and that top communicators must have broad general management skills, which are necessary to achieve a wider understanding of the businesses about which they are communicating. The Argenti research concludes with these remarks:

> Companies that continue to take a laissez-faire approach to communication will find it increasingly difficult to compete. Although there will be a continuing need for tactical execution, the addition of an integrated strategic focus will be critical to success.[16]

The idea of integrated corporate communication at a strategic level brings together a number of concepts, such as corporate identity, image and reputation, all of which are tools for communicating corporate strategy, visually as well as through values, actions and communication content. The functions that are included under the banner of corporate communication are structured differently across corporations and can include public affairs, investor relations, media relations, marketing and internal communication. One writer describes this move towards integrated communication as a historical progression. As Joep Cornelissen looks at the history of public relations, he notes a move from publicity-seeking in the 1900s to information dissemination in the 1930/1940s, relationship management in the 1960/1970s, organizational positioning in the 1980/1990s, and integrated communication in the twenty-first century. This continuum, he notes, is a move from the tactical to the strategic, which has become more emphasized as strategic communication has taken hold.[17]

Cornelissen also argues there are three drivers that have led to the emergence of the idea of integrated communication. He categorizes them as market- and environment-based, communication-based and organizational. From the market and environmental perspective, stakeholder groups, such as customers, employees and activist groups, have shown two characteristics, becoming more vocal and organized on the one hand and less homogeneous on the other, indicating a fragmentation of their views. Both of these trends have placed greater demand on organizations to develop a coordinated response in terms of marketing and public relations. Added to this is the market influence of corporate social responsibility, which has meant that corporations are expected to provide a transparent response embracing the activities of the corporation as a whole. Cornelissen's communication-based driver for integrated communication stems from the massive number of communication messages in the marketplace every day, making it increasingly competitive to attract attention. Cornelissen quotes one statistic that claims that the average person is hit with 13,000 commercial messages, including logos, a day. This places pressure on corporations to deliver consistent messages, delivered across a variety of media, which can only come about from an integrated approach to communication. Cornelissen's organizational driver for integrated communication is an outcome of corporations seeking to become more efficient while at the same time being required to be more accountable, driving a strategic direction to communication. The intention became to position the organization with various stakeholders by developing messages distinctly for them while embodying the same corporate values and overall corporate strategy in those messages.[18]

Corporate story frameworks – two approaches

In the era of integrated communication, investor relations is at the end of the spectrum where its function is based on communicating a holistic story about a corporation, shaped for key stakeholders like the investment community, shareholders and the business media. Before looking at the creation of this type of story, it is useful to consider more generally the work that has been done in the area of applying storytelling to corporations. While there is a crossover, with a business orientation applying in the financial and investor communication area, structures of stories developed for more widespread stakeholders provide helpful templates in considering how to approach the task for investment-oriented stakeholders. Of two differing approaches that have emerged in the area of corporate storytelling, one begins with a reputation platform while the other takes authenticity as a starting point.

For van Riel and Fombrun,[19] if corporate stories are to be sustainable and a vehicle for creating consistency among the many messages corporations send out each day, then reputation is where the process should start. For many corporations, the encapsulation of a corporate story is in a symbolic representation of its name and accompanying slogan, with this quite often having four possible sources, representing corporate activity, ability, location or responsibility.[20] As this is extended into a longer form story, it works to bring out a company's history, strategy, identity and reputation in a way that "rings true to internal and external observers".[21] This combination of topics is the reputation platform and its effectiveness is determined by whether it can be seen as being relevant, realistic and appealing.[22] When companies apply this platform in creating corporate stories they tend to rely on generalized themes to allow them to emphasize what they see as the essence of their corporate stories. Some focus on an activity, like car companies, others on benefits, such as those that flow to customers, and another common theme is an appeal to the emotions in trying to establish a personal connection between corporation and stakeholders.[23]

As a corporate story is developed in textual form, it sometimes develops a plot, such as tracing a company's history of venturing into new markets or perhaps recovering from a crisis or difficult economic circumstances. It will use words that reflect what is special about a company and its history, its strengths and the way it connects with stakeholders. Van Riel and Fombrun describe six steps for the creation of a sustainable corporate story.[24] The first is positioning a company, both in relation to its rivals in a market and also with its stakeholders. It will account for the competitive nature of its markets and also a prioritizing of the most prominent among its various stakeholders. The second step is to link a story with a company's identity, which is a reflection of beliefs from those on the inside of a company and what they see as distinctive. A third step is the link to reputation, a concept that essentially reflects the perceptions of those outside a company. There are a number of drivers of reputation from outsiders, depending on their perspective. This can include experiences from those who use company products, the extent to which a company is considered trustworthy, well-managed or as having a reliable record of financial performance, and whether a company might be seen to demonstrate social responsibility and provide an attractive workplace environment. The fourth step involves plotting the story and usually encompasses providing proof points for positioning, adopting an appropriate tone of voice and weaving a story around abilities, activities and accomplishments. Steps five and six involve implementing the story, possibly by testing drafts with key stakeholders and then monitoring feedback for further refinement.

Ultimately van Riel and Fombrun conclude that "the true purpose of the corporate story is as a framework for guiding interpretations and conveying the essence of the company across multiple media".[25] They also develop four criteria for judging the effectiveness of a corporate story: the extent to which it is relevant, demonstrating that it has added value; that it is realistic, describing what the company really is and does; that it is sustainable in recognizing and balancing the competing demands of various stakeholders; and that it is responsive in encouraging open dialogue with the company. Ultimately these characteristics are intended to show that any gap between what a company claims and what it actually does is minimal.

A contrasting framework for developing a corporate story, while bringing out many similar characteristics, is from Janis Forman,[26] for whom the foundation is authenticity as the first of four tiers in constructing a story. While Forman's test for authenticity is that words must match deeds, the two components that underlie authenticity are facts and the voices of others who have direct experience of the corporation and what it does. Facts provide the evidence and stability of the story while the voices of others can be from employees, customers or communities who become "accidental spokespeople"[27] for the corporation from the stories they relate of their experiences with the company. In this way they can voice in their own words their knowledge of how a company has acted that has had a positive effect on them personally, with the authenticity of the corporate story combining the personal and the organizational. Forman also issues a warning about corrupting the authenticity of a corporate story by associating it too closely with a celebrity rather than genuineness or from insisting on too close a scripting of a story line for spokespeople so that the story descends into artificiality.

The second tier of Forman's framework for constructing a corporate story is what she calls fluency, in which the effectiveness of story is assessed by how well it engages people's emotions and intellect, or the way it touches the heart and mind.[28] The extent to which a story can achieve this, Forman points out, is whether it meets a definition from the poet Coleridge in which a successful story should evoke a "willing suspension of disbelief", enabling it to be implanted in our imagination.[29] Components of this process involve general aspects of the craft of storytelling, such as developing stories for the right purpose, with flexibility to adjust them for types of audiences and varying categories of storytellers. While a CEO might be a storyteller in relation to corporate strategy, this content also needs to be versatile in being presented to reflect the differing needs of audiences and also allow other spokespersons to adapt it to their style. An interesting example Forman gives is of a consulting firm where consultants are not expected to take company literature to meetings with potential clients but rather use the information they glean from these meetings to allow them to weave their company story into how they would address client concerns and develop solutions.[30] The use of new technology and social media also affords new ways of developing the fluency of storytelling.

The third tier of Forman's storytelling framework is the way a story can be developed to reflect general business objectives of building trust, informing, persuading and inspiring. The most effective way of achieving these objectives is to meet the expectations of stakeholders, Forman argues. Since most people have expectations of receiving high-quality products, recognizing transparency or dealing with a company they can trust, then companies need to listen to what these stakeholders are saying. From this, they need to align their actions with expectations, so that their stories reflect values stakeholders recognize. In informing stakeholders, stories need to explain simply what a company does and the art of persuasion involves developing stories that "teach without preaching".[31]

Forman's fourth tier of corporate storytelling is the way it is intended to meet specific business objectives, such as communicating corporate strategy, culture and branding. While a strategy is forward-looking, it can bring in the characteristics a company has that will contribute to it breaking into new markets or meeting the needs of customers. Corporate culture is a reflection of common assumptions within a company, such as how it does things or thinks about things, with its encapsulation in a story intended to connect this with the perceptions of external stakeholders. Incorporating brand into a corporate story is a way of creating differentiation from competitors, with the brand also representing a promise to deliver on expectations, whether with a product, experience or with financial performance. In this way, a brand becomes a device for developing trusting relationships with stakeholders.[32]

Common features of these two storytelling frameworks – from a reputation platform or authenticity starting point – are the way facts and stakeholder perspectives are woven together to add a new dimension to information. Facts on their own cannot meet the objectives of developing interest in a corporation or building concepts such as trust and motivation. In the investment sphere, numbers need to be added to facts to meet the objective interests of certain groups of stakeholders, which increases the burden that this type of material carries if it is to be converted into communication. It is through the device of narrative, or the corporate story, that factual and numerical information is enabled as a vehicle for engaging with the imaginations of stakeholders so that they are motivated to create a picture of how a corporation can develop into the future. While reputation can be a starting point for developing a corporate story, it is also a factor in investment decision-making, as some researchers have found.

Reputation from an investment perspective

The concept of reputation has had a widespread influence on the theory and practice of communication. From a corporate perspective, it is something that is bestowed on a corporation by outsiders, leading to the idea of enhancing reputation becoming a common objective of many communications programmes. One of the aims of integrated strategic communication is to focus on the corporation as a whole and, in the process, contribute to building reputation. For many, the discipline of public relations is centred on building reputation and protecting it. Reputation is a longer-term concept and it matters, according to Argenti, who describes it in this way:

> Reputation differs from image because it is built up over time and is not simply a perception at a given point in time. It differs from identity because it is a product of both internal and external constituencies, whereas identity is instructed by internal constituencies ... Reputation is based on the perceptions of all an organisation's constituencies.[33]

Reputation has an influence on customers, the community, employees and also investors. Argenti quotes one survey showing that for four out of the five years between 1994 and 1999, an investor who owned stock in Fortune's most admired companies would have earned returns that beat the S&P 500.[34] However, the link between investor returns and reputation is not so clear cut, according to later research by Helm,[35] which shows there is a diversity of loyalty effects of corporate reputation. A company's reputation may well be a strong influence on individual investors' investment decisions but institutional investors are more influenced by financial factors. Where investors make a choice of stock based on a company being one with a reputation for being safe and offering high future earnings, they can often be disappointed. However, a company's reputation has a positive effect on investor loyalty, Helm finds, and this in turn is a factor in reducing volatility of a firm's stock and also its cost of capital. Helm also highlights three streams of research that indicate the role of corporate reputation in financial markets. One relates to financial performance and indicates that firms with relatively good reputations are better able to sustain superior profit outcomes. A second stream indicates that investors are more willing to pay higher prices for shares in companies with better reputations. While return is important in investment decisions, corporate reputation is also highly influential. A third stream relates to financial services markets in which reputation has a positive influence on customer satisfaction and loyalty.

Allied to the idea of reputation, especially in financial services markets, is that of trust. Since the 2008 global financial crisis, community distrust of banks has become widespread. According to ANZ Australia CEO Phil Chronican, this trust can only be restored by a considerable shift in transparency and discipline, with leaders demonstrating integrity and personal accountability.

> Values and behaviours are important ... [and banks] need to get back to basics – accept the new environment as our new reality and adopt new business models and practices to demonstrate we're in touch with customer and stakeholder expectations. We have to demonstrate that, as a sector, we've learned from the experiences of the past five years. ... Trust will only be restored if we work hard to earn it.[36]

Some possible effects on stock price of corporate reputation have also been highlighted from data-mining, brought to light in an interesting *Business Week* article in 2007. While there is some scepticism about this from investment professionals, an issue which does require explanation is the baffling extent to which intangibles can have an effect on share price. As *Business Week* puts it:

> [Corporations] are finding that the way in which the outside world expects a company to behave and perform can be its most important asset. Indeed, a company's reputation for being able to deliver growth, attract top talent and avoid ethical mishaps can account for much of the 30 per cent to 70 per cent gap between the book value of most companies and their market capitalisation.[37]

A difference in reputation is part of the explanation for varying price-earnings ratios applied to companies in a similar industry. At the time of the *Business Week* article, it was differing perceptions of reputation that explained Johnson & Johnson having a higher price-earnings ratio than Pfizer, Proctor & Gamble being preferred over Unilever, and Exxon Mobil having a higher share price than Royal Dutch Shell. While recognizing that it is hard to value an intangible asset such as reputation, and also that financial results are a more powerful determinant of stock price, data-mining specialists have been developing a form of analysis to seek ways of quantifying reputation. In doing so, the aim is also to be able to predict effects on stock prices when changes to reputation take place.

The way some science is added to the process of connecting reputation to the stock market involves sifting through various pieces of information from many sources over a period of time and assessing them in relation to stock price movements. In looking at financial disclosure and economic conditions and their effects on stock prices, it becomes possible to isolate non-financial factors from these stock price movements. Among these factors can be large amounts of data that can relate to media coverage, opinion surveys, investor interviews, a company's public statements, reputation rankings in magazines and many other reputation-related issues. In assessing them and connected stock price movements, it becomes possible to make estimates of possible reputation influences in terms of cents per share.[38]

While this explains the techniques behind the science, the methods do not have universal support among market professionals who have stronger beliefs in their financial analysis techniques than being concerned about reputation issues. However, in one example quoted in *BusinessWeek*, related to Southwest Airlines, the data-mining experts estimated that a public relations switch to emphasizing long-haul flights and frequent services between many cities instead of budget fares would move Southwest's stock 3.5 per cent, equal to $400 million in market value.[39]

One of the difficulties about these examples is that they are intended to induce a generalization that a universal truth is being presented, that this is how things work all the time. If there were such a magic formula, it would be commonly known and followed. However, it is a compelling example that shows a connection between communication and stock price. Of course, there are in fact many influences on stock price, not just one factor and it is worth examining some of these issues before looking at other research that considers how aspects of communication affect stock price or markers of stock price. This also establishes a vantage point for looking at the positioning of investor relations in the communication function and its role in communicating corporate strategy.

Influences on stock price

A stock unit or share is a part ownership of a business. The price of that stock unit on a stock exchange is subject to many influences and also there are many views about how those influences work. Under the efficient market hypothesis, investors are rational and all existing information about a stock is known to the market, which factors it in to determine price. As new information is released randomly, it affects stock price randomly. The outcome of relying on this view of markets is passive investing, reflecting a view that stock prices are unpredictable and the soundest form of investing is a broad-based basket of stocks.

For active investors who believe there is value from analysing information around individual stocks, there are two pieces of information that have the greatest influence on stock prices. The first is a company's profit, often expressed as earnings per share and representing net profit after tax divided by shares on issue. The second is its valuation multiple, expressed as the P/E or price to earnings ratio, which is calculated as price per share divided by earnings per share, leading to an expression like a share trading at "ten times current earnings". There are also two influences on this valuation ratio – the expected growth rate of earnings and the discount rate used to discount to present value the estimates of future earnings. This discount rate is a reflection of perceived risk of achieving estimated earnings and also inflation. In a later chapter we explain a variety of financial measures, including how to understand that discount rate, which is expressed as a company's cost of capital.

All these factors relate to individual companies but there are also other categories of information, external to companies, which have an effect on the overall stock market and so flow on to individual stock prices. These can relate to economic information, generalized factors relating to the stock market and other competing investment opportunities. Inflation and interest rates, and views about their directions, have a significant influence on stock prices. So to do economic statistics, which can affect views about market direction and particular effects on individual stocks. Competing investments to stocks can be property or interest bearing securities, which can be more attractive at certain times and become larger proportions of wider investment portfolios as market conditions change. Large investors sometimes make investment decisions about buying or selling stocks for their own reasons, with large transactions influencing prices irrespective of stock fundamentals. Demographics can affect stock prices as people adjust portfolios in relation to retirement objectives. Liquidity can also influence price, with larger stocks being easier to sell, which can add to their attractiveness compared to smaller stocks where liquidity is lower.

All of these factors are objective and unrelated to psychological factors such as investment sentiment. The emergence of behavioural finance has presented a challenge to the efficient market hypothesis, with the argument that markets are not rationally based and that sentiment and subjective factors can also influence stock prices. An example of this is the way trends or views about them can affect stock prices, such as over-exuberance for technology stocks or, in the current era, for social media stocks because investors see this sort of stock as the way of the future. Popular stocks can become even more popular as investors jump on a bandwagon that adds to stock price momentum.

While there are many influences on stock price, the proposition that communication has an impact has, for a long time, been more conjecture than being able to be verified. However, in recent years, more evidence to substantiate the value of communication has emerged.

Communication influences on stock price

Before examining the evidence, several areas of qualification around some of this research need to be considered. The topic of "corporate communication" is hard to quantify in relation to an objective measure like stock price. Consequently, the research relates to various aspects that connect with communication and that can be measured. The majority of research relates to US stock prices, with some from other countries. Some of the data relates to markers of share price, such as liquidity, trading volumes, volatility, and buy-sell or bid-ask spreads so these terms need some brief explanation.

Liquidity is an attractive feature for stocks. If they are liquid, it makes it easier for investors to buy and sell. Research also shows that greater transparency of disclosure adds to liquidity, another self-perpetuating benefit of liquidity. If effective corporate communication adds to disclosure quality it is adding to liquidity. Some small-sized

Case study

CAM Commerce: a public company CEO's guide for successfully managing the public markets

By Geoff Knapp[40]

Background

I was 24 when I founded software and payments company CAM Commerce Solutions in 1983. We completed a tiny NASDAQ IPO in September 1987 at $5 per share. The market cap after the IPO was under US$10 million. We had no business going public but it was the only way we were able to raise money at the time to expand the business. Shortly after our little IPO the stock market crash of 1987 hit, the stock went to $0.50 and we began our life in "microcap purgatory". The investment bank that took us public provided no support, the stock barely traded and we would discover the hard way that due to our size and small float that most investors would never be interested in us. Any original shareholders that didn't or couldn't bail out had pretty much written off their investment.

Over the next 12 years we worked hard at building the business and to create interest in our stock. I did roadshows, participated in three or four microcap investor conferences every year and took every opportunity to present the company to anyone who was interested, especially brokers who traded in microcap companies. The business itself grew but profitability was up and down. We did not succeed with any consistency and the stock would trade between $1 and $5 over that time period on small volume, when it traded. I had one broker tell me our stock was a "ToWhoma". "Once you buy it, to whom are you going to sell it?"

In August 2008 we would sell the company to a private equity firm for $40.50 per share or $180 million. The stock traded as high as $45 that year. The biggest barrier to the sale was that the market consistently valued the company higher than strategic or financial buyers as a result of our successful investor strategy. We couldn't get a big enough premium to our stock price because the market, small as it was for our stock, loved our company and especially our dividend strategy (more on this below).

During my more than 20 years of experience as the CEO of a small public company I tried everything possible to figure out how to succeed as a public company. Most of what we tried the first 12 years didn't work, in no small part because the company wasn't exciting. The strategy I ultimately settled on came from the lessons learned about what didn't work and why. I thus have some very strong beliefs about the best way for a small public company stuck in microcap purgatory to maximize shareholder value, and also what not to do. It comes from 20 years of experience that finally resulted in success.

Getting started

It all starts with thinking about your company differently. You may not realize it but when you went public you added a new product, the value of which greatly affects everything else in the business over the long run. This product is the shares in your company that trade in the public markets. This "product" has a value, an image … a brand. You have customers for this product, better known as shareholders and sales prospects, which are, of course, investors that might buy your product. Shareholders and prospective shareholders assign a value to your product (shares) based on many factors but one is the strength of your public market brand. Your brand is influenced by many things, especially considering that most investors will not be directly familiar with your actual products. You have competitors for your product, which in the bigger scope are every other possible investment, but in reality are probably just your public company peers. So you have a product (your shares), customers (your shareholders), prospects (potential buyers of your stock) and competitors (other public companies). When you look at things in this way everything else falls into place as you contemplate how to succeed as a public company.

Building your brand

In the traditional sense, a successful company has happy customers who ideally have a very positive relationship with the company's products and employees. A customer who "loves you more than family" will be your advocate. They will tell others. They will be your best salesperson. You obtain that status with the customer by meeting and exceeding his or her expectations and by being better than the competition over the long haul at doing this. And of course your product needs to perform as expected or better and deliver the features that were advertised. It is no different with your stock and your shareholders. So what do customers (shareholders) want and expect? What would you expect as an investor in someone else's company?

Before you can answer the first question you have to answer the question of who your target market is for your product. Who are you building your product for and how do you meet their needs? The biggest mistake I made during the first several years of being a public company was believing the entire market was available to me. I made investor presentations to anyone that would let me and attended any conference that would have us. I would eventually realize that we were too small for most investment firms and analysts, no matter how much they liked our story. In 20 years no significant analyst ever covered us and I think we had two research reports written by smaller firms over that 20-year period. Analyst coverage is highly overrated and often detrimental for a microcap company, but more on that later. The bottom line is that the analysts and investment firms weren't going to recommend us to their clients for fear of affecting the price too much because there just were not enough shares trading. They couldn't make a large enough investment to make it worth their while without owning too much of the company. I was wasting my time. I was offering my product to buyers who were not really prospects once they understood what I was selling. Thus, it seemed to make sense to identify the type of investor that would be interested in what we had to offer.

The target market for microcap investors

Only a small portion of the investment universe is willing to invest in microcap companies in any serious way. Forget about the big firms. If they want what you have, they will find you. I will address how to target potential customers but first a brief discussion about things you might think you want, that you actually don't.

What seems good can also be bad

A high stock price – At first it may seem that having a high stock price is always a good thing. And if you are about to sell your stock and not look back then it is probably true. I would argue that if your view is long term, you want a stock price that is at the high end of "fair". You don't want a stock price that is too high because it won't stay there if you believe markets are ultimately efficient, which they are.

Very high trading volume – It may seem that lots of trading volume in your stock means liquidity, which is always desirable. I would argue that volume that is disproportionate to your float over a sustained period can be unhealthy to your long-term goals. You want your stock to trade regularly in proportion to your float but you don't want your stock to trade too much because it inevitably means you have "traders" in your stock and thus volatility. While some trading is healthy, what you are mostly looking for are loyal long-term shareholders. When a stock rises too fast it turns loyal shareholders into sellers (profit takers), who wouldn't otherwise consider selling. Steep drops are also obviously bad and they are the natural back end of the steep rise. Furthermore, if your stock is overpriced it is hard to be out telling new shareholder prospects they should buy it, at least if you want them to end up as happy customers. The message here is to look at the long term and resist the temptation to "promote" the stock to the type of shareholder that may not be healthy for the long term.

Research reports and analyst coverage – Every company seems to try so hard to get a research report (we did for a while) on their company and some resort to paying for it (we thought about it). Paying for research damages your brand and is a huge mistake and a waste of money. Don't do it! An analyst's research report sets expectations that you may or may not agree with. It sets limits that may put you in a box. I am not saying these cannot be helpful but they are a double-edged sword and you don't need one to succeed. Furthermore it can actually be a plus not to have any research written on your company because it helps your company fit the profile of the target investor who is looking to "discover" the next undiscovered stock gem. If there is research on the company it means someone else already discovered it and others know! I used to make a point of noting in my investor presentation that "nobody followed us" … there was no research coverage. This was a positive for the investor we were targeting.

What do customers (shareholders) and prospective customers (shareholders) want?

Investors think they have an advantage in dealing in small companies they can talk to and understand. They probably want the same things you would want, such as:

- a compelling business model that is easy to understand;
- financials that are easy to model;
- management with experience that they believe to have the highest ethics;
- timely and complete information – transparency;
- good public company standing – all filings timely and complete and regulations met;
- regular and open communication (the ability to get their questions answered);
- an acceptable degree of safety – limited downside;
- yield (income) for many – a dividend will greatly expand your market potential.

Winning a new customer (shareholder)

Targeted investor presentation – It is very important you are able to simplify your story and create a logical presentation that anticipates questions and objections, and answer them. Each time you give your presentation you have an opportunity to improve it by listening to the questions you get and seeing where investors might be having trouble following it. And are they coming away with the impression you are shooting for? Can the presentation stand alone on the web, because if it can that is a big plus. This presentation is the most important tool you have for winning new customers. It needs to be highly professional, very well-organized and easy to understand. After an investor sees it they should be able to say "I get it" and be excited about your company. If your presentation is filled with TLAs (three-letter acronyms) that only someone familiar with your industry will understand, you need to fix this.

Make shareholder communication sincere and a priority – I made it a point to take every shareholder call, answer every shareholder communication promptly and to go out of my way to make sure I was setting reasonable expectations. I wouldn't let shareholders get too carried away with big numbers that I knew were not possible. Within the constraints of the rules, I did everything I could to make sure that shareholders and prospective shareholders understood the company properly.

Managing the chat boards – The Yahoo! and other "chat boards" are a touchy subject due to the limitations you have in dealing with them. They are far more important and influential in the microcap market than company management realizes or wants to admit. With a small company, where information is hard to come by, you can bet that most investors will check the chat boards now and then. And if the stock goes up or down dramatically and it isn't obvious why, then investors will seek out the chat boards to see if they can get a clue as to what is going on. Chat boards are another way your brand image can be affected. I always assume everyone I talk to might post what I said on the chat board or might one day be a regular poster giving opinions about the company. I found if I took the time to treat shareholders with respect it would result in positive posts about the company on the chat boards. An active chat board with supportive shareholders can be positive for the company but it is a situation that can also turn ugly and be out of your control. All you can do is the best you can within the rules but you can definitely influence it in a positive way and minimize the chances for a negative result.

Overcoming unspoken objections – Most investors will never say "I don't trust you". Due to a significant number of bad actors among microcap companies and the low level of companies that meet investor expectations, investors start out with a high level of scepticism. The more comfortable you can make investors with the risk, the more likely they are to invest and to assign a higher value to your product. If you assume investors start out not trusting you and you set out to earn their trust in every way you can, this can only benefit you. Don't take it personally, but rather see it as a challenge and just another objection to overcome in the sales process. An unspoken objection, if you can overcome it, offers significant financial reward for all shareholders.

How do you attract the shareholders you want?

After many years of trying everything and anything I settled on a simple strategy:

Investor conferences – Most conferences for microcap companies we went to were poorly attended and I often saw the same people. Over time I found three that I felt were worth doing and I did them every year. By consistently going to the same ones I also found it was a way to connect with shareholders, which helps build long-term relationships that promoted the "word of mouth" campaign for new shareholders. Only one of the conferences was really good for us, but doing these conferences was also good practice for staying on message and keeping me sharp in presenting our story.

One-on-one broker and boutique investment firm presentations – I worked with an IR firm I felt had good contacts in this area and was willing to make the appointments for me. They did a great job for me in that regard. The only thing I expected of them was to open the door to new investor contacts for me, it was up to me to create and make the presentation, with helpful feedback from them. The thing I value most in an IR firm is its contacts. Nobody knows my company better than I do and nobody should be able to articulate it better than I can. I have yet to see the IR firm that can spin straw into gold. Most border on being worse than worthless. If they are not opening doors for you then you need a new IR firm. However, don't expect them to work miracles or sell something that you can't.

Stock screening tools – Over time I realized that most of the investors I was looking for were looking for me by using various stock screening tools. They had certain criteria they were interested in and their preferred method for managing the large universe of small companies was to use a software tool to pull the diamonds out of the rough. I began to focus on how, when and why we would or wouldn't show up in a particular search of companies. What were investors searching for and did my company fit the criteria? How could I position the company in the future to show up more often? I started to think in terms of "managing my charts". My revenue growth chart, my profit growth chart, my margin growth chart, etc. And finally I focused on "yield".

Why a "meaningful" dividend strategy is your best option if your company results warrant it

Nothing worked better for us than implementing a dividend strategy. With the dividend strategy we had found a way to truly differentiate ourselves and to reward all investors. We paid out a significant portion of our profits and grew the dividend every year and this resulted in even better "charts", which resulted in even better search results for investor screening tools. It took about six quarters before there was enough historical information for it to really catch on but I can tell you it worked very well! And our investors loved it. Of course the business was succeeding with margins and profits growing every year. Even with paying out the majority of our earnings as a dividend our cash still grew dramatically.

I would add one caveat, and that is if you start a dividend programme it needs to be for the long haul. Cutting or cancelling dividends is a big problem and in most cases you would have been better off never having started in the first place.

Insider buying – If you think your stock is too cheap, why aren't you buying? Isn't that a logical investor question? Once I realized our company was going to succeed for the long term and that our business model was strong, I began a pattern of purchasing shares in the company over several years. I thought our stock was way too cheap and it was. Every time the stock would drop to a level at the low end of fair value or lower and I was in a window where I could buy I would buy some shares. And it turned out to be the best investment I could ever have made.

In summary, I built a reputation over many years of talking to shareholders honestly and being accessible to them. I was buying our stock in the open market on a regular basis at ever higher prices and we were paying a majority of our ever-increasing profits out to investors. At the same time we had lots of cash that allowed us to sleep well at night (important with a small company). We were doing things differently and investors were noticing. We created a better investment opportunity with less perceived risk than our competition. I had long ago decided we didn't need to appeal to the whole market. We only needed to appeal to a very small segment of the investing population to be successful and we did. Not every investor will like your strategy but they don't need to. You can't build one product that fits every customer, but even niche markets can have huge potential! The bottom line is that we gave our target group of investors what they wanted and we earned loyal, long term customers. The result was a sustainable stock price that represented the high end of the fair value range.

company stocks suffer from what the market calls a "liquidity discount", reflecting a lack of visibility of a stock among potential investors. Volume of trading can be a proxy for liquidity and also for corporate communication, since it is a reflection of attracting further attention from the media and investment community, leading to greater trading of the stock, measured in terms of the volumes of stock units traded. Volume is a reflection of a willingness to trade and invest. Volatility is a concept associated with risk in financial markets. A measure of this market risk for a stock or portfolio is referred to as its beta, or its risk of return in relation to the market as a whole. High beta stocks have higher risk but offer potentially higher returns while low beta stocks offer lower risk and consequentially lower returns. Common objectives of investor relations programmes are to reduce a stock's volatility, measured by its beta, and to improve its liquidity. Effective corporate communication can be a contributor to lowering volatility and expanding liquidity, although neither of these topics are part of the content of corporate communication.

Buy-sell or bid-ask spreads are a reflection of supply and demand for a stock – the closer the spread the greater the demand and the wider the spread the lower demand. The breadth of the spread is also a reflection of information about a stock, with it being wider if information is not widespread. Better known stocks have closer spreads, also illustrating a marker on which communication can have an input.

Some of the stock market data analysed to reach conclusions about the effects of communication on stock price, or its markers, refers to these terms. Set out below is a summary of research articles and their conclusions, with all of them picking up on aspects of communication having an impact on stock price. The list of research references is not meant to be exhaustive but it focuses on easily researched papers connecting with work around corporate communication and investor relations and their effects on stock price or markers. The papers are by academics in established institutions, giving them authority as well as being anchored in research of market data. The content of the research is summarized briefly below.

News dissemination and the business press

Soltes, University of Chicago[41]

How information is distributed, even when it is public, is important. Compared with announcements just made to an exchange platform, those that are disseminated to the media and investment community have a positive effect on reducing the cost of information and in increasing company visibility. Achieving media coverage for this news adds to this effect because of its broader distribution to investors. The evidence is that greater dissemination of news lowers bid-ask spreads, increases trading volumes and lowers volatility.

Publicity and stock prices

Solomon, University of Southern California[42]

While models of market efficiency assume investors can costlessly receive and process all relevant news signals, implying there would be no reason for companies to spend resources on promoting new coverage, Solomon finds evidence to the contrary. His research shows investor relations firms generate greater media coverage around positive news compared to negative news and that positive media coverage increases stock price returns. Media coverage affects the price response to news, with investors relying on the media because media coverage carries the imprimatur of importance for a story.

Media coverage and stock returns

Fang and Peress, INSEAD[43]

For companies suffering from reduced analyst coverage, mass media coverage and public relations efforts aimed at creating awareness and familiarity can pay off in terms of generating investor interest and reducing the cost of capital.

Disclosure quality and investor relations

Chang, D'Anna, Watson and Wee, University of Western Australia[44]

Firms with higher disclosure quality through their investor relations activity have enhanced market exposure, higher analyst following, more institutional shareholders and are larger in terms of market capitalization.

Analyst coverage and the cost of capital

Bowen (University of Washington), Chen (University of British
Columbia) and Cheng (University of British Columbia)[45]

Gaining analyst coverage lowers the cost of raising equity capital, reduces the information gap between investors and companies, and improves financial reporting and voluntary disclosure.

Determinants of coverage in the business press

Solomon (University of Southern California) and Soltes (Harvard)[46]

Coverage by the financial press significantly affects both the trading and pricing of securities, and firms that engage an external investor relations firm receive differential coverage. Media engagement is not simply a strategic change in the way a firm issues a single release but more a sustained set of interactions that changes a firm's relationship with the press. Among factors determining whether a company announcement achieves media coverage are its news value, the timing of the release, the effectiveness of news distribution and whether company spokespersons are available to the media.

Business press as an information intermediary

Bushee (Wharton), Core (MIT), Guay (University of Pennsylvania)
and Hamm (Ohio State University)[47]

The press serves an important role in shaping firms' information environments. Greater press coverage reduces the information gap about companies, leading to lower spreads and greater depth of trading. This is especially the case around earnings announcements. Broad dissemination of information to the market and media can have a bigger impact than the actual quantity or quality of press-generated information. Nevertheless, media coverage can help reduce information problems around earnings announcements.

Investor relations, firm visibility and investor following

Bushee (Wharton) and Miller (Harvard)[48]

When companies increased investor relations activities, proxied by hiring an outside investor relations firm, results showed these companies exhibited increases in disclosure, media coverage and analyst following. Companies also showed substantial and ongoing increases in institutional ownership. In the year following initiation of investor relations activities, the firms showed improvements in valuation. Overall, results indicated that investor relations activities focused on increasing firm visibility are successful in having an impact on market participants' interactions with companies.

The effect of news on investor buying behaviour

Barber and Odean, University of California[49]

Individual investors tend to buy stocks that have been in the news. This is a result of the difficulty these investors have in searching the thousands of stocks they could potentially buy. Consequently they only tend to consider purchasing stocks that have first caught their attention, irrespective of a firm's size.

How investor relations contributes to the bottom line

Laskin (Quinnipiac University, Connecticut)[50]

The study combines a literature review and a Delphi Panel of investor relations practitioners. It found four key areas of investor relations contribution: fair share price, improved liquidity of stock, enhanced analyst coverage and building and maintaining investor relationships. "Wall Street has so many information sources but all those numbers don't mean much if you don't trust those who are running the company. The only way to establish that trust: build relationships and consistently communicate clearly."

CEO interviews on CNBC

Kim (Nanyang Business School) and Meschke (University of Kansas)[51]

Since TV interviews are not major corporate events, an analysis of the market response can be viewed as a simple test of the conjecture that enthusiastic public attention may move stock prices away from fundamentals. Kim and Meschke find stocks experience a strong run-up and reversal during the ten trading days following an interview. These price dynamics suggest that the financial news media is able to generate transitory buying pressure by catching the attention of enthusiastic investors.

Familiarity breeds investment

Huberman (Columbia)[52]

While theory suggests that investors should diversify, this paper shows people prefer to invest in the familiar. People look favourably on stocks that they are familiar with and think of them as more likely to deliver higher returns at lower stock-specific risks. This view tends to tilt portfolio weights toward familiar stocks.

Benefits from increasing the size of the investor base

Merton (MIT)[53]

Merton's model counters the theory that returns are larger from investing in neglected firms. He notes there are benefits for a firm in increasing the size of its investor base since this contributes to a fall in the cost of capital. Consequently his model justifies the expenditure on public relations in bringing the firm to the wider attention of potential investors and in increasing the firm's visibility. He sees the cost of this as being similar to marketing the firm's products.

Engaging with stakeholders builds value

Henisz, Dorobantu and Nartey (Wharton)[54]

Engagement with stakeholders, with a view to increasing cooperation and reducing conflict, enhances the financial valuation of a firm.

Business media coverage and earnings guidance

Twedt (Texas A&M University)[55]

When earnings guidance is distributed to the media and receives coverage, it has a significant impact on market reactions.

What are we meeting for? The consequences of private meetings with investors

Solomon (University of Southern California) and Soltes (Harvard)[56]

Assessing data over a six-year period covering 900 one-on-one meetings between 340 institutional investors and a NYSE-listed company, the research showed that subsequent trades achieved better returns and more informed trading decisions. The analysis does not suggest that companies were providing material information at these meetings that should have been disclosed publicly but rather that the information gleaned provided a better mosaic of a picture to inform investment decision-making. Meeting with investors consumes a considerable amount of executive time, estimated at 17 to 26 days a year plus preparation time, and the research indicates benefits flow from this.

Content and source of disclosure makes a difference

Kothari (MIT), Li (University of Texas) and Short (University of California)[57]

When content of disclosure is favourable, it reduces cost of capital but when negative, it increases risk measures. Negative disclosures in the business press increase cost of capital while favourable press coverage reduces cost of capital.

Analyst following and market liquidity

Roulstone (University of Chicago)[58]

Firms receive cost of capital benefits from increasing analyst following and the precision of analysts' beliefs – another benefit of increasing disclosure.

Financial analysts in the media

Kuperman (Minnesota State), Athavale (Ball State) and Eisner (Pace University)[59]

The news media are generators of attention cascades and when analyst comments are reported in the media, they support exaggeration of price trends.

Information and the cost of capital

Easley and O'Hara (Cornell University)[60]

The quantity and quality of information affects asset prices, with firms being able to influence cost of capital by selectivity of accounting standards, analyst coverage and location of stock exchange listing.

The way a number of these articles are written is that they build in an acceptance of the value of communication and its direct relationship with effects on stock price. The research has been published and consequently subjected to peer review, establishing an acceptance of documenting elements of what influences stock prices. Communication is not the only influence on stock price but its now established inclusion is an indicator of progress from views of yesteryear that it did not contribute demonstrable value.

Investor relations, the corporate story

The growth of the investor relations profession has not come about because of the research findings given above but the research does legitimize and provide objective confirmation of the value of investor relations. It also reinforces the objectives and content of investor relations programmes, which we will examine in later chapters. As the term implies, investor relations treats investors as stakeholders that have a relevant relationship with a corporation. Here's how the term is defined by the National Investor Relations Institute (NIRI) in the United States, the largest organization of its kind, with many other counterparts in most stock market economies:

> Investor relations is a strategic management responsibility that integrates finance, communication, marketing and securities law compliance to enable the most effective two-way communication between a company, the financial community, and other constituencies, which ultimately contributes to a company's securities achieving fair valuation.[61]

Essentially, the job of investor relations is to communicate a corporate strategy to relevant stakeholders. This implies investor relations is integrated with corporate communication efforts, encompassing reputation and brand and the values the company represents. Among the objectives of investor relations programmes are those highlighted from the research as influences on securities pricing, to achieve the fair valuation to which NIRI refers. These include using communication to improve a stock's liquidity, increase trading volumes, reduce volatility and narrowing bid-ask spreads. Along the way, investor relations seeks to build a following with stock analysts and attract media coverage. While information has a role in influencing stock price, investor relations is actively involved in converting information into communication and then disseminating it to stakeholders to help them reach a better understanding of the corporation.

Accepting that in the modern corporation, investor relations is part of an integrated corporate communications effort, then a starting point needs to be established for the work of building those relationships with relevant stakeholders. This begins with developing the corporate story in a way that combines facts, numbers and narrative, since this is the content that investor relations deals with and converts into communication.

There are a number of pointers towards the style, content and communication of this story. It needs to blend education and business context along with providing information about an individual corporation. Conveying the information takes many forms, in writing, in casual conversation and formal presentation. It involves the rhetoric of storytelling as much as the principles of rhetoric. Our next chapter looks at the composition of this corporate story from the investment perspective and the influences involved in communicating it.

Notes

1 Steyn, B, "From 'Strategy' to 'Corporate Communication Strategy': A Conceptualisation", paper at 9th International Public Relations Research Symposium, July 2002
2 Steyn (2002), pp 1–4
3 Steyn (2002), p 5
4 Steyn (2002), p 6
5 Steyn (2002), p 8
6 Steyn (2002), p 11–12
7 Steyn (2002), p 17
8 van Ruler, B, "The Communication Grid: Introduction of a Model of Four Communication Strategies", *Public Relations Review* 30, 2004, pp 123–143
9 Steyn (2002), pp 18–19
10 Argenti, P, Howells, RA and Beck, KA, "The Strategic Communication Imperative", *MIT Sloan Management Review*, Spring 2005, p 84
11 Argenti et al (2005), p 85
12 Argenti et al (2005), p 86
13 Argenti et al (2005), p 88
14 Argenti et al (2005), p 88
15 Argenti et al (2005), p 88
16 Argenti et al (2005), p 89
17 Cornelissen, J, *Corporate Communication: A Guide to Theory and Practice* (Sage, London, 3rd edn: 2011), pp 15–17
18 Cornelissen (2011), pp 22–28
19 van Riel, CBM and Fombrun, CJ, *Essentials of Corporate Communication: Implementing Practices for Effective Reputation Management* (Routledge, Abingdon: 2007)
20 van Riel and Fombrun (2007), p 134
21 van Riel and Fombrun (2007), p 136
22 van Riel and Fombrun (2007), p 136
23 van Riel and Fombrun (2007), pp 136–137
24 van Riel and Fombrun (2007), pp 148–158
25 van Riel and Fombrun (2007), p 158
26 Forman, J, *Story Telling in Business: The Authentic and Fluent Organisation* (Stanford University Press, Stanford, CA: 2013)
27 Forman (2013), p 26
28 Forman (2013), pp 31–44
29 Forman (2013), p 32
30 Forman (2013), p 40
31 Forman (2013), p 47
32 Forman (2013), pp 47–52
33 Argenti, P, *Corporate Communication* (McGraw-Hill, Boston, MA: 2009), p 83
34 Argenti (2009), p 84
35 Helm, S, "The Role of Corporate Reputation in Determining Investor Satisfaction and Loyalty", *Corporate Reputation Review* 10 (1), 2007, pp 22–37
36 Chronican, P, "Trust in Finance – Banking for the Future", FINSIA Speech, 23 October 2012
37 Engardio, P and Arndt, M, "What Price Reputation?", *BusinessWeek*, 9 July 2007, www.businessweek.com/stories/2007-07-08/what-price-reputation
38 Engardio and Arndt (2007)
39 Engardio and Arndt (2007)
40 This is an abbreviated version of a longer paper written by Geoff Knapp, who summarized his approach and thoughts for other CEOs of public companies to learn from his experiences. The case study was supplied by Ted Haberfield and John Mattio of the MZ Group (www.mzgroup.com). The MZ Group is a multinational company and the world's largest independent investor relations, market intelligence and applied technology firm. MZ provided investor relations advice to CAM Commerce Solutions when Geoff Knapp was CEO.

41 Soltes, E, "News Dissemination and the Impact of the Business Press", University of Chicago, Booth School of Business, June, 2009, http://mms.businesswire.com/bwapps/mediaserver/ViewMedia?mgid=167154&vid=1

42 Solomon, D, "Selective Publicity and Stock Prices", *The Journal of Finance*, April 2012

43 Fang, L and Peress, J, "Media Coverage and the Cross-Section of Returns", *The Journal of Finance*, October 2009

44 Chang, M, D'Anna, G, Watson, I and Wee, M, "Does Disclosure Quality via Investor Relations Affect Information Symmetry?", *Australian Journal of Management* 33 (2), 2008

45 Bowen, RM, Chen, X and Cheng, Q, "Analyst Coverage and the Cost of Raising Equity Capital: Evidence from Underpricing of Seasoned Equity Offerings", *Contemporary Accounting Research* 25 (3), 2008

46 Solomon, D and Soltes, E, "The Determinants of Coverage in the Business Press", Working Paper, University of Southern California, April 2011, www.kellogg.northwestern.edu/accounting/papers/Soltes.pdf

47 Bushee, BJ, Core, JE, Guay, WR and Hamm, SJW, "The Role of the Business Press as an Information Intermediary", October 1, 2009, http://ssrn.com/abstract=955021 or http://dx.doi.org/10.2139/ssrn.955021

48 Bushee, J and Miller, G, "Investor Relations, Firm Visibility and Investor Following", *The Accounting Review* 87 (3), 2012, pp 867–897

49 Barber, B and Odean, T, "All That Glitters: The Effect of Attention and News on the Buying Behaviour of Individual and Institutional Investors", *Review of Financial Studies* 21 (2), 2008, pp 785–818

50 Laskin, AV, "How Investor Relations Contributes to the Corporate Bottom Line", *Journal of Public Relations Research*, June 2011

51 Kim, YH and Meschke, JF, "CEO Interviews on CNBC", Fifth Singapore International Conference on Finance 2011, December 2011, http://ssrn.com/abstract=1745085

52 Hubermann, G, "Familiarity Breeds Investment", *The Review of Financial Studies* 14 (3), 2001, pp 659–680

53 Merton, RC, "A Simple Model of Capital Market Equilibrium with Incomplete Information", *The Journal of Finance* 42 (3), 1987, pp 483–510

54 Henisz, WJ, Dorobantu, S and Nartey, L, "Spinning Gold: The Financial Returns to External Stakeholder Engagement", Working Paper, The Wharton School, University of Pennsylvania, June 2011, www-management.wharton.upenn.edu/henisz/hdn.pdf

55 Twedt, B, "Spreading the Word: Capital Market Consequences of Management Earnings Guidance Dissemination through the Business Press", Texas A&M University, Mays Business School, Working Paper Series, May 2013, http://dx.doi.org/10.2139/ssrn.2182162

56 Solomon, DH and Soltes, EF, "What Are We Meeting For? The Consequences of Private Meetings with Investors", September 6, 2012, http://ssrn.com/abstract=1959613

57 Kothari SP, Li X & Short JE, "The Effect of Disclosures by Management, Analysts and Business Press on Cost of Capital, Return Volatility, and Analyst Forecasts: A Study Using Content Analysis", *The Accounting Review* 84 (5), 2009, September 2009

58 Roulstone DT, "Analyst Following and Market Liquidity", *Contemporary Accounting Research* 20 (3), 2003

59 Kuperman JC, Athavale M & Eisner A, "Financial analysts in the media: Evolving roles and recent trends", *American Business Review* 21 (2), 2003

60 Easley D and O'Hara M, "Information and the Cost of Capital", *The Journal of Finance* 59 (4), 2004

61 www.niri.org/FunctionalMenu/About.aspx

5 Investment perspectives on the corporate story

Building a corporate story from an investor relations perspective brings in many of the concepts we have covered so far. It is underpinned by a theoretical framework, from communication, public relations and applied finance. It is at the centre of describing corporate strategy as well as communicating it. It combines elements of marketing and selling and yet some striking differences in these concepts as well. Its content needs to bring in ideas of reputation and brand that underlie the progress of a business. It cannot be focused solely on a corporation but has to cover its industry, wider business context, stakeholders and trends. Its overall content needs to be capable of being represented in phrases, key messages, presentations, lengthier pieces of writing and website images, as well as encapsulations for social media. It needs to be able to be conveyed orally and in writing. Its essence needs to come through in news announced by a corporation as well as in its logos and slogans. Content needs to be shaped for the varying components of stakeholder audiences, some of which are better informed than others. It needs to be educational, covering elements of the past, present and future. While we have seen how communication of the corporate story can influence stock price, the content of the corporate story is about the business and its context, not the stock price. The story needs to be conscious of behavioural elements of stakeholder markets, which have expectations of what they want to hear from corporations. While story is a word with many connotations, a business version of a story has its own characteristics, not all of which are identical for every company. As a starting point for looking at these issues, the history of the evolution of investor relations is instructive. This leads to considering the many elements of a corporate story and its similarities and differences with selling and marketing as these disciplines apply to other aspects of a corporation's business. It is also useful to consider what represents effective persuasion with well-informed investor audiences and how their specific information interests lead to elements of co-creation of corporate stories.

Evolution of investor relations

The evolution of investor relations has involved a progression of several levels of communications practice. Laskin[1] provides an interesting perspective on this evolution, categorizing it into three eras. While this classification is generally reflective of trends over this period, the history of the National Investor Relations Institute (NIRI)[2] in the US adds some embellishments to his categorization. Laskin's three eras comprise the communication era (1945–1970), then the financial era (1970–2000), followed by the synergy era (after 2000). In Laskin's view, the communication era was more focused on achieving mass media coverage for a corporation, with practitioners less noted for financial expertise and not necessarily involved in strategic or managerial activities. Shareholding patterns were not researched and feedback from shareholders was not collected. The stream of information was one-way, outwards from the corporation to anyone who might be interested and particularly to the mass media.

While this might reflect general trends in the market during those years, the NIRI history adds some interesting insights. It traces the origins of the term "investor relations" to 1953 when the chairman of General Electric, Ralph Cordiner, established a specialized function to deal with the needs of shareholders. The focus then was on retail shareholders, since they were rapidly growing in numbers, while institutions were not the substantial shareholding force they are today. Large corporations, such as Ford, GM and Chrysler, had already picked up on this trend, seeing that rising numbers of individual investors could be both potential customers as well as a source of new capital. Increasingly, these new shareholders saw themselves as owners of corporations, demanding some attention as they began to attend annual meetings and actually read documents such as annual reports. In this era there were two extremes of corporate views about shareholders – either they represented a marketing opportunity or were something of a nuisance. An influence on these views was the issue in 1951 of the third edition of the classic investment textbook *Security Analysis* by Benjamin Graham and David L Dodd. These two authors were the champions of value investing and were the primary influence on the way Warren Buffett invests. In this early edition of their book they stated a view, under the heading "Management may properly take some interest in the market price of the shares", which has become an established justification for the investor relations profession:

> The most obvious indication of an unsatisfactory state of affairs is a market price which is persistently lower than the stockholder's investment or the indicated minimum value of the business as judged in some other reasonable way. When the price is consistently too low, it is proper for the stockholders to raise questions as to why this is so and what can be done to remedy the situation. Fair price is essential to proper marketability. It is true of course that a company's officers are not responsible for the fluctuations in the price of its securities. But this is very far from saying market prices should never be a matter of concern to the management. The idea is not basically wrong, but it has the added vice of being thoroughly hypocritical. It is wrong because the marketability of securities is one of the chief qualities considered in their purchase. But marketability must presuppose not only a place where they can be sold, but also an opportunity to sell them at a fair price. It is fully as important to the stockholders that they be able to obtain a fair price for their shares as it is that dividends, earnings and assets be conserved or increased. It follows that the responsibility of managements to act in the interest of their shareholders includes the obligation to prevent – in so far as they are able to do so by proper corporate measures – the establishment of either absurdly high or unduly low prices for their securities.[3]

The NIRI history describes this as "the clarion call to arms for investor relations – the intellectual, moral and philosophical foundation of the profession: an obligation on corporations to do what they properly can to achieve a fair price for their securities".[4]

It was well into Laskin's financial era that this point of view was fully taken up by corporations. Other driving forces were that the communications era had seen an over-reliance on using the media to boost interest in company stocks, sometimes without due consideration to the ethics of this, and also that the rising power and prevalence of stock analysts was only just beginning to be appreciated. Laskin described the financial era as a shift of emphasis in communication from private shareholders to professional investors, reflecting the growing recognition by institutions that they needed to increase their exposures to equities. As this was taking place, corporations also moved their communications emphasis away from specialists in dealing with the media, to accountants and finance professionals who became focused on providing financial disclosure to investors. This was accompanied by changing priorities away from the mass media to one-on-one meetings with institutional shareholders and financial analysts, introducing more interpersonal communication and a two-way exchange of information. While corporations gathered feedback from these meetings, Laskin notes it was often more for the purposes of using it to craft more persuasive messages to "sell" the organization and achieve higher stock prices than for more objective purposes.

Laskin's third era, post 2000, he describes as one of synergy because it recognizes the value of combining communication and finance skill-sets in investor relations. The common goal of this era is more about improving understanding of corporations with investors, analysts and the media, involving two-way communication with feedback being analysed in a way that it becomes a valuable input to corporate strategic planning. This involves assessing both positive and negative information with a view to achieving a fair value of a stock. There is a recognition that "overvaluation can be as negative as undervaluation because it can lead to a sudden drop in price as well as to increased price and volume volatility when additional information becomes available".[5] As companies seek to bring about a broader understanding of their businesses, they are also realizing their communications efforts need to embrace not only financial aspects, but also non-financial information about how businesses are managed, their strategies and marketplace issues. This reflects also a recognition of views about investing that go beyond a common acceptance that markets might be efficient.

This evolution of investor relations also points up some of the differences and similarities with general principles of marketing.

Marketing, selling and investor relations

Sales and marketing are vital components of any business. They are focused on selling products and services that make up the revenue of a corporation. While revenue is a key topic of investor relations as it seeks to present the corporate story to investors, there are distinctions in how these differing elements of marketing are implemented.

A lot of guides about selling products and services are about preparing a salesperson to win over potential buyers. Selling involves an understanding that people buy from people. So the selling process means building a rapport with buyers, recognizing that many buying decisions are based on emotions, not logic. For the salesperson, there needs to be an understanding that people do not buy product features so much as the benefits they deliver. They tend to buy solutions and results rather than products or services. From this perspective, a sale is less about price and more about the value and experience that is on offer. This sentiment does not correlate exactly with investing in stocks, where price is critical, but there is a parallel with the idea of reputation, which can add a premium to what may be considered basic value. Separately, as we cover later, price is not ideally the subject matter of investor relations since it is achieving fair value – recognizing all the factors that contribute to stock price – that is usually a primary objective of investor relations. However, there are other selling principles that can apply to investor relations. Selling can be a process of building agreement and enhancing understanding over time rather than bullying towards a sale at a first meeting.

While selling is about closing a deal, the wider field of marketing is about creating the conditions and support for selling. A common abbreviation of the principles of marketing is the four Ps, involving a focus of marketing effort on a target market with a mix of product, price, promotion and place (or distribution). While the focus here is on product, there are parallels with marketing a corporation. One investor relations commentator, Palizza, who sees parallels with sales, marketing and investor relations, describes it this way:

> You want the right type of customers (investors) to buy a piece of your company (stock) and to have a good ownership experience (own the stock for a long period of time).[6]

Palizza describes investor relations as consultative selling since it can involve a number of parties, separate from companies and investors, such as analysts, dealers who sell stocks, portfolio managers and traders. This complexity as well as the variety of competing choices of stocks means a sale can take some time, often involving companies presenting their story to potential investors over a period of years as they build relationships and allow their performance to be monitored. As in other types of selling, building relationships means companies investing time in helping investors and analysts understand the company and its industry, often tracking down information that helps investors overcome uncertainty. Once investors have become shareholders, if they have built a relationship with and understanding of the company, they can tend to remain longer-term investors over times when share prices fluctuate. Similarly, if companies have not invested the time in cultivating the right type of investor for their company, another function of investor relations, then these investors – possibly index funds, hedge funds or day traders – will sell stock at times of changing market conditions.

Building the corporate story for investors

The evolution of the discipline of investor relations shows the financial and communications components of the process coming together in the current era. Involved with this are the similarities and differences of selling and marketing in the financial and investment sphere. How companies implement these elements in practice also highlights that a theoretical framework can be an influence on the way financial communication is applied in investment markets.

The corporate story is a vehicle for how corporations present information about themselves. In shaping this story, the reputation and authenticity based models we referred to in the previous chapter still apply but the content takes on more of a business and investment orientation for the key stakeholders of shareholders, the investment community and business media. The story is a body of information that has many components. It brings in company history, the structure of the business, development strategy, financial performance, the competitive and market context of the business and issues that relate to reputation and branding. Along with this content is the way it is presented, since this connects with how investors develop impressions about the quality of a company's management. The circumstances in which this information is imparted is also relevant, since it can vary from being in writing, from a phrase to quite lengthy documents, to oral presentations for groups or one-on-one, and also to social media encapsulations.

One of the concepts underlying construction of the corporate story is that of layers, building outwards from phrases to larger pieces of information. This larger body of information is like a background landscape, with pieces brought forward from time to time for closer examination and elaboration. Bringing forward the whole landscape at one time runs the risk of not aligning it with any current news or information and so can make for a very dry presentation. For example, if a chief executive were to begin an interview, investment presentation or annual meeting with the idea that the corporate story must be told in some detail, then the risk of losing an audience entirely is very high. This corporate story information, if it is to equate with effective communication, needs to be used judiciously. The two words, "corporate" and "story", connote the bringing together of information and the way it is imparted. The element of story relates to how aspects of information from the corporate landscape are brought into focus. Since the information combines facts and numbers, they cannot just stand in isolation if they are to come alive and be interesting. They have to be presented so people can understand how the facts and numbers came into being, which is in effect a story. The story, in its classical structure would have a beginning, middle and end, with its content being selective.

This selectivity is similar to the processes of an editor, choosing the best information for the space available and for the audience. Stakeholder audiences, whether listeners or readers, have varying states of knowledge about a corporation and this influences content and how the story is presented. Providing the information is also a two-way communications process, since stakeholders have a powerful means of reaction, which can be to buy or sell stocks, so their views and ability to question corporations also influence information content and style. The corporate and stakeholder perspectives require closer examination.

Corporate objectives

From the corporate perspective, there are a number of influences on developing investor relations objectives. One direction of influence is from investors like Warren Buffet, who are looking for companies that are easy to understand and run by people investors can trust. NIRI presents a key objective of investor relations as being to achieve fair value of a company's stock. While stock exchange-listed companies are faced with mandatory requirements for disclosure of information, meeting the most basic of disclosure requirements will not equate with the corporate objectives Buffet and NIRI would expect. This basic disclosure needs a conversion process, enveloping it within the corporate story, with its building blocks of facts, numbers and narrative, as a way of achieving these objectives.

An example of this is the basic number of profit that all companies are required to disclose. Profit is not a number in isolation. It is a number with an up or down direction in comparison with the same number a year ago. It is a number with a story that evolves from market conditions, industry dynamics, divisional contributions, the wider history of corporate performance and the strategy a company is executing. An elaboration of the story around profit performance leaves an audience with a significantly more educated understanding, irrespective of the up or down direction of the profit number. They do not just see profit as a static number but one driven by a management team with an understanding of what is involved in improving performance into the future. If the information around it is excuses, it is not as convincing as an educative explanation that brings an audience into the perspective of how a corporation is managing into the future. Explaining profit in this way is not only providing an understanding of corporate strategy but also an exposition of the corporate story. In this sense, it goes further than meeting the basics of disclosure requirements. What is being developed is the context around a corporation, not just viewing it in isolation. The explanation is more powerful if it acknowledges the market forces about which Michael Porter wrote and also the sense of landscape that historian Simon Schama developed. Schama argues that nature and human perception are indivisible, not separate concepts. In a corporate context, market conditions affect performance, not only of one corporation but also the competition. This is the way analysts view companies. They see them as part of an industry sector and their view of the management qualities of an organization is going to be enhanced if they see management showing an awareness of market forces, rather than being a company that is focused only on its own performance, indicating it is a company without a convincing story.

Among other objectives of investor relations, which point up differences with marketing and public relations, are trying to pass on a sense of enthusiasm to others about a company's prospects by conveying a picture of the future in a way that will not subsequently attract criticism if performance falls short of promise. Companies can develop differing approaches to these topics. At one extreme, companies can be overcautious and simply meet basic disclosure requirements. At the opposite extreme, companies can use the language of hyperbole to boost explanations of what they might achieve in the future. As a more effective middle course, there is an opportunity to develop the corporate story and provide an interesting picture of a company's present position and performance. From this, those who listen to the story can develop for themselves a view of a company working to achieve objectives of a prosperous future, perhaps along the lines Buffet and NIRI might expect. What is taking place is a passing on of a sense of enthusiasm about the future by outlining an effective present-day strategy, possibly attracting new investors, customers and supporters along the way. How this is achieved in investor relations is often the reverse of common selling techniques. Salespeople in most walks of life need to establish what is unique about their products. Sometimes this is achieved by exaggeration and hyperbole to boost their selling proposition, possibly also by pointing out the shortcomings of competing products. The language of this type of selling is often accompanied by many adjectives and adverbs to embellish what is being sold. The world of investor relations, while it has selling components, requires more subtlety than standard selling techniques. In fact, the listeners and hearers of corporate messages are quite often sophisticated consumers of this type of information. They may have been investors in many companies over the years and have become familiar with corporate messages that tend to exaggeration in the hope of building enthusiasm. One of the clichés of investment markets is that companies that are most admired are those which "under-promise and over-deliver" and in a way this is a form of selling by underselling, not using the language of hyperbole but almost the opposite, to build a longer-term enthusiasm from investors by adopting a realistic form of openness.

This form of reverse psychology in presenting a picture of the future reflects the pressure the market applies to listed companies. Investors buy stock on the basis of positive expectations and expect companies to deliver. The consequences of non-delivery can be swift and harsh, resulting in a falling stock price. While some companies remain determinedly optimistic, there is a general tendency in corporate communication to avoid being specific about future performance. Some companies do make definitive forecasts of future performance or give a range of likely outcomes for the year ahead, although this is not mandatory disclosure. In circumstances where companies realize actual financial performance at a point in time is likely to be quite different from what the market is expecting, whether up or down, they usually issue earnings guidance to prepare the market for what is to come. What needs to be appreciated about any information relating to the future is that analysts in the investing marketplace use it to form firmly held and widely publicized views of companies' prospects, since this is a key part of investment decision-making. Investors are not necessarily looking to companies to make forecasts but, if they do, then they become a basis for expectation, with an allied presumption that sound communication will accompany any variations. In the absence of specific forecasts, as is often the case, analysts can glean information about how a company sees its position in its markets and this becomes the material they need to make their own leaps of imagination about how a company will perform in years to come.

Among other common objectives of investor relations programmes are those of conveying an impression of good management, seeking a fair stock price and building trust with key stakeholders. For each of these objectives, similar reverse expectations of what might be standard communication principles can be discerned. Good management is displayed more by performing the task well, and explaining strategy and how it has been implemented, rather than by simply asserting how well managed a company is. Regarding stock price, it is usually a topic that effective investor relations avoids, recognizing it is an outcome of market action, reflecting the results of decisions made in the face of information provided by a company. Trust is also a characteristic awarded by the market rather than it resulting from companies insisting on their own trustworthiness. Management capability is a concept that can be conveyed though the corporate story. By providing information about a company and its markets, and explaining the challenges for management and how management is dealing with them, a story is being presented. Again there is a choice of language to be used. Hyperbole can be adopted to explain how well management is performing but the more objective the language of investor relations the more it can contribute to the concepts of trust and credibility. Stock price is a consequence of these actions, and can be influenced in a negative way from an exaggeration of capability, especially when it does not deliver the performance expectations the language might imply.

Stakeholder needs

Understanding the information needs of the primary stakeholders of investor relations – the investment community, shareholders and the business media – is an important influence on how the corporate story is presented. An appreciation of these information needs does not mean companies need to meet them in every respect but it is certainly not helpful to ignore them altogether. Stakeholder characteristics are covered in later chapters but their information interests have relevance to corporate story formation.

Case study

Stockland – evolving beyond the "three Rs" story

Stockland is a substantial Australian listed property company or REIT (real estate investment trust). For 60 years it has been one of the leaders of Australia's property industry, ranking as the nation's largest developer of land for housing, owner of a A$5 billion shopping centre portfolio and the country's third largest operator of retirement villages. Additionally it owns and develops office and industrial property. In 2010, Stockland's CEO coined the term "three Rs" to describe the group's strategy, reflecting its intention to focus on three property sectors – retail, residential and retirement – with its A$2.7 billion office and industrial property portfolios to be sold to fund expansion of the three Rs.

The logic behind this self-funded focus to achieve higher returns seemed well-founded. It also tied in with the company's belief in the importance of sustainability as a value driver. This was influenced by the views of Harvard professor Michael Porter and his shared value business philosophy. The Stockland view was that creating happy residents in housing projects and retirement villages led to happy shoppers in community shopping centres built by the group. As Stockland managing director Matthew Quinn put it: "Creating shared value means our business benefits from creating value for other stakeholders."[7]

When Stockland announced its half-year results in February 2011, the company's strategy received positive accolades, with one media headline reading: "Three 'Rs' Strategy Pays Off for Stockland", as the company "emerged from the global downturn with its three core divisions performing ahead of expectations, leading it to issue an earnings upgrade".[8]

Six months later, when Stockland announced its full year results, there was further evidence of the strategy working, with profit up, but that was in comparison with a previous year involving significant property write-downs. Stockland also announced a flat outlook for the year ahead. At the same time, Quinn ruled out a buyback as just a short-term solution and indicated capital would be better invested in the long-term strategy.[9] As the result was absorbed, it led to some questioning from the market. One stockbroker was reported as saying investors were "losing patience with the focus on long-term strategy at the expense of poor relative share price performance",[10] while others thought a share buyback would be just the thing to help the share price. A few days later came an awkward moment – Stockland "bowed to investor pressure"[11] and announced it would initiate an on-market buyback of up to 5 per cent of its issued capital. Stockland justified this on the basis that its credit rating would be unharmed, some debt funding had been arranged for the buyback and that there was "additional visibility on assets sales". Despite the corporate embarrassment, the market welcomed the move as "common sense".[12]

While Stockland moved on from this hurdle, property market conditions remained stubbornly tough, meaning a slide in half-year earnings in February 2012 but at least a statement to maintain guidance for a full year result similar to the previous year. This outlook did not settle market questioning of the three Rs strategy and a poor contribution from the smaller retirement sector led one fund manager to describe the strategy as "two big Rs and one little r".[13] A frustrating aspect of articulating its strategy for Stockland was that it felt there was often a misinterpretation of seeing the three Rs as being equal, although that was never the case, with the company's aim being that by 2017, the asset mix would be 65 per cent retail, 23 per cent residential and 12 per cent retirement.[14] As Stockland tried to streamline its message, Quinn was quoted as saying, "our business will always be two-thirds rents and one-third trading profits, not a third each from the three segments".[15]

In a third quarter update in May 2012, Stockland clung firm to a view about improving markets in the longer term but in the short term, Stockland had to concede ongoing difficult market conditions and announced it was cutting its workforce. This led one media columnist to headline a story about it as: "Stockland's Fourth R is for Redundancy"[16] and an analyst to say that along with three Rs comes three Ss, "shrinking, streamlining and saving".[17] However, at least the analyst acknowledged the move made sense in implementing the overall strategy.

As Quinn headed off on his annual mid-year family holiday to Bali he had a lot on his mind and when he returned, he announced he would retire after nearly 12 years at the helm of Stockland, far above the average CEO term of tenure of four and a half years.[18] Quinn had been popular and respected and his chairman was supportive when his retirement was announced, saying the three Rs strategy remained in place and was the right strategic setting. He did add, however, that a new CEO would not be prevented from reviewing the strategy.[19] In a media interview, reflecting on his achievements, Quinn lamented that the market had been too focused on financial metrics and not sufficiently on the non-financial proposition of sustainability, in which Stockland was creating "better places to shop, to live and to retire", a strategy expected to deliver "exemplary" financial results when markets recovered.[20]

By November 2012, the board announced that the search for a new CEO was over, with the appointment of Mark Steinert, a former global head of research with UBS and a property specialist. He began the new role in January 2013 and by early February rumours had commenced that there would be a clearing of the decks with property write-downs[21] and that the industrial portfolio might be spun off into an IPO.[22] When Stockland did announce its half-year results in mid-February, it confirmed write-downs, which led to a half-year loss, but the share price went up with the market sensing a turnaround, especially as the new CEO said that, in terms of strategy, "everything is on the table".[23]

By mid-2013, the recasting of the corporate story at Stockland was under way, with a reversal of a decision on industrial property into an intention to boost involvement in that sector, a commitment to increase retail development and a capital-raising, to fund expansion and reduce debt.

A generalized aim of the investment community is to establish a valuation of a company, in per share terms, for comparison with market price, to establish whether a stock represents a buying opportunity or sell signal. Information for these valuation models comes from many published sources, principally company accounts, but the models are also better informed if companies are forthcoming about their businesses and surrounding contexts. To meet these requirements, companies do not have to make forecasts or provide information that might be harmful to their competitive positions or disclose sensitive internal information. The investment community has access to industry information that allows for estimates of likely growth rates and product pricing trends. The extremes of minimal disclosure and exaggerated disclosure are not as useful as companies telling their corporate stories in a way that is informative about management decision-making. The investment community survey mentioned below highlights the gap between what companies tend to disclose and what the investment community is really looking for.

Providing information to the media and shareholders brings in the concept of telling a story in layers. Some journalists and investors will be quite well-informed about a company while others may have scant knowledge of what a business does and the characteristics that make it successful in its marketplace. Journalists will want a story presented in the context of current news developments and shareholders want reassurance that their investment still represents value among the many competing investment choices. Assessing the current knowledge of these stakeholders is useful in making corporate information purposeful. While the content of many annual reports and annual meetings can meet the requirements of reporting on past periods, many do not meet the information needs of stakeholders, resulting in very low values for readership of annual reports.

Persuasion and presentation

Building a corporate story takes shape differently with each company. The content and context will of course be different. However, there is common ground among some of the principles, purposes and objectives. Persuasion in the sphere of investor relations is different to the fundamentals of many aspects of selling but it does bring in some of the ideals of rhetoric. An attempt at persuasion through the use of a biased corporate perspective and an overoptimistic view of the future is not the two-way exchange of information for which key stakeholders are searching.

For some, persuasion may seem out of place in investor relations, a realm of facts and figures, with objective investment decisions based on models of future earnings to discern value in the stock market. Persuasion is also a controversial concept in the theory of communication. However, investor relations also has a human dimension in which non-financial information becomes part of the decision-making process. Since there are also important differences between standard selling practices and presenting an investment story, it is worth considering some of the principles underlying persuasion and how they might apply to financial and investor communication.

If we consider persuasion as "human communication designed to influence the judgements and actions of others",[24] then there are reflections of this as companies report financial performance and spell out business strategies. In the psychological study of persuasion, there are debates about the extent of reason required for persuasion, but in the financial arena it requires stronger emphasis, given the nature of the information and characteristics of key stakeholders who are mostly well-informed. Two scholars who have researched widely around the topic of persuasion, Simons and Jones, have developed several principles common to persuasion generally and then refined these further as they apply in special circumstances where audiences are of a more independent frame of mind and require convincing. On a general basis, their principles of persuasion are:

- human beings project images of themselves as they communicate about important matters;
- communicators are not entirely in control of the effects they produce;
- messages make connections with things – for example, in an investor relations context, descriptions of market conditions can be taken as applying to competitors as well as a particular company;
- message recipients can become co-creators of meaning and may even self-persuade in ways unintended by communicators;
- messages communicated are verbal and non-verbal and encompass context as well as text.[25]

To apply to areas of specialized persuasion, Simons and Jones developed the term "coactive persuasion". This relates to persuasion in which both sides are aware of each other's standpoints but are open to techniques of persuasion being applied. An example from the investment perspective might be where corporate presenters have substantial information to support their explanations of financial performance and their well-informed investor audiences equally understand the wider business environment as well as the company's circumstances. The audience may be sceptical about how a company has performed but may be persuaded to a better appreciation of the corporate perspective if they are treated in an appropriate way. The relevance of this for investor relations is better illustrated in Table 5.1, which sets out the Simon and Jones principles of specialized or coactive persuasion,[26] giving examples to amplify their meaning and showing how they can apply to circumstances of investment presentations.

These principles are present when CEOs give presentations of their corporate stories to informed groups like financial analysts. These audiences are not persuaded by minimal disclosure, glossing over issues or presentation of unsubstantiated futures. If the objective is to have these audiences understand the corporate perspective of performance and strategy then there needs to be recognition of what represents a route to persuading them to a view of how management sees the world. These principles of

Table 5.1 Principles of specialized or coactive persuasion

Principles	Examples	Financial applications
Being receiver-oriented rather than topic-oriented.	Since not all receivers are alike, persuasion involves adapting messages for the circumstances.	Using awareness of particular investment community interests to adapt the corporate story.
Adapting messages for situations.	Messages that are persuasive in the boardroom are not necessarily persuasive in a public forum.	When performance does not meet expectations, persuasion involves a full explanation, not minimal information.
Responding to an audience's desire to be addressed by a credible and not just likable source.	Since most people cannot separate a message from its author, recognize that credibility is based on perceived expertise and trustworthiness.	Build understanding of the corporate story by showing complete knowledge across products, markets, industry trends and financial performance.
Building from shared premises.	Look for areas of agreement to build a persuasive argument, adopting a "yes, but" approach.	Acknowledging criticisms of management decisions while explaining the evolution of strategy development.
Move audiences by appearing reasonable and providing psychological support.	While not letting emotion override facts, give people a feeling for problems so they are persuaded by facts being presented.	Explain company strategy from a market forces perspective, letting an audience see decision-making around problems and issues.
Use many communication resources.	Persuasive arguments can be carried in many forms, from oral to written and visual.	Use many devices for conveying the corporate story, from website to one-on-one meetings and media coverage.

persuasion provide a guide to improving effectiveness in building support for a corporate story.

Another related aspect to the study of persuasion is what is termed "cognitive shorthands", which are psychological principles that influence aspects of decision-making. A scholar in this area, Robert Cialdini, has developed seven principles of influence[27] which his research from many examples of real life persuasion has shown are commonly present when people are influenced to decide in a way suggested. Cialdini's principles, with examples added from financial and investor communication as a way of showing how investor audiences can be influenced to understand a corporate perspective, are outlined in Table 5.2.

As companies begin to prepare presentations to key stakeholders it would seem inappropriate to begin with a list of persuasive principles and develop content from there, since it would almost seem a denial of the genuineness these presentations require. However, it would also be a mistake to overlook the persuasive element and cognitive shorthands that are necessary if companies are to convey a convincing story to stakeholders that they in turn can pass on to their stakeholders of investors and media audiences.

Table 5.2 Cialdini's seven principles of influence

Principles	Examples	Financial applications
Contrast	Presenting less palatable alternatives, to be eliminated in reaching a preferred decision.	Highlighting various strategic choice options as a way of influencing agreement with management's chosen strategy.
Reciprocity	Providing a benefit in seeking agreement.	Providing a discount to existing shareholders as encouragement to invest in a new issue of stock.
Consistency	Having made a choice, affirmation comes from sticking to it.	Having developed a logic for corporate strategy, build support from consistent application.
Social proof	Develop common ground by showing wide agreement.	Applying, and explaining, proven commercial and accounting principles, gains approbation.
Liking	People tend to believe praise and will return it.	Applying sound principles of corporate governance will be respected by investors.
Authority	In the medical field, respected authority leads to people following advice.	Displaying corporate leaderships builds confidence with investors.
Scarcity	Appreciating that products are scarce can increase demand for them.	Presentation of a convincing corporate story can make investors see potential for growth and stock being attractive at current prices.

The role of persuasion is acknowledged as a contentious topic in the theory of public relations. Grunig, in his original encapsulation of public relations theory, argues that the most effective form of communication is a two-way symmetrical communication between stakeholders and corporations and that persuasion in this sphere is not ethical. Challenges to this view have been developed by Pfau and Wan,[28] with their argument having two grounds. One is that Grunig assumes goal compatibility and a level playing field between stakeholders, which Pfau and Wan do not see as applying in the real world corporate arena. They contend that persuasion plays a critical role in negotiation between stakeholders and corporations. Their second proposition, in contrast with Grunig's view about the ineffectiveness and low ethical value of persuasion, is that persuasion is usually applied in the form of shaping messages to influence views over a period of time. In this way it is a common form of human exchange and can only be unethical if used for unethical ends, such as marketing harmful products, which all would agree is inappropriate. Pfau and Wan argue that persuasion plays a critical role in strategic communication, which is the way it is commonly applied in practice. They see instances of it in the way people receive information and form views, whether from key facts and figures or peripherally from expert views. They cite the way corporate communication affects changing perceptions, in promotional campaigns and sponsorships. They also note how differing types of media, such as television and print, can have differing degrees of influence on how people understand messages and pictures. Persuasive elements of corporate communication can also surface in the way corporations seek to influence investors through their attitudes to the environment. Establishing a basis of corporate goodwill through communication is also a practice implemented by corporations as a form of damage limitation in advance of possible crisis events.

From an investor relations perspective, persuasion involves putting forward a corporate view, involving objective and corporate elements, in a form of subjective objectivity.

It uses objective facts and numbers and surrounds them with a narrative, delineating a company's strategy in the context of the markets in which it is operating. This is intended to achieve a superior level of persuasion, since it connects directly with the concerns of investors. Underlying this process is a connection with rhetoric, Porter's market forces and an appreciation of the value of information in investment markets. Essentially it is a structure for the corporate story. This story, across the layers of phrases, websites and PowerPoint slides, as well as combining written and personal presentation, is a way for companies to lay out their development strategy, conveying a view of the future while incorporating a means for improving understanding and building trust.

If this form of communicating the corporate story is effective, it is providing material to be used for the secondary force of selling in investment markets, which is stockbrokers, as they sell stocks to wholesale and retail investors. The telephone conversations between brokers and clients are really about the elements of the corporate story. If it has been effectively presented, then these key points will be repeated in these conversations. If a corporation's business has been explained in a way that makes it easy to understand, then these messages are easily adopted by others who can pass them on. It is for the secondary sales force to offer opinions about the quality of management, whether a company can be trusted and whether its stock price represents value. They do not react well to being told these things by corporations, which is what makes the indirect selling techniques of investor relations different to standard product-selling. The secondary sales force is affected by the persuasive capacities of corporate communication when they are given interesting information from the corporate story, which makes their own jobs of persuading investors more effective.

One group of researchers (Hoffmann, Pennings and Wies) has taken this a step further and discovered the benefits that come from corporations recognizing the investment community as customers, with whom relationships are built and to whom helpful information is provided as part of marketing a stock to investors.[29] They see investor relations as a function that integrates finance, communication and marketing. It adds value through taking into account the variations in behaviour and preferences of differing investor types. This in turn has an influence on building relationships in differing ways with each separate type of investor. This research looked at five dimensions of building relationships and the extent to which they were achieved as a contribution to meeting primary investor relations objectives. These five dimensions were: an orientation towards being cooperative; a preparedness to evaluate the quality of relationship; a willingness to provide information that is not always positive in the firm's interests; a commitment to ongoing exchange of information; and an understanding of the reciprocal nature of relationship-building and information-sharing. Where these characteristics were exhibited, there was a positive correlation with achieving quality investor relations outcomes, such as lowering cost of capital, improving stock liquidity, increasing analyst coverage and reducing incidents of shareholder activism. In achieving these outcomes, investor relations, viewed from this perspective of "investor relationship marketing" becomes a function that can "drive shareholder value" and be "a strategic tool to build a sustainable competitive advantage".[30]

In their conclusion, these researchers argue that, by viewing investor relations as relationship management and investor relationships as market-based assets, then there is a change in the way investor relations is conducted. In relation to existing shareholders, this supports regular meetings aimed at building a collaborative relationship, intended to nurture trust and commitment. Additionally, this relationship orientation need not imply a total dependence on existing relationships since it is also the basis for evaluating the appropriateness of the shareholder base and exploring opportunities to find new investors.[31]

These elements – persuasion, relationship-building and communicating information – are the building blocks for the corporate story from an investment perspective.

The gap between information and story

While the investment community is just one of a number of stakeholders in investor relations, it is one of the most influential and demanding. There is often a tension between companies wanting to favour the release of good news and analysts wanting as much information as possible so they can assess not only what is going right but also consider what might happen if strategy is not implemented as planned. One of the more revealing surveys of what analysts want was conducted by two US academics, Epstein and Palepu,[32] of the top 140 Wall Street analysts. While it is a little dated now, it still gets to the nub of what financial analysts are seeking and what they find helpful in performing their function of making assessments of stock price and future performance.

The three primary sources on which analysts rely for information, according to Epstein and Palepu, are private meetings with companies, meetings of companies and groups of analysts, and a company's annual report. However, they also complain that these sources provide little information on strategies of the business units of a company and the risks they are likely to encounter. Analysts believe companies do not do enough to provide this sort of information nor do they make it easy for analysts to obtain this information, with boards of directors too often absorbed in representing the interests of management than those of other stakeholders like investors, bondholders, creditors, employees and community interests. With annual reports, analysts say they rely most on what the chairman and chief executive have to say and find pictorial and descriptive elements least helpful. The most useful financial information is the three main statements: the balance sheet, except where assets are valued at historical cost and where intangible assets are written off arbitrarily; the income statement; and the cash flow statement. Data on the performance of individual business segments is particularly insightful, providing historical information that guides views about possible future performance. However, what is too often missing is information around the strategy of these units as well as the overriding corporate strategy. A comment from one survey participant from an investment bank, which is also often a current view today, was:

> The more financial information a company can provide to present the dynamic and accounting of the business is a positive change. We obviously understand the protection of competitive information in the role of an analyst, and I am sensitive to that. But I think any information that you can provide an investor or analyst that speaks to the primary drivers of revenues and expense and the dynamics of what the primary expenses are helps you to understand really what makes the profits.[33]

The survey also found that companies find it a lot easier to be forthcoming when things are going well than when they are not:

> Analysts commonly believe that companies tend to provide only information that is legally required plus additional good news they want to trumpet. If corporate disclosures are to be credible, full disclosure must occur in good times and bad, they

say. A corporate communications strategy that recognises the importance of open and honest communications to both financial analysts and shareholders is important to the fair valuation of a company's stock.[34]

Epstein and Palepu say their survey strongly suggests corporations need to change the way they communicate. They see a pressing need for an improvement in quantity and quality of disclosure and point out that if leading analysts have difficulty in understanding notes to accounts, which are essential to understanding financial statements, then ordinary shareholders will have even greater difficulty. They argue that financial reports should become more central to communications strategy, which would not only achieve better relations with stakeholders and analysts but also, as they say, reflect what other studies have shown, which is that communication can have a significant positive effect on stock prices. They observe that corporations devote substantial effort to developing an overall corporate strategy as well as strategies for functional areas, including marketing, finance and operations, and for all significant business units.

> Yet they often are ineffective in communicating those strategies to those who make investment recommendations and investment decisions. Also, they often neglect to develop a comprehensive corporate communications strategy that is important in telling the corporate story. Our survey captures the resulting dissatisfaction of analysts regarding the adequacy of corporate communications. Financial managers can improve communications with analysts and investors by adopting a new attitude and new strategies to communicate more effectively with financial analysts and other stakeholders.[35]

Among suggestions Epstein and Palepu make are to:

- use the chairman's statement in the annual report to communicate a company's strategy, the key elements of its business model, success factors and risks and the value proposition around a company's products and services;
- use the chief executive's report to provide an insider's assessment of the effectiveness of its strategy and value proposition and relate this to the financial statements, providing non-financial metrics as well as a way of linking management actions to results and guide views about future performance;
- use notes to the accounts to explain the links between a company's business strategy and financial reporting choices;
- go beyond accounting technicalities and conventions to report on business factors, such as a company's customers, products and competition;
- reflect these changes to annual reports in other communication, such as presentations to analysts, conference calls and other investor relations efforts.

What Epstein and Palepu say their survey really shows is:

> The bottom line is that financial analysts want companies to be more forthcoming with their financial information and to provide more voluntary disclosures that "tell the corporate story" to external users.[36]

In the decade or so since this survey, there has been significant progress in the quantity of disclosure that listed companies are required to make. It has been an important element of how authorities have improved regulation of financial markets. However, it is not uncommon to hear echoed today many of the core criticisms from analysts reflected in the Epstein and Palepu survey, which is essentially about the missing elements of the corporate story.

In a more recent survey of the information needs of financial analysts, two Swiss researchers, Hoffmann and Fieseler, interviewed analysts who followed stocks on the Frankfurt Stock Exchange and found that non-financial information was equally as important as financial. Their research followed earlier findings from an Ernst & Young survey of analysts and investors, which found that "financial metrics are usually a lagging indicator of a company's performance, whereas non-financials actually provide information about a company's future success".[37] In pursuing their investigation of the content of the non-financial information that analysts want, the Swiss researchers also explored the extent to which investor relations is an image building function, focused on increasing "a company's visibility in capital markets to enhance its impact on investors' perceptions and opinions".[38] Their findings from their survey were:

> Equity analysts consider the following eight categories of non-financial information when forming an impression of a company: the stakeholder relations of an organisation, its corporate governance, its corporate social responsibility, its reputation and brand, the quality of its management, and its strategic consistency. One of the most important factors, however, is the quality of a company's communication, which underscores the strategic role that the investor relations function should play in fostering positive capital market relations.[39]

Their research highlights that, since capital markets participants strongly believe in the power that a company's management team has over the success of the organization, they are keen to form a personal impression of the people in charge of the business. This in turn emphasizes that not only is the image of a company's top management critical to market perceptions but also that a core task of investor relations is building that image.[40] In assessing this image, the research shows that the investment community pays attention to "the persuasiveness of top managers, their personal appearance and their communications skills" on the basis that "convincing leaders are expected to be able to deliver on their promises".[41] For the researchers, this elevates the importance of the role of investor relations and its pervasiveness throughout an organization because the centrality of its function, as shown by investment community views, is to be involved in building an organization's overall reputation and influencing public perceptions of it.

What this survey across investment influences on the corporate story shows is that marketing, persuasion, relationship-building and reputation all play a part in the way investor relations works in companies conveying their corporate stories. The language used in this communication combines words and numbers, and in the next chapter we will look more closely at this process to appreciate how numbers can escape their accounting straitjackets to become part of the narrative.

Notes

1 Laskin, AV, "Investor Relations", 14 November 2008, www.instituteforpr.org/topics/investor-relations

2 Origins of NIRI, www.niri.org/FunctionalMenu/About/Origins.aspx

3 Quoted in Origins of NIRI, Chapter 2, www.niri.org/FunctionalMenu/About/Origins.aspx

4 Origins of NIRI, Chapter 2, www.niri.org/FunctionalMenu/About/Origins.aspx

5 Laskin, AV, "Investor Relations", 2008, www.instituteforpr.org/topics/investor-relations

6 Palizza, J, "Sales, Marketing, Relationships and Investor Relations", *Investor Relations Musings*, 2 March 2010, http://investorrelationsmusings.blogspot.com.au/2010/03/sales-marketing-relationships-and.html?m=1

7 Harley, R, "Pressure Test", *BOSS*, 12 May 2012, p 24

8 Cummins, C, "Three 'Rs' Strategy Pays Off for Stockland", *Sydney Morning Herald*, 10 February 2011

9 Carapiet, L, "Buy Back Rejected for Safe Strategy", *Australian Financial Review*, 11 August 2011

10 Carapiet, L, "Stockland Strategy Questioned", *Australian Financial Review*, 12 August 2012

11 Carapiet, L and Harley, R, "Quinn Backflips on Buy Back", *The Weekend Financial Review*, 20–21 August 2011

12 Carapiet and Harley (2011)

13 Friemann, G, "Difficult Times Hit Stockland's Profit", *Australian Financial Review*, 10 February 2012

14 Boyd, T, "Stockland at the Crossroads", *Australian Financial Review*, 30 July 2012

15 Chong, F, "Stockland Upbeat on Affordable Housing Despite Earnings Slide", *The Australian*, 10 February 2012

16 Rochfort, S, "Stockland's Fourth R is for Redundancy", *Sydney Morning Herald*, 15 May 2012

17 Fielding, Z, "Stockland Revamp Welcomed", *Australian Financial Review*, 16 May 2012

18 Durie, J, "Nothing Like the Mighty Quinn", *The Australian*, 26 July 2012

19 Boyd, T, "It Really is Tough at the Top", *Australian Financial Review*, 26 July 2012

20 Harley, R and Fielding, Z, "Quinn Hangs up his Gloves", *Australian Financial Review*, 26 July 2012

21 Cummins, C, "Headwinds Hit Property", *Sydney Morning Herald*, 11 February 2012

22 Thompson, S and Macdonald, A, "Stockland Weighs Industrial Change to Portfolio", *Australian Financial Review*, 5 February 2013

23 Harley, R, "Stockland Turns, Despite Payout Doubts", *Australian Financial Review*, 14 February 2013

24 Simons, HW and Jones, JG, *Persuasion in Society* (Routledge, New York: 2011), p 34

25 Adapted from Simons and Jones (2011), pp 112–113

26 Simons and Jones (2011), pp 121–145

27 In Simons and Jones (2011), pp 210–237

28 Pfau, M and Wan, H, "Persuasion: An Intrinsic Function of Public Relations", in Botan and Hazleton (2006), Chapter 4

29 Hoffmann, AOI, Pennings, JME and Wies, S, "Relationship Marketing's Role in Managing the Firm-Investor Dyad", *Journal of Business Research*, September 2010

30 Hoffmann, Pennings and Wies (2010), p 897

31 Hoffmann, Pennings and Wies (2010), p 901

32 Epstein, MJ and Palepu, K, "What Financial Analysts Want", *IR Update*, NIRI, May 1999

33 Quoted in Epstein and Palepu (1999)

34 Epstein and Palepu (1999)

35 Epstein and Palepu (1999)

36 Epstein and Palepu (1999)

37 Quoted in Hoffmann, C and Fieseler, C, "Investor Relations Beyond Financials: Non-financial Factors and Capital Market Image Building", *Corporate Communications: An International Journal* 17 (2), 2012, pp 138–155

38 Hoffmann and Fieseler (2012), p 141

39 Hoffmann and Fieseler (2012), p 138

40 Hoffmann and Fieseler (2012), p 149

41 Hoffmann and Fieseler (2012), p 150

6 Numbers and the corporate story

The world of investor relations brings together many disciplines, across accounting, finance, law, marketing and public relations. It is not the purpose here to become immersed in the intricacies of financial, accounting and stock analysis. However, there does seem value in narrowing down the aspects of the numerical side of financial communication to reveal the basic fundamentals that are part of the investor relations armoury and to bring out how they connect with developing a corporate story. For those from a non-financial background, this is intended to be a short cut through a wealth of detailed accounting and investment information and, for those for whom this is second nature, perhaps reveal the story that can be drawn from numbers to hone communication values.

The broad context for this is that there is an argument for an alternative to believing that stock markets price all stocks efficiently. While the three forms of the efficient-market hypothesis – weak, semi-strong and strong – assert that stock market prices reflect all available information, the emergence over the years of anomalies to this general hypothesis has led to widespread questioning of its validity. The adoption of fundamental analysis of the numbers around what makes up a stock price is a common part of how stocks are compared and talked about in the marketplace. This makes it mandatory for those involved in investor relations and the development of corporate stories to have an understanding of the key numbers in the process.

The main components to understand are the three primary financial statements of listed companies – the balance sheet, income statement and cash flow statement – as well as the fundamentals around stock price, the concept of cost of capital and an appreciation that stock price represents the market's assessment of the present value of future cash flows. While extensive financial knowledge is helpful in investor relations, it is also possible to appreciate the communications aspects of the role without a fully-fledged financial background. For minimalists, it is possible to argue that the basic financial component of the corporate story can be covered by understanding just five numbers and one principle, the time value of money. These five numbers come at the end of the chapter. An understanding of these financial elements unlocks the language of the marketplace and provides a platform for credible communication of corporate stories. In many cases, capability to derive these numbers is less important than an appreciation of the parts of the story they represent, and to which they contribute.

Financial statements

Stock exchange-listed companies are required to issue audited accounts annually and half-yearly. In some jurisdictions they also issue quarterly financial statements, which are usually subject to audit review rather than being audited. The three main financial statements are: the balance sheet, an indicator of financial health; the income statement, showing earnings; and the cash flow statement, culminating in cash held at the end of the period. Large listed companies would be audited by one of the big four global accounting firms and accounting standards applied to accounts have become basically common across jurisdictions in recent years, under International Financial Reporting Standards (IFRS) and generally accepted accounting principles (GAAP) in the US.

The balance sheet

A balance sheet is a summation of the assets a company owns and the way those assets have been funded. It is also an indicator of the financial health of a company. A balance sheet has three components: a company's assets; liabilities in relation to those assets and running a business; and the equity a company has in those assets after subtracting liabilities. It is called a balance sheet because these components balance out. The total value of assets (A) is equal to the sum of liabilities (L) and equity (E), also called shareholders' funds or net equity. The simple formula for a balance sheet, which can guide a lot of understanding about corporate finance is:

$$A = L + E \text{ or } A - L = E$$

There are a few key elements of a balance sheet that require understanding but often the most illuminating are the ratios that its components deliver. It is the ratios and their implications that become key elements of communication. For example, some clichés used in relation to balance sheets are that they can be "strong", indicating a company is in a sound financial position, "lazy", suggesting a company has spare capacity to increase borrowings to make acquisitions or "risky", implying borrowings may be too high and could imperil the existence of a company. Descriptive terms such as "lazy" and "risky" would not usually be used by a company itself but if a company wants to convey it is in a sound financial position, perhaps with a capacity to expand by acquisition, then it needs to be able to incorporate financial elements into these aspects of description to add credibility to this part of a corporate story.

The balance sheet example shown in Figure 6.1, from a top 50 Australian company, helps to highlight key balance sheet terms. Assets are in two categories – current assets are those that can be converted to cash within 12 months and non-current or fixed assets are those that are not easily converted to cash. Within current assets, which are also known as liquid assets, are components such as cash, inventories and accounts receivable, which are amounts owed to the company. Non-current assets comprise plant and equipment, property, financial assets such as investments and intangible assets, which can comprise items like patents, trademarks or goodwill, which represents the difference between price paid for an acquisition and the net asset value of a business acquired. So long as goodwill represents a realistic market value, it remains an asset with indefinite life but if market value that it relates to falls, then an impairment has to be taken into account. A feature of investment markets is that they tend to attribute value to intangible assets not on balance sheets, with market values of companies often in excess of the values of net assets in balance sheets. In the case of a couple of large listed companies, such as Coca-Cola and Pfizer, which have substantial values based on brands and patents, neither lists such intangibles on their balance sheets at all.[1]

CONSOLIDATED BALANCE SHEET
as at 30 June 2012

	Note	2012 US$m	2011 US$m
ASSETS			
Current assets			
Cash and cash equivalents	14	174.2	138.5
Trade and other receivables	15	1,054.8	1,050.3
Inventories	16	48.2	56.5
Derivative financial instruments	17	8.9	11.3
Other assets	18	66.2	56.9
Total current assets		1,352.3	1,313.5
Non-current assets			
Other receivables	15	8.5	9.6
Investments	19	17.1	16.8
Property, plant and equipment	20	4,138.6	4,279.0
Goodwill	21	1,607.4	1,694.3
Intangible assets	22	362.2	403.7
Deferred tax assets	9	37.6	36.3
Derivative financial instruments	17	19.0	14.1
Other assets	18	3.0	0.7
Total non-current assets		6,193.4	6,454.5
Total assets		7,545.7	7,768.0
LIABILITIES			
Current liabilities			
Trade and other payables	23	1,176.8	1,264.3
Borrowings	24	86.4	325.6
Derivative financial instruments	17	5.0	6.1
Tax payable		46.5	102.9
Provisions	25	90.1	189.3
Total current liabilities		1,404.8	1,888.2
Non-current liabilities			
Borrowings	24	2,777.7	2,811.7
Derivative financial instruments	17	0.8	3.2
Provisions	25	30.4	20.0
Retirement benefit obligations	26	58.8	37.4
Deferred tax liabilities	9	505.7	529.1
Other liabilities	23	27.1	27.0
Total non-current liabilities		3,400.5	3,428.4
Total liabilities		4,805.3	5,316.6
Net assets		2,740.4	2,451.4
EQUITY			
Contributed equity	27	6,484.1	14,370.2
Reserves	29	(6,689.1)	(14,716.8)
Retained earnings	29	2,945.4	2,797.6
Parent entity interest		2,740.4	2,451.0
Non-controlling interest	29	-	0.4
Total equity		2,740.4	2,451.4

The consolidated balance sheet should be read in conjunction with the accompanying notes.

Figure 6.1   Example of a balance sheet

Liabilities are also in two categories – current and non-current, indicating liabilities that have to be met within 12 months or those that are outside that period. Common items within liabilities are amounts payable to creditors, borrowings or debt and tax liabilities. Balance sheets are commonly set up as shown in Figure 6.1, with total liabilities subtracted from total assets to give net assets or the equity a company has in those assets. Common categories within equity are contributed equity, which represents the number of shares issued by a company multiplied by the face value at which they were issued, retained earnings and reserves, which are usually funds set aside for a specific purpose. Balance sheets also show two columns of figures for each category, for the current year and previous year, to allow comparisons and assessment of changes to key components.

On the face of it, a balance sheet is just a list of accounting categorizations and numbers, not obviously communicating anything about a company. However, that is before a communicator, with just the small amount of description given above, begins to look for a story within those numbers. Effective financial and investor communication is not about creating a story despite the numbers. On the contrary, the numbers provide the back-up and evidence for describing how a company is progressing with its strategy, the sort of company it is and the characteristics it displays from its numbers. For example, investors do not want to invest in companies with precarious financial health nor should they be encouraged to ignore the key signs of a company's wellbeing.

Balance sheets generally are a guide to a company's financial position, principally because they give a picture of debt in relation to assets. The use of debt is fundamental to the way companies grow and the amount of debt is contained under the heading of liabilities. If debt levels are too high, it can mean that servicing the debt takes up too much of available income. An advantage that companies have in using debt is that interest on debt is deductible from income, which has the consequence of reducing the amount of income that is taxable. A concept that applies to balance sheets in relation to debt is that of gearing or leverage, which refers to the proportion of debt in comparison with the value of total assets. A rule of thumb that can be applied generally to balance sheets in determining an acceptable level of gearing is that debt, or assuming that debt is equivalent to total liabilities, can be 50 per cent of assets. Another way of expressing this same percentage is that it would represent a gearing ratio of 2:1, since assets would be two times liabilities or debt. Alternatively, debt can be expressed as a debt to equity ratio, which in this example would give a 1:1 ratio. More specific versions of gearing ratios are achieved when actual numbers for debt are extracted from liabilities. There are also a number of exceptions to this simplified example, since a lot depends on the industry sector in which a company operates. For example, the business of banks is that of borrowing from depositors and providing loans, leading to comparatively high gearing ratios for banks, ranging from debt being between 3 to 10 times assets, with Lehman Brothers before it collapsed showing debt to equity ratios of 30 to 60 times.[2] For many companies, gearing is a comparative ratio to be judged in relation to industry peers, with the rule of thumb varying across industry sectors and the attitude of board and management to debt and corporate strategy.

As well as being an indicator of overall financial health, the balance sheet is a guide to a company's ability in the short term to meet its obligations. Two tests of short-term liquidity are the current ratio (total current assets/total current liabilities), for which a conservative rule of thumb is that this should be 2:1, and the quick ratio (total current assets – inventories/total current liabilities), an indicator of immediate liquidity and for which a rule of thumb is 1:1. Higher ratios than these rules of thumb would indicate a company has high levels of cash, possibly a pointer to being able quickly to implement strategic initiatives such as acquisitions or share buybacks.

The income statement

The income statement shows how profitable a company is as well as the expenses involved in achieving profit. This statement is the focus of a lot of inquiry for those involved in investor relations and it is also the source of a lot of fundamental analysis of stocks and their prospects. While there are accounting standards requiring uniformity of the main elements of income statements, sometimes not all of the items of interest are included in the statements themselves but may appear in notes to the accounts published in annual reports. To help familiarity with the terms used, the following is a generic form of income statement, with an actual corporate version shown in Figure 6.2:

Revenue (principally sales but sometimes includes other income, such as interest income)
- cost of goods sold
= gross profit
- selling and administrative expenses
= operating profit or EBITDA (earnings before interest, tax, depreciation and amortization)
- depreciation
= earnings before interest and taxes (EBIT)
- interest expense
= profit before tax (NPBT)
- tax
= profit after tax (NPAT)

Profit after tax is also referred to as the bottom line. Occasionally companies may have additional items affecting the bottom line, of either a positive or negative nature, and these are referred to as extraordinary or abnormal items since they do not occur on a regular basis as part of the ongoing business operations. Under current accounting standards, they are not separated out in income statements but they may be part of a separate statement showing underlying profit, with accounting standards requiring a reconciliation with the underlying figures and statutory profit. Providing both numbers meets requirements while also creating an opportunity for companies to develop a surrounding story in explaining financial performance.

Items at various levels of the income statement above are also the source of some common ratios and additional terms. A common term in assessing the viability of a company's products in its market is margins. A gross profit margin is gross profit divided by revenue, expressed as a percentage. Comparing this year to year indicates how products are coping with competition. Net profit margin is calculated similarly, as profit after tax divided by revenue, and provides the added information of how a company is keeping all its expenses, or overheads, under control. While margin information is interesting, it is more meaningful when compared with other companies in the same industry, since varying industries can have strikingly different margins. For example, in the US in 2011, profit margins for S&P 500 companies were 8.9 per cent and were expected to be slightly

CONSOLIDATED INCOME STATEMENT
for the year ended 30 June 2012

	Note	2012 US$m	2011 US$m
Continuing operations			
Sales revenue	5A	5,625.0	4,672.2
Other income	5A	142.6	135.0
Operating expenses	5B	(4,833.9)	(4,004.4)
Share of results of joint ventures	19C	5.5	6.4
Operating profit		939.2	809.2
Finance revenue		21.5	17.2
Finance costs		(173.5)	(144.7)
Net finance costs	8	(152.0)	(127.5)
Profit before tax		787.2	681.7
Tax expense	9	(212.3)	(209.9)
Profit from continuing operations		574.9	471.8
Profit from discontinued operations	12	1.4	3.6
Profit for the year		576.3	475.4
Profit attributable to:			
- members of the parent entity		576.3	475.3
- non-controlling interest		-	0.1
Earnings per share (cents)	10		
Total			
- basic		38.9	32.9
- diluted		38.6	32.7
Continuing operations			
- basic		38.8	32.6
- diluted		38.5	32.5

The consolidated income statement should be read in conjunction with the accompanying notes.

Figure 6.2   Example of an income statement

less in 2012, while computer company Intel recorded margins of 62 per cent.[3] It is how competitors fare in their marketplace that gives rise to the story element around margins and opens up the market forces issues Michael Porter has developed. Another common ratio from the income statement is interest cover, which reflects the extent to which current earnings are available to meet commitments on both short-term and long-term debt. It is calculated as NPAT divided by annual interest expense (an item from the cash flow statement) and usually expressed as the number of times earnings cover interest expense. While company and industry comparisons are the most revealing, a common rule of thumb is that ratios above 2:1 are acceptable. Since the global financial crisis, a sound margin of safety of interest cover is an essential part of a corporate story.

A number of items in the income statement are also considered on a per share basis, which we cover below. However, the interaction between balance sheet and income statement also provides some key ratios. Apart from profitability items such as margins, the amount of profit a company makes is a reflection of how much money a company has invested in its operations. This amount of investment is the item of equity or net assets from the balance sheet. A company's return on equity is net profit after tax divided by net assets, expressed as a percentage. As a rule of thumb, companies showing a return on equity of 15 to 20 per cent are performing well, with this also reflected in their stock prices.

The interaction between balance sheet and income statement also gives insights to two measures of a company's efficiency. As a guide to how quickly a company converts its inventory into sales there is the inventory turnover ratio, which is cost of goods sold divided by average inventory (the average of the two inventory numbers from year to year in the balance sheet). This shows how frequently inventory is turned over in a year and can be divided by 365 to give a measure in days. Another efficiency ratio reflects how quickly customers pay for goods sold, calculated as average accounts receivable (the average between the two years in a balance sheet) divided by total sales. If this number is divided by 365, it shows how many days it takes for a company to collect cash from its customers. These measures of efficiency also suggest ways the information could be used in a corporate story sense, especially when compared with competitors.

Cash flow statement

Many investment analysts place greater faith in the cash flow statement than the income statement to give a guide to actual cash profit. This is because income statements can reflect accounting practices of accruing future costs and income while the bottom line of a cash flow statement shows the actual cash that is generated from the business, after its expenses and investment in capital items for its future. As the cash flow statement example shown in Figure 6.3 demonstrates, the statement has three components – cash flows from operating activities, from investing activities and from financing activities. Operating cash flows reflect sales less the amount of cash needed to make those goods and services. For most companies, it would be expected this would produce a positive net cash flow, although some companies in high growth or development phases of their businesses, like in software or biotechnology, might produce negative operating cash flows in early years. For any company, changes in operating cash flow from year to year provide a glimpse of the future, either positively or negatively. Differences in net profit after tax and operating cash flow are also worth observing – if profit is significantly higher it may be because a company has slowed down recognition of costs.

CONSOLIDATED CASH FLOW STATEMENT
for the year ended 30 June 2012

	Note	2012 US$m	2011 US$m
Cash flows from operating activities			
Receipts from customers		6,217.7	5,210.2
Payments to suppliers and employees		(4,759.2)	(3,815.6)
Cash generated from operations		1,458.5	1,394.6
Dividends received from joint ventures		4.2	5.6
Interest received		5.8	5.1
Interest paid		(164.2)	(169.6)
Income taxes paid on operating activities		(215.1)	(222.2)
Net cash inflow from operating activities	31B	1,089.2	1,013.5
Cash flows from investing activities			
Payments for property, plant and equipment		(949.4)	(764.7)
Proceeds from sale of property, plant and equipment		93.5	100.8
Payments for intangible assets		(53.8)	(46.3)
Costs incurred on disposal of businesses		(0.4)	(2.1)
Acquisition of subsidiaries, net of cash acquired		(22.7)	(1,050.2)
Net cash outflow from investing activities		(932.8)	(1,762.5)
Cash flows from financing activities			
Proceeds from borrowings		1,721.5	3,184.3
Repayments of borrowings		(1,710.0)	(2,487.7)
Net inflow/(outflow) from hedge instruments		4.6	(9.5)
Proceeds from issues of ordinary shares		326.6	231.1
Dividends paid, net of Dividend Reinvestment Plan[1]		(397.7)	(224.0)
Net cash (outflow)/inflow from financing activities		(55.0)	694.2
Net increase/(decrease) in cash and cash equivalents		101.4	(54.8)
Cash and deposits, net of overdrafts, at beginning of the year		80.4	123.3
Effect of exchange rate changes		(29.1)	11.9
Cash and deposits, net of overdrafts, at end of the year	31A	152.7	80.4

[1] The Dividend Reinvestment Plan was suspended on 17 August 2011.

The consolidated cash flow statement should be read in conjunction with the accompanying notes.

Figure 6.3   Example of a cash flow statement

Cash flows from investing activities principally reflect capital expenditure on new equipment or items that are required to keep the business growing. It also includes acquisitions or investments. Surpluses in this aspect of cash flow are not necessarily a good thing, since investors want to see companies continuing to reinvest in their businesses, at least at the rate of the depreciation of existing assets.

Cash flows from financing activities show money coming in from borrowings or loan repayments made and dividends paid to shareholders.

The net result of these three items of cash is shown as a bottom line, mostly as a positive item for companies progressing well and profitably, representing cash at the end of the period. A significantly positive amount of cash flow generated by companies is an encouraging sign from an investment perspective. It indicates funds available for growth, paying back debt and paying dividends. For some analysts, there is a closer correlation between cash flow and dividends than with earnings which can be more volatile.[4] The main item for investment focus is termed "free cash flow", which in a short cut form is calculated as operating cash flow – capital expenditure. There can be other adjustments in calculating free cash flow but essentially it represents money available to be spent immediately, which is a different concept to net profit in the income statement, which is the result of historic accounting transactions. The amount of free cash flow a company generates, and the sources and reasons for this, provide raw material for making a company story interesting.

Per share information

A number of the key elements of information from the three main accounting statements are also expressed on a per share basis. This unit of information is common in investment analysis and is often used in the media, so is an important aspect of information for companies to provide and make part of their story. The actual number of shares issued is occasionally found on the balance sheet statement but usually the item of equity or net assets on the balance sheet will have a note to an item later in the accounts that sets out shares on issue and how this has changed during the year. Armed with this piece of information, a number of per share ratios can be calculated, with the most common being:

Earnings per share = net profit after tax/shares on issue

The answer to this sum enables the calculation of the price-earnings or P/E ratio:

Stock price-earnings per share

The P/E ratio is expressed as a multiple of earnings, such as ten times earnings per share. This means it would take ten years of earnings at this rate, ignoring inflation and the time value of money, for earnings to pay back the original stock purchase price. The historical P/E ratio average of the US S&P 500 is approximately 16,[5] with the Australian Securities Exchange showing a similar historical average of 15.[6] While averages fluctuate over periods and can be misleading, they tend to highlight something of a dividing line between value stocks, seen as relatively cheap with a P/E lower than 15, and more expensive growth stocks with a P/E higher than 15. This does not mean stocks in either category are by definition better than the other, since there may be a good reason for a stock trading at a low multiple since its prospects may be poor while a higher P/E stock may have attractive growth prospects but could also be considered as expensive by value investors. From these perspectives, a P/E ratio and how it compares with other companies in an industry sector is an important input to how companies pitch their corporate stories to investors.

Dividend per share is an indicator of the rate of income return an investor receives from having purchased stock in a company. Dividend paid to shareholders will be shown in the cash flow in the component headed cash flows from financing activities.

Dividend per share = dividends paid/number of shares on issue

This is usually a prominent item shown in up front summaries of annual reports and so will not always need a manual calculation. Dividend is also important in two other ratios, yield and the payout ratio.

Dividend yield = dividend per share/stock price (expressed as a percentage)

Yield indicates the income rate of return an investor would receive from buying a stock, often an influential factor in an investment decision as it provides a comparison with rates of return on fixed interest investments, bank deposits or other stocks. A high yield might be an indicator of attractiveness or perhaps a stock with a low price and out of favour, while a low yield can indicate a growth stock.

Investors also want to know how much a company is paying out of its earnings in the form of dividends to shareholders who own the company. This is referred to as the dividend payout ratio, calculated as:

Dividend payout ratio = dividend per share / earnings per share

This is usually expressed as a percentage, with a common payout ratio being 50 per cent, with the rest becoming retained earnings to fund further growth.

Each of these per share ratios is part of the market language in financial communication. However, while providing the accounting information components around this is something companies are required to do, it is the stock market that makes judgements on stock price, with comparative ratios being part of the process. Market judgements reflect perceptions of the content of the corporate story, which is focused on business characteristics, and in turn it is this story content and how it is told and presented that can influence those judgements and perceptions. The resultant stock price is what the market determines but value per stock unit is a different concept. The value of a stock is determined by a company internally, on the basis of the inside information it has, and externally by investors on the basis of information made public as well as perceived values for intangible items, such as reputation and brand. Since the objective of investor relations is to achieve a fair value for shares in the market, it is appropriate to consider the varying ways to determine stock value.

Valuation of stocks

There are many differing methods for valuing shares but it was the influential investor, Benjamin Graham, in the first edition of *Security Analysis* in 1934, who highlighted the difference between stock price and value and introduced the term "intrinsic value". Graham believed intrinsic value was principally based on facts and he defined it as:

> the value which is justified by assets, earnings, dividends, definite prospects and the factor of management … In essence, the intrinsic value of the firm is its economic value as a going concern, taking account of its characteristics, the nature of its business(es) and the investment environment.[7]

When intrinsic value per stock unit is calculated, it provides a comparison with stock price and if it is well above stock price, it is an indicator of value for the investor. Theoretically, based on the efficient market hypothesis, which says in its semi-strong form that all public information is recognized in a stock price, intrinsic value should equal stock price. In actuality this is not often the case, which substantiates the viewpoint of those who undertake fundamental analysis of stocks. Separately, one of the aims of financial communication is to work towards closing the gap between value and price. Undervaluation or overvaluation are equal communications challenges but to assess them requires an understanding of ways to value shares.

Two concepts underlying the process of calculating intrinsic value are the definition of a share, representing the present value of future cash flows, and an appreciation of the time value of money. The simple concept underlying time value is that an amount of money can be invested at an interest rate that will mean that amount will be worth more in the future, especially if the interest is added to the principal and the combined amount is reinvested each year. Conversely a promise to receive an amount in the future does not have the same equivalent present value since there is a period to wait. So the present value of a promised future amount is calculated by discounting the future value at an interest rate to derive a lesser present value.

A simple example illustrates the point. A discount rate is simply an interest rate that works backwards. If there is a promise to receive an amount of $100 in a year's time and the discount rate applied is 10 per cent, the present value of that amount is $100/1.10 or $90.91. Similarly, if the promise is to receive $100 in two years' time, then the present value is $100/(1.10 × 1.10) or $82.64 since there is a two-year period over which interest is earned with the original principal plus interest reinvested after the first year.

What is being implemented here is the present value and future value formula, expressed as:

$$PV = FV/(1 + i)^n$$

where i is the interest rate expressed as a decimal and n is the number of years.

If this example is extended to the concept of a company producing free cash flow over future periods, at demonstrated growth rates, and remembering that stock price is the present value of future cash flows, then deriving a present value of those cash flows is a principal component of calculating intrinsic value. A common way of estimating these forward cash flows is to do so for five years ahead and, recognizing that the firm will be operating for many years afterwards, a present value of this perpetuity value beyond five years is added to the present value of predictable cash flows to achieve a single present value number. This is then divided by number of stock units on issue and gives intrinsic value per stock unit to be compared with current market price.

Case study

Enron – when words and numbers went beyond reality

At the end of December 2000, Enron was ranked as the seventh largest firm in the S&P 500 in terms of sales and its stock price was US$83.125. A year later, Enron filed for bankruptcy, with its closing market price at 60 cents a share and leaving investors and creditors counting losses in the billions. What brought this about? It was the market finally catching up with misleading numbers and a story that never really had any connection with reality.

According to one group of researchers,[8] there were three bases for the unravelling – Enron created bogus numbers, it never complied with its own model of managing risk and, in telling its story based on these factors, it set out to deceive Wall Street analysts, regulators, investors and the financial media.

On the first charge of bogus numbers, there was also a link with the story Enron was presenting. The numbers were suspect on two grounds – the way assets were valued and off-balance sheet transactions. Enron created a story that it was an energy bank, being an intermediary between sellers and buyers of natural gas, making a profit between buying and selling. The analogy was that it was just like a commercial bank, with gas producers being the depositors and consumers of energy were the borrowers. Along with the analogy was the implication of safety in the business model. However, the natural gas market was unregulated at the time and forward prices, on which Enron based its transactions, came to be seen more like guesswork than actual prices. In line with accounting standards at the time, Enron valued its transactions at market values, except that it was also the creator of those values. While the longest publicly traded contracts for natural gas were six years in duration, Enron created ten-year contracts and consequently its own forward price curve. From this it artificially inflated its profits.

Enron CFO Andrew Fastow was also adept at creating "special purpose entities", which became "a dumping ground for under performing assets that he could 'sell' to generate cash and revenues while keeping the related debt off the Enron balance sheet. ... As a result, Fastow was able to maintain a high credit rating, which lowered the cost of Enron's borrowing ... Eventually, however, this short-term scheme could not be maintained."[9]

As part of selling this story, Enron also trumpeted its risk management skills. It had a senior manager in charge of risk who was supposed to operate independently of other senior managers and answer to the board. However, in practice, this risk manager did not get on with Fastow and was sent to "corporate Siberia"[10] if he highlighted risk issues. Additionally, the board did not appear to fully understand the risk being created nor how to exercise any oversight. Enron's risk policy was spelled out and made public as a way of building market confidence but the way it worked tended to corroborate the practices in which Enron was engaged. Enron's risk model was based on the idea that there should be a 95 per cent confidence in the amount of money that was at risk at any point in time.[11] However, given it was based on volatile energy markets and predictions about uncontrollable factors such as weather, it was a wildly overoptimistic risk rating that could not be predicted with any confidence. Even based on its own risk estimates, amounts that could be lost or won on any day were substantial. However, the illusion created was one of controlled risk.

On the rhetorical side, perhaps the most outrageous storytelling was the creation of trading days intended to educate analysts about how the Enron trading process worked. These took place each year, from 1998 to 2001, and involved Enron setting up a simulated trading floor: "According to former Enron employees, on the sixth floor of the company's downtown headquarters was a set, designed to trick analysts into believing business was booming ... Former employee Carol Elkin said that it was all an act, and that no trades were actually made there. The people on the phones were talking to each other."[12]

Ultimately the regulators began to investigate the off-balance sheet transactions but even then it did not stop the storytelling as teleconferences were scripted for damage control. Towards the end, chairman Ken Lay paid himself a cash advance, which was later described as his "ATM approach"[13] to how the company was run.

When it all unravelled, many outsiders and even employees were still baffled about how Enron actually made money, let alone how it hid the facts for so long. The way it used numbers and story to replace transparency in financial reporting will long be remembered as a valuable case study.

Postscript

In June 2013, a court decision resulted in a ten-year reduction of the 24-year prison sentence given to former Enron chief executive Jeffrey K Skilling, for Enron-related crimes. The court deal, which could result in Skilling being free by 2017, also involved a US$40 million distribution from Skilling to victims of the Enron collapse.

Former Enron chairman Ken Lay died of a heart attack while on vacation in Colorado in 2006, three months before his sentencing hearing, which was likely to lead to a 20- to 30-year prison sentence.

Former Enron chief financial officer Andrew Fastow pleaded guilty to fraud in 2004, served five years in prison and now earns a living from the speaking circuit.[14]

Simpler versions of calculating intrinsic value can be used by estimating growth in earnings per share and discounting future values by an average P/E ratio. Alternatively, estimates of future dividends can be made based on average dividend payout ratios. A short cut approximation for estimating intrinsic value is shown on the formulas page at the end of this chapter.

If a derived intrinsic value from these methods was $12 a share and compared with a market share price of $10, then the 20 per cent difference is referred to by Benjamin Graham as a margin of safety,[15] a concept also adopted by Warren Buffet. For an investor looking for value in the stock market, a company selling at less than its intrinsic value is an attractive investment, with the margin of safety protecting an investor from market fluctuations and the inherent guess work involved in deriving an intrinsic value based on assumptions about future growth. Alternatively, for growth investors, there is not the same expectation that intrinsic value should be higher than stock price, with it being just one of the factors in an investment decision.

While understanding these terms is helpful, effective financial communication is more focused on using the language of the marketplace and knowing what terms mean rather than being immersed in calculating them. The corporate story is around the end result and its implications, rather than the process. The intent of the corporate story is not that it should dwell on stock prices and intrinsic values but, since they are critical issues for investors, accepting that they are also inextricably bound with the objectives of investor communication.

Two other important concepts to consider in relation to stock valuation, both of which have communication implications, are the actual discount rate used and also the influence of non-financial factors in valuation. In the discount example above, where future cash flows were discounted to present values at the rate of 10 per cent, the present values would have been significantly different if a discount rate of, say, 5 or 15 per cent were used. For example, if a discount rate of 5 per cent was used, the present value of $100 in a year's time would be $95.23 and $100 to be received in two years' time would have a present value of $90.70. These are significantly higher present values compared with those calculated at a discount rate of 10 per cent. If the future values being discounted were company cash flows, the present value, or intrinsic value per share, would be higher if a lower discount rate were used.

Calculating the actual discount rate to be used has some complexity about it, as we explain below in relation to a company's weighted average cost of capital. However, the underlying principle is that in considering future cash flows, there is some risk around estimating the actual amount that will be received and actual growth rates that will be attained. If risk were minimal, then a low discount rate would be used but that discount rate increases as the element of risk is perceived to be higher. The concepts applied here are that of a risk-free rate, usually a government bond rate as a guide to minimal risk of repayment, to which is added an equity risk premium, assessed according to several factors relating to individual corporations, such as their size, credit rating, industry sector, the quality of management and corporate governance. Risk premiums in the US used by institutional investors were estimated at 4.08 per cent in early 2012 compared with averages of 8.4 per cent in 1990 and 5.7 per cent in 2008 and 2009.[16] The outcome has a significant impact on discounting to present values. While the calculation of a risk premium is mostly based around objective factors, it is also an outcome of perceptions about companies, bringing it into the realm of communication.

The process of deriving intrinsic stock values is an element of what is called fundamental analysis, a school of thought that value can be discovered in the stock market from analysing the numbers around individual stocks. Fundamental analysts include those who are described as value investors, who see intrinsic value as a pointer to cheap stocks, and growth investors who are prepared to buy at prices above intrinsic value if they are confident in future growth. However, both types of investors also account for qualitative factors in their ultimate stock selections. They look at who runs the companies and how well they are performing, the industry sector and how companies fare against competitors and also larger economic factors and trends. In essence, both types of investors are looking for company stories that combine facts, numbers and narrative as inputs to their investment decisions. It is the job of financial communicators to bring relevant components of all this to their attention.

Cost of capital

As investor relations managers set out their programme of objectives each year, high up on the list is that their communications efforts should contribute to lowering a company's cost of capital. The cost of capital is the cost of funds to invest in new projects that would have a similar level of risk to the firm itself. It can also be seen as the discount rate at which future cash flows are discounted to present value and consequently it represents a benchmark or base rate of return that companies seek to achieve. Lowering cost of capital is not only a primary investor relations objective but, when it is achieved, it adds to the lexicon of communicating about corporate initiatives. When cost of capital is lower, it makes a greater range of capital investment and acquisitions possible because they would only be embarked on if estimated returns from them exceeded cost of capital, creating a platform for communicating about them. As with stock price, there are many factors that contribute to companies achieving a lower cost of capital but, as we have seen earlier with our summary of research findings, there is evidence that communication plays a role in reducing cost of capital. The concept of cost of capital is not complex, nor is its ultimate arithmetic calculation, although there are layers of complexity in understanding the derivation of the components that make up the formula for the calculations. The formula brings in the capital asset pricing model, known as CAPM. While we describe its various components in words and show a formula at the end of the chapter, the intention is not to become immersed in these issues when there are many other sources for this information. Our primary purpose is to bring out the communications aspects of a number such as cost of capital.

A company's cost of capital can be determined by external analysts from published accounts. It is also derived internally by management, using information that may not be public and so often arriving at different number that is used internally. One of the reasons it is not made public is that while it might be a tool for management teams to analyse performance and guide decision-making, it is not necessarily material that companies want in the hands of outside observers. There are other measures in published accounts that managers prefer to have as public metrics for explaining performance and these concepts are covered below.

The cost of capital is the cost of a company's funding. Consequently, it is the average cost of its debt and equity. Cost of capital is a useful management concept since it provides a guide to how a company should use its funds. It represents a minimum rate of return a company should expect from any investment it makes. For example, when a company considers buying new equipment, building new premises or making an acquisition, it has to calculate a rate of return on this investment, with the answer, in terms of its level above the cost of capital, being the guide as to whether it should proceed. From an external perspective, when an investor calculates a company's cost of capital, it gives a guide to the expected return an investor should expect from providing capital to a company.

There are significant advantages for a company in having a lower cost of capital. It provides a greater variety of projects it can consider because of a low hurdle rate of return for these projects. Where companies achieve a lower cost of capital than competitors, then investors consider them to be lower risk which in turn makes their stock more liquid and consequently easier to trade. A higher cost of capital indicates companies having a higher risk and liquidity premium. Competing for capital is an aspect of financial markets and it is to a company's advantage if it has a lower cost of capital. Consequently, if investor relations and effective communication can contribute to a company lowering its cost of capital, it is an important contributor to higher growth and returns.

Since the cost of capital has two components, debt and equity, it is often referred to as the weighted average cost of capital, or WACC. One definition of WACC is that it is "the discount rate, or time value of money, used to convert expected future free cash flow into present value for all investors".[17] The cost of the debt component is relatively straightforward since it is the interest rate a company pays on its borrowings. This may need to be averaged across a few different items of debt if this information is available. Often this information is hard to obtain for external analysts so an approximation needs to be made based on an expected borrowing rate for a particular type of company given its size. Corporate interest rates are usually at a margin over a base rate, with the margin reflecting a company's credit rating. A short cut approximation that can be applied is to derive an interest rate, by using the interest expense component from a company's cash flow divided by debt shown on the balance sheet. The derived interest rate could be applied across all a company's debt to give the debt cost component of cost of capital. Since interest cost on debt is tax deductible, this element of tax effectiveness is accounted for in the total calculation.

The cost of equity can be calculated in two ways, using the dividend growth model or the capital asset pricing model (CAPM). The dividend growth model looks at the cost of equity as being the dividend paid and so provides a way of discounting to present value the likely cost of future dividends. However, the more common, and more complicated, approach is to use the CAPM, which allows for the market price of risk as well as an individual company's risk in calculating the expected return on a stock, which is effectively the equity component cost of capital. While there is a wealth of learning around the CAPM, the basic element to be understood is that an individual stock, with its individual expected return and individual measure of risk, is compared with an average return and risk for the overall market. The formula that calculates the expected rate of return for a stock under CAPM incorporates a term called "beta", which is a measure of the sensitivity of a stock's return in comparison with movements of the market as a whole. The formula is shown at the end of the chapter and, while there is a wealth of learning around its derivation, it is the end number that is relevant here. The cost of equity becomes an input to calculating the WACC (formula also shown at the end of the chapter), accounting for the proportions of debt and equity that make up total capital. A point to be noted in this calculation of the proportions of debt and equity that make up a company's total funding is that there can be a number of differing types of debt and equity and a closer approximation to total cost of capital is achieved by using market values of debt and equity.

The outcome of calculating cost of capital is a number that is a discount rate, for discounting cash flows and for being a hurdle rate to assess the viability of projects, with only projects showing a return above cost of capital being worth pursuing. Earlier we encountered the P/E ratio. While it is a different concept, the P/E is a pointer to cost of capital issues. A high P/E indicates investors being prepared to pay a high price for the available earnings, indicating the company would have a low cost of capital.

These calculations and formulas are just intended to provide a background setting, to inform communications activity and direction. Considerable research has shown that liquidity is an important factor in cost of capital. Liquidity is effectively a measure of how long it takes to buy and sell an asset. Stocks that are expensive to trade are considered less liquid than those that trade cheaply. If a stock is less liquid, then it implies that an investor would want a higher rate of return because of the higher implied risk. Higher expected return and higher risk means higher cost of capital. Measures that reflect costs of liquidity are brokerage fees, the bid-ask spread and the costs of selling large amounts of stock. Each of these measures can involve added risk and each is lower with more liquid stocks. One of the most important factors contributing to increasing liquidity, and hence lowering costs associated with low liquidity, is information. The more that is known about a stock, in the form of quality disclosure to the market, then the more a contribution is being made to increasing liquidity, decreasing trading costs and lowering cost of capital. Another factor contributing to liquidity is a growing number of shareholders. The more investors there are, the more there are opportunities to trade stock. These two factors combined, namely growing numbers of better informed shareholders, can both be outcomes of communication, underlining why increasing liquidity and lowering cost of capital have become important investor relations objectives.

Painting with Numbers

In his book, *Painting with Numbers*, Randall Bolten invents the term "quantation", a combination of the words "quantitative" and "communication" to represent his view that numbers, if presented well, can tell a story. Bolten notes many mistakes in the presentation of numbers, ranging from having too many numbers after a decimal point, to too many columns or line items in tables, poor labelling of charts, uninformative use of pie charts and the creation of unreadable PowerPoint slides through cramming too many columns into them. He argues that if numbers are to be "valuable and meaningful to your audience, you need to have a sense of what decisions the people in your audience are making, what problems they are facing, how they think about these decisions and problems, and your own ultimate goal in preparing your report(s)".[18] He also points out that numbers on their own do not have meaning but it is comparisons, highlighting of trends and development of key indicators that tell people things. While a company's balance sheet might be an indicator of financial condition at a particular date, for Bolten it is the income statement that reflects an organization's decision-making. Labelling of line items in the income statement, their sequence and the trends they represent, point to where attention should be focused in gaining an explanation of the drivers of profit or reasons for performance not meeting expectations. To help this understanding, Bolten also acknowledges that numbers need accompanying words to create a full picture.

Some analysts have also looked at how numbers can be manipulated in the interests of perpetuating a story and seeking to meet market expectations. These manipulations are not necessarily contrary to accounting principles although it depends how far the process goes. The two main devices used are decisions made around timing and classification of accounting items. For example, in the income statement, revenue and expenses can be shifted from one period to another to achieve a desired result, and in the cash flow statement, classification of items as operating or financing can also produce a different picture.[19] In its straightforward form, this practice is known as "earnings management", which some investors and analysts view positively on the basis they can differentiate good practices from bad.[20] Some research has shown positive market reaction to management of earnings[21] but the fact it can be detected is not necessarily a positive contribution to corporate reputation. A different version of a similar process is companies focusing on "underlying profit", which is statutory profit with one-off or unusual items stripped out, as a way of explaining performance. The Australian regulator has described this process as "cherry-picking" results and a survey in 2011 of Australia's top 100 companies by accounting firm KPMG, found that nine of them that claimed an underlying profit actually made a loss in statutory terms.[22] As one regulator has put it, "confidence in the quality of financial reporting is fundamental for investors, lenders and also market regulators".[23]

Business performance metrics

In addition to the main accounting notions of business performance covered above, many businesses develop individual metrics that are indicators to describe how a business is performing. These will vary across companies and industries and can be quite specific for individual companies. Some companies prefer to keep these metrics as internal information rather than make public a piece of information by which analysts might make judgements separate from standard accounting measures. However, these metrics are an important tool for conveying a story. They indicate how management teams make decisions about their businesses and are a pointer to strategy. The words around these metrics are equally important in implying their meaning and interpretation. Some can be of a general nature, like customer and employee satisfaction, productivity, repeat business, margins or the speed of cash flow. Others can be company-specific that build a direct connection to and understanding of the performance component of a company story. Two examples are GE Capital and Brambles, the world's largest pallet supplier.

GE Capital

GE Capital leases aircraft to customers. Leases last for 7 to 12 years, after which GE will redeploy the aircraft by negotiating a new lease. That process creates a time period when the aircraft is not under lease and therefore not generating revenue. When measuring the costs of downtime for aircraft leases, GE Capital's FP&A team spends time with the operations team so that they understand the process and activities involved with transferring an aircraft from one lessee to the next one. This process involves activities such as inspection and maintenance, which have to be factored into the necessary time and cost of downtime measurement. The FP&A team then develops a baseline calculation of necessary downtime that is included in the financial plan, and then monitors the days off lease and dollar value of lost rental income compared to the baseline amount in the plan. That metric is included in a weekly "dashboard" report of performance statistics and reviewed with senior leadership and the operations team to identify root causes of incremental downtime. All participants can then work together to devise a plan of action to ensure the negative effects of off-lease aircraft time on operating profits are lessened.[24]

Brambles

Cost leadership is also about maximizing capital efficiency. Our focus on asset utilisation continues to increase, in particular in Pallets. The three main drivers of asset cost in equipment pooling are loss, cycle time and damage – that is, what proportion of the pool leaves our network control, how quickly we can retrieve our assets, and the extent of wear and tear that those assets endure while they are under hire. During the Year, we continued to invest in projects aimed at addressing these three key issues so we can improve control of our assets over the long term. For example, in CHEP USA, we have worked with some customers in the grocery manufacturing sector to reduce the number of pallets sent into distribution and retail channels that do not participate fully in the CHEP pooling network. This means fewer of our pallets get lost, we are able to retrieve and return them more quickly and – because they spend less time in the field – damage rates should reduce. We are pleased to report a modest reduction in the size of the Irrecoverable Pooling Equipment Provision – which provides for non-compensated pallets that have leaked from our system – in the Americas region of the Pallets segment as a result of these initiatives.[25]

Both these examples link communication and business understanding, with narrative incorporating facts and numbers, or metrics.

Combining words, numbers and narrative

A corporate story is an opportunity to bring together points of distinction about a company. Not every version of this will bring in numbers but a story needs to be shaped for differing groups of stakeholders so some versions will involve more numbers than others. Since a corporate story is individual for each company, there is not a common defined structure or list of contents for every circumstance but a variety of aspects of story construction are given below.

A phrase

A descriptive phrase for a company is a critical piece of communications strategy. It is a guide to how the media can succinctly describe a company and how the investment community and investors can talk about it. The phrase essentially is a minimalist description of what a company does but also includes a component of positioning a company in its market. Examples could be:

- a national banking organization;
- a global packaging company;
- a diversified renewable energy company.

The phrase becomes how companies can begin announcements, with a short but meaningful summary of corporate purpose. It is a self-description that is different from wording that might accompany a logo which has an alternative marketing intention.

Strategic direction

Some companies use front covers of annual reports and website front pages to establish themes that sum up strategic direction and corporate priorities. Some examples of this are:

- Telstra, 2012, telecommunications company – "It's how we connect."
- Westpac, 2012, bank – "Strength, Return, Growth, Productivity."
- QBE, 2011, global insurer – "A clear vision supporting a diversified, entrepreneurial, specialist, global business."
- AGL, 2012, energy company – "Energy in action."
- Brambles, 2012, global pallets and logistics business – "Momentum."

Sentences

Expansion of the phrase into a sentence or two is how detail is added to the story. The sentences could be on a company's website or in a paragraph headed "About us", which might form an ending to a stock exchange announcement. A temptation here can be to add adjectives, adverbs and superlatives to describe how a company is the best in its market or is world leading or has unique technology. These claims, in lacking objectivity, are not convincingly persuasive. Alternative words such as "distinctive" or "significant" can convey a greater degree of persuasion, with actual achievements being more influential than claims. The aim is not so much to say how great a company is but to describe it persuasively so that readers or hearers of the description will be better informed and not feel they are being subjected to a sales pitch. Numbers, percentages and statistics can enhance the picture being painted by the words and in the process combine to create a succinct narrative. The idea of these sentences is that brevity and simplicity are more likely to add to understanding than tortured prose that aims for exhaustive completeness. Some examples of effective story sentences are shown below in these examples from Goldman Sachs and Nestlé.

Goldman Sachs

The Goldman Sachs Group, Inc. is a leading global investment banking, securities and investment management firm that provides a wide range of financial services to a substantial and diversified client base that includes corporations, financial institutions, governments and high-net-worth individuals. Founded in 1869, the firm is headquartered in New York and maintains offices in all major financial centers around the world.[26]

Nestlé

Nestlé has 468 factories in 86 countries around the world and around 330,000 employees. Nestlé is the world's leading nutrition, health and wellness company with an unmatched portfolio of more than 2,000 global and local brands.[27]

Context

The placement of a company in the wider context of its market, industry and trends can be a forcefully persuasive element and more effective than superlatives. It affords an opportunity to bring out positioning, comparative description, market share and branding to add colour to the story. Some examples are shown below.

GlaxoSmithKline

GSK is currently the largest healthcare company in the UK with offices in more than 100 countries and major research centres in the UK, USA, Belgium and China. In recent years, GSK has focused its business around three strategic priorities which aim to increase growth, reduce risk and improve long-term financial performance. We are succeeding in our strategy to create a more balanced business capable of addressing the market challenges we face, delivering sustainable financial performance and providing new value to patients and consumers. In 2011, we delivered underlying sales growth, strong cash generation, significant R&D progress and increased shareholder returns. We are committed to using free cash flow to support increasing dividends, share repurchases or, where returns are more attractive, bolt-on acquisitions.[28]

General Electric

GE is building the world by providing capital, expertise and infrastructure for a global economy. GE Capital has provided billions in financing so businesses can build and grow their operations and consumers can build their financial futures. We build appliances, lighting, power systems and other products that help millions of homes, offices, factories and retail facilities around the world work better.[29]

Capabilities, direction

Particular characteristics that highlight a company's competitive advantage are elements to bring out in story descriptions as well as guide understanding of where a company is heading. There may be aspects of a company's operations that need to be downplayed because they may be intended for sale or there may be aspects of a business that are of particular interest to investors. Alternatively, some aspects of a business may be more substantial contributors to profit, or they may be faster growing. Words and numbers that bring out the shape of a business, presently and how it is likely to be in the future, are influences on how the sentences are drawn together. Examples are shown below.

Noble Group

> We are Noble Group, a market-leading global supply chain manager of agricultural and energy products, metals and minerals. Our objective is to build long-term value for our shareholders. Noble Group was established 25 years ago in the belief that urbanisation would drive demand for the products and services that we aimed to provide. We connect low cost producing countries with high demand growth markets. Our investments focus on key stages of the supply chain to create and extract additional value, manage risk and secure long-term flows of products and information. Noble is listed in Singapore (SGX: N21), with headquarters in Hong Kong and operates from over 140 locations. We are ranked number 91 in the 2012 Fortune 500.[30]

Amazon

> We seek to be Earth's most customer-centric company for four primary customer sets: consumers, sellers, enterprises, and content creators.[31]

Connecting with people

Any business, in whatever industry, ultimately has to connect with customers and the people who buy its goods and services. Corporate story sentences that are abstract and distant from this connection with reality miss an opportunity to be inclusive of the audience they are trying to reach. The examples below show how this can be achieved.

Google

> It's really the people that make Google the kind of company it is. We hire people who are smart and determined, and we favor ability over experience. Although Googlers share common goals and visions for the company, we hail from all walks of life and speak dozens of languages, reflecting the global audience that we serve. And when not at work, Googlers pursue interests ranging from cycling to beekeeping, from frisbee to foxtrot. We strive to maintain the open culture often associated with startups, in which everyone is a hands-on contributor and feels comfortable sharing ideas and opinions. In our weekly all-hands ("TGIF") meetings – not to

mention over email or in the cafe – Googlers ask questions directly to Larry, Sergey and other execs about any number of company issues. Our offices and cafes are designed to encourage interactions between Googlers within and across teams, and to spark conversation about work as well as play.[32]

Walmart

Since the first Walmart store opened in 1962 in Rogers, Arkansas, we've been dedicated to making a difference in the lives of our customers. Our business is the result of Sam Walton's visionary leadership, along with generations of associates focused on helping customers and communities save money and live better.[33]

Track record

Past achievements may be what have underwritten a substantial business today or maybe the recent past has not lived up to expectations, with particular circumstances having temporarily derailed a steady growth pattern. Bringing out any of these elements can give a sense of history or consistency or provide a thoughtful recognition of how management is addressing a correction to its business model or a way of regaining trust if it has been lost through poor past performance. Adaptation to change is an interesting element that may need description, or simply giving an example of a company in action can highlight its attributes. Some examples are below.

Goldman Sachs

When the Brooklyn Navy Yard Development Corporation (BNYDC) wanted to further revitalize its 300 acres and continue to create local jobs, it needed additional funding and expert advice. Goldman Sachs helped BNYDC identify previously untapped sources of funding, invested its own capital, and helped manage the complexity of many different parties working together. The result: the renovation of Building 128, which will house innovative and growing businesses and create jobs for Brooklyn residents.[34]

General Dynamics

General Dynamics is a market leader in business aviation; combat vehicles, weapons systems and munitions; shipbuilding and marine systems; and mission-critical information systems and technology. The company was formed in 1952 through the combination of the Electric Boat Company, Consolidated Vultee (CONVAIR) and several others. The company grew organically and through acquisitions until the early 1990s, when we sold many of our defense-related businesses. Starting in the mid-1990s, we began expanding by acquiring combat vehicle-related businesses, additional shipyards, information-technology product and service companies and Gulfstream Aerospace Corporation. Since then we have acquired and integrated more than 60 businesses, including six in 2011. Our revenue has grown from $4 billion to approximately $32 billion in that time and our workforce has increased from 29,000 to approximately 95,000 employees today.[35]

Risk

There may be a need to bring out how a business manages elements of risk to take on directly impressions outside observers may have of how a business operates or builds in management of risk to its operations. Examples could be:

BP

> BP is following a 10 point plan to grow value for shareholders – ten things you can expect and measure as we work to rebuild the company. The plan starts with a relentless focus on safety and centres on playing to BP's strengths. These are: exploration, giant fields, deepwater, gas value chains, a world-class downstream, technology and relationships.[36]

Volkswagen

> Superior value, social responsibility and a practical commitment to sustainability are hallmarks of our corporate culture. We take a far-sighted approach to the key issues of the future, such as climate change. We pursue a broad range of research and development activities and generate the pioneering technology that the mobility of the future will demand. In all of this we are assisted not least by the process of dialogue with our stakeholders. By 2018 the Volkswagen Group aims to be the most profitable, fascinating and sustainable automobile manufacturer in the world. We are ready to accept the responsibility that goes with this status. Across the globe. The Volkswagen Group with its twelve brands provides solutions in all vehicle segments from sub-compact cars to heavy-duty trucks and buses. We use the most efficient technologies and pave the way for fundamental innovations. We take our guidance here from sustainability and responsibility – the basic principles underlying Volkswagen's corporate activities.[37]

Reputation, standards, the social connection

Aspects of reputation, standards of behaviour and adhering to corporate social responsibility and ESG (environment, social and governance) guidelines can be worth highlighting but are less effective if done in a self-congratulatory way. Objective touchstones like winning awards or aspects of external recognition are more convincing. Some examples are below.

Volvo

> The Volvo Way shows what we stand for and aspire to be in the future. It lays the foundation for developing the Volvo Group into the world's leading provider of commercial transport solutions. It is a recipe for success in which we strongly believe. It expresses the culture, behaviours and values shared across the Volvo Group. The Volvo Way is based on the conviction that every individual has the capability and the determination to improve our business operations, and the desire to develop professionally. The Volvo Way is the lively dialogue between leaders,

within teams, and among colleagues around the world. This is the way we conduct business and deliver results. This is how we partner with customers and suppliers, how we work and change, and how we build the future together.[38]

Caterpillar

Sustainable Development for Caterpillar means leveraging technology and innovation to increase efficiency and productivity with less impact on the environment and helping our customers do the same – enabling their businesses to become more productive by providing products, services and solutions that use resources more efficiently. Of course, it starts with our own operations, with our customers in mind.[39]

Investment community perspectives

Any corporate story description needs not only to reflect an internal perspective but also to recognize how outsiders might see a company. For example, a company may be proud of its dominant market share. However, to a canny analyst, this might represent a mature market with limited growth prospects, indicating there might be better investment prospects elsewhere. Story elements may need to hint at new directions for diversification. Possible examples follow, from Walmart and DuPont.

Walmart

Walmart helps people around the world save money and live better – anytime and anywhere – in retail stores, online and through their mobile devices. Each week, more than 200 million customers and members visit our 10,700 stores under 69 banners in 27 countries and e-commerce websites in 10 countries. With fiscal year 2013 sales of approximately $466 billion, Walmart employs 2.2 million associates worldwide.[40]

DuPont

In this DuPont (DD) stock overview, you'll see how the challenge of providing for the food, energy and protection needs of a growing population provide DuPont with opportunities to bring unmatched science to the marketplace. We are focused on market driven innovation, cost and working capital productivity around these three global megatrends. As an overview of DuPont stock and its potential, we expect to grow faster than market rates over the next few years by focusing on the most promising businesses, growth in developing markets and continued productivity improvement.[41]

Connecting with strategy, audiences

Corporate stories also need to connect with a company's overall strategy and how it is being expressed in other aspects of the business, through marketing and public relations. The audience is also relevant. A presentation to the investment community has to be focused on financial performance and company metrics that are indicative of how management assesses its own progress. Presentations to shareholders at an annual meeting or to groups of employees need to have a more general assessment of a corporation in its environment. Journalists may be focused on a particular angle of news and need to have a context of a company's story in relation to this. These nuances are covered in succeeding chapters as we consider the corporate story in its financial market context and the way disclosure is shaped for key stakeholder audiences.

Five numbers to know

Those involved in financial and investor communication come from many backgrounds. Some have the dual role of chief financial officer, making them intimately involved in analysing a corporation's financial performance. However, for those less familiar with accounting and applied finance, it might be helpful to zero in on just five numbers that can unlock a lot of the complexity of financial information. Allied with this is an appreciation of the principle of time value of money, which we covered earlier, since this underlies the process of discounting future cash flows. The five key numbers are highlighted below, along with explanations of how those numbers can be used to create additional meaning, all of which are components for developing the corporate story.

1. Net assets

Net assets on the balance sheet are an indicator of the balance of ownership and responsibilities in a corporation. It is net assets that allow calculation of gearing ratios, an important story element in a corporation's financial health and capacity to take on additional debt that might contribute to growth. Net assets on balance sheets are the difference between assets and liabilities and is sometimes labelled equity or shareholders' funds. If tangible assets are deducted from net assets the term net tangible assets is used.

2. Net profit after tax (NPAT)

A company's profitability is at the basis of all financial analysis and, like all numbers, is more meaningful as a trend and as part of ratios that form key indicators of performance. NPAT is the bottom line of income statements.

3. Stock price

This is a basic piece of information anyone involved in financial and investor communication needs to know, especially how it trends within a day and over time. Price on a particular day is a reflection of volume of stock traded which is also another relevant piece of information to follow. Stock price is key to important ratios covered below.

4. Shares on issue

Shares on issue is sometimes given in highlights sections of annual reports. Otherwise it is found by looking at notes to the accounts that relate to net assets given on the balance sheet. It is sometimes expressed as the weighted average of shares on issue if new shares have been issued during the accounting period. Knowing the number of shares on issue is the basis for calculating "per share" ratios, although some of these will be given also in the highlights sections of reports.

Informative items derived from knowing the first four key numbers are net assets per share (NAPS, also referred to as NTAPS if intangible assets are deducted from net assets), earnings per share (EPS), P/E ratio and market capitalization.

Net assets per share (NAPS)

This provides a comparison with stock price, indicating a margin of safety if stock price exceeds NAPS. NAPS also enables calculation of the "price to book ratio", which is stock price decided by NAPS, indicating the number of times the market values a stock above its balance sheet value and providing a basis for comparison with other stocks.

Earnings per share (EPS)

Knowing this number is a component of other ratios while also making a comparison of earnings in previous years on the basis of varying amounts of equity having been issued.

P/E ratio

Dividing stock price by EPS gives the P/E ratio, describing stock price as a multiple of earnings per share, which is a pointer to whether a company is a growth or value stock.

Market capitalization or market cap

This is the multiplication of shares on issue and stock price and so is the market value of a company's equity. Knowing market capitalization is the starting point for many conversations with prospective investors and the financial media. "Market cap" is a simple size comparison number among listed companies and immediately positions a company into groups that analysts follow, like large cap, mid cap and small cap stocks.

5. *Dividend*

This is usually given as an item in the cash flow statement and, divided by shares on issue, gives dividend per share, which is also often provided in the highlights section of reports. Dividend per share divided by stock price gives the yield on a stock, for comparison with the income return on alternative fixed interest investments as well as other stocks. The amount of dividend paid divided by NPAT and expressed as a percentage gives the dividend payout ratio, another item for comparison with other stocks and an indicator of board policy about sharing rewards with shareholders. Knowing dividend per share over previous years provides a basis for calculating an earning rate and for estimating future earnings rates of stocks, a basis for the dividend growth model which can be a short cut for calculating intrinsic value per share.

While attempting to reduce the entirety of accounting and applied finance to just five numbers is a large simplification, it does point to some key numbers for focus when developing a corporate story. It is the trend in these key values that are at the basis of discerning how a company is performing and progressing with its strategy.

Numbers, facts, words and narrative all come together to bring out key story elements around a corporation. In combination, they can represent the legal term, "disclosure". Listed companies are required by law to make statements from time to time and to disclose how they are performing. However, they are not required to build in all these story elements but instead the legal focus tends to be on what represents minimum disclosure, allowing companies to exceed this voluntarily. For companies that want to give a priority to communication, disclosure can become an opportunity rather than an obligation. The topic of disclosure and its connection with story and stock price are the next aspect of the stock price story to consider.

Capital asset pricing model (CAPM)

The capital asset pricing model calculates the expected return on an asset based on its level of risk. The formula accounts for the level of risk of an individual stock, which is its "beta", and in combining this with an estimate of the return for the market overall, calculates an equity risk premium for a stock above what might be considered a risk free rate. As a formula, the CAPM is expressed as:

Expected return = risk free rate + beta of an individual stock x (the market return – the risk free rate)

$E(ri) = Rf + \beta i(E(rm) - Rf)$

$E(ri)$ = return required on financial asset i

Rf = risk-free rate of return

βi = beta value for financial asset i

$E(rm)$ = average return on the capital market[42]

Calculating the formula for beta can be complicated and the beta can be more easily obtained by simple Internet research, especially for large companies. In short cut calculations, an average beta of one can be assumed, which simplifies the formula greatly, as average market returns can also be easily searched.

Weighted average cost of capital (WACC)

The weighted average cost of capital provides a discount rate for calculating the present value of future cash flows. It also represents a hurdle rate of return for companies as they assess whether to proceed with capital investment. The formula accounts for the weights of the two sources of finance for a company, equity and debt. The weights are based on the proportions of the market values of these two components. Where there is no market value of debt, the balance sheet value is used but for equity, the value used is the market value of a company's issued capital (stock price × stock units on issue). The formula uses the CAPM, described above, to calculate the cost of equity.

WACC = (weight of equity × cost of equity) + (weight of debt × cost of debt)

If we know the values of debt (D) and equity (E, using market cap) and add them together to give a total value (V), the proportional weights are easily calculated:

Weight of equity = E/V
Weight of debt = D/V

When companies use debt, the interest is deductible as an expense and so there is a tax advantaged effect of using debt, which is reflected in the WACC formula as: 1 – the company tax rate.

While debt may have a number of components, if we assumed a simple outcome of using debt as nominated on a company's balance sheet, and then used the item of interest expense from the cash flow, the cost of debt is interest expense divided by debt, expressed as a percentage rate.

From this information, a simplified way of calculating WACC, using the CAPM outcome to calculate the expected return or cost of equity above, and assuming a tax rate of t, is:

$$\text{WACC} = [(E/V \times E(r_i))] + [D/V \times \text{Interest expense}/D \times (1 - t)]$$

Intrinsic value per share – short cut calculation

$$\{[\text{ROE}/\text{RR} \times D/\text{NPAT}] + [\text{ROE}^2/\text{RR}^2 \times 1-(D/\text{NPAT})]\} \times \text{NAPS}$$

Where:
ROE = return on equity = NPAT/E
RR = investors required return = risk free rate + equity risk premium (say, 10% for ease of calculation)
D = Dividend   NPAT = net profit after tax   D/NPAT = dividend payout ratio
NAPS = net assets, or equity, per share

Note:
This formula is an approximation and uses notation already used in this chapter. It can be refined using normalised earnings instead of NPAT and using average equity over the period instead of end of year equity.[43]

Notes

1 Lev, B, *Winning Investors Over: Surprising Truths about Honesty, Earnings Guidance and Other Ways to Boost Your Stock Price* (Harvard Business Review Press, Boston, MA: 2012), pp 155–158
2 Berman, K and Knight, J, "Lehman's Three Big Mistakes", *HBR Blog Network*, http://blogs.hbr.org/financial-intelligence/2009/09/lessons-from-lehman.html
3 Schwartz, ND, "Earnings in United States Are Beginning to Feel a Pinch", *New York Times*, 16 September 2012, www.nytimes.com/2012/09/17/business/earnings-outlook-in-us-dims-as-global-economy-slows.html?_r=0
4 Cottle, S, Murray, RF and Block, FR, *Graham and Dodd's Security Analysis* (McGraw-Hill Book Company, New York: 1988), p 240
5 Ferri, R, "P/E Doesn't Predict Future Earnings", Forbes, 29 October 2013, www.forbes.com/sites/rickferri/2013/10/29/pe-doesnt-predict-future-earnings
6 Kidman, M, "Sharemarket a bargain by historical standards", Sydney Morning Herald, 5 March 2012 www.smh.com.au/business/sharemarket-a-bargain-by-historical-standards-20120304-1uaz1.html

7   Cottle et al (1988), pp 41–42

8   Boje, DM, Gardner, CL and Smith, WL, "(Mis)using Numbers in the Enron Story", *Organisational Research Methods* 9 (4), 2006, pp 456–74

9   Boje, Gardner and Smith (2006), pp 461–462

10 Boje, Gardner and Smith (2006), p 464

11 Boje, Gardner and Smith (2006), p 466

12 Boje, Gardner and Smith (2006) p 468

13 Boje, Gardner and Smith (2006), p 470

14 Hays, K and Driver, A, "Former Enron CEO Skilling's Sentence Cut to 14 Years", *Reuters*, 21 June 2013

15 Cottle et al (1988), pp 128–129

16 Damodoran, A, *Equity Risk Premiums (ERP): Determinants, Estimation and Implications – The 2012 Edition Updated: March 2012*, Stern School of Business, http://people.stern.nyu.edu/adamodar/pdfiles/papers/ERP2012.pdf, pp 18 and 21

17 Copeland, T, Koller, T and Murrin, J, *Valuation: Measuring and Managing the Value of Companies* (John Wiley & Sons, Hoboken, NJ: 2000), p 201

18 Bolten, R, *Painting with Numbers: Presenting Financials and Other Numbers So People Will Understand You* (John Wiley & Sons, Hoboken, NJ: 2012), p 171

19 Schilit, HM, "Financial Shenanigans: Detecting Accounting Gimmicks That Destroy Investments", *CFA Institute*, December 2010, www.scribd.com/doc/77727688/Financial-Shenanigans

20 Martorelli, MA, Book Review of Giroux, G, *Detecting Earnings Management* in *Financial Analysts Journal*, May 2004, www.cfapubs.org/doi/full/10.2469/faj.v60.n3.2626

21 Felleg, R, Moers, F and Renders, A, "Investor Reaction to Higher Earnings Management Incentives of Overoptimistic CEOs", Maastricht University, Department of Accounting and Information Management, August 2012, www.econ.core.hu/file/download/korosi/2012/felleg.pdf

22 Durkin, P, "Profits of Top Companies Come Under Surveillance", *Australian Financial Review*, 30 November 2011, p 5

23 Gibson, B, Deputy Chairman, Australian Securities and Investments Commission, quoted in *Australian Financial Review*, 22–27 December 2011

24 www.gecapital.com.au/common/documents/access-ge/ge-capital-measuring-success.pdf

25 www.brambles.com/PDF/Annual_Reports/Brambles%20Annual%20Report%202012-2-3.pdf

26 www.goldmansachs.com/investor-relations/index.html

27 www.nestle.com/media/facts-figures

28 www.gsk.com/investors/investing-in-gsk.html

29 www.ge.com/company/building

30 www.thisisnoble.com/index.php?option=com_content&view=article&id=29&Itemid=50

31 http://phx.corporate-ir.net/phoenix.zhtml?p=irol-irhome&c=97664

32 www.google.com.au/about/company/facts/culture

33 http://corporate.walmart.com/our-story/heritage

34 www.goldmansachs.com/our-firm/progress/brooklyn-navy-yard/index.html

35 www.generaldynamics.com/about/corporate-overview/index.cfm

36 www.bp.com/sectiongenericarticle800.do?categoryId=9021974&contentId=7072362

37 www.volkswagenag.com/content/vwcorp/content/en/sustainability_and_responsibility.html

38 www.volvogroup.com/SiteCollectionDocuments/VGHQ/Volvo%20Group/Volvo%20Group/Our%20values/volvo_way_eng.pdf

39 www.caterpillar.com/sustainability

40 http://corporate.walmart.com/our-story

41 http://investors.dupont.com/phoenix.zhtml?c=73320&p=irol-homeprofile

42 www.accaglobal.com/content/dam/acca/global/PDF-students/2012/sa_jj08_head.pdf

43 Derived from Whitehouse G, "Demystifying Intrinsic Value: Step by Step", www.clime.com.au/articles/demystifying-intrinsic-value-step-by-step

7 Disclosure and the communication context

Corporations law and the listing rules of stock exchanges make it mandatory for all stock exchange-listed companies to make public disclosures of information, quite a lot of which is sensitive to stock prices. A survey of company announcements on any one day shows that they may well meet the regulatory information disclosure requirements but not necessarily jump the communication hurdle. While understanding this disclosure regime and principles of corporate governance are critical components that shape corporate communication, the disclosure process also combines opportunity and pitfall. It can be a filter for determining what is important to communicate but doing this ineffectually can mean that companies are overlooked in the competitive race for capital or worse, they can damage reputation. Appreciating these nuances is a critical element in effective corporate communication.

Information and markets

We have covered earlier the important role information has in markets, for adherents of the efficient market hypothesis and also fundamental analysts. In fact, wherever sympathies may lie, information is the lifeblood of markets, governing the movements of stocks. Given this influence, the way information is released and its content has increasingly been the subject of regulation in all recognized stock market jurisdictions. A fundamental principle governing markets is that there should be fairness in trading, that all market participants have the same information at the same time so there is an equality in the way in which decisions can be made about stocks. This is not to say that everyone will make the same decision from the same information and in any event there are many stocks from which to choose. However, the trend since the 1930s has been for governments to introduce legislation and give regulatory authorities the power to implement rules for the ways companies release information to stock exchanges. This process governs the minimum information companies release or disclose about their businesses. The extent and style of this disclosure has increased over the years, although some companies prefer to adhere to minimum standards while there are also many other shades of disclosure developing along the way. Communication principles providing a pathway though the maze of disclosure can sometimes be lost somewhere between the extremes of minimum information and an excess of detail.

Evolution of disclosure

The onset of regulation around the information process was borne out of disaster. In the United States, the beginning of securities legislation was as a response to the Wall Street market crash of 1929 and the Great Depression that followed.[1] Before then, securities oversight was the responsibility of the states but two pieces of federal legislation in 1933 and 1934 were the start of the national government taking over the governance of securities markets. The two pieces of legislation were the Securities Act and then the Securities Exchange Act. The principles within the legislation were those around trying to make company information more transparent and encouraging companies to make fulsome disclosure around their activities. The underlying idea was that "sunshine is the best disinfectant" and so disclosure of information meant that companies were protecting themselves from doing the wrong thing at the same time as building in safeguards for investors.[2]

Over succeeding decades this disclosure process has become more refined and similar regimes have been implemented in other countries, such as the UK and Australia. There have been three main milestones in disclosure in the US, triggered by two significant clusters of market disasters. These crises were a number of major corporate and accounting scandals in the early 2000s, such as those affecting Enron and WorldCom, and the credit and economic crisis of 2008. The corresponding legal developments in relation to disclosure have been the implementation of the SEC's Regulation Fair Disclosure (Reg FD), which became effective in 2000, the Sarbanes-Oxley Act of 2002 (SOX) and the Dodd-Frank Wall Street Reform and Consumer Protection Act of 2010, known simply as Dodd-Frank.[3]

The general idea around Reg FD was that there should be full and fair disclosure by listed companies as a way of preventing insider trading. This meant that any information given by companies to the likes of people in the investment community that might have an influence on stock price should be disclosed simultaneously to the market as a whole or if the information was given inadvertently, it should be made public soon afterwards. SOX mandated internal procedures within companies to ensure they would make accurate disclosures, including off-balance sheet items. This was intended to overcome the Enron situation in which a company fraudulently used off-balance sheet instruments and then failed to report them. Dodd-Frank covered a range of reforms, including oversight of systemic risk, regulation of over-the-counter derivatives markets and broadening shareholder voting power in relation to executive compensation.[4]

The effect of these legislative and regulatory developments has been to lay down quite strict rules around the ways listed companies manage the release of information, with similar regimes operative in most stock exchanges jurisdictions globally.

Structures and practices

The general rule around disclosure in relation to stock exchange-listed companies is that they are required to release publicly any information that might be considered sensitive or material in relation to stock price. While there can be many different shades of legal opinion around what should or should not be disclosed, a saying often applied to these circumstances is, "when in doubt, put it out".[5] This does not mean that companies are required to release information that may be damaging to their competitive positions in markets. In this sense, companies have reasonable discretion around what information they choose to disclose. Some events are mandatory disclosures, such as earnings announcements or transactions of major significance. To manage this process, most listed companies have a written disclosure policy and a disclosure committee that has the responsibility to determine what become disclosure events and how information is provided. Oversights and mistakes in the disclosure process can have serious consequences, such as large damages suits against companies, class actions by shareholders who may have lost money from irresponsible disclosure, fines against directors and the company and banning of directors from future board membership. There is a rich set of case law around mistakes across most jurisdictions, with some from the US perspective effectively summarized in NIRI's disclosure paper of November 2011.[6]

The overall intention of continuous disclosure imposed on listed companies is that stock exchanges want to ensure an efficiency and integrity in capital markets, to give confidence to investors and improve the accountability of company management, in the interests of minimizing insider trading and market distortions.[7] In helping companies with their decision-making about what constitutes market-sensitive information, a common test is that management should ask two questions:

1.   Would this information influence my decision to buy or sell securities in the entity at their current market price?
2.   Would I feel exposed to an action for insider trading if I were to buy or sell securities in the entity at their current market price, knowing this information had not been disclosed to the market?[8]

If the answer to either question is "yes", then information of which the company is aware is price-sensitive and should be released to the market. A company is assumed to be "aware" of the information if its management ought to have come into possession of it in the normal course of duties and there is an obligation to release it "immediately", which is taken to mean "promptly and without delay" rather than "instantaneously".[9] If the information being considered at the time relates to an incomplete transaction, it may be necessary for a company to seek a temporary halt to trading of its stock until the issue is settled. External information of which companies are expected to be aware from a price-sensitivity perspective includes social media and chat room content, which places more emphasis on the monitoring responsibilities companies are expected to assume.

In relation to earnings guidance, while there is general market encouragement for the practice, listing rules also point out some of the regulatory dangers, such as:

> As a forward looking statement, earnings guidance must have a reasonable basis in fact or else it will be deemed to be misleading, with all the significant legal consequences that entails. For this reason, appropriate due diligence needs to be applied to the preparation of earnings guidance. The underlying figures and assumptions should be carefully vetted and signed off at a suitably senior level before the guidance is released.[10]

Companies that do not provide earnings guidance do not entirely avoid risk since they can fall into the trap of making statements which might be considered "de facto" earnings guidance. Examples of this might be companies saying to analysts or being quoted in the media as stating they expected earnings to be "in line with analysts' forecasts" or within a particular percentage range in relation to previous period earnings. In these circumstances, stock exchanges or regulators may ask companies to confirm the comment with a disclosure release so the whole market is informed.

Companies are expected to be aware of what market expectations are in relation to earnings, from assessing analysts' forecasts, and make public disclosure if they believe their actual results will differ materially from these expectations. A generally accepted definition of "material" from accounting standards is a variation equal to or greater than 10 per cent, although companies are generally advised to wait until nearer a balance date to be reasonably sure that differences will actually be material.

Along with these disclosure obligations, there are also extensive communication implications. Disclosure needs to be accurate and timely as well as being an informative and interesting component of the corporate story so that it contributes to overall communications objectives. Looking at the crossover between disclosure and communication can be achieved by examining various steps in the disclosure process that become key issues in investor relations.

Disclosure issues

Given the value of information in markets, listed companies usually have policies and procedures around how information is released, what this information should contain, rules around what can be disclosed and what is reasonably confidential to be retained internally, recognizing the positions of industry competitors. Set out below are a variety of issues that relate to the disclosure and communications process, accepting that these will vary from company to company.

Information development and communication

Often company news announcements have their origins in communications departments but their preparation needs to have guidelines around the accuracy of information contained in the release and for final versions to be approved at the highest level. Companies also need rules around who can speak to releases publicly, involving a spokesperson policy that usually requires approval by the board. In this way, companies build in protection against unauthorized public comment and reduce the potential for unintentional disclosure that would need to be rectified by subsequent announcements to avoid possibly damaging consequences. Once announcements are made, there should also be guidelines about how this information is disseminated publicly. Distribution would be to the investment community, shareholders who opt to receive the news, the media and, increasingly, social media.

Mandatory disclosure

Listed companies are expected to demonstrate from their procedures they have a good understanding of releasing any information that is price-sensitive and material to stock price, while not making any misleading statements. These are duties under the law, requiring release of information within a short period after it is known to a company. Among mandatory disclosures are earnings announcements, which are at least half yearly or quarterly in some jurisdictions such as the United States. There are usually time limits around information having to be released within certain periods after balance dates. In Australia, it is mandatory to issue earnings releases within two months of balance date and annual reports within three months of balance date. Failure to do so results in a suspension of trading of the company's stock until documents are finally produced.

Annual reports

These annual documents are structured to meet statutory reporting requirements, with companies having alternatives of producing quite plain versions or more colourful productions that include pictures of people and operations. Since they are mostly devoted to a year in review they can be seen as historical documents but they also provide an opportunity to shape perspectives around the future by giving a view of the business through the eyes of management. They naturally contain a full, audited disclosure of numbers, with balance sheet, income and cash flow statements, and notes to the accounts. The reporting component in words is an opportunity to elaborate on the corporate story and to put it into a market and industry context. Among expected disclosures are reporting on business segments, principal products and major customers, all in the context of reporting on financial performance and the factors that influenced it. Risk factors are also part of this explanation. Separately from reporting on financial performance, the annual report also gives details about directors, senior management, their shareholdings in the company and remuneration and an explanation of the company's approach to corporate governance.

Forward-looking statements

Where companies do make disclosure about the future and provide earnings guidance, these statements usually contain an explanation of various risks that may affect achieving predictions and also about the risks investors take in relying on statements about the future. Most announcements to stock exchange platforms are accompanied by a risk management paragraph. These paragraphs are often referred to as providing a safe harbour in which forward-looking statements can be made. The legal liability companies can incur from not achieving predictions tends to lead to cautious language when being forward-looking.

One-on-one meetings

The investment community appreciates having one-on-one meetings with listed company executives. It is how they develop perceptions of individual stocks and their prospects, how analysts build their models and how stockbrokers develop a marketing edge in introducing listed companies to their institutional network. From the company perspective, executives need to be careful about what they disclose in these meetings. The meetings are a common way in which communication with the investment community is conducted – companies need to be close to sources of capital and the conduits for providing this capital need to have sound relationships to build trust in the users of that capital. Nevertheless, both parties need to be cognisant of the law, since it is illegal to trade on inside information about stocks and it is not good for a company's reputation to be a provider of selective briefings.

An example of one-on-one briefings gone wrong occurred in Australia in mid-2013 when a substantial resources company seemingly gave selective briefings to analysts in advance of a large asset write-down brought on by a falling gold price. A "rolled-gold disaster" is how one media headline described the aftermath of a significant stock price fall with some in the investment community having had warning of it.[11] Several leading analysts met with the company in the lead up to the announcement and issued earnings downgrades before the news was made public. The ramifications have been widespread, including angry investor reaction. In response, the regulator has launched an investigation as well as the company instigating its own, bringing in an outside expert to review investor relations practices. As market outrage grew, the regulator decided to go further and commence a process of having its own staff sit in on one-on-one briefings to see whether there was a market-wide problem that needed fixing. Some critics saw this as an overreaction but it shows how careful the disclosure practice has to be with price-sensitive information. In an unrelated example in the UK at the same time, a listed engineering firm decided, after a communications review, to stop giving one-on-one briefings so that it could give a better impression of treating all investors equally. It intends to replace them with expanded information on its website, group shareholder meetings and continue its annual investor day. While these moves may be well-intentioned, the investment community reaction has not been positive. One institutional investor wrote to *The Financial Times*, saying: "We strongly disagree with corporate policies that seek to halt one-on-one meetings between existing, or prospective, institutional investors and executives. These meetings are a vital part of the dialogue with providers of risk capital."[12]

One-on-one meetings are likely to be a focus of disclosure discussion in coming years. Precautions companies can build into those meetings are to manage the timing of them to follow close after major announcements, to begin them with a statement that the discussion will be based only on information that is public and that a company has more than one representative in the meetings to add formality to the process. This builds in risk management and also allows analysts to form impressions from body language and how managers talk about their competitive environment. Shapers of the corporate story can also easily work within these parameters, so long as they are accompanied by boundaries and ground rules about disclosure.

Analyst reports

As a result of earnings or news announcements or meetings with companies, sell-side analysts will write reports, headed by a recommendation to buy, sell or hold a stock. Where these reports are favourable, it is often tempting for companies to display them on their websites since they can present as third-party endorsement of a positive investment view abut a company. While nothing prevents companies taking this action, upholders of standards of investor relations behaviour, such as NIRI, discourage this procedure, as well as companies actually contributing to the content of analyst reports. As NIRI writes:

> The practice of distributing analysts' reports is fraught with potential legal problems. First, analysts' reports are proprietary and should not be distributed without the approval of the analyst or analyst's firm. In addition, distributing an analyst's report, even with permission, may expose the company to the appearance of "entanglement" with the report, meaning the company runs the risk of appearing to embrace or endorse the report's contents and inclusions. Further, the distribution of analysts' reports, particularly those that are more optimistic about a company's

prospects for performance than may be warranted, may be cited as evidence in shareholder suits of a "conspiracy" between the company and the analyst (or perhaps the analyst's firm) to defraud investors.[13]

A policy many companies follow in relation to this is to list on their websites the names of analysts and their firms that follow the company and have published reports on them so that investors can contact those firms directly.

The usual regulatory regime regarding content of analysts' reports and forecasts is that companies are expected to monitor and be aware of them but are not under any obligation to correct them to align with their own forecasts. When companies become aware of a forecast that differs materially with their own, it is usually suggested companies contact the analyst to explore the reasons and to see if it might be based on error or having missed a relevant announcement so that these things can be pointed out. It is in everyone's interests for all analysts to be working from the same public information and, in the same vein, it is inappropriate for companies to provide preferential treatment to preferred analysts just as it is to ban from briefings an analyst a company does not favour.[14]

Public comment

Since listed companies are in the public spotlight, their activities attract widespread interest, especially if they have potential to affect stock price. Among these events might be a possible merger or acquisition, capital-raising, refinancing or restructuring. Rumour of any of these events could lead to requests from the media, investment community or investors for comment on what they have heard. While companies obviously prefer these transactions to proceed in secret until they are ready to be announced, it poses a problem from a disclosure perspective of how to respond when negotiations are incomplete. Providing a "no comment" response can actually imply something must be going on, particularly in media terms where it can virtually amount to a confirmation of rumours. An alternative such as "we don't comment on rumour" can be tried but if rumours gather strength and begin to affect stock price then wider disclosure responsibilities take over.

The usual disclosure regime that applies to companies commenting on rumour is based on determinations about materiality – idle speculation can be dismissed but if the rumours themselves or the movement in stock price is material, then a formal disclosure is expected. Even if rumours are partially accurate but are having a material effect or the wider market is uninformed without some response from a company, then some public clarification or correction is usually required.

Third-party forums

While companies are responsible for comment they make in any forum, such as in blogs, electronic investor forums or on social media, there is a growing awareness of liability that can arise from third-party comment on these sites. A recent landmark legal decision in Australia in 2012 determined that "businesses are responsible for third-party comments posted on their Facebook and Twitter pages, and may be in breach of consumer laws and advertising standards if those comments are misleading or offensive".[15] On external websites, where retail investors might discuss their perspectives on stocks, sometimes with outlandish views, either positive or negative, companies cannot be held accountable for those discussions taking place. Most companies tend to keep a distance from these forums, even if inaccurate rumours or information is being exchanged while others prefer to correct any misleading information on a public record. In any event, it is informative for companies to monitor these discussions. If inaccuracies seem serious enough, they are most simply corrected by disclosing information through conventional channels rather than taking on new liabilities from venturing into the third-party comment arena.

Media interviews

While the media is not subject to the same legal requirements as listed companies in how they report news, companies need to have disclosure issues in mind when media interviews are conducted. Being in the media has value for companies and there are pressures in responding to searching questions from journalists as they seek news angles. Succumbing to this pressure may lead to the disclosure of information that has not yet been made public. While the ideal in interviews is not to reveal non-public information, the appearance of a media story that makes such revelations should lead to swift disclosure to the appropriate exchange platform.

Company websites

Company websites are an important disclosure platform for information around the corporate story. They are a vehicle for housing the disclosure made to exchange platforms. Additionally they are an outlet for disclosing information that does not have the same urgency associated with news that has to be announced and yet illuminates understanding of how a company operates. This information can provide the context around a company's story and industry sector and also its policies that relate to various stakeholder issues, such as the environment and employees. A recent survey of NIRI members found that 88 per cent of respondents had no immediate intention of making their corporate websites the exclusive domain for material disclosure, with most of them using more than 15 different channels for disclosing material information.[16]

Roadshows

The process of companies visiting various locations to present their stories to key stakeholders is often referred to as a roadshow. A common practice is to devise a PowerPoint presentation that can be released to an exchange platform and that reflects a uniformity of how the story is told and presented so there are built-in disclosure boundaries. Making disclosure beyond these boundaries does not make the information public, in a legal sense, even though it may be made to a large forum, with the media possibly present. Companies need to be on guard that going beyond the agreed guidelines can trigger obligations to make a separate public exchange platform disclosure.

Shareholder meetings

At shareholder meetings, similar rules apply to those of roadshows, in the sense that statements to this type of forum, even if a large audience, do not represent disclosure if there is a release of new information that has not been made to an exchange platform. If new information of a material nature is released at a meeting of this type then it is prudent for companies to make a release to the exchange shortly after the meeting.

Social media

The advent of social media presents an important opportunity for a company to broaden dissemination of its corporate story. However, the process is not without risk and requires surrounding policy because of the instant broad reach that social media can have, along with inadvertent slips of information that can be released by people at all levels of a company. While many companies might have corporate Facebook pages and release announcements on Twitter, employees also use these platforms privately and so need to have an understanding of what constitutes disclosure if they make comment about company operations and performance. Companies also need to monitor this sphere of media, not necessarily from the perspective of taking on added responsibility to correct third-party comment but rather to ensure that information sourced from the company is being used accurately and reflects authorized disclosure.

In something of a landmark decision in April 2013, the US regulator, the SEC, said that if companies used social media outlets such as Facebook and Twitter to release key information about progress they would be complying with Regulation Fair Disclosure "so long as investors have been alerted about which social media will be used to disseminate such information".[17] The SEC also indicated that personal social media accounts of corporate executives "would not ordinarily be assumed to be channels through which the company would disclose material corporate information".[18]

While this decision points a way to the future, regulatory authorities in Australia and the UK have not rushed to follow suit, preferring announcements to be made to an exchange platform first before heading off into the social media sphere.

Conference calls, webcasts

For significant news announcements such as earnings and large transactions, many companies adopt the practice of conducting conference calls or webcasts for the market. Those interested in participating are mostly the investment community but notification of the event is made through public announcement to an exchange platform, allowing anyone to participate. The events are an opportunity for participants to ask questions of management and for management also to give some colour to announcements to enhance understanding of how a company is performing. To ensure broad access to information disclosed, transcripts and opportunities to view the webcast at a later date are usually provided by companies. The calls or webcasts are usually preceded by safe harbour statements and also statements that release a company from updating any information that might be disclosed. While some companies script these events quite strictly, they are opportunities to make a corporate story interesting and to add communication value to it in reaching out to the audience that has taken the trouble to dial in.

An interesting aspect to note about these conference calls is that they are invariably conducted by the CEO, often in company with the CFO. So it is an important task for the corporation and not one that is delegated. Given this importance, it underlines the value of having content of the call reflect a company's story. The information is coming from the top and so represents corporate strategy in action, an invaluable opportunity to implant strategy and story around initiatives and performance, all aimed at giving disclosure a communications direction.

Earnings announcements

Among the mandatory disclosures companies must make are those around earnings, a crucial influence on stock price. While minimalist reporting does occur, best practice in investor relation is towards fuller disclosure, allowing for financial results to be put in the context of the evolving corporate story. There are many audiences for this information, each with differing requirements. The investment community is looking for consistency and conformity with accounting standards. The business media is looking for a concise summary of key information along with quotes from the CEO. Regulatory authorities are looking to ensure material disclosure has been made in the appropriate way. The general public with an interest in this information would be looking for insight into how the company operates and performs. As well as basic information and comparisons with the previous corresponding period, all stakeholders are seeking guidance on what has been important in the period and what trends might be apparent. There is an expectation that financial information conforms to accounting standards and that definitions of profit are made clear and reconciled with any extraordinary items. In relation to accounting measures, it can be helpful to refer to common performance metrics in an industry, with examples being cash burn rate for developing companies or same store sales for retail companies.[19]

Explanation of company performance can be put in the context of a company's own expectations, goals and strategies. Indicating the main drivers of performance highlights how results have been achieved and this understanding is enhanced if there is reference to industry conditions. This also enables analysts to assess how competitors have performed under the same conditions. Connecting performance with management actions is also instructive. As NIRI suggests, performance explanations should answer the question, what is management doing to maximize results in the current (and long-term) situation?[20] Releases around earnings information usually include quotes from the CEO. Phrasing these in a way that is genuinely explanatory, rather than self-congratulatory, creates a connection of performance with strategy, while adding to credibility at the same time. Expression in plain English that connects with the corporate story also gives these quotes an improved chance of being used in media reporting.

How the segments of a business contribute to performance is also a way of enhancing understanding of a business for outsiders. It is these contributors to group results that are a pointer to how a corporate story is told, since it provides a way of ordering their importance to group development and achieving longer-term goals. What makes disclosure around segments helpful is where there is information about sales, profit, business mix, market factors and growth strategy of a business segment. While the overall corporate story is important it cannot be told properly without taking into account the contributions of the parts of the corporation that make up the whole.

Earnings announcements are expected to conclude with some comments on the outlook. These need not be specific in terms of giving earnings guidance but wording of this section is a critical guide to how stakeholders form an investment view of a stock. Often outlook comments are of a quite general nature so that a company is not anchored in the future to past predictions. The wording of these comments is also a

Case study

QBE – when CEOs change…

When a longstanding and successful CEO retires, several things can happen to the corporate story. There might be a market concern whether corporate progress will be perpetuated in the same way, there could be acceptance that it was time for a changing of the guard leading to expected adjustments by a new team or there could be a need for a substantial revision to strategy. When one of Australia's most successful CEOs called it a day in 2012, there was almost a combination of all these alternatives. When Frank O'Halloran announced his retirement from the world's 18th largest insurer, QBE Insurance Group, he had recorded some formidable achievements. He had been admitted to the Insurance Hall of Fame two years earlier and was considered an industry legend for what he had achieved at QBE. He had been at the company for 37 years, the last 14 as CEO, and was directly responsible for 125 acquisitions. Growth by acquisition began when he was CFO and, in partnership with the then CEO, they took market capitalization from US$20 million to US$2.1 billion, by which time O'Halloran became CEO and took market cap to US$22 billion at its height. He had taken QBE global, giving it operations in 52 countries and was lauded in the industry for introducing "vision, values and essential management behaviours" to the group.[21] As a stock, QBE had become a market darling.

However, conditions in insurance markets had become tougher in 2011 and this, along with several natural disasters, meant QBE was in the position in January 2012 of having to announce that profit for financial year 2011 would be down 40 to 50 per cent. Adjustments within the group were made and the story at the time was that margins would return to previous levels and the drive for acquisitions would be maintained.[22] Just a month later, O'Halloran announced his retirement, with his deputy, an 11-year QBE veteran and former head of underwriting, to succeed him, with O'Halloran guiding him over the succeeding six months.

The feeling then was that the worst of a tough market was over. O'Halloran's achievements were praised, his growth model was to be perpetuated, an experienced man was to be at the helm and a former insurance industry equities analyst with a respected reputation had been convinced to join QBE as its new investor relations manager. On his first day as the new CEO, John Neal was able to announce a 13 per cent rise in profit for the first half of FY12 and that the company began the second half of the financial year "feeling bullish and very confident about the fundamentals of the business and our ability to meet or exceed the expectations the market has of us".[23] In mid-October, QBE stepped up its communication efforts, possibly to overcome "perceived poor communication with stakeholders" and embarked on a roadshow in New York and London to provide "improved visibility into QBE's management".[24] A matter of weeks later, Hurricane Sandy hit the East Coast of the US, meaning significant claims for QBE.

By mid-November, as these claims were counted, QBE announced that Sandy would cost it between A$350 million and $450 million, meaning projected insurance profit margin for 2012 would need to be revised downwards from a previous estimate of 12 per cent to 8 per cent.

Despite this, QBE said it expected to report a 2012 profit of $1 billion, an increase of 30 per cent compared with its poor year in 2011, enabling the new chief executive to say: "It is frustrating to be reporting disappointing news at a time when the vast majority of our ongoing businesses are performing in line with, or better than, expectations. QBE has a unique franchise in the global insurance and reinsurance markets and we remain positive that we can achieve the level of return our shareholders expect."[25]

However, with market expectations of a profit of A$1.75 billion and the news representing the second major profit downgrade in the year,[26] the stock price dropped 8 per cent and media headlines included "Shareholders Dump QBE on Profits Shock"[27] and "Storm Clouds Gather for QBE".[28]

These developments were a tough baptism of fire for a new CEO and as 2013 began, there was an indication of a changing hue to the corporate story. Early in 2013, news leaked out in a media report,[29] not a stock exchange announcement, that QBE was considering significant job cuts, which would contribute to a cost reduction programme that had already been foreshadowed. The market reacted positively to this news, with the stock price rising, and the indication was that a story revision of consolidation was under way.

Acquisitions had made QBE a significant global insurer but it would seem the time had come to usher in the integration phase. While the new CEO had wanted QBE to continue to be seen as a growth stock when he was appointed, it was time now to rebuild earnings and adjust the story to the circumstances. With announcement of FY12 results in February 2013, the focus was on value creation, with acquisitions "not high on our agenda".[30] The way the new story was expressed was that QBE was "evolving from a regionally-focused multinational business to a fully integrated global insurer".[31] The new vision was for QBE "to be *the* most successful global insurer and reinsurer in the eyes of our customers, our people, our shareholders and the community."[32]

significant determinant of media reporting, often to the extent of taking over as a headline in reporting results.

Communication values are not specified as mandatory under any stock exchange rules and yet they can be the most important factor in how earnings disclosure is interpreted. Expressing descriptive information in plain English is a start but putting results in the context of the corporate story, and surrounding industry issues, are how communication can guide interpretation. For some companies, their earnings statements show a lack of understanding of how genuine communication can be a way of connecting with key stakeholders. The overuse of adjectives, adverbs and superlatives, as well as excuses around poor performance, display a far too subjective perspective from corporate communicators, not realizing that most stakeholders have heard and seen this type of exaggeration before and been disappointed. From this perspective, the companies that try the hardest to boost their own positions around earnings statements do not gain the support of astute investors looking for sound long-term investment value. The cliché of "under-promise and over-deliver" seems a simple proposition and yet, while overlooked by some companies as they try to win over stakeholders, is a lesson that has been hard learned by investors over many years. It is not unreasonable for companies to use persuasion around how they interpret their financial performance but it is more effectively conveyed if anchored in building a context of narrative around the facts and numbers.

Beyond the numbers

While the numbers of financial performance are an inescapable component of disclosure, they are not the most influential element. Disclosure essentially combines numbers, facts and narrative, and research is showing that numbers do not always have the primary role commonly attributed to them. Professor Baruch Lev brings this out in his work. He looks at disclosure from the perspective of hard and soft information, with hard information representing core accounting data and soft information involving other facts around a business and the narrative that ties them together. He has found that hard corporate data, such as earnings and book values (net assets), account statistically for no more than 10 per cent of stock price changes around the financial report release.[33] Consequently, it is the soft information that is more influential and so the challenge for managers is to unlock this formula in the information they disclose. Lev also found that in the 1970s and 1980s, reported earnings and book values accounted for around 75 to 85 per cent of the differences in capitalization across companies, indicating that almost the entire difference in share value across companies was due to accounting data. His research up to 2005 shows that this same data now only accounts for 30–40 per cent of differences in capitalization, or a 50 per cent decline in the importance of reported earnings and asset values.[34]

A further statistic Lev provides to support his view about the importance of information beyond basic accounting data is the market to book ratio.

> The average market to book ratio (companies' total market value or capitalization divided by their balance sheet value of net assets or book value) of the S&P 500 companies prior to the free fall of stock prices in 2008 was close to 3. This means that of every \$3 of share value paid for or received by investors, only \$1 was reported on the companies' balance sheets as net assets. So why were investors

paying a $2 premium for every dollar of book value? A massive rip off? Hardly. The $2 premium primarily reflects the presence of intangible (intellectual) assets as the dominant value creators of business enterprises. The dramatic rise of intangibles was initiated by emerging key economic sectors that are almost entirely intangible – software, biotech, and later Internet enterprises – as well as by the increased use of intangibles (like patents, brands, or business processes) by traditional sectors using these value drivers to compete successfully.[35]

Treatment of intangibles has been a longstanding argument in the accounting profession but one that investment markets have moved beyond as they have become aware of the way these assets are accounted for in stock prices. From a communications perspective, if companies are to disclose the information that investors want, then covering this aspect of a company's business is another angle on conveying the corporate story.

Along with noting investors' heightened interest in soft information about listed companies, Lev brings out other interesting research findings that support these trends. These include findings such as:

• media coverage can make stock prices jump;
• headlines guide interpretation of earnings releases;
• footnoting earnings adjustments rather than including the adjustments in earnings statements means less attention is focused on them;
• the tone of the narrative around earnings releases has a significant impact on stock price;
• releasing bad news on a Friday can lead to it receiving less attention from the market.[36]

A lot of judgements around soft information by the market are made in conference calls that follow earnings announcements, with analysts and institutions dialling in to hear management discuss corporate performance and have them answer questions. Lev and his colleagues conducted an extensive analysis across thousands of transcripts of these calls. Their focus was on calls that created significant stock buying after their conclusion, including whether the news was good or bad. Among their findings was that positive outcomes resulted when there was wide participation by the market, when there were specific quantitative responses to questions rather than falling back on generalities, when there were straightforward responses to adversity rather than vagueness and when guidance about the future had elements of directness rather than flights of fancy. Their overall conclusion was that tone mattered, whether optimistic or negative, and that honesty was more effective than obfuscation.[37]

Lev notes that all these ingredients of communication have an effect on stock price, resulting from a combination of them in conference calls, earnings announcements and through the work of "information facilitators",[38] such as investor relations practitioners and the business media. The positive effects they have include reducing the costs of information and increasing the number of analysts following the stock, as well as making institutional investor interest more visible, enhancing the liquidity of a stock and improving volume of trading. In combination, all these factors contribute to increasing stock price.[39] Among the communication techniques Lev recommends to bring these things about are to offset the soft information with an infusion of facts and numbers, pay attention to tone and style (with a move towards certainty, whether optimistic or pessimistic, being most effective), to foster interactive communication in conference calls, to enhance company recognition and visibility through media coverage and even to use humour when appropriate.[40]

Lev also argues that one of the big advantages from companies being frank and fulsome in disclosure is that it reduces information asymmetry that, in relation to stocks, comes about when the company knows far more about how its business is operating than it is telling the market.[41] The loser from this situation is the company since it leads to lower prices. An example Lev quotes is the second-hand car market where, since the risk of buying a lemon or poor quality car is quite high, because the seller knows more about its condition than any buyer, then all prices in the market are brought down because of this information asymmetry. The outcome is that buyers then question the quality of any second-hand purchase they make. Similarly with listed companies, and hence the decreasing reliance on the basic hard numbers of earnings and asset values. To counter information asymmetry and to provide the type of disclosure investors are increasingly looking for, Lev argues for companies developing standardized measures that directly link to their own performance and a description of how their business model works. He describes this as a path to growth report, in which companies explain the value drivers of their businesses and the outputs they deliver, as a way of explaining their combination in contributing to long-term growth. He is not advocating the disclosure of secret, future development plans but just relevant facts that would be mostly known to competitors but presented in a way that enhances understanding of a company. His argument also links with a body of research that highlights the benefits of improved disclosure, in the form of lower cost of capital and debt, lower stock price volatility, increased analyst following and closing the bid-ask spread gap.[42]

These additional disclosures Lev advocates are voluntary. Supporting Lev's view about the value of making voluntary disclosure is research from Europe, when there was a change in accounting standards to introduce more transparent financial reporting in 2005. The research showed there was a demonstrable example of improved disclosure having a positive effect on stock price. When companies adopted the standards, voluntarily in advance of the deadline, and then announced their decision, they experienced an increase in stock price and an upgrade in analyst stock recommendations after the announcement.[43]

Legal responsibilities, corporate governance

Boards of directors and senior management have legal responsibilities to ensure proper disclosure. This not only includes providing audited accounts and financial information according to accounting standards but it also involves the concept of "continuous disclosure". This means making announcements to stock exchange platforms when there is price-sensitive information that should be made public. Ensuring disclosure is proper and timely is a critical role of boards and enshrined in most legislative regimes. It is a legal recognition of the importance of information, and communication, in markets. The responsibility of boards to act properly in this way is also the essence of corporate governance. In exploring the role of directors in corporate governance, one legal authority has drawn a distinction between, on the one hand, the "enterprise" and "ownership" issues in corporate decision-making and, on the other, "oversight" issues in the board's non-decision-making monitoring role.[44]

Enterprise issues are essentially the decision-making province of senior management in pursuing a strategy that has been endorsed by the board. Ownership issues, which usually arise in mergers and acquisitions and capital-raising where decisions affect dilution of ownership, can be a significant legal test for corporate governance and boards. Oversight issues do not involve so much board decision-making as exercising a duty of care that company executives carry out their managerial responsibilities and comply with the law. The general guideline directors follow is known as the business judgement rule which US Chief Justice Veasey states as: "In making a business decision, the directors are presumed to have acted independently, on an informed basis, in good faith, and in the honest belief that the decision is in the best interests of the corporation."[45]

The requirement for management and boards to act responsibly in the way that they deal with information is not only high but ignoring it can also have severe consequences, including penalties such as prison sentences and fines. While there is extensive case law on this topic, two quotes from judgments highlight the intertwining responsibilities of boards and management and are applicable across varying legal regimes. Former Australian Federal Court judge Justice Austin notes "the fundamental importance of senior executives providing their boards with all the information they have that is material to the board's decisions".[46] Now retired Australian High Court judge Justice Kirby, in relation to directors, says that being a director is a "privilege to be earned each day, which may be withdrawn for misconduct but also for incompetent, improper or lax activities in the functions of corporate management".[47]

Getting disclosure right is not only an exercise in meeting legal obligations but increasingly has implications for stock price. Pricing corporate governance has potential as an investment strategy, with certain companies favoured when they adopt governance reforms.[48] Separate research, which equates good corporate governance with shareholder rights, has also shown that "firms with stronger shareholder rights had higher firm value, higher profits, higher sales growth, lower capital expenditures and made fewer corporate acquisitions".[49]

Disclosure directions

A common feature of disclosure regimes in many countries is a move towards having companies move beyond the statutory minimum of disclosure towards voluntary disclosure, which increases understanding of how companies actually work, make money and implement strategy. As one example indicative of trends globally, the Australian regulator ASIC, in March 2013, released a new regulatory guide[50] encouraging companies in this direction, especially with information in the operating and financial review sections of annual reports. The guide encourages companies to provide more information in three areas – current operations, analysis of results and information that would enable investors to make an informed assessment about the future. Overall, ASIC wants more information that would reasonably be expected by investors and, in relation to these three areas, the regulator is also asking for more information around a company's narrative.

In relation to current operations, ASIC is asking companies to explain not only their strategies but also the industry context around them in a way that improves understanding of what a company does, its comparative size and history. This information also needs to be connected to performance so that investors have an appreciation of the financial effectiveness of strategy implementation. While some of this information may have been given, and disclosed, in presentations to the investment community,

ASIC's expectation is that the annual report should become a "single location" where any investor can find this type of information. In connecting with financial information, investors should be given an appreciation of the underlying drivers and reasons for performance, "rather than simply restating information that may be readily determined from the financial statements",[51] such as "revenue has increased x%" which is "self-evident"[52] from the financial statements. ASIC also wants companies to explain the features of their business models – "that is, how the entity makes money and generates income or capital growth for shareholders, or otherwise achieves its objectives".[53] Included in this would be how business segments perform, their products, competitors and market positions, along with any significant changes or events that have had an impact on the organization's business units during the year.

Discussion of financial information, as well as pointing out any significant changes to assets, liabilities, funding or dividend strategy, should encompass the impact of any unrecognized or undervalued assets and mention any unusual contractual obligations or whether financial performance might be depending on maintaining certain primary sources of contractual income. While financial statements are required to conform to accounting standards, information beyond the standards should be included if it would help understanding.

Regarding the future, ASIC believes strategies and prospects should be considered for periods beyond just the next financial year but there was no insistence on including financial forecasts. The outlook should consider factors related to the company and industry sector that might affect performance as well as considering material business risks. While encouraging companies to provide more information, ASIC was also prepared to include an "unreasonable prejudice exemption", allowing companies not to disclose information that might harm their competitive positions.

An important feature of these disclosure directions is that they are not compulsory but a regulatory encouragement towards voluntary disclosure that adds value. Implementing disclosure professionally, as an aspect of corporate governance, is not only a direct influence on stock price but also a vehicle for conveying the corporate story. A cliché in investor relations is that "companies should not just comply but communicate". This sums up the opportunity. Lev's research shows that investors want more than just basic compliance and accounting information and this is supported by current regulatory guidelines. Value lies in combining these facts and numbers with narrative, which is the essence of the corporate story. To understand how this value can be applied in financial markets, it is helpful first to understand how markets work, who the key players are and how they interact.

Notes

1 NIRI, *Standards of Practice for Investor Relations, Vol III – Disclosure*, November 2011, www.niri.org/media/News-Releases/NIRI-Releases-Standards-of-Practice-for-Investor-Relations-Vol-III--Disclosure.aspx, p 12
2 NIRI (2011), pp 12–14
3 NIRI (2011), pp 12–18
4 NIRI (2011), p 19
5 NIRI (2011), p 8
6 NIRI (2011), pp 49–59
7 ASX Listing Rules, Guidance Note 8, 1 May 2013, p 6

8 ASX (2013), p 10

9 ASX (2013), pp 12–13

10 ASX (2013), p 42

11 Chambers, M, "Rolled-gold Disaster at Newcrest", *The Australian*, 8–9 June 2013

12 Murphy, C, Aviva Investors, quoted by Guthrie, J, "Calibration Error", *The Financial Times*, 25 July 2013, www.ft.com/intl/cms/s/0/7a232224-f524-11e2-b4f8-00144feabdc0.html#axzz2abyqbzTk

13 NIRI (2011), p 30

14 ASX (2013), pp 48–49

15 Travis, D and Guadagno, N, "Focus: Beware of Liability for Third Party Posts on Social Media", Allens Linklaters, 18 September 2012, www.allens.com.au/pubs/ldr/foldr18sep12.htm

16 NIRI, Use of Corporate Websites for Disclosure: 2012 Survey Report, 17 October 2012, p 3, http://www.niri.org/NIRIAnalytics/CorporateWebsites.aspx?Site=niri

17 NIRI, *Executive Alert*, 3 April 2013, p 1

18 NIRI (April 2013), p 2

19 NIRI, *Standards of Practice for Investor Relations, Vol 1 – Earnings Release Content*, 2009, pp 3–7

20 NIRI (2009), p 7

21 Insurance Hall of Fame, Frank O'Halloran, Induction Year 2011, www.insurancehalloffame.org/laureateprofile.php?laureate=144

22 QBE Market Update on 2011 Preliminary Results and 2012 Outlook, 12 January 2012, www.asx.com.au/asxpdf/20120112/pdf/423qr6mm48vj2n.pdf

23 Bingemann, M, "QBE Heads for Recovery After Natural Disasters", *The Australian*, 18 August 2012

24 Liew, R, "Road Show Reaches Out to Investors", *Australian Financial Review*, 15 October 2012

25 QBE Market Release, Market Update on Superstorm Sandy and 2012 Forecast Results, 12 November 2012, www.asx.com.au/asxpdf/20121112/pdf/42b3yf1hppgjm1.pdf

26 Patten, S, "QBE's Losses from Sandy Could Hit $450m", *Australian Financial Review*, 13 November 2012

27 *Sydney Morning Herald*, 13 November 2012

28 *Australian Financial Review*, 13 November 2012

29 Liew, R, "QBE Joins Cost-cutters: 700 Jobs Face the Axe", *Australian Financial Review*, 21 January 2013

30 QBE, "QBE Announces 2012 Results and Senior Management Succession", 26 February 2013, www.asx.com.au/asxpdf/20130226/pdf/42d8d19xmh0qjf.pdf, p 2

31 QBE (2013), p 7

32 QBE (2103), p 7, emphasis in original

33 Lev (2012), p 46

34 Lev (2012), p 147

35 Lev (2012), pp 155–156

36 Lev (2012), pp 42–43

37 Lev (2012), pp 50–51

38 Lev (2012), p 57

39 Lev (2012), p 57

40 Lev (2012), pp 58–59

41 Lev (2012), Chapter 7

42 Lev (2012), p 169

43 Research quoted in Lev (2012), p 170

44 Chief Justice E Norman Veasey quoted in Ramsay, I, "Corporate Governance and the Duties of Company Directors", in I Ramsay (ed.) *Corporate Governance and the Duties of Company Directors* (Centre for Corporate Law and Securities Regulation, Monograph Series, 1997), p 10

45 Veasey, EN, "The Defining Tension in Corporate Governance in America", in Ramsay (1997), p 17

46 Quoted in Lucy, J, "Directors' Responsibilities: The Reality vs. the Myths", address to Australian Institute of Company Directors, 17 August 2006

47 Quoted in Lucy (2006)
48 Bebchuk, L, "Pricing Corporate Governance", 29 November 2010, www.project-syndicate.org/commentary/pricing-corporate-governance
49 Gompers, PA, Ishii, JL and Metrick, A, "Corporate Governance and Equity Prices", *Quarterly Journal of Economics*, February 2003
50 ASIC, "Effective Disclosure in an Operating and Financial Review", *Regulatory Guide 247*, March 2013
51 ASIC (2013), p 10
52 ASIC (2013), p 13
53 ASIC (2013), p 13

8   The financial marketplace

Just as the surrounding business context is what makes a corporate story interesting, it is the financial marketplace that provides the context in which communication of the story is implemented. This makes it important to understand that context, including how the market works, who the key players are and what the influences are on their decision-making. In financial markets, information has value, especially in how it influences stock prices and wider perceptions. From a communications perspective, it is how that information is presented that unlocks real value. While a lot of communication intent is focused on shaping perceptions, it is in the financial marketplace that those perceptions come up against a hard reality that has many guises. "Perception is reality" is a common cliché, implying that communication conquers all and that image overcomes substance. In the tough world of financial markets, peopled with astute investors who are focused more on finding stocks that perform than those reflecting talk of potential performance, communication needs to account for the reality that markets understand. It is not that perceptions are irrelevant – far from it – but communication of a corporate story has to be conscious of how those in the market see the world. A corporate story is about how a stock exchange-listed company presents itself to key investment stakeholders. This presentation is ultimately converted into a number, its stock price, but that number is the outcome of how stocks are traded and the myriad of views that guide the thinking of why those trades take place. Consequently, it is unfolding the mysteries of the financial marketplace, across equities and debt, that informs how communication with these markets might be most effective.

How stock markets work

Stock markets are a meeting place for many shades of retail and wholesale investors, with stockbrokers providing the mechanism for buying and selling. A company's stock is a share in the ownership of a company. It is represented in the marketplace as the price per stock unit. If you buy a number of these units, you are building up a percentage of ownership of a company. As an owner, you share in the company's fortunes, good and bad. If a company pays a dividend, usually announced as a dividend per stock unit, you receive that dividend for each unit you own. In terms of security, a stock unit ranks after a company meets its obligations to employees and secured creditors. So in terms of risk, an investment in the equity of a listed company does not rank as securely as owning a government bond or bank deposit but the offset for a higher level of risk is a higher potential reward. This higher reward for taking on a level of risk above a government bond is known as the risk premium, with a long-term government bond often used as a proxy for the risk-free rate in applied finance calculations.

As in any market, the laws of supply and demand are a primary influence on price. Stock prices depend on demand for those stock units in supply but there are also many other influences on stock price, with corporate communication among them. Motivations for buying stocks can vary but any investment decision is based on judgements about how to get the best risk-adjusted return on funds available for investment. Investors have differing time horizons for making these judgements, with some planning to be shareholders for the long term while others are traders with a short-term view.

Most stocks are traded electronically, through online accounts, utilizing funds the stockbroker knows are available. In this way, investors have made a decision about which stocks to buy. For example, retail investors who have made a decision about which stocks to buy can go to an online broking site or account, key in account details and insert the number of stock units in line with the amount they want to invest. Funds are then transferred to a stockbroking firm, which settles the trade and takes a commission in completing a transaction.

While institutions can also transact investing electronically and in some circumstances anonymously, most institutional trading is done through stockbrokers, involving more personal relationships and discussion between investor and stockbroker about stocks and parcels of stock available. Similar relationships develop with larger retail investors. These relationships result in conversations about market conditions, when might be a good time to invest and views about particular stocks. These sorts of connections entitle stockbroker clients to see research the stockbroker may have done on particular stocks. From these relationships, stocks can be traded on the basis of a telephone call or emailed instructions. Settlement arrangements, by market convention, are a few days after an order has been made, with a stockbroker being assured funds will be transferred to cover settlement of stocks purchased.

Ownership of stocks is managed electronically by stock exchange systems, with older processes of stock ownership certificates, or scrip, having become outmoded. Stockbrokers are responsible to regulatory authorities for their behaviour in trading stocks, with this including trust arrangements around settling trades initiated by clients.

Sell-side, buy-side

One way of looking at the stock market is through the roles of two sides to the trading equation, the buying and selling of stocks. The sell-side comprises the stockbrokers. They are the agents for selling stocks to buyers. The principal components of a stockbroker's office are the dealing desk, back office, research and corporate. The dealing desk takes the buy and sell orders and advisers talk to clients about stocks. In a sense, they are also salesmen. Their interests are in trying to convince investors about buying stocks. Like any salesperson, their integrity is tied up with the sales process and seeking repeat business so they don't achieve this if they do the wrong thing by clients simply to transact one sale. Their front of office role in selling stocks means they are generators of commission for the firm and so the personal remuneration of those who are on the dealing desk is usually linked to the amount of trade they generate. A key component of how the dealing desk sells stocks is based around the corporate story they have absorbed about the stocks with which they become familiar. This makes them important in the corporate storytelling process because ultimately this story becomes broken down to a few key phrases and descriptions by the dealers and governs the buying and selling process.

Supporting the dealing desk once trades have been made is the back office, which manages transactions through to settlement. Another important area of support is the research team of stock analysts. Analysts are the people who make company visits, interview company executives and write reports, not only analysing the company but, importantly, concluding with an investment recommendation. These recommendations involve terms such as "buy", "sell" or "accumulate", which are fairly clear. They also include terms like "overweight" or "underweight", which indicate a portfolio perspective of whether a particular stock should have its position increased or decreased in relation to the proportion of the market as a whole that an individual stock represents.

The corporate department of a stockbroker's office becomes involved in capital markets transactions for listed companies. This involvement is greater where a stockbroking firm also includes investment banking operations, which is the type of business that many of the larger brokers operate. The type of transactions involved are capital-raising, mergers and acquisitions, company restructuring and general corporate advice around levels of capital and debt appropriate to a listed entity and the implementation of fund-raising to achieve economically effective solutions.

Some stockbrokers focus purely on the institutional or wholesale market while others also have retail clients. Collectively these clients of stockbrokers are known as the buy-side. Institutions represent investment funds, insurance companies and banks that have investment portfolios while retail investors can be "mums and dads" or the larger investor known as "high net worth" individuals.

Investment funds can have a number of differing forms. Ultimately they have funds to invest on behalf of individuals who choose them as an agent for investing their funds, or they may be pension funds investing massed superannuation contributions from individuals. Superannuation funds in most countries have a structure in which boards of trustees receive advice on how to allocate investment funds across various asset classes, with a proportion, commonly around 50 per cent,[1] allocated to equities across domestic and international markets. This allocation is broken up into differing components of equities investing and specialist fund managers are chosen to invest proportions of the portfolio. These fund managers might have specializations in large capitalization companies or small companies, global equities, property securities or an industry sector focus.

Institutions make up the majority proportion of the buy-side and consequently are important clients of the sell-side, the stockbrokers. A common organizational structure within a fund manager is to have a chief investment officer, portfolio managers who manage portfolios on behalf of clients and research analysts who follow particular stocks, similarly to the industry sector focus of sell-side analysts. For any particular fund manager, different investment strategies might apply to particular portfolios. Alternatively, a fund manager may be committed to being a particular type of investor, such as a value or momentum manager, with this style being how a fund markets itself to prospective clients who give them funds to manage. These styles of investing are described further below.

Where fund managers are investing funds in equities markets on behalf of individuals they are also known as mutual funds. A requirement for these funds is that they maintain liquidity so that investors can withdraw funds when they would like to. The value of an investment in these funds, in which investors would own units, is described as net asset value per unit.

An increasingly prominent component of the buy-side in recent decades has been hedge funds. While conventional fund managers mentioned above invest long, which means they buy shares on the basis they will increase in value, hedge funds, in line with derivation of their name, invest long and short, which means they also sell shares short on the expectation they will decrease in value. In this way they are hedging their bets in relation to equities markets directions, hence the name. Hedge funds typically increase the funds they have available to invest by taking on borrowings, or leverage. This enables them to invest a large amount, sometimes focused on small movements in markets over a short period as they seek to maximize returns. Returns from hedge funds are known as absolute returns, which net out the effects of investing long and short as well as borrowing costs. The investing styles of institutions and hedge funds are covered below. Hedge funds are often managed by individuals who have a particular following among investors for the way they are able to maximize returns. Since these returns are absolute and can be neutral to how markets move because of the various correlations of assets within a hedge fund, they have built significant funds under management, with a capacity to move markets because of the volumes they represent. Total funds managed by hedge funds around the world are approximately US$2 trillion, with around half this accounted for by US hedge funds.[2]

Stock exchanges

The trading of stocks, and how the buy- and sell-sides interact, is governed by stock exchanges. Stock exchanges have rules that apply to market participants, including listed companies, stockbrokers and investors. Principal among these are that listed companies are required to disclose information regularly, the sell-side has to manage liquidity to achieve settlement of stock trading and all market participants are prohibited from insider trading. Stock exchanges have a primary role of ensuring an orderly market for trading, with policing functions usually managed by other regulatory authorities. Some markets have several stock exchanges, such as in the United States where there is the New York Stock Exchange, NASDAQ and the OTC markets. Competition in the UK has increased to the extent that the London Stock Exchange now only has a 56 per cent market share of the top 100 listed stocks.[3]

Two elements of how stock exchanges operate that have added to complexity in recent years are dark pool trading and high frequency trading. While stock exchanges generally operate to make stock trading public, the emergence of dark pool trading has been a cause of concern in recent years as it has increased in volume. Dark pools are so called because they represent trading outside the public arena, usually in large volumes and by financial institutions that see value in masking their investing intentions. Mechanisms for achieving this are through organizations such as the US-based Liquidnet, which is an independent buy-side-only exchange process, or crossing networks operated by large institutions. Ultimately pricing for these trades becomes public but not at the time of transaction, indicating both their advantages for investors while being a source of frustration for regulators.

Another unregulated phenomenon is high frequency trading, which involves the use of algorithms to trigger high volume trades when potential price aberrations are detected. Since these trades are triggered electronically they bypass traditional broker networks and also have potential to cause market mayhem because of their large and mechanical nature. In Australia, high frequency trading accounted for between 15 and 25 per cent of equity market turnover in 2011, up from 3 to 4 per cent in 2009, indicating why it is of increasing concern to stock market regulators.[4]

Who owns equities?

An increasing trend in recent decades is that institutions increasingly are the major shareholders in listed companies. In the US, institutional ownership of the market as a whole is around 70–75 per cent[5] while in Australia it is closer to 80 per cent, which includes local and foreign institutions.[6] A more recent 2013 survey with a focus on the top 300 stocks in Australia showed institutional investors owned 90 per cent of issued capital of those companies, up from 85 per cent just over a decade earlier.[7] While retail investors are a smaller component of the total market, some 54 per cent of Americans own stocks, down from 65 per cent before the recession and financial crisis,[8] while 43 per cent of adult Australians own shares.[9]

These components of share ownership are a pointer to listed company communications effort and message formulation, since they indicate the increasing importance of communication to the investment community. While retail investors might own less of listed companies, they are still relevant stakeholders in the communications process. A survey of retail investors in Australia in 2010 by the Australian Securities Exchange revealed some interesting attitudes among this type of investor,[10] with several of them having relevance for communication.

- An increasing number of investors want to make their own investment decisions, with only 12 per cent wanting to delegate them.
- The likelihood of share ownership increases with age, education and household income, with more males owning shares than females.
- Retail investors are active seekers of information about the markets, eager to build their knowledge and to become more personally involved in decision-making, with newspapers being the most commonly used source of information.
- Retail investors were considered to be of four main types:
  - cautious consulters – the largest segment, they have some knowledge of markets but lack confidence in their own decision-making capabilities and so consult professionals, family and friends to get second opinions;
  - prudent investors – knowledgeable but being careful in rebuilding portfolios since the financial crisis;
  - agile investors – also knowledgeable but prepared to take more risks, seeing the markets as exciting and challenging;
  - disengaged delegators – the smallest segment, preferring to leave decisions to experts in the absence of their own market knowledge.

Supporting the importance of the media for institutional investors as well as retail investors, Rivel Research found that 83 per cent of wholesale investors said they discovered new companies as investment ideas through the media.[11]

A further piece of the jigsaw of describing the make-up of investors in stocks comes from a Reserve Bank of Australia report,[12] which shows differences in portfolio weights between institutional and retail investors. For institutions, 30 per cent of portfolios are in financial stocks and 70 per cent in non-financials, while the exact opposite is the case for retail investors, with 70 per cent of their portfolios in financial stocks. A partial explanation of this is that institutional portfolios reflect the composition of the stock market as a whole while retail investors favour the high dividend yielding financial stocks.

Among the communication lessons from these statistics are that there is a ready audience for companies that are prepared to tell their stories, to investors directly and through the media.

Market information

While our overall focus is on how companies tell their stories, it is also important to understand the market context in which this information is received. While ultimately both retail and wholesale investors make decisions about individual stocks, they are also swayed by prevailing market conditions and the basic statistics about stocks that are published daily in the media.

Each major stock market has an index that is an indicator of how that market is performing and movements in these indices are part of daily news bulletins, across print, electronic and online media. They show the temperature of the market and direction of market sentiment. The US market is measured by the Dow Jones index, the UK by the FTSE index and the Australian market by the S&P/ASX 200. Percentage or points moves in these indices is how market conditions are described.

A common pointer to market sentiment is the futures index of any market, with it indicating an upward view of market direction if the futures index is higher than the current market index, or downward if below the current level.

In stock market data columns published in daily metropolitan newspapers, common information across several countries is:

- a company's code, which is needed for trading shares and data-searching;
- volumes of stock units traded, indicative of market interest in the stock;
- high and low value of the stock over the past year or week, allowing comparison with current price to help in forming a view about value and trends;
- a P/E ratio, which we have previously explained as price to earnings, representing the most recent share price divided by earnings (or net profit after tax) per stock unit, with the market's long term average P/E of 15 representing a dividing rule of thumb between high P/E growth stocks and lower P/E value stocks;
- dividend yield, being the stock price per unit divided by dividend per stock unit, indicating the rate of income return on a stock unit.

Stock market information pages in the media also contain information about certain larger stocks where it is possible to trade futures, options and contracts for difference (CFDs) in relation to them. Since the underlying security for these derivatives is the stock itself, communication about the stock is equally as relevant for its derivatives.

The global financial crisis

The onset of the global financial crisis, usually marked by the collapse of Lehman Brothers in the US in September 2008, has been followed by more market uncertainty globally. An observable communication effect of these events has been one word emerging to infiltrate common language and in particular the realms of corporate storytelling. It is the word "debt". It is well understood that leverage was the cause of the many issues that led to the global financial crisis. It was an outcome of a housing bubble in many world markets that led to investors taking on too much debt and financial institutions not only fuelling this but taking on too much debt themselves. The ultimate outcome was a widespread and growing inability to service debt, which in turn led to a downturn in asset prices and the compounding of the problem into a worldwide financial crisis.

The impact for many companies was to look closely at their debt levels and balance sheet covenants relating to debt commitments and, if necessary, implement capital-raising to achieve more prudent debt to equity ratios. While debt may have rated a mention in past investment presentations, changing times have meant it has become more of a headline item and a figure that has increased in prominence as analysts and the media made judgements about corporate survival.

In a sense, the word "debt" became a key that unlocked a number of terms in the way companies began to describe themselves and their management practices. While debt is an acceptable component of achieving growth from a corporate finance perspective, company descriptions have begun including terms like "conservatively geared", "virtually debt free", "rigorous risk management practices", "costs reduced from lower interest expense due to debt reduction", "implementation of cost cutting programmes" and many similar terms. Descriptions of corporate performance have increasingly taken in how all industry competitors were affected by changing economic circumstances, so that individual company performance is not isolated from a widespread economic downturn. The changing storytelling focus has in a sense increased the scrutiny on management actions in coping with deteriorating business conditions as well as preparing for improving times. Baruch Lev quotes two contrasting examples of companies managing the process of deteriorating financial performance.[13] One provided little explanation around declining sales and profit and gave greater but vague reassurance around a likely improvement, with the market treating this information disdainfully and cutting stock price significantly. By comparison, another company faced with declining performance gave detailed explanation of the reasons behind it and specific actions management was implementing to achieve a turnaround. After this explanation in a conference call with analysts, stock price went up, despite a poor financial result. In highlighting the differences between these two examples, Lev notes the benefits that come from being prepared to provide facts and figures to back up the narrative, delivering information in a tone and style that is frank about the actual situation and in being clear in describing what is being done about it. What he sets out is an interesting example of the corporate story in action, as it is modulated to suit the changing circumstances of variable financial performance.

Another effect of the financial crisis on financial communication has been on disclosure. Widespread understanding of derivatives and their implications really only took place when there was greater appreciation of the impact derivatives had on actually causing the crisis. As sub-prime lending increased with the housing bubble in world markets, particularly the US, these sub-prime mortgages were bundled into pools to become an underlying level of security, with their poisonous nature partially offset by other better quality securities in the pool, and the combined creation known as collateralized debt obligations (CDOs). These structures ultimately collapsed as viable instruments in extremely large volumes, with reverberations in markets around the world.

Case study

Coles vs. Woolworths – retail rivalry brings out story nuances

For decades, Australia has had two fierce rivals in food retailing, Coles and Woolworths. The rivalry extends across several other levels as well, with both involved in liquor retailing and, in separate businesses, hardware retailing. The two competing public companies in this mix are Wesfarmers, the parent company of Coles, and Woolworths, and in recent years their extended rivalry has led to varying nuances in their corporate stories.

In 2007, Wesfarmers made a substantial acquisition, buying the Coles group, with its national chain of supermarkets and other businesses, for A\$20 billion. While Coles was an iconic brand in Australia, it had underperformed for a decade, leaving it with "a bloated head office and poorly managed, [with] every aspect of the business … in decay".[14] On the first day after the acquisition, there was no one in reception to meet Richard Goyder, CEO of Wesfarmers and new owner of the business, indicating attitudes at Coles and the challenges ahead.[15] Responsibility for the turnaround was given to a new manager Wesfarmers imported from Scotland, Ian McLeod. McLeod later reported some shocks he discovered in Coles' haphazard ordering procedures, giving the business a four-year supply of coat hangers and enough Italian olive oil to fill Lake Como.[16]

The real challenge for Coles was to make up the ground it had lost to arch rival Woolworths. In 2008, Coles food and liquor sales were 25 per cent lower than those at Woolworths and margins were less than half those of its rival. By 2011, the gap on both these measures had improved substantially, reflecting 12 consecutive quarters of comparable store sales growth, but there was still a way to go.[17]

A year later, sales continued to improve at Coles, helped along by a successful advertising campaign built around a reworking of a 1975 hit song by British pop group, Status Quo, called "Down Down", with the lyrics changed to focus on how prices were going down at Coles, which was one form of attack on Woolworths. When Wesfarmers announced its financial year 2012 results, it gave emphasis to the way Coles and other businesses were improving, with margins at Coles up to 4.6 per cent, but still short of the 7 per cent levels at Woolworths.[18] However, the analysts were more concerned about focusing on returns on capital. Return on shareholders' funds increased to 8.4 per cent, but with analysts calculating Wesfarmers' cost of capital at around 12 per cent pre-tax and 10 per cent after tax: "Richard Goyder will continue to face charges that he destroyed value by paying too much for the Coles group almost five years ago."[19]

Meanwhile, over at Woolworths, where there was satisfaction with how the supermarket chain was performing under its "fresh food people" slogan, the focus was moving to how the company could take on Wesfarmers in the hardware market. Wesfarmers subsidiary Bunnings is a highly successful national chain, prompting Woolworths to initiate a joint venture with US home improvement giant Lowes to take a bite of market share in the home handyman and trade market. By August 2012, under the Masters brand, the joint venture had 20 stores operating with 112 in the pipeline,[20] with one analyst predicting Woolworths would have a 6 per cent market share by 2017 compared with Bunnings at 19 per cent.[21]

Sensitivity about rivalry in the hardware market boiled over in September 2012 when the *Australian Financial Review* published findings from an industry consultant who said Woolworths needed to change its "female-friendly" Masters format if it wanted to avoid missing out on business from trade and serious hardware users.[22] Woolworths responded strongly, claiming in an article the next day that the report was part of a dirty tricks campaign.[23]

In another area of rivalry, Woolworths has been successful in liquor retailing and benefits from a boost to sales through hotel ownership. A sidelight of this is that hotels revenue includes a component of income from poker machines, which led to protests at the 2012 annual meeting and Woolworths surviving a vote that may have led to a restriction of income from gaming. Possibly seeking to gain a reputation advantage, a story leaked into the media in November 2012 suggesting that Coles might be seeking a joint venture partner for its hotels portfolio. This would enable it to separate out income from liquor, leaving beneficial ownership of gaming with a partner. [24]

When rivalry is so close between two large companies sharing allied markets, their corporate stories take on an anticipation of a competitor's moves as much as outlining a singular path ahead.

Additionally, what seemed like a risk management tool in the form of credit default swaps also became unstable as the risks they were meant to be covering became too large in the face of debt levels out of step with a market where asset values were declining. Many of these derivatives, and so-called insurance over them in the form of credit swaps, were able to be located outside balance sheets and so escaped disclosure in a discernible way. What emerged was what was described as a "shadow banking system".[25] These developments prompted Warren Buffet to describe derivatives as "financial weapons of mass destruction".[26] As investors have become aware of the havoc created by these instruments, companies and institutions have increasingly been obliged to explain whether derivatives and any off-balance sheet obligations might be part of their operations in a post-crisis era.

Styles of investing

Understanding various styles of investment is an important factor in communication since it also has an influence on how companies present their corporate stories as well as define potential investors. There is little to be gained from companies reshaping their stories in an attempt to appeal to particular types of investors, but they can highlight aspects of their stories that bring out what specialist investors are seeking. While there are many differing types of strategies pursued by investment managers, a few key types are outlined below.

Growth and value

The most common but differing perspectives on investing in stocks is growth compared with value. A simple difference between the two is that value investors look for stocks they consider to be cheap while growth investors are driven by what they see as the demonstrated growth capability of stocks and choose them because they see this trend continuing. A focus on value stocks can mean buying those considered out of favour by the market or at the low end of a business cycle. Characteristics of stock that might seem to be at a low price are that a stock might have a low price-earnings ratio, or book value of net assets per share might be higher than stock price. Growth stocks would have higher price-earnings ratios than value stocks. While some investment managers have a distinctive value or growth orientation, others argue that these two types of investment approaches have a low correlation of returns so it can be beneficial to combine them in the one portfolio to enhance returns. Correlation of returns is the extent to which differing stock prices move in the same direction, or not, at the same time. Portfolio theory says that if investors combine stocks with a low correlation, that is one has a tendency to go up while the other might go down in the same market conditions, then return from the portfolio achieves maximization of return with minimization of risk. Among the more renowned value investors are Warren Buffet and his mentor, Benjamin Graham. Their method principally involves analysing stocks to determine intrinsic value and to buy when this is below current market price, building in what they describe as a margin of safety against market fluctuations. One of the better-known growth investors is Peter Lynch. Growth investors are prepared to buy stocks some might consider expensive from the belief they offer higher growth prospects, with some spectacular returns achieved when the right choices are made as tiny companies with a good idea or business model grow into substantial companies. In the wake of the dotcom bubble in the late 1990s, a variant of growth investing, known as growth at a reasonable price (GARP), emerged, taking in some characteristics of value investing into the growth model. While fundamental stock analysis is a component of all value and growth investing, the appeal of a corporate story is also a driver of the investment logic of value and growth investors.

Active and passive investing

Another two differing perspectives of investing relates to time frames. Active investors take a short-term view and trade stocks regularly while passive investors take a longer-term view of buy and hold. Active investors believe they can pick stocks that will outperform the market while passive investors see safety in the longer-term growth prospects of equities as an asset class, often investing in a portfolio of stocks that are representative of the market index as a whole. Both styles have their adherents and the mutual funds market offers many fund choices that adopt these differing perspectives.

Small and large cap stocks

Market capitalization ("cap") refers to the value of a company's equity on the stock market. A rule of thumb for breaking listed stocks into size groups is that large caps have a value of US$10 billion and above, small caps are between US$250 million to $2 billion, with mid caps being between the two and micro caps having a value of less than $250 million. The two principal investing views are whether returns are greater from small caps or big caps exclusively or from a mixture of them in a portfolio. Advocates of small caps argue that there is greater opportunity for growth investing in this area, picking on smaller companies that have the opportunity to grow substantially. A feature of smaller caps is that they can have higher volatility, which is a measure of risk. At times of financial crisis, as has been seen since 2008, a flight to safety by investors can see smaller cap stocks go out of favour in preference to larger stocks. There can be cycles of the market where focusing on a particular size of stock can show superior returns but these can also average out over the longer term.

Momentum, trend-following

Following the price momentum of stocks in the market is another way of making investment decisions. The idea is to follow trends up and sell when the momentum changes. "The trend is your friend" is the philosophy that guides this practice and many successful devotees of the style, such as Michael Covel, have shown it can yield consistently positive returns. The great economist Keynes is often quoted in support of this style, with his aphorism being "when the facts change, I change my mind".[27] The prevailing strategy is to seek to make money whether markets are going up or down by combining shorting of stocks with going long. On the face of it, the existence of momentum investing as a possible successful investing strategy appears to run counter to the efficient market hypothesis since it implies, in contradiction to the hypothesis, that past price behaviour might have some influence over future price movements. Since the existence of momentum investing suggests some inefficiency in markets, proponents of momentum investing have put forward possible explanations for this. One is that, while the efficient market hypothesis assumes new information is available instantly to influence prices, investors tend to react to new information in differing ways and time frames. Second, they cite the psychological phenomenon of the "disposition effect". Stock owners tend to act prematurely to crystallize a profit on good news or hang on too long when there is bad news in the hope of avoiding a loss, with the disposition effect creating an artificial headwind that limits potential up or down moves because of these investor reactions. A third explanation is the bandwagon effect, with the tension between short- and long-term reactions to news taking a while to reach equilibrium.[28] While debates about the viability of momentum investing continue, it is more likely to work an advantage for professional investors than individuals.

Hedge fund investing styles

The increasing size of hedge funds, and their propensity to commit to quite large bets based on their analysis, makes their investing styles worthy of study, especially when they come to the attention of investor relations officers as new entrants on the share register. There are many differing styles of hedge fund investing but one London School of Economics study grouped them into four types.[29] One is long/short funds, with an ability to short (betting on a price fall) stocks being a distinguishing factor with most long-only portfolio managers who invest for capital appreciation. Within this group of hedge funds, styles can include market neutral strategies that have a bias to stock picking or pairs trading, which involves choosing two similar or different stocks, with arbitrage earned from predicting their similar or divergent stock movements. A second group of hedge funds looks for special situations or opportunities that could have an impact on securities pricing, usually over a short-term period. This can include corporate restructuring, stock buybacks or earnings surprises. Two main categories of hedge funds within this group are those focused on distressed securities and others that focus on risk or mergers arbitrage. A third group of hedge funds encompasses a variety of tactical trading views, often with a macro view of market directions and ranging across several market types, not just equities. A fourth group relates to a variety of relative values, essentially looking for market mispricings, with examples being value differences in convertible securities or between a company's debt or equity securities. The advent of a hedge fund on a company's share register is often not due to a company seeking this sort of interest, especially if the fund is shorting the stock. A communication response needs to take into account the particular investment style that a hedge fund represents and also consider, after weighing hedge fund views in relation to the market as a whole, the extent to which added disclosure might benefit all investors.

Analysts' models

While there may be a plethora of differing investment styles, there is common ground around how analysts build a financial picture of a company's value per stock unit and how this might trend in the future. It is a process that leads to calculation of the intrinsic value per stock unit and is followed by buy side and sell side analysts. The process involves building an Excel spreadsheet of a company's three key financial statements: the balance sheet, income statement and cash flow statement. A simplification of how all this works is that the model might include most of the key line items of these statements for the past five years to discern a growth trend for making projections for future years. Future estimates are discounted at the rate that approximates a company's cost of capital, with a net present value per share and multiples of earnings per share derived for comparison with current market price. From a corporate communications perspective, it is important to understand how these models are put together. They can explain why analysts are seeking specific information around individual financial items, such as planned capital expenditure, because they are critical inputs to cash flows and reaching conclusions from the model. Providing disclosure that helps with this process is also part of the transparency analysts are looking for in listed companies.

Buy-side investment decisions

Understanding how the buy-side is judged by its investment performance is also an input to developing appropriate communications strategies. Depending on a particular investment style an investment manager is following, short-term performance may be a critical factor, outweighing the longer-term perspective on a stock, which investor relations officers might prefer. Essentially, investment managers are running businesses based on attracting investors who follow their style and performance. Consequently these managers need to be able to demonstrate that they can outperform standard stock market indices. Investment managers are seeking to demonstrate they are adding a component of alpha to their returns, which is a direct result of their skills, in addition to beta. The term "beta" reflects a return from the market overall, with individual stocks having a beta that indicates how closely their returns correlate with that of the market. Investors might expect that a fund manager's portfolio of stocks would at least provide a return that equates to that of having just invested in a market index of stocks. These returns provided by a manager are usually measured against a market benchmark, reflecting how well a manager has performed in relation to an objective measure. Particular benchmarks are chosen to parallel the style of a portfolio's investment strategy. Fund managers are under constant pressure to outperform these benchmarks, quite often on a short-term basis that can conflict with a manager's personal preference for taking a longer-term view. An alternative to assessing investment manager performance that does not refer to a benchmark is the Sharpe ratio, derived from the capital asset pricing model, which measures a capability to provide a risk-adjusted return.

However performance is measured, it is also compared with other competing managers and so when a performance deadline is approaching, at the end of a month or quarter, fund managers might sell particular stocks to crystallize investment profits to demonstrate improved returns. This can be frustrating for companies since a shareholder might sell regardless of how well a company might be performing and communicating. Other aspects of how managers build portfolios involve the concept of asset allocation, ensuring a diversification across stock types, again reflecting a decision to buy or sell that is quite often unrelated to individual company issues. Fund managers on their websites usually refer to their investment philosophy, the processes they adopt in implementing it and the skills of the people managing the portfolio and strategy. Each of these items, along with performance, becomes part of how investment managers are rated. As investor relations managers go about the process of targeting potential investors, they also take these factors into account as influences on how they communicate with them.

"What's happening with our stock price today?"

Those in the position of being investor relations managers for listed companies are often asked to answer the quite difficult question of why a company's stock price might be fluctuating at a point in time. It is not an easy question because there are so many factors that influence prices. However, a general grasp of the basics of how the markets work is often sufficient to narrow down the field of possible reasons. Since stock prices are like those in any other market, subject to supply and demand, the volume of stock units traded is one indicator, whether the movement has been up or down. Prices can move on little volume, which may indicate an isolated movement, or if there are substantial volumes, it is a stronger indication of market sentiment about the stock overall. A measure of this is volume traded on a day compared with average daily volume, with marked differences being a major part of the explanation about stock price movement.

The identities of the buyer and stockbroker are also an indicator of motivation around the trading that has sparked a price movement. Sometimes this information is not known until a few days after the trade but a number of conclusions can be drawn when identities are known. If the trade is through a stockbroker that is an established follower of the stock and it is a buy initiated by a recognized fund manager, then it is quite a positive sign for the stock. If the fund manager can be identified as a value or growth investor then more is known about motivation, which contributes to answering the question. If the trade is a sell and the price has gone down, then it may be cause for concern regarding a change to market sentiment. The advent of shorting a company's stock can be shown from daily stock exchange reports, which usually indicate the value of short-selling as a percentage of market capitalization. This type of event can trigger a broader communications programme on its own, involving shoring up relationships with other major shareholders and ensuring news flow is keeping the market informed about corporate progress.

Depending on whether the stock price movement has been up or down, it will have an effect on a basic ratio such as the P/E ratio, which can make the stock look cheap or indicate that there is buying power to support a company's growth prospects. This perspective adds to the context in explaining possible motives around market action.

Debt and communication with lenders

The stock market is not the only focus for the corporate story, particularly in an era when there is also market interest in a company's debt levels and its relationship with its lenders, whether they are banks or investors in corporate bonds. Debt instruments can also be convertible to equity at some stage, which adds another level of interest from the market in wanting to understand attitudes of debt providers. Issues around which the market expects disclosure is the amount of debt facilities companies have, cost and maturity dates and any covenants that accompany debt obligations. Examples of covenants might involve a company agreeing to commit to maintaining sales or profits or total indebtedness at certain levels, with a breach of covenants usually making a loan repayable immediately rather than at maturity.

These arrangements with debt providers raise several communications issues. One is that debt providers are an important stakeholder in the process of financial communication. Consequently they are also targets for receiving the corporate story, which has to be shaped to give them an overall perspective of how a business is implementing its strategy to compete in its markets, bringing out its competitive advantage and its plans for growth in a market context. In a sense, this is the same as the story presented to investment-oriented stakeholders, with a change of emphasis being to bring out a more holistic view of the corporation.

Another communications issue around relationships with debt providers is the extent to which corporations disclose to the market the exact nature of covenants to debt arrangements. The desire for analysts to know this is obvious. They need to understand the margin of safety before a company might breach its covenants and also the impending maturity dates of loan facilities, which may or may not be easily renegotiated in tightening financial markets. As with many financial issues, some companies are prepared to make full disclosure around debt covenants, which will endear them to financial analysts, while others are more reticent, preferring confidentiality around what can be sensitive information that can have a significant impact on stock price if all the nuances around it are not fully appreciated.

A further communications issue related to debt is in connection with credit ratings agencies, since credit rating is a critical issue in determining the price of debt. While ratings agencies essentially base their conclusions on financial analysis, they too become involved in the company presentation process as they listen to chief executives and chief financial officers explain their business strategies. While objective financial analysis might be the primary influence, it is how a company presents its story about its position in a competitive market that places a context of confidence around the financial information. This makes credit agencies a critical stakeholder in communication of the corporate story as well.

Communicating with financial markets

Financial markets are dynamic, changing constantly with many views and attitudes shaping trading. The connection of this with corporate communication is that corporate stories need to be flexible in relation to changing markets while maintaining an underlying thread of consistency. There are of course immutable aspects to a company's story. Its financial performance is recorded in audited accounts and so that cannot change. However, what is changing around a company is its operating environment and how a company reacts to these circumstances is a big influence on ongoing financial performance. There are many aspects of a company's story that can move in and out of the foreground as the story is presented to differing audiences and explains a corporate response to changing financial markets. The topic of debt has become more prominent in the wake of the global financial crisis. Feedback from the buy-side and sell-side after a company gives investment presentations can also shape how the story might be presented differently in the future. There might be a call for explaining growth potential more specifically, or perhaps people might want to know more about innovation and how a company might be using research and development to create new market opportunities. Perhaps the media might be highlighting industry trends that are relevant to a particular company and so the investment community might want to hear how a company is coping with exposure to these underlying market shifts. All these aspects call for some flexibility in how a company story is presented from time to time. It is not as though a company story is chameleon-like in being different to different hearers, since that can be harmful in displaying an inconsistency of business strategy. However, in keeping a company story interesting and in illustrating a company's adaptability to changing markets, there are many differing emphases that can be highlighted in telling the story.

How this story is presented effectively to the key stakeholders – the investment community, media and shareholders – is covered in the following chapters.

Notes

1 Large Super Fund Asset Allocation, *APRA Annual Statistics*, June 2012
2 www.firstresearch.com/Industry-Research/Hedge-Fund-Management.html
3 Moulakis, J, "Broker Criticises Multiple Exchanges", *Australian Financial Review*, 7 June 2012
4 Moulakis (2012)
5 "Institutional Ownership Nears All-time Highs: Good or Bad for Alpha-seekers?", http://allaboutalpha.com/blog/2011/02/02/institutional-ownership-nears-all-time-highs-good-or-bad-for-alpha-seekers, February 2011
6 Black, S and Kirkwood, J, "Ownership of Australian Equities and Corporate Bonds", *Bulletin – September Quarter 2010*, Reserve Bank of Australia
7 AIRA survey quoted by White, A, "Mum and Dad Investors Ousted", *The Australian*, 11 February 2013
8 Jacobe, D, "In US, 54% Have Stock Market Investments, Lowest Since 1999", *Gallup Economy*, www.gallup.com/poll/147206/stock-market-investments-lowest-1999.aspx, 20 April 2011
9 Australian Securities Exchange, "2010 Australian Share Ownership Study", p 3
10 ASX (2010), pp 3–4
11 Nash, J, "Investor Relations Could Mean More to your Stock Price than you Think. Like 25% More", *Financial Week*, 27 April 2009, from www.rivel.com/financial%20week.pdf
12 Black and Kirkwood (2010)
13 Lev (2012), Chapter 2, pp 39–41, 57–58
14 Norman, A, "Against the Odds Wesfarmers Has Taken Coles to the Top of the Supermarket Tree", *Sydney Morning Herald*, 29 January 2013
15 Norman (2013)
16 Stensholt, J, "Coles Coathanger Legacy", *Australian Financial Review*, 13 July 2012
17 Mitchell, S, "Coles Carries Weight of Wesfarmers' World", *Australian Financial Review*, 1 August 2011
18 Mitchell, S, "Solving the Capital Problem", *Australian Financial Review*, 17 August 2012
19 Mitchell (2012)
20 Woolworths ASX Results Announcement, 24 August 2012, www.asx.com.au/asxpdf/2012 0824/pdf/42877d1bvngt84.pdf

21 Mitchell, S, "Hardware Gains Forecast for Bunnings, Masters", *Australian Financial Review*, 10 October 2012

22 Mitchell, S, "Masters 'Needs a Makeover'", *Australian Financial Review*, 12 September 2012

23 Mitchell, S, "Woolworths Lashes Out at Poor Forecast", *Australian Financial Review*, 13 September 2012

24 Thompson, S and Macdonald, A, "Coles Looks for $900m Joint Venture", *Australian Financial Review*, 14 November 2012

25 Pozsar, Z, Adrian, T, Ashcraft, A and Boesky, H, "Shadow Banking", *Federal Reserve Bank of New York Staff Reports*, no. 458, July 2010: revised February 2012, www.newyorkfed.org/research/staff_reports/sr458.pdf

26 Buffett, W, "Chairman's Letter", *Berkshire Hathaway Annual Report*, 2002, www.berkshire-hathaway.com/letters/2002pdf.pdf

27 Quoted at IM Asset Management, www.imassetmanagement.com/institutional-services/investment-process/Pages/default.aspx

28 Berger, AL, Israel, R and Moskowitz, TJ, "The Case for Momentum Investing", *AQR Capital Management*, Summer 2009, www.aqrindex.com/resources/docs/PDF/News/News_Case_for_Momentum.pdf

29 Connor, G and Lasarte, T, "An Introduction to Hedge Fund Strategies", London School of Economics – Financial Markets Group, November 2010, http://www.iam.uk.com/Portals/0/pdf/lse-publications/An-Introduction-to-Hedge-Fund-Strategies.pdf

9 Communicating with the investment community

The investment community, comprising the buy- and sell-sides of the financial market, is arguably the most important stakeholder for a listed company, with the relationship between them having many variations. For large companies, there is an extensive following by analysts. At the other end of the spectrum, small companies struggle to achieve attention. For companies in between, there are gradations across meeting analysts' insatiable information appetites and marketing to them in an attempt to spark investor interest. Within the sell-side, there is a duality of relationship, often divided by a "Chinese wall", a self-imposed dividing line within an organization to separate potentially conflicting interests as investment bankers, stockbrokers and analysts vie for corporate relationships. Sell-side analysts need to maintain an objective stance for their research, which is intended to create investing insights for the buy side. Other activities within the same firms are focused on building relationships with listed companies so they can raise capital, advise on mergers and acquisitions and provide corporate finance advice. On the buy-side, analysts and portfolio managers want to build corporate relationships to round out an industry picture as much as they might want to invest in individual stocks.

Across these multifaceted connections, the investment community is a powerful stakeholder that companies cannot afford to ignore nor fail to cultivate even in the face of occasionally critical comment on management strategy or as analysts might display a preference for other companies. The connecting thread between listed companies and investment community – information – is where companies have an opportunity to influence the quality of stakeholder relationships through converting information into communication.

Companies have a legal obligation to provide information to the market. This information enables the investment community to make financial assessments that are the basis of investment decisions about companies. However, the amount, extent and type of information companies provide, and how they present it, is a significant influence on those decisions. Companies may decide they will only provide the bare minimum of financial information, with limited wording to accompany financial basics. In doing so, they may meet statutory requirements but in the process miss the opportunity to engage with the investment community and influence their thinking, decisions and ongoing waves of influence that flow on to other investors. Not engaging with the investment community, or adopting a "letting the numbers speak for themselves" approach, is an opportunity missed. It ignores the value companies can achieve from actively communicating about their businesses.

If companies accept the inevitability and economic necessity of needing to communicate with the investment community, then several consequential issues arise. The "why" of communication has been considered earlier in the light of research that substantiates the contribution communication makes in a positive way to various markers of share price. However, the how, what, when, where and who of communication are significant issues to consider since they each in turn add to the way in which companies are perceived by the investment community and consequently, how they are valued. Each of these perspectives is covered below but perhaps an interesting starting point might be not just a corporation's objectives in taking a strategic approach to communication but also aspects of theory and research around this. Does understanding theory really apply to how companies and the investment community view the way in which they engage? Neither side of this communication equation really ponders theoretical perspectives when they embark on the process but considering the theoretical and research framework around it nevertheless helps the analysis of what is taking place.

Theory informing practice

Theory is not a driver of communication with the investment community but it does have interesting things to say around the language that is used. This includes the way arguments are framed, how information is placed into a narrative context, the extent to which audiences are drawn into participating in arguments being presented and the way in which communication is an element of organizations pursuing their goals. These perspectives are the outcome of research across many examples of corporate communication and some key elements relevant to investor communication, combining theory and practice, are brought out below.

Language and tone

The outcome of one piece of research, by Elaine Henry, is that investors, measured by market reaction, are actually influenced by how earnings press releases are written. They are influenced by the tone of the language, on the basis that "framing financial performance in positive terms causes investors to think about the results in terms of increases to reference points", and also, if releases are too long, they can have the opposite effect – "longer press releases reduce the market impact of unexpected earnings".[1] An interesting context around this research is that earnings press releases are not compulsory but a voluntary addition to lodging financial information with a stock exchange. This financial information must conform to accounting principles and reporting requirements but there is greater licence around how facts, figures and numbers are presented in a press release. As Henry points out, the content of these releases, from a rhetorical perspective, can combine an informational and promotional purpose. As an example, accompanying the numerical content in earnings releases is explanation in words. This provides context around the economy and marketplace that can shift the emphasis away from the corporation to surrounding external factors in relation to financial performance, thus fulfilling a promotional purpose. Numbers themselves can also have a dual function in the way they are presented. Numbers that are the outcome of accepted accounting principles can be accompanied by adjustments in earnings releases to give them an educational interpretation, also highlighting a distinction between simply providing information compared with adding a guide as to how to interpret it. While the numbers themselves have to be accurate and authentic, it is the selectivity around which numbers are highlighted that sets up the surrounding story. The accompanying text can create impressions, perhaps highlighting those that connect with longer-term strategy, while negative numbers can be within a context that provides management perspective. The selection of a comparative benchmark for performance can also skew interpretations to enhance a comparative understanding of performance.

In looking at the language of earnings releases, Henry also notes a number of examples of what she describes as "impression management". In these cases, language becomes a pointer to drivers, external to the company, as primary causes of financial performance. For example, "press releases with negative evaluative comments can still reflect some aspects of promotion", by using words such as "challenging", "disappointed" and "lower".[2] The use of the passive voice and references to nonhuman agents such as the weather and the economic environment can build in some distance between the message and messenger in attributing blame or providing reasoned explanation.[3] Disseminating these releases directly to investors, rather than just relying on media interpretation, can also enhance the impact of language and tone.[4]

Henry links her consideration of individual releases to a statistical analysis that bears our her conclusion "that the tone of earnings press releases, even controlling for [actual] financial performance, influences investors, as indicated by market reaction. Specifically, abnormal market returns are higher as the tone of the press release becomes more positive, up to a point."[5]

Communication theory and reporting strategies

Another area of research around corporate reporting has been to examine the extent to which companies link the theory of "image restoration" to how they explain performance. In 1995 WL Benoit developed a theory of image restoration around how companies tend to manage crisis and explain it in terms of how they want stakeholders to perceive the corporation. More recently, three researchers, Erickson, Weber and Segovia, have used the Benoit framework to examine corporate reporting strategies, especially when addressing weaknesses in financial performance. Their starting point is that since communication is a goal-directed activity with a purpose, a central goal is to maintain a positive image. Consequently, when financial results are not showing a continual upward rise, corporations feel compelled to adopt some measure of image restoration as a central goal of communication to receive support or approval from stakeholder audiences.[6] Benoit developed five categories of image restoration, involving denial, evasion of responsibility, reducing the offensive act, taking corrective actions and mortification (meaning apologizing for wrongful behaviour and asking forgiveness), with each category leading to specific communication response strategies.[7] Each of these categorizations of image restoration is a form of persuasion and, while many people may want to know who to blame, they also find it more reassuring to know that steps have been taken to eliminate or avoid future problems.[8]

In linking this to corporate reporting, Erickson et al point out that management must first acknowledge why material weaknesses exist before they can correct them. By studying how management responds, in relation to the Benoit framework, it is possible to gain insights into how serious management is in taking action necessary to eliminate weaknesses.[9] The researchers found from their sample that 87 per cent of companies used corrective action as their most frequent response. Interestingly, where non-corrective action was adopted, the most common strategy implemented was scapegoating, a form of evading responsibility. What this strategy ignores is that other companies faced similar challenges at the same time but dealt with them in a more effective way.[10]

Among lessons from this research are that reporting financial results must be accompanied by cogent explanations of reasons for or drivers of performance, within and external to the company, to achieve supportive reaction from the investment community.

Strategic application of storytelling

Building on Fisher's narrative paradigm, which essentially proposes storytelling as a basis for analysing human communication as an alternative to a rational or reason-based paradigm, two researchers, Barker and Gower, developed an application of storytelling to corporate communication. They see storytelling as a key communication strategy in linking individuals to a wider corporate view. The impact of the narrative paradigm is that it describes a common method globally of how people actually communicate in their daily lives. Barker and Gower argue that a reason for many international business failures is an inability to grasp intercultural differences and not to recognize that corporations are responsible for making themselves sensitive to the diverse needs of different groups of people.[11] An application of this to financial communication, especially in relating to the investment community, is that companies need to understand the content and tone of the information they provide in reaching out to the buy- and sell-sides and the way to achieve this effectively is through the corporate narrative. Among the advantages of narrative that Barker and Gower bring out are that stories are memorable, easy to understand, can communicate values and create credibility.[12] The way narrative works, particularly if we consider it from the perspective of financial communication, is that since everyone has within them the capability to be a storyteller, we "use rationality and logic to assess stories as listeners and recreate a reality based on what is presented".[13] Stories have a persuasive function, in establishing common ground, reducing organizational uncertainty and in creating a future vision.[14] In this sense they can have an organization-making function rather than just an organization-maintaining one.[15] Barker and Gower also bring out that how stories are told affects how they are received. They need to have a relevance that is reinforced with an appropriateness of content, style and tone so there is a connection with actual events and narrative. While stories are capable of generating action, they are primarily a vehicle for sharing knowledge and in showing cause and effect. Their basic content has to be true as well as reflecting the authenticity of the storyteller and when these ingredients are combined, storytelling can be applied in a strategic corporate context to enhance connections with key stakeholders.[16]

This research reinforces the value and power of narrative, combining facts and numbers, as being a guide for companies in communicating with the investment community. It can be a way of helping analysts and investors see the world in the way management does and to appreciate the industry constraints in implementing strategy.

The investment story and narrative analysis

When company financial performance is mixed rather than sailing along on a continual uptrend, there is added pressure on how these circumstances are communicated. One researcher who has assessed the written form of communication by companies in these circumstances is Daphne Jameson, who traces a thread between narrative analysis and the way company reports connect with readers. Her starting point is to look at this form of corporate communication as a narrative because "the way a story is told, as well as what it says, matters".[17] She breaks down narrative into three levels: fabula, story and text. Fabula is the underlying material of the story, including events, actors, time and place. The story is the fabula presented in a certain way in terms of sequence, duration, frequency, focus and point of view, with a fabula containing many sub-stories. The text is the realized story, structured and converted into words, with the idea that a story can be presented by a variety of narrators in different ways, yielding many texts.

This narrative structure can be seen in a number of ways in financial and investor communication, across announcements and annual reports as well as in face-to-face investment presentations. Another aspect of narrative theory Jameson highlights in this context is that the preparation of a story involves a selection from all the material available, leading to the shaping of the story, and then its manifestation, in writing and verbal presentation. This process emphasizes that structure is integral to narrative and that "the shaped story is never the same as the raw materials"[18] or, in other words, the numbers aspect of a story cannot stand alone or speak for themselves.

A second aspect of narrative theory Jameson brings out is the impact of the narrative on audiences, which is the field of phenomenology, which sees meaning as being within the communication process and not a derivative of it. From this perspective:

> phenomenological theory sees the audience as implicitly portrayed in the text, actively involved in the temporal flow of reading, and centrally positioned as a kind of co-author. In the case of shareholder reports, then, phenomenology suggests that audience analysis involves understanding how the reader is depicted in and interacts with the text. Audience is what readers do as well as who they are.[19]

A third aspect of narrative theory Jameson brings to light is dialogism. While phenomenology focuses on the reader's experience, dialogism looks at the object of that experience, involving the diversity of voices within a story revealing its meaning. Visual symbols, such as charts and diagrams, are also part of how differing narrators get across their perspective of the story.

In her analysis of investment reports, Jameson saw evidence of these three components of narrative theory. She noted the "kernels" of narrative unfolding towards the main story, the interaction of theme with the levels of directness of expression, the use of differing narrators, such as the chairman, CEO, CFO and managers, to add a range of voices and a broader attempt to reach out to audiences to have them respond emotionally as well as intellectually. In this way the audience is drawn into a personal relationship with the narrators. "The reader's response is not to the words themselves but to the words as spoken by the narrators. Thus the reader cannot be passive but must actively contribute to the making of the text through imagination."[20]

Jameson is essentially highlighting three critical aspects of how companies communicate with the investment community. The structure of a narrative is important. Second, it should account for the information needs of the audience in a way that involves them within a narrative. And third, storytelling can have many voices from within a company in bringing out its strategy, context and financial performance.

Objectives

Each of these aspects of narrative theory evokes a powerful connection with how companies can achieve effective communication with the investment community. Communication theory would not be a starting point for how chief executives and investor relations practitioners start their conversations around how to talk about their companies but it provides objective reference points and confirmation around what works for effective communication to this key stakeholder group.

While in many ways "theory" is a descriptive term in creating a template for practice, it does outline general objectives that companies must consider in reaching out to the investment community. Companies need to recognize the cultural divide and, while wanting to convey their story, also need to acknowledge what the investment community wants from them. Reflecting theory, audiences determine message content as much as the company is seeking to have them absorb its perspective. If a primary objective, from the corporate perspective, is to achieve understanding of the company, its strategy, performance and direction, then conveying the corporate story convincingly in encompassing these topics meets this objective. If companies are to demonstrate an audience sensitivity, as theory suggests, then understanding what investors and stock analysts want to hear, and the cultural environment in which they have to survive, is a sound starting point.

How analysts work

Analysts, whether on the buy- or sell-side, work in a competitive environment. Unlike their colleagues on the dealing desk or working as portfolio managers, analysts do not earn income directly for the firm or demonstrate earnings, even though their analytical reports of companies may be the raw material for generating stockbroking firm or institutional earnings. In some environments there is recognition that analyst reports might have generated revenue-based activity but in any event, analysts are under pressure to be recognized in the industry as people with insights and whose skills are acknowledged in industry surveys. This requires being productive in terms of writing company reports and giving those reports points of difference so they can be noticed and provoke investor action. Making company visits is an important part of the job, with institutions often saying to sell-side analysts they really only want to hear from them after they have visited a company so they can check their own intuition. An analyst making an earnings revision of a company is a particularly important piece of news for the market and so needs to be based on not just a company impression but also one of the wider sector. Analysts are not immune from the need to undertake marketing themselves. Their reports need to be distributed to a client base with insights brought to their attention and they also need to be attentive to an ongoing connection with the companies they are analysing to ensure a communicative relationship is maintained. When a company does release financial results to the market it can be a dawn to well beyond dusk length of a day for analysts, as they absorb the information, analyse and report on it in relation to their own forecasts and then communicate their perspective to clients and colleagues, often globally. A central focus of analysts' jobs is valuation, in particular a thorough and independent assessment of the quality of earnings, the E that is the major influence on the P of stock price and which together form the P/E ratio. Analysts also have to be conscious of compliance issues, especially in relation to the confidentiality of information they receive and insider trading implications of this.

For listed companies, recognizing that analysts want to have a close relationship with them as much as companies want to ensure they connect with analysts is a valuable starting point for the corporate investor relations perspective. The most effective relationships are those that are mutually beneficial, reflecting the theoretical public relations perspective of Ledingham. From successful relationships, analysts have access to management within a company and for the company, analysts in turn can provide access to buy side institutions. Both sides recognize the constraints of continuous disclosure but this does not prevent analysts gaining insights from conversations around business and markets as well as making judgements about body language.

Opportunities and structure

Within regimes of continuous disclosure there are structured opportunities for companies to communicate about financial performance and strategy. With updates on earnings being a critical piece of information, half yearly and annual results announcements are primary events, supplemented by quarterly earnings announcements, the issue of the annual report and the annual meeting of shareholders. These key events provide the main opportunities for listed companies to communicate their messages to the investment community but they are not the only ones. Others are analyst days, roadshows and more informal relationship-building between the investment community and listed companies. Along the way companies are also making announcements around progress and achievements with operations so these too bring about investment community contact. While it helps companies to have an understanding of what analysts want to know, the main communication challenge for companies is to get across their own messages within the surrounding corporate story context. It is also competitive for companies to attract the attention of the investment community, which adds to the need to make the surrounding story interesting, moving beyond a minimalist focus on bare information around a company in isolation and taking in its wider environment and a strategy to grow a business in that market. Below we cover these various opportunities for listed companies to reach out to the investment community.

Earnings announcements

Many companies build in a formal process in the lead up to these announcements. It begins soon after accounts close with financial analysis taking place, accompanied by drafting descriptive information to bring together events as well as reasons around performance. Investor relations people usually become involved in putting this basic earnings and performance information into a story that fits with a company's strategy and broader competitive position. An earnings release is usually the first document drafted. It is a document that is released to the stock exchange and media and forms a summary of the key numbers and performance explanation, as well as positioning the material within the corporate story. It will include quotes from the CEO, to give a personal flavour of interpretation and for use by the media. This draft will be reviewed by the CFO and auditors before a draft is finalized for consideration by legal counsel and ultimately the CEO. A review process like this with many hands can lead to messages becoming mixed so again it becomes the responsibility of investor relations professionals to distil key messages and create a headline. This will guide input for a PowerPoint presentation, which has become a common way for companies to communicate their story to the investment community. It also provides an opportunity to introduce the symbols of communication, such as charts, tables and diagrams, to put graphic explanation around performance and make it more easily understood.

Earnings announcements usually comprise three documents being released to a stock exchange: accounts for the period in a form complying with exchange requirements and accounting principles; a news release that combines words and numbers, possibly using an interpretation of the numbers differently from those resulting from accounting principles; and a PowerPoint presentation. The only document that is compulsorily released to the exchange is that setting out accounting numbers but if companies want to spread an understanding of their businesses and performance then these other accompaniments are the tools with which to do it. Before any documents are released they will have been through appropriate internal approval channels, with most companies having rules about disclosure, involving committees that oversee the process and agreed guidelines about who can speak publicly on behalf of the corporation to the investment community and media.

Companies also commonly arrange a conference call with the investment community, either on announcement day or a few days afterwards. The earnings release will have provided dial-in information, making it possible for anyone interested in the call to dial in. These calls provide an opportunity for analysts to ask questions of management about performance and strategy and the way management responds can be critical to market interpretations of performance and to stock price. While question and answer sessions in these conference calls may lead to the release of new insights, companies usually try not to make significant disclosures in these calls that would necessitate another announcement under continuous disclosure obligations. To decrease this likelihood, companies usually script an introduction and summary statement for the calls and also seek to anticipate possible questions and answers. Preparing this material is usually the role of investor relations people, including obtaining all relevant approvals within the company and often conducting rehearsals of the script and questions and answers.

Content

In a recent exchange of views through an online discussion among NIRI members, one practitioner asked her colleagues about the primary role of investor relations during the earnings announcement process. One reply went as follows:

> My primary role is to collect and analyse all the financial data and then synthesize it into a "story", relating the current quarter to the prior history and to where we think the company will be going in the future.[21]

This story element in an earnings announcement shines the spotlight on how strategy is being implemented and how the company itself explains its progress. It brings out the metrics that a company uses to judge its own performance and it provides an opportunity to create an aura of competence and leadership around where a company is heading. From research mentioned above, there is value from using positive language but there are also pitfalls in going too far with superlatives that leave little room for objectivity. The audience assessing this, the investment community, is discerning and judgemental so preparing material that makes a story interesting, convincing and possibly inspiring about the future involves considerable thought and preparation. In some ways it is like preparing a rhetorical case before a court of law in which the logic of an argument is presented in a way that shows a company has implemented sound business decisions in the face of the economic and market environment with which it has been dealing.

Announcement day processes

In today's competitive world, listed companies face competition in attracting the attention of the investment community. Consequently, it is helpful for companies if they implement processes that achieve wide dissemination of their story to this stakeholder group. Research has shown that dissemination, beyond just leaving an announcement on an exchange platform, has a positive influence on stock price. Dissemination can take the form of subscribing to news wire distribution services or companies can build their own lists that cover the media, investment community and shareholders. For companies of a reasonable size, there is also an expectation they will present their results story face-to-face, either to groups of analysts or a series of individual presentations across several cities. On announcement day, there will also be presentations to the media, through individual interviews or telephone calls, a press conference or conference call. Smaller companies have to work harder to find analysts who are prepared to pay attention to their story, with this often managed simply by waiting until there is time in the calendar for presentations to be fitted in. Some conference calls for larger companies are accomplished through webcasts, with PowerPoint slide material also accompanying a conference call. Companies usually have sections of their websites where announcements are posted and there is also an increasing trend to use social media mechanisms such as Twitter to distribute news. All of these processes are managed by investor relations professionals.

Within a short time after a company releases an earnings announcement, sell-side analysts covering the stock and journalists will usually release short reports, followed by lengthier versions later in the day or overnight. An analyst will have a model, which enables predictions of earnings, and divergence from this will be the basis for having a view about how a company has performed, with surprises on the downside or upside having a significant influence on stock price. In days before regulation became tighter, listed companies would drop hints to analysts that might help to bring their earnings estimates into closer alignment with actual earnings. It is not to say that veiled hints do not get dropped in a more heightened regulatory atmosphere but the risks of doing so have become significantly greater. This has led to many companies providing earnings guidance through the continuous disclosure process when they know in advance that earnings are likely to diverge from market consensus.

Through closer relationships with some sell-side brokers, contact with the investment community can also take place in more informal settings over lunch, with selected buy-side institutions making up the group. While the setting might be informal, the stakes are just as high since a company and CEO are dealing at close quarters with institutions that may or may not be large shareholders who own the company or whose decisions could have a significant influence on stock price. Often these events involve a large amount of preparation, belying the casual atmosphere. In more carefree days the events might also have involved imbibing alcohol over lunch but the more serious current times make this less frequent. The preparation involves a company, and the hosting sell-side broker, considering the key messages and story in advance. Any results announcement has highlights and those that are relevant for the investment community can differ from those that are for more general consumption by the media and wider marketplace. In these gatherings, the focus is on earnings, what drives earnings and where future opportunities for growth might be. The sell-side broker will anticipate questions, and help the company with answers from two perspectives. The broker knows what issues of interest and concern might be in the minds of buy-side institutions, which happen to be the broker's clients, and so needs to ensure this information is brought into discussion. This might involve the broker asking leading questions to prompt a company to cover these topics. The broker also needs to prepare companies for the more difficult questions it anticipates some institutions might ask. In some of these gatherings, analysts do not hold back, with their hard-hitting questions having the potential to disorient some CEOs and CFOs. In these circumstances, the company story and preparation are essential fallback positions.

Some companies, even though they may have a spread of sell- and buy-side interest, prefer to host their own events to provide a results presentation rather than attend sell-side organized lunches. Alternatively, they may arrange a series of one-on-one meetings. Implementing individual briefings in several cities can be hugely time-consuming and distracting for company management, which has led to more time-efficient practices such as group events and conference calls. However, for all parties closely involved in the process of connection between companies and the buy- and sell-sides, relationships are critical and, while they might come at a time cost, it is important at some stages of the year to make the personal connections that are vital to having the corporate story more widely appreciated. As the NIRI definition of investor relations reminds us, there is an element of marketing in the process.

Targeting and discovering investors

While there is a democratic randomness in equities markets, in which anyone can buy shares in a company, investors approach the concept of ownership with differing motives. From the corporate perspective, investors ideally are a stable army of shareholders who are supportive of a company's strategy and direction, whatever the circumstances. However, there is an unreality about this ideal of the homogeneous shareholder. In fact, investors have differing time horizons, with some buying stock for short-term trading purposes, others possibly anticipating a takeover target and quite often a smaller percentage of shareholders fitting the buy-and-hold investor with a longer-term perspective. Some investors might even be prepared to lend their stock to a prime broker, which makes it available for short-selling purposes, enabling an investor such as a hedge fund to bet on a company's stock price going down rather than up. Recognizing this reality, companies need to have consistency in how they tell the corporate story while also thinking about how they can achieve some of their ideals by targeting investors that are a match for the type of business they represent from an investment perspective.

In an earlier chapter we covered how companies can shape their story to reflect the interests of particular investors, such as those with a growth or value orientation. From research and relationship-building with the investment community, companies can also find analysts and institutions with a longer-term perspective. While these relationships can be beneficial, it is not to say that institutions will permanently hold this view since they too have many pressures to provide returns to their investors and may easily take the "Wall Street walk" and sell to invest elsewhere in search of better returns or simply to balance their portfolios to a different direction. Retail investors can provide an alternative and as a group are often considered more likely to be longer-term investors. As a component of investor targeting, companies often begin retail investor campaigns through stockbrokers with large retail client bases.

For the investor relations professionals, targeting investors is an important aspect of assessing a company's register of stockholders and analysing it for investor type and attitude with an ongoing view of finding new investors to create demand for the stock. Part of this process can involve searching the identity of new shareholders whose origin can be masked under a nominee designation. Many listed companies use the consulting services of organizations that search the background of nominee holdings to identify the ultimate beneficial owner. While ownership discovery may not ultimately be a route to discovering motive for share purchases, it is a step towards companies being able to make a more informed guess at likely investing intention and assessing whether short-selling or takeover might be on the agenda of new shareholders coming onto the register. In this sense, discovery is both a tool for marketing and corporate defence.

In a membership survey in 2012, NIRI[22] found that 84 per cent of respondents engage in investor targeting, a process they take seriously by measuring their progress, and increasingly extending their targeting efforts outside the US to reach investors globally. They are assisted in their targeting efforts by the sell-side as well as from commercial databases and consulting groups that take them to meet new potential investors. Among the measures used to judge the effectiveness of these targeting programmes are examining the extent to which potential investors are converted to shareholders, the percentage change in current investors who could own more and surveys of investor attitudes. In assessing potential investors, companies are looking at the potential of an investor to buy a significant stake, investment style, peer company holdings, holding periods, investor type (such as whether an institution might be a mutual fund or hedge fund), the amount of funds under management and the institution's knowledge of the industry. Among the reasons companies are involved in investor targeting are to diversify the investor base, broaden understanding of the company story and attract long-term shareholders with a view to decreasing short-term volatility in a company's stock price. Investor targeting is not without its challenges – it can be costly and takes up management time. As one survey respondent put it:

> One challenge to [our company] engaging in targeting is the level of resources needed to identify potential targets, understand their investment strategy, and determine if they should own our stock. Also, finding the time to meet with buy-side analysts can be difficult.[23]

For companies not involved in investor targeting, the survey showed it was not that they did not understand the value of the process but cost and lack of time prevented a more active pursuit of the task. As the survey showed, most companies do not take for granted the ownership make-up of their companies and see the corporate story as a tool for building a shareholder base that sees an alignment between story and the investment proposition.

Meeting the information needs of the investment community

Investment analysts have an insatiable appetite for information. That is their job. They never run out of questions. If companies provided information on the basis of what analysts would like to see, vast volumes of information would need to be produced. While analysts confront individual companies for their information needs, they are also building models of how an industry is performing so their interest in companies is not always for the purpose of persuading clients to buy or sell a company's stock but in building a picture of where it fits into its sector and how its growth compares with others. For example, some analysts will commission industry surveys to discern customer habits or pricing directions as a way of identifying early an industry trend.[24] As one analyst put it, in commenting on a survey about how analysts go about their work: "You need to understand how the industry thematics impact the numbers."[25]

While the end point of analysts' work is to make earnings predictions for companies, they are also interested in the quality of information provided since this is part of their value judgement about companies. Underlying the search for the variables that are part of the earnings equation is an assessment of how well companies are telling their story and whether it is being done genuinely or with a certain amount of wishful thinking about the future. Some analysts take seriously the study of body language as they assess how managers respond to questions about their business and how it is performing. Studies of body language also indicate that first impressions count, right down to the initial handshake and greetings, with some research indicating that 10,000 non-verbal clues can be conveyed in a single minute.[26] It is not just analysts who are paying attention to this, with it also being of increasing interest to investor relations professionals as they seek to make the most of any meetings with analysts. To paraphrase Warren Buffett, investors should be looking for companies they can understand run by people they can trust, a proposition well-supported by stock analysts.

While analysts may want volumes of information, companies need not be passive instruments in this process. As an information provider, companies are in the powerful position of being the storyteller. They can shape how the message is presented and the financial metrics by which they are prepared to be judged. They can know what information is commercially confidential and what they can provide that makes their story convincing. A company's forthrightness and directness around what information is public and what is not can be a key ingredient around displaying the genuineness analysts are seeking. Analysts are making judgements across a variety of topics and it is also important for them to see that companies take corporate governance seriously in not providing information in one-on-one meetings with analysts that has not been provided to the market generally.

As well as seeking financial information that helps them assess earnings drivers and growth factors, analysts want to gain an impression of the quality of management. This is a frequently cited variable, after earnings, that analysts give in making investment assessments of companies.[27] Earnings predictions have an inherent human quality. Can management actually deliver the earnings an analyst believes a company is capable of producing? This is a question inextricably connected with financial analysis and it is where companies have an advantage in preparing a corporate story that points to a guided conclusion about potential achievements. Among the volume of facts, figures and narrative that can fill investor communication, it is often a few simple metrics that can sum up business capability from a management perspective. It is a reduction of complexity to simplicity that conveys a management team is on top of its business and communicating this to analysts is a key component of the confidence-building process. For example, a health care business that owns hospitals, across varying types and in differing locations, would have a key metric of cost per bed, which would enable analysts to assess margin and analyse the complexities of the business in a simpler way. Performance of manufacturing businesses can be measured by units produced over comparative periods. Service businesses can be measured by the amount of repeat business. Business metrics on their own are not a story but they are an example of combining facts and numbers within a narrative.

Investment presentations

A common vehicle for conveying a corporate story directly to the investment community has become the investment presentation, often in PowerPoint format, selected from a company's "slide deck". There is not an identikit version of these presentations that guarantees success. So many differing companies bring much thought and input to the process, all of which make progress towards communicating their corporate stories. No doubt many are also involved in the process of gathering feedback afterwards to ascertain how effectively they have been communicating to the investment community. For many analysts, investment presentations will not give them all the information they need but they pay close attention to all that is said and how it is presented to glean clues about how management sees its world and growth trajectory. Analysts often can be reticent to ask questions at presentation gatherings where many of their competitors are present because they do not want to give away their own trends of thought and how they will present the stock to their own target market. From a company perspective, much effort is put into these presentation events because they involve the CEO and CFO being under the spotlight and wanting to perform well. While there are standard topics many presentations cover, analysts also look through the actual slides to gain an impression of genuineness of the presenters and how well they appear to be on top of the information by which their performance is being judged. Of course analysts are helped if the presentation is able to step away from being overly company-centric and bring in information around the business context of the company and its sector. Presentations that just go over published financial information do not really add value. Those in formats that are without any graphic design values and are in a type size too difficult to be comprehended from a distance are going to be among the least insightful presentations. CEOs at these events can also adopt differing personas, with some being nervous, some opting to put on a show and others laboriously reading what can be easily seen on the screen. Again, analysts who have seen so many of these presentations are able to read these personality types as they make assessments about genuineness and competence and they seek to define in their own terms what can be a difficult to define characteristic of management quality.

If companies are able to bring interesting and educational qualities of their corporate stories to light in presentations they are going to exercise a greater influence on the investment community. The macro view of a company, linked with themes that connect with a company's products and performance, is always going to add elements of persuasion and narrative to facts and numbers. A company cannot perennially be a top performer but it can aim to be a top explainer of its business and its context, conveying management quality in the process. This outlines a higher objective of investment presentations, since analysts are quite capable of analysing what is the easily obtainable public information.

Case study

Qantas – story wars and the rules of communication

Running an international airline in the current era would have to be one of the hardest CEO jobs around. The challenges are immense – rising costs, strong competition, customer demands for cheaper fares and better service, industrial relations issues and the hangover of debt from when it was easier to service. In the midst of this, Australia's national airline Qantas, nicknamed the flying kangaroo, was reporting dismal financial results early in 2012 and its dividend drought was entering its third year. Half-year profit then had fallen over 80 per cent and was only eight times the pay packet of the CEO Alan Joyce.[28] Not surprisingly, the share price fell and several months later was driven to record lows by hedge funds shorting the stock on the prediction of the need for capital-raising. Qantas CEO and managing director Alan Joyce was at a conference in Beijing at the time and when asked about the share price by some Australian journalists there, he let fly with his views: "We don't need to raise equity … So we continue with the messages, we continue with the strategy and I believe fundamentally that the underlying value of the company will come through in the share price. And it's very clear that the underlying value of the company is worth a lot more than the share price is today."[29]

Reaction to this by one commentator was quite critical: "Most CEOs know that the first rule of communications is never to comment on your share price. It is a pointless exercise unless you back up the comments with something concrete such as better profit performance. Other ways to get market attention are to reveal a takeover approach or capital management. None of these options are on the table at Qantas at this stage."[30]

Part of the Qantas argument was that share price of 97 cents did not reflect fair value when tangible book value a share was A\$2.45. However, several analysts felt the discount to book value was about right for a company that would record return on equity of 3 per cent for the financial year.[31]

Sticking to his guns and with the backing of the board, the Qantas CEO in November 2012 was able to announce several measures intended to close the discount gap. Among these were a reiteration of the strategy of managing costs and turning the international business around to profitability by a proposed alliance with Emirates, along with some financial measures. These included using A\$750 million from asset sales to pay \$650 million off debt and institute a \$100 million buyback of shares. The market reacted positively, with share price up 4 per cent.[32]

While these moves halted a downward spiral, they also coincided with a new battle emerging around the Qantas story. A rival group of shareholders had begun agitating for change. The Qantas strategy promulgated by the CEO and board was for its discount airline Jetstar to lead growth in Asia, for an alliance with Emirates to achieve a sounder footing internationally and for a continued tough position with unions who were demanding job security in the face of Qantas pursuing cost-cutting and outsourcing positions more cheaply outside Australia.

An alternative strategy, put forward by a group of dissident shareholders and some wealthy backers, was to push for the sale of the Qantas Frequent Flyer rewards business and to launch a partial float of Jetstar. This strategy would include a more aggressive expansion of the mainline carrier into Asia, adding more routes and frequencies, especially into Asia's booming business capitals. While the dissidents recognized there might be some value from the Emirates alliance in solving network issues in Europe, they questioned the likely financial returns. Their view was that a more productive alliance might be with a partner in Asia to help them lock down this region.[33]

Weighing into the strategy war was the head of Emirates who not only endorsed the Qantas CEO's strategy but said that it was essential in dealing with a lot of inherited issues and that not only would it achieve a financial turnaround but in three years, those proposing an alternative strategy would be eating their words.[34]

Joining the argument from a different perspective was one anonymous shareholder who was quoted as saying: "There wouldn't be room for shareholder activism if shareholders were happy."[35]

Shareholder support for the activists was not widespread and in January 2013, the strategy war ended, with the dissident group selling out at a reported profit of A$18 million from its sortie.[36] In February, there was also good financial news, with half year profit up 164 per cent to $111 million and losses in Qantas International down 65 per cent.

Just a few months later, the Qantas strategy achieved official government endorsement and by April it launched, with Qantas and Emirates now flying 14 times a day from Australia to Dubai, and providing "one-stop" access to 65 destinations. The stock market responded positively and the Qantas stock price soared to A$1.90, its highest price for nearly two years and perhaps reflecting CEO Joyce's optimism nearly a year earlier when stock price was less than half that value.

While conditions remain tough for international airlines, it seems stars are finally beginning to align for Qantas, across story, strategy, financial performance and stock price. There is no commitment yet about when the dividend drought might end but at least the battle over strategy seems to provide another interesting example of the connection between stock price and story.

Investor tours, analyst days

An effective way for companies to reach out to the investment community is to have analysts visit their operations to see for themselves how a company works. For analysts, the value that often comes from these events is to meet a broader range of the management team and to gain insights from on-the-ground explanations of how a company produces the goods and services it sells. Some companies like to impose rules on these tours, like limiting access to managers, not including the media and being cautious in which parts of operations analysts can see. There may be a sound basis for these attitudes but often the more effective briefings are those that are more open and inclusive. It is also educational for people whose lives are usually centred in an office environment to see how assembly lines or manufacturing operations work. These events also involve a social element and an opportunity to move away from a standard investment presentation to bring out more practical elements of how a company works, adding more elements of interest in the process. Where operations tours are geographically inconvenient, analyst days also take place in city conference venues. Analysts invariably say these events are worthwhile, even if they are only an annual fixture on a corporate calendar.

The future and the stock price

Two elements on which the investment community is always fixated in relation to listed companies is how they are going to perform in the future, both short- and long-term, and the implications of this for stock price. It is usually the case that companies and the investment community will not share the same view on stock price. Companies commonly believe they are not properly appreciated by the market and that they are undervalued. However, voicing this concern publicly is never the best policy. The simplest rule, often contrary to the view of management, is not to talk about the stock price at all. Markets determine price on the basis of information available and many other external market influences. As the investment community firmly believes, the market is the forum in which stock price should be determined, not investment presentations where companies might complain that price does not reflect potential. Companies need to have developed an objective assessment of stock price at which their communication is aimed but it should be communication of the story that leads the argument, not an expression of views about why the market is wrong on price. At a time when there are so many influences on stock price, with monetary and political intervention being the biggest movers of markets, one commentator argues that the traditional price to earnings ratio is giving way to the price to expectations ratio as markets vie to predict another round of central bank intervention or election outcome.[37] In recognizing these influences, another investor relations professional argues that, while it is a feature of modern capital markets that companies cannot discuss their stock price, the hallmark of effective investor relations is "to separate your story from the noise" and provide a level of knowledge and detail around a company that becomes the main influence on stock price.[38] Here we have another contribution to the argument that stock price is more of a story than a number.

Another perspective on stock price and investor relations is from Baruch Lev. He argues that, since earnings guidance is so highly valued by the investment community, providing earnings guidance is ultimately the way to win investors over.[39] However, it could be some time before cautious management as a group adopts his view as a universal truth.

News flow

An effective way for companies to build communication with the investment community is to maintain a flow of news announcements to the exchange platform. Some companies are reluctant to do this, preferring only mandatory half-yearly or quarterly earnings announcements as a way of updating the market. At the opposite extreme, other companies overdo a flow of announcements seeking to highlight how well the company is progressing, since there is never such a flow of negative news. However, if companies are judicious in making announcements, there is much to be gained from this form of straightforward communication. It indicates that steps are being made towards milestones companies have outlined in investment presentations. The announcements become evidence of good management as there is concrete confirmation of goals being achieved. Giving these announcements a news angle, also contributes to the likelihood of them receiving media coverage. Regular news flow means that companies do not have to keep going back to the investment community to make sure there is an understanding of their company since the announcements tend to do that job for them.

Activist investors

For investors to use voting power to express a point of view and seek to impose it on a company is not something new but in recent years it has become more prevalent and widespread. Motives can be varied, from financial self-interest, to seeking board representation or even reflecting a politically motivated stance. These occurrences are covered in more detail in Chapter 11, but there is also a crossover with the wider investment community. From a corporate perspective, the appearance of activist shareholders can be seen as a threat but, as Lev points out, it can often have a positive effect on share price, as investors see a shake-up of entrenched corporate attitudes on the horizon.[40] The common thread in a lot of investor activism is that companies tend to be singled out if they are seen to be undervalued and, consequently, vulnerable.[41] In a sense, this underlines that the best defence against activism is seeking to ensure stocks are appropriately valued, which is one of the main aims of any investor relations programme. Strategies for dealing with activists will be covered later but activism can become an opportunity, not a threat.

Many activist investors are hedge funds, which might go short or long on a stock or have a short-term holding period in mind. One practice, recently highlighted by *The New York Times*, is the extent to which hedge funds use surveys of analysts to gain advance notice of company earnings directions, so they can take a position for a short period in advance of information becoming public.[42] The effect on companies of this is that their stock price might move suddenly and they might be forced into disclosure when perhaps they should have done so earlier. Communication in a timely and informative manner with the market is a way companies can prevent this volatility in stock prices and avoid the unwanted attention of activists, which can prove to be distracting from the primary focus of management.

Clichés of the market

There are many sayings used by people in investment markets that convey simple and fundamental communications truths. Some of them may seem trite in stating the obvious but they are also borne out of experience by seasoned investors who have seen many companies make promises that they were not ultimately able to keep, with a resultant slide in the stock price. While circumstances change over time, some of these sayings are worth highlighting since they form a guide to some of the basic ideas in financial communication. As well as providing communications signposts, these sayings indicate the behaviour the investment community expects from listed companies. Among some common market clichés are listed and analysed below.

People invest in what they understand

To paraphrase Warren Buffet and Peter Lynch, a company worth investing in should be simple to understand and give the impression that any fool can run it, because some day one will. A primary corporate communications task is to convey a clear understanding of a company's business model and growth strategy so that it is educational in going beyond abstract explanations of purpose.

Be quick with the bad news and slow with the good

The investment community expectation is that companies will be up front when things might not be going exactly according to plan and that they ease up on boastfulness when things are going well. Analysts and investors are also too well aware that the temptation for companies is to do the exact opposite, to show reluctance in admitting to not meeting expectations and to trumpet achievements even if they lack importance for the big picture. The cliché reflects an ideal that is respected by the investment community.

Under-promise and over-deliver

A connected cliché is that the market does not like surprises, although those on the upside can be forgiven. Any comment about the future by companies creates expectations. So not meeting expectations can be punished severely by the market. While analysts do not like to be embarrassed for not being accurate forecasters of company earnings, the market as a whole likes to see companies doing well and achieving growth, perhaps beyond what might have been expected, reflecting good management. Effective communication around these elements involves the reverse psychology factor of delivering performance better than expected while not promising too much in advance.

Elevate basic values

An advantage the investment community has over the management of many companies is in seeing a huge range of companies in the space of a year, providing many comparisons of style. This makes it relatively easy to identify companies putting salesmanship ahead of being frank about performance. All the investment community wants is straightforwardness about these issues and to hear a presentation that makes the corporate story compelling. Companies that divert from these basic values make themselves less favoured comparatively.

Keep shareholders in the picture

If companies are not communicating regularly or effectively then shareholders, and the market, will not value them appropriately, which is what everyone wants to achieve. A related cliché is that companies benefit if they set out to achieve a long-term relationship with their register of stockholders.

Buy the rumour, sell the fact

A feature of stock markets is that they are forward-looking. This explains why rumours about things potentially happening with a company can have a significant influence on stock price. It often confounds companies that their stock price will rise on the anticipation of good news and then fall when it is actually announced. The cliché explains a characteristic of markets and there is not a lot companies can do about it except to maintain a flow of communication to the market and pursue a responsible attitude to corporate governance that seeks to keep rumour to a minimum. After all, the cliché essentially represents a short-term view of stock price and not the longer-term corporate perspective.

Accountability goes beyond financial results

The investment community expects that companies are well managed in every respect. Outcomes from this would be a satisfied and productive workforce, a company being a responsible citizen and upholding ethical behaviour. Ignoring these factors and not taking responsibility for them, on the basis that financial performance is all that counts, is not reflective of the style of company well-favoured by the investment community.

There's no benefit to shareholders from a personality cult

Many CEOs love the limelight of public attention and media interest in listed companies. If the investment community gains an impression of this becoming a priority rather than a focus on financial performance, it is not well accepted.

Managers should manage and let the stock price look after itself

The investment community does not take kindly to companies that want to tell them that the market has it wrong when it comes to stock price and that their potential has been overlooked. A related cliché is that the market delivers value, not management. What the investment community respects is a management team focused on making its business work well, for which the reward is an appropriately valued company. Lecturing the investment community about how it should be valued can quite often achieve the opposite effect and represent a breaking of one of the primary rules of investor communication.

While communicating with the investment community can involve both art and science, many CEOs feel that at least there is a common ground with the audience because they all share an involvement in the business world. By contrast, the media represents foreign territory for many CEOs and dealing with the media can create a greater trepidation for CEOs as they venture into the midst of journalists. However, the process need not be so daunting, as we explain in our next chapter.

Notes

1 Henry, E, "Are Investors Influenced by How Earnings Press Releases are Written?", *Journal of Business Communication* 45 (4), 2010, p 363
2 Henry (2010), p 374
3 Henry (2010), p 375
4 Henry (2010), p 375
5 Henry (2010), p 396
6 Erickson, SL, Weber, M and Segovia, J, "Using Communication Theory to Analyse Corporate Reporting Strategies", *Journal of Business Communication* 48 (2), 2011, p 210
7 Erickson et al (2011), p 212
8 Erickson et al (2011), p 214
9 Erickson et al (2011), p 214
10 Erickson et al (2011), pp 216–217, 219
11 Barker, RT and Gower, K, "Strategic Application of Storytelling in Organisations", *Journal of Business Communication* 47 (3), 2010, p 297
12 Barker and Gower (2010), p 299
13 Barker and Gower (2010), p 300
14 Barker and Gower (2010), pp 302–304
15 Barker and Gower (2010), p 305
16 Barker and Gower (2010), pp 306–308
17 Jameson, DA, "Telling the Investment Story: A Narrative Analysis of Shareholder Reports", *Journal of Business Communication* 37 (1), 2000, p 9

18 Jameson (2000), p 10
19 Jameson (2000), p 11
20 Jameson (2000), p 30
21 Brewton, L, "Preparing for the Earnings Release", *NIRI General Discussion eGroup*, 19 June 2012
22 Morgan, JD, "NIRI Explores Global Investor Targeting Practices", *NIRI Executive Alert*, 4 June 2012
23 NIRI (2012), p 3
24 Johnston, E, "Buy, Sell and Hold: How Analysts Shape Our Views on Stocks", *Sydney Morning Herald*, 11–12 August 2012
25 Cousins, S (JP Morgan), quoted in Johnston (2012)
26 Weidner, D, "The Meaning Behind Body Language", *IR Update*, NIRI, February 2011, p 22
27 Chugh, LC and Meador, JW, "The Stock Valuation Process: The Analysts' View", *Financial Analysts Journal* 40 (6), 1984
28 Sandilands, B, "Qantas Ditches Share Dividend Again – and 500 Jobs", *Crikey*, 16 February 2012
29 Quoted in Creedy, S, "Qantas Says Key Holders on Board", *The Australian*, 12 June 2012
30 Boyd, T, "What's Really Ailing Qantas", *Australian Financial Review*, 12 June 2012
31 In Boyd (2012)
32 Smith, M, "Qantas on Right Path as Debt Falls", *Australian Financial Review*, 16 November 2012
33 Cleary, A and Chessell, J, "Rivals May Challenge Joyce", *Australian Financial Review*, 19 November 2011
34 Cleary, A, "Qantas Will Turn Around, Says Clark", *Australian Financial Review*, 15 November 2012
35 Quoted in Cleary, A, "The Qantas Club is Back", *Australian Financial Review*, 24–25 November 2012
36 Korporaal, G and Creedy, S, "The Qantas Strategy Appears to Have Paid Handsomely", *The Australian*, 31 January 2013
37 Hachtuel, R, "So Long Price-Earnings, Hello Price-Expectations", *The Wall Street Journal*, 10 October 2012
38 Quast, T, "Discussion of Stock Price", *NIRI General Discussion eGroup*, 11 October 2012
39 Lev (2012), Chapter 6
40 Lev (2012), Chapter 11
41 Lev (2012), p 257
42 Morgenson, G, "Surveys Give Big Investors an Early View from Analysts", *The New York Times*, 15 July 2012

10 Communicating with the business media

Stock exchange-listed companies are in the public arena, making them objects of public interest to the media, with the consequence that there are benefits for companies if they reach an understanding of how to engage effectively with the media. The media that covers business news is extensive, across TV, radio, newspapers, magazines and online outlets. For listed companies the stakes are high, since media coverage can influence reputation and stock price. Consequently, dealing with the media can be a minefield for companies or it can deliver significant understanding of the corporate story, which in turn can lower the cost of capital and have a positive effect on stock price. Creating a media profile requires management, involving distribution of stock exchange announcements, news flow on achievements and journalist contact to achieve media coverage. While there are many texts that provide advice on dealing with the media, there are special considerations for a stock exchange-listed company that govern how and when news is released. The media marketplace can be daunting for some CEOs and, while it is also competitive to achieve coverage, it offers significant opportunity for reaching out to potential investors. Since there is value for companies in being in the media, the focus here is to discern a road map through the media minefield to deliver that value.

Value of being in the media

There is a body of research that substantiates a connection between media coverage and stock price. It shows that media coverage increases the importance of news related to a company and brings the news to a wider audience. It reduces information problems around stocks and makes them more familiar, which in turn leads to more investment, and investors. Even though not every announcement from a company can receive media coverage, research has found there are positive outcomes from disseminating news to the media, especially as it enhances the likelihood of unlocking the benefits that flow from media coverage.[1] This value for listed companies of being in the media warrants a closer examination of what the media is looking for when it receives announcements from companies, and how companies can embark on the process of making their news, and company story, of interest to the media.

Who is the media?

In the era of the 24-hour news cycle and the increasing presence of online news coverage, there are many components of the media beyond the daily newspapers that can influence stock prices. To achieve coverage, dissemination needs to be widespread, whether it is through companies subscribing to services, like PR NewsWire, or being diligent in managing their own databases to ensure a diversity of media is covered in distribution. While diverse scattering of news has a purpose, there is also a hierarchy of importance among media outlets, with some having greater authority than others. Many online news outlets have their own process for picking up on news released through stock exchange platforms and, while each has its own following, the outlets of primary importance that deal with the news first are the news wire services. These include international organizations like Dow Jones, Reuters, Bloomberg, Agence France-Presse and, in Australia, Australian Associated Press. These organizations have experienced editors and journalists who specialize in dealing with business news and so are familiar with rating and ranking news in competition with the many events that take place in a day. The customers for these wire services are other media outlets and corporate buyers who see value in having a regular feed of business news on a daily basis. The news judgements of wire service editors can flow on to the print media that may buy stories from these wire services. However, print news editors make separate judgements that relate more to the specific nature of their readers. Online outlets, with their varying specializations also make assessments of news they might cover by considering what may be relevant to their followers and subscribers. The ability to store many stories on websites means that online outlets can cover more stories than newspaper print editions. While newspapers cover large numbers of stories in their online editions, editors are selective about what appears in print. Magazines have longer deadlines and are able to take more time with stories. They also need to make their output distinctive to what has already appeared in print or online. Many magazines, whether, weekly, monthly or quarterly, have adopted the practice of having daily electronic newsletters to pick up on the daily news flow of relevance to their subscribers. The electronic media, of radio and television, tends to take its lead from what is on the agenda from other news outlets during the day and then exercise editorial judgement in relation to the news they feel their listeners and viewers will find interesting. An additional factor for television news is that it needs vision to accompany a news story. This means TV producers need to send crews to cover stories or they may take footage from corporate sources, assuming the video has been sufficiently objectively prepared.

Within each media outlet there are reporters, many with particular topic specializations, editors and opinion writers. While editors quite often allocate stories to reporters, reporters also initiate stories they believe will be of interest to their editors. From the corporate perspective, relationship-building over time covers all these components of a newsroom.

Factors around being in the media

From the media perspective, there is only one criterion for information being in the media and that is whether it is sufficiently newsworthy. While news judgements can be personal, there are many objective factors that contribute to determining what makes news. Two researchers who looked at determinants of coverage in the business press discerned seven factors – company size, level of unexpectedness of the news, industry relevance, the extent of negativity of the news, timing of the release, effectiveness in the dissemination process and ease of access to a company for comment on the news.[2] These factors highlight some purely objective factors – that large companies with relevant news have an advantage in achieving media coverage. The research also points to some of the mechanics of providing information to the media – it needs to be received by the media in a timely fashion for the daily news cycle and a spokesperson needs to be available to speak to journalists. The survey also highlighted the media's predilection for negative news, which can often take precedence over good news.

These factors provide some guidance to companies around how to increase the likelihood of media coverage when they release information publicly to stock exchange platforms. Companies cannot change the actual nature of what it is they are announcing but they can pay attention to giving the information a news angle and interesting headline while presenting the information in a format that encapsulates it within the wider corporate story. Making an announcement early in the day is always going to increase likelihood of media coverage than later in the day. Implementing dissemination to media outlets and journalists likely to find the news relevant is also helpful for improving chances of coverage. Having a spokesperson available to speak to journalists is an essential part of the process of achieving coverage. Unavailability means journalists will move on to other stories to cover. Time pressures can mean that news announcements containing quotes written in ways journalists find helpful can be adopted when journalists are facing deadline pressures to complete their stories. Negative news requires companies preparing in advance for how a spokesperson engages with the media to provide a broader perspective around the news, especially since uncooperative or combative attitudes in dealing with journalists around negative news can inflame attention and achieve unwanted, and perhaps unwarranted, coverage.

While company size is an objective determinant of whether an announcement has a high likelihood of being covered, its news value and the input of public relations techniques can also make a difference that helps achieve media coverage, despite company size. Media relationships play a part, as does presentation of the announcement within a news-oriented framework. It is these processes that can help smaller companies achieve media coverage, overcoming the disadvantage of their size.

Some surveys of the Australia media show that public relations sources play an important role in media coverage. Two different surveys found that between 60 to 75 per cent of stories in the up-front sections of newspapers had a public relations source while in finance sections, between 50 and 80 per cent of stories had public relations sources. One of the surveys found 24 per cent of articles were republished press releases but under a journalist's by-line.[3]

The combination of research findings and the way the media works highlights several layers of interconnectedness between the media and corporate financial information. Company announcements provide the raw material that comprises media coverage. Companies can enhance the likelihood of coverage if they introduce news values to their announcements. While journalists may not want to acknowledge in too public a way how much they rely on corporate information, it is a valuable resource in helping them do their jobs. For companies, there are clear lessons that well-prepared corporate announcements are of value to the media and ultimately to shareholders as they contribute to media coverage of the ongoing corporate story.

How the media views companies

Given the value for companies from being in the media, it is helpful to have an understanding of how the media goes about its processes in assessing the massive amount of information it absorbs and converts into news coverage in the course of a day. While what actually happens in the media is the outcome of experienced editors over the years passing on their knowledge to younger journalists, one news outlet in 2012 published its guidelines for reporters and editors after keeping it as an internal document for many years. Matthew Winkler's *The Bloomberg Way* sets out how Bloomberg News seeks to provide definitive coverage of economies, markets, companies and industries worldwide. Its guidance on how reporters should assess information and then construct headlines, leading into the all-important first four paragraphs[4], is a helpful guide to companies when considering the presentation of their own announcements. While companies have an obligation to present their announcements in a way that reflects legally the information they are seeking to convey, the Bloomberg process provides guidance about information that it is helpful to include. It is necessary for journalists to interpret corporate news in the context of other events in markets and the surrounding environment but if they are given effective raw material in the first place, then companies are becoming involved in the process of helping their announcements achieve media coverage.

Many corporate announcements provide quotations from the chief executive and, while journalists may need to add other quotes that are more relevant to their reports, quotes in a corporate release that reflect a conversational tone combined with relevant content are more likely to be reported.

Bloomberg reports reflect a "show don't tell" style of reporting, with an emphasis on nouns and verbs, not adjectives and adverbs. "Let nouns, verbs, facts, figures and anecdotes do the work", says the guide, quoting Mark Twain approvingly: "When you catch an adjective, kill it."[5] Precision and brevity are hallmarks of the style, as well as doing away with jargon and clichés. The past tense and active voice are how Bloomberg expects writing should be presented. Successful Bloomberg headlines should reflect five elements: surprise, what's at stake, names that make the news, conflict and conflict resolution.[6] These may not be the way corporations want to present their information but the guideline shows how company announcements will be interpreted and what the media deems interesting.

One pointer to corporate media relations is that Bloomberg wants its reporters to get to know the important companies, executives, investors and experts that are relevant to areas they are covering and find out what makes them influential.[7] This supports companies reaching out to reporters to build relationships since it is mutually beneficial, a reflection of the way public relations theorist Ledingham views how public relations can be described. Bloomberg also encourages its reporters to show enterprise in developing story ideas,[8] making them receptive to ideas from companies around trends and issues that might connect with company stories. Since reporting starts with research,[9] background factual material is also helpful when relevant to story ideas.

Journalists at Bloomberg are expected to recognize news and explain it so there is no mistaking its importance. At the heart of a reporter's job, Winkler says, is the interview, for which preparation is necessary as well as displaying good manners. While the strategy for an interview is to gain good information and the key quote that supports the theme of the story, listening to what people say can stimulate follow up questions that will yield detail and examples.[10] "The best reporters know how to collect the details and anecdotes that will give their stories colour and credibility."[11] Reporters are responsible for the accuracy of their stories, which they need to verify with editors, whose role is to be guardians of language and information, ensuring each story is clear, logical and accurate.[12]

> Editors, as Bloomberg's gatekeepers for news judgment and language, can never be too rigorous. Nothing asserted in a story should get by without questions: How do we know this? What are the facts? Are you sure about this? How do you know it's true? What are the examples? Have you seen it? If you haven't seen it, how do you know it's true?[13]

Bloomberg's structure includes team leaders, who are the equivalent of a section editor in a newspaper or magazine, and also a bureau chief, all of whom are expected to create an environment for the pursuit of news.

When it comes to reporting company news, Bloomberg, like any news outlet, is on the receiving end of thousands of company press releases each day. When companies make news, Bloomberg sees its job as being to provide the detail and perspective of daily newspapers with the real-time speed of a news service. Technology helps with the speed of this process but it "can't judge the importance of the news in the release. It can't discern what was left out of the release that people need to know."[14] The role of corporate communications professionals in developing the corporate story can be helpful to reporters in providing elements of this surrounding context. However, reporters also need to cover how the company's stock price has been affected by the news and occasionally what analysts think of the news as well. Market reaction to a company announcement can become the lead to how the news is reported.[15] The extent of a company's debt has also become a key item in reporting any news, particularly in the current post-financial crisis era, since debt is a guide to a company's health.

> Any story about the fortunes of a company – earnings, acquisitions, bankruptcy, executive changes, regulatory investigations, a change in its bond rating or change in capital structure such as share or debt sale – needs to include at least one paragraph about debt. Evaluating debt helps us understand whether a company is becoming a safer or more risky investment.[16]

When it comes to reporting company earnings, Bloomberg likes to focus on the element of surprise in the announcement and those without any tend to receive minimal attention.[17] The search for a surprise begins before announcements are made, with reporters reviewing previous announcements to anticipate whether forthcoming news might contain a surprise. Analysts make forecasts of what earnings they expect companies to produce and Bloomberg, and most other news outlets, like to compare these estimates with a company's actual performance as a gauge of the market's likely reaction to surprise. Bloomberg reporters look beyond the earnings statement to the balance sheet and cash flow statement to discover other news angles, as well as looking for comments on forecasts, acquisition intentions, industry trends, the economy's impact and the direction of commodity prices.[18] These connected aspects of news are a pointer to where media priorities lie and so companies can make themselves useful to reporters by including information on these topics in their releases.

Reports on earnings are expected to focus on the bottom line, despite how a company might present its explanatory information around financial performance. This approach "ensures that investors aren't subjected to manipulated numbers in ways that don't meet accounting standards. Net income/loss measures all companies by the same parameters, giving our global audience a uniform scale for comparison."[19] Bloomberg reporters are urged to:

> read company releases with scepticism to ensure that the information is transparent … So-called cash earnings and ebitda, or earnings before interest, taxes, depreciation and amortisation, are among measures of financial performance that confuse more than clarify. Beware of the labels *pro forma*, *special*, *one-time* and *adjusted*. All are warning flags that the earnings numbers have been massaged to look better than they would be under a standard presentation. Companies often try to disguise costs or expenses that are a regular part of doing business.[20]

This attitude is a lesson to companies concerned about their reputation in providing financial information. With reporters under instruction not to be taken in by companies seeking to divert their attention away from conforming to accounting standards, companies achieve a better media relations outcome by accepting a bottom-line focus while providing cogent surrounding explanation to aid understanding.

In terms of style, it is the Bloomberg preference to make comparisons with a year earlier and to give the percentage change for profit and revenue. Active verbs are preferred in describing directions of the key figures. It is also the most recent reporting period that can give the most meaningful understanding of the trend in performance, often involving extracting a quarterly performance from nine months' performance figures. Stories tend to keep numbers to a minimum and include descriptions that put the numbers into perspective, such as the biggest increase in ten years. The industry perspective needs to be included as well as any personal angles that can add flavour to the story, such as the tenure of the chief executive.[21]

Media mechanics

When stock exchange listed companies release announcements publicly, engaging with the media requires a combination of judgement and understanding of the basic mechanics of how the media works. The media consists of many outlets that deal with news in differing ways. With most print media outlets also having websites, they are dealing with news instantly just like wire services and dedicated online news outlets. If companies want to make their news available to the media for consideration they need to have in place a distribution mechanism. In the US, most companies utilize the services of PR Newswire, which distributes announcements to journalists and editors and some online news outlets publish these announcements in that format as they select news relevant to specialized readerships. There are the equivalent of PR Newswire revives in most countries. An alternative is for companies to establish their own media distribution lists, which, with the help of software that enables individually addressed group emails, enables a news distribution to be personalized to journalists and editors. The advantage of this method is that it also creates an opportunity to craft a message to accompany an announcement attached to an individually addressed email. This message, in conforming to disclosure requirements, cannot add new information but it can encapsulate the news into the context of the corporate story and provide useful background information that may aid media reporting.

Timing of making an announcement is another factor that can influence whether news might be reported by the media. An announcement earlier in the day allows more time for consideration by journalists and editors than if it is made late in the day or evening. Some basic mechanics of companies releasing news to the market as it relates to the media is that there are certain times of the day and week when the likelihood of attracting media attention can be increased. A general rule is that "early in the day and early in the week" is a way of improving media prospects. This emanates from how the media day evolves. While wire service journalists work in shifts and are covering the news of the world around the clock, the metropolitan daily newspapers have traditionally been more focused on the production of news in time for the papers to be printed for next-day delivery. While this is changing as newspapers pay increasing attention to online editions, with some journalists beginning early in the day to pick up on overseas markets news, the traditional print journalist day for a daily newspaper would be from around 10.00 am to 7.00 pm, with many exceptions involving late or early breaking stories. However, while the ultimate deadline for a metropolitan daily might be around 9.00 pm, the majority of what appears in the newspaper is decided by the 4.00 pm news conference. This conference involves all editors and section editors, with the layout and advertising reviewed and ultimate space for each section determined. Flexibility has to be maintained for late and important news, with some later stories swamping those written earlier. An advantage for companies of being early in the news process is that stories can at least be written, quotes exchanged with journalists and stories in the system, sometimes appearing a day or two later if their news value outranks other stories on subsequent slower news days.

A common tendency is that news builds as the week progresses. Thursday is often the busiest day for daily newspapers and Friday is a day when deadlines come forward earlier to meet print deadlines for larger weekend editions. Some sections of the large weekend editions are printed well ahead of the rest of the paper's final deadline and to reach regional locations, some Saturday editions are on the plane during Friday afternoon.

Some companies like to think that by announcing bad news late on a Friday they can escape scrutiny. What this strategy does not appreciate is that financial journalists also work on a Sunday to produce Monday's edition. With very little news breaking on a Sunday, journalists have the spare time to trawl the "bad news avoidance" efforts on Fridays, with the outcome that they can achieve publication in Monday's edition. For companies that like to pursue some form of playing down their bad news with the media, a better option is probably late Thursday, the busiest day of the week, with little time left for a hangover of scrutiny on the next day.

Some research on attempting to hide bad news on a Friday has concluded it might not be such a good idea. While more bad news is announced on Fridays than any other days, investors have become more aware of this phenomenon and stock returns reflect a higher sensitivity to this type of news, especially for firms with high financial visibility. What the research shows is that the benefits of seeking to avoid the spotlight by a Friday announcement have disappeared over time.[22]

The mainstream electronic media of radio and television, apart from specialist programmes, does not devote a lot of space to daily business news unless it is about significant transactions or large company results. In terms of news programmes on television, the news-gathering process starts early in the morning with the day consumed with producing vision to make up a half-hour news bulletin. By the time a TV news programme covers international events, local, state and federal political developments, the weather and sport, there is little time left for business stories. Some occasional exceptions are human health stories, which can have relevance to life sciences companies. While chances may be slim of business items making it to the TV news, the process is to notify the TV news chief of staff to see if an item might have a chance of making it to the newsroom's whiteboard list of events. Radio newsrooms have more frequent news bulletins but they are briefer and so again business news is often overlooked.

With the electronic media, coverage opportunities are more often with specialist business programmes, such as Sunday morning programmes, late evening business programmes and pay television business news, which often runs in city dealing rooms. While the focus is mostly on larger companies it is important to remember these programmes are run by journalists who have a sense of news. Corporate developments can be made newsworthy when put into the wider context of a corporate and industry story, supported by independent expert commentary.

What companies want to achieve

Most management teams of listed companies are focused on implementing their business strategies, looking to achieve growth and improving returns for investors. When they think of the media, they see a powerful force in society, which they hope may be favourable to their objectives. As announcements are being prepared, a question often asked is how will the media interpret this? Companies are aware of the power of criticism that can appear in the media and how it can have an impact on stock price. As one researcher found, media content can be a proxy for investor sentiment, with high levels of media pessimism predicting downward pressure on market prices.[23] Companies wanting to see a positive flow of media coverage every time they make an announcement have an expectation that is not aligned with how the media works. Media definitions of what is considered newsworthy are governed by company size, how company news fits into the pattern of the day and the personalities involved. The media wants to interpret company news into a bigger picture story, which might bring in the views of other investors and relevance of the news to the wider economy. Companies do not always see things this way. They often have a view that their announcement should be printed just as they released it. They are also not always prepared to have their news ignored and while their preference might be to have negative news disappear, to their annoyance this is just the news the media likes to find and make prominent.

When it comes to earnings announcements, companies provide their interpretation to the market along with quotes from the chief executive and expect to see this repeated in the media. When this does not happen, companies tend to be critical of journalists and point to their lack of close knowledge about a business and their inexperience. What is missing from this perspective is an appreciation that journalists are working to different priorities to those of companies and some thought needs to be applied to bridge this gap.

Companies also have an expectation that journalists work in the same way they do. For example, appointments made to meet journalists or have journalists attend a corporate event can be seen as immutable from a corporate perspective but journalists have to respond to the news cycle, which governs how they order their priorities, often leading to last-minute changes to previously given commitments.

Matching media and company needs

Matching the way the media works and the corporate perspective is more a case of building understanding on the part of companies around how they can adapt to media processes that are unlikely to change. One particular initiative companies can take, which meets a media need, is move beyond viewing individual announcements in isolation and to make a connection between them and the company's larger story. The media in reporting news does exactly that. The media needs to report what a particular item of news means, for a company and the market, rather than regurgitating a company announcement that is based on assumptions that everyone is following a company's story and progress. For companies, putting their news into this wider context themselves means they are increasing the likelihood of achieving media coverage because they are providing information in a more useful way for the media, and also for the market, as their announcements become more informative in embracing the wider corporate story.

While the media does not often adopt a company's announcement headline, companies can nevertheless move towards writing media-oriented headings to their announcements to give them a boost in attracting initial attention. Writing styles will vary but using a media orientation that leaves out adjectives and adverbs is another process companies can use to make their material more easily adopted by the media. Similarly with quotes, those written in plain English have a greater chance of being reproduced than the stilted self-congratulatory tone that many announcements can slip into. These processes all have a similar orientation, which is to present information as news in a style the media can adopt so that its value as media content is enhanced.

Getting into the media

While news of a negative nature is something many companies might like to have unreported in the media, there are many times companies do want to achieve media coverage because of the value it can deliver in increasing recognition, with flow on effects to stock price. It is competitive to achieve mainstream media coverage, since there is not the space for all company news to be covered nor does every announcement have news value that might outweigh other competing news.

While company announcements on a particular day are subject to the news weighing machine of the media, the techniques of public relations can contribute to higher levels of media coverage for companies. Among the reasons some announcements are covered by the media is that companies have built relationships with journalists, making it easier to talk to them about news that has been announced. Conversations like this provide an opportunity to give background information and position the news into a broader and more interesting context. These conversations need to be managed around when journalists are not consumed with deadlines and also require an ability to impart genuine information rather than make the inquiry journalists find infuriating, which is "did you receive our news release?"

One of the premises underlying public relations is that the media is a marketplace of ideas. This means creating ideas around companies that make them of interest to individual journalists can also enhance the likelihood of achieving media coverage. The process requires research around trends and wider topics beyond a company since this is the type of information journalists need, with a particular company being a reference point to a larger story. This public relations process may require patience and perseverance in finding a journalist who takes up the idea with enthusiasm. An advantage of this type of coverage is that it contributes to companies achieving a higher profile, which in turn is helpful when announcements are made since there is wider recognition of the firm. Editors are always asking journalists if they have some stories to develop and report. In the busy world of the media this is hard as journalists short of time are busy with daily announcements and often do not have the luxury of time to research related issues. Companies able to develop good storylines and provide research to back them up are providing information of genuine value to journalists and are helping them in their jobs by contributing to a story flow that journalists can present to editors.

Listed companies also have the advantage of presenting opportunities for journalists to participate in events, such as investor days, operations tours, press conferences around earnings announcements or earnings calls. These all contribute to building media relationships if invitations are extended to journalists as well as analysts. Some companies prefer to keep the media separate from these events, thinking that it creates enhanced opportunities for journalists to obtain independent commentary on a company but journalists do this anyway and are often encouraged by editors to obtain diverse views.

Developing news flow

While regulations around disclosure require public release of information that is price-sensitive, the extent of what fits this definition is met with varying interpretations by companies. Some companies veer towards just focusing on earnings announcements and not much in between while others can release too much, perhaps containing much that is less important. What many investors want is a flow of information around how a company's strategy is progressing and if this is contained within the bounds of genuine information release and sound communication values, it will represent a news flow that will have value for the media. In the process, it contributes to adding to a company's media profile if it achieves coverage.

A critical part of developing news flow is that the information has to conform to a definition of news if it is to be effective. It would be news if it represented developments within the business that have an effect on strategy and additionally it has to be written and presented as news if it is to have an impact on the market and have a chance of being reported by the media.

While news needs to be current, sometimes items of newsworthy information in a company release can be overlooked in the wake of other diverse company news released on the day. Repackaging these overlooked items and using them in interviews with journalists can also contribute to news flow and achieving media coverage. At times of the year when many companies are releasing earnings information, journalists have too much information to contend with. In quieter times, they can often be looking for stories and a collection of overlooked company news can then be fashioned into a definition of a newsworthy story.

Meeting the media

The role of chief executive of a stock exchange-listed company brings with it an obligation to have contact with the media. Some chief executives like the prospect and process while others can be more reluctant and see it as risky. For journalists, it is an essential part of reporting if they are covering a story on a company that they have access to the company's main public figure. The requirement for a journalist is to make an interview yield key details for a story and quotes that will provide a theme for it. For many chief executives it can be an exercise in risk management, in trying not to make mistakes and to avoid being misreported as a result of the conversation.

Both sides of the equation, when companies meet the media, have differing objectives. Company spokespersons have the advantage of knowing their subject matter and being fully conversant with operations, announcements made and the industry sector into which the company fits. The challenge for companies can be how to make this body of information interesting to a journalist. If a company's objective in a media interview is to make itself a small target to reduce the likelihood of error, then objectives can come down to responding briefly to questions asked. However, if objectives shift to wanting to ensure journalists understand the company story, then this information needs a news edge and to be told with anecdotes to enhance storytelling values.

Journalists have the objective of gathering information that fits a storyline they have developed. Their questions to achieve this could come from many differing directions or be persistent in a particular direction. A common objective for journalists in reporting news is to explain why something has happened so they need to explore background reasoning. Journalists talk to many sources and some of them may have suggested a particular line of inquiry to a company to gather further explanation around news that has been announced.

While journalists know that companies want to maximize positive media coverage while minimizing risks, companies can learn a lot when they meet the media if they also conduct some questioning with journalists around what they need to know and what their objectives are. If companies are able to glean this information in advance of beginning an interview then it helps in understanding how to marshal information that answers the questions. It may also help to influence the line of inquiry a journalist is following and establish an opportunity to mould a company's story to fit with what a journalist wants to know. Understanding a journalist's objectives helps to establish a more level playing field between the two sides and can convert an interview into more of an opportunity than a threat.

Achieving positive outcomes in dealing with the media has advantages for companies because of the way positive media coverage can influence the various markers around stock price. It is not possible that every experience in dealing with the media can be positive since the media has a different agenda to that of companies. However, there are a number of steps companies can take to enhance the likelihood of achieving media coverage that is more beneficial than if it had not occurred. Among the opportunities a company can grasp in meeting the media are to enthuse journalists about a company story and to build relationships with them for the future. Both sides gain from preparation in advance of meeting. While journalists know their media perspective, they cannot know a company as thoroughly as those within a company. This should not be seen as a journalist being insufficiently prepared but more an opportunity to provide a story in an interesting way to bring about understanding.

One of the risks for journalists in conducting interviews with chief executives is returning to the newsroom and having to tell an editor that a chief executive really had nothing interesting to say. Editors see this as the fault of a journalist for not asking the right questions but the blame can equally lie with companies in not making their

Case study

James Hardie – a press release and lessons for corporate governance

On 15 February 2001, the directors of ASX-listed James Hardie Industries Limited met in Sydney. In one of several court cases over the next decade emanating from this meeting, a defence barrister for one of the directors described it as "perhaps the most important meeting in the company's corporate history".[24] That history had been lengthy, with the company established in 1888 and becoming a blue chip stock. In 1920, the building products company incorporated a subsidiary, James Hardie Asbestos Ltd.,[25] which in decades to come would be a cause of many problems which came to a head in the 2001 board meeting.

During the twentieth century, James Hardie became Australia's biggest asbestos manufacturer with factories in each state, mines in South Africa and Canada, and factories in Indonesia and Malaysia. Its products were widespread and in 1978, Hardie chairman John Reid a descendent of the founder of the company, said: "Every time you walk into an office building, a home, or factory; every time you put your foot on the brake, ride a train, see a bulldozer at work ... Every time you do or see one of these things the chances are that a product from the James Hardie group of companies has a part in it."[26] Over the years, awareness began to build about the health hazards of prolonged exposure to asbestos, causing lung disease that over time could become fatal. In 1979 the company placed health warnings on its products and in 1987 Hardie stopped manufacturing any asbestos-related products.[27] Subsequently, health claims about asbestos began to mount and Hardie found itself facing quite significant rising liabilities. It was estimated that by 2020, at least 55,000 Australians would have died from asbestosis or mesothelioma, with many having a claim against Hardie.[28]

As claims began to escalate, Hardie in 2001 decided to take steps to protect its shareholders from the rising damage. In the lead up to its February board meeting it prepared two measures. One was to transfer its asbestos liabilities to a separate vehicle, known as the Medical Research and Compensation Foundation. The other was to move the domicile of the remainder of the company offshore, to the lower taxing Netherlands. It was the press release announcing these moves that contained the seeds of danger for the board and senior executives. The statement issued to the ASX said "the foundation 'has sufficient funds to meet all legitimate compensation claims' and the scheme would deliver 'certainty' because it was 'fully funded'"[29]. As it turned out, the fund ran out of money within three years, with Hardie having provided A$293 million, which was $1.5 billion short of what was needed.[30]

The press release and the claims it made were the subject of litigation for the following decade, ultimately reaching the High Court. At the January and February 2001 board meetings, which decided on the terms of the release, there was some urgency to approve the trust fund because of an impending change to accounting standards that would require Hardie to assess not just present but also future asbestos liabilities if they were still in the Hardie accounts.[31] The board also considered a media strategy around the announcement, adopting the ploy that news of the new fund should be included with a quarterly results announcement so that the news would be covered by finance journalists and not come to the wider attention of general news reporters.[32] When the High Court judgment was finally handed down in May 2012 in relation to the press release, seven non-executive directors and three executives received fines and bans for making a misleading statement to the market. They had approved the statement at a board meeting and subsequently approved minutes of the meeting, making them liable for what had been released.

The business community reaction was that this sort of legal decision had raised the bar and made the role of being a director of a public company just that much harder. However, the regulator, which instigated the legal action, saw it more as a timely reminder for directors to ensure they do not release information that is inaccurate. It was not that the law had changed but instead: "This ruling clarifies the obligations of directors, but it's nothing more than common sense", the chairman of the regulator said.[33]

The inadequacy of funding of the Medical Research and Compensation Foundation became the subject of a public inquiry leading to an eventual agreement between Hardie, government and unions for the establishment of a new fund to provide long-term compensation for asbestos claims. This was approved by Hardie shareholders in 2007.[34]

Today, reflecting adherence to high standards of corporate governance, James Hardie carries information on its website about its asbestos history and claims, along with the story around its current operations. James Hardie is a substantial company, the largest manufacturer of cement fibre products in the US, Australia, New Zealand and the Philippines, has annual sales of US$1.3 billion and employs 2,700 people.[35]

stories interesting enough. While chief executives might be in the position of having to answer questions from journalists they also have the advantage of being able to shape responses that can enliven the interview with interesting information. This is part of the preparation corporate communications professionals can contribute in helping chief executives with this process. The risk management approach to preparing for interviews comes down to preparing key messages, which is appropriate for some aspects of the interview but they also need to be backed up by convincing facts, figures and anecdotes. This brings out the components of a corporate story, combining facts numbers and narrative, while adding elements of human interest through anecdotal examples.

Meeting the media has similarities to giving an investment presentation. It is more informal but contains similar disclosure boundaries. Being clear about these boundaries can be combined with politeness and a sense of storytelling. By making disclosed facts interesting and by giving insights around pursuing a business strategy within a sector that has characteristics that can be outlined, the sense of a corporate story can be woven in to answering a journalist's questions. Some interviews take place because of a journalist initiative or news announcement being an attraction, while others are the outcome of relationship-building from a public relations perspective. In either sense, there is a selling component in the interview from the company's perspective, since the objective is to convey not only understanding but to have a journalist return to the newsroom with a sense of having a story that will meet an editor's definition of news.

Among other aspects of preparation for a media interview from a corporate perspective are considering areas of information a company does not want to cover, such as comments on competitors or hints about new developments that might be in the pipeline, and being reminded to avoid them. Allied to this is whether to give journalists information off the record, on the understanding that it is not to be published but as an aid to explanation and understanding of how a company might be dealing with particular issues. Some company spokespersons like to follow this practice as a way of strengthening a relationship with a journalist and there are many public relations practitioners and journalists who like and respect the process. However, it is a practice that can be avoided since it does bring an added element of risk in dealing with the media and is not seen as essential by many journalists. Relationships can be built in far more straightforward ways, such as returning phone calls when journalists are seeking quotes or information and providing useful background information as it arises. This straightforwardness in itself is a reflection of integrity and genuineness and can be a far more effective tool than going off the record.

In meeting journalists there can be obvious differences depending on the type of media they are representing. Print journalists are looking for good quotes and information, TV and radio journalists are looking for an articulate presenter who will answer questions as asked, regional media journalists are wanting a subject to connect with their local audience and specialist publications are looking for details relating to a select and well-informed group. Communication professionals would brief a chief executive on these nuances, which can also be platforms for slight variances to presenting the corporate story.

Preparation for all these occasions of meeting the media will allow bringing together a combination of news and anecdotes relevant to a particular media outlet. Television and radio appearances that are live can have an added degree of nervousness but all interviewers are essentially looking for is interview subjects who can just be themselves while being articulate around topics they know well. This is not an insurmountable task for a chief executive, especially when there is time to have a briefing on a journalist's needs and a reminder of the key facts, numbers and narrative to bring together for the occasion. This type of preparation suits the naturalness of the occasion rather than prepared scripts, which can add formality and limit capability to bring in appropriate anecdotes in response to questions.

A media briefing involving a group of journalists can have differing dynamics. Just as with groups of analysts, these briefings mostly tend to go smoothly but it is also possible they can be derailed by a questioner out to seek particular answers to issues. The public nature of the event requires considered but natural responses, representative of a leader able to outline a strategy and corporate story. A more common occurrence with media briefings is journalists arriving at various times and the group as a whole needing to be informed around the background to news. The storytelling approach of combining facts, numbers, narrative and anecdotes is a useful formula for managing all these eventualities.

An issue that arises for some chief executives in dealing with the media is that of media training. Media training can take the form of filling in chief executives on how the media works but it can also introduce an element of stage management that can be frustrating to journalists and audiences who want to hear a genuine voice rather than one that bridges too glibly to key messages. Most chief executives who rise to that position are quite prepared for the actual circumstances of meeting the media but can benefit from a briefing before the event to sharpen their approach around content, likely question areas and awkward issues to avoid. This content-oriented preparation can be more effective than superficial training, which can tend to encourage an approach towards providing information despite questions being asked.

Managing bad news

For corporations, having to reveal bad news publicly is not an enviable position, especially for chief executives who have to take responsibility for it. Bad news means that things have not gone according to plan, that expectations have not been met and that the future will turn out to be different to that previously portrayed. As companies think about this in terms of communicating with the media, they naturally become concerned about potential negative headlines and the disastrous effect this could have on stock price. There is a recognition from the corporate perspective that the media likes bad news. It has a greater news value and will achieve more prominence than good news. Among the alternatives companies have are to play down the negative aspects, offsetting it with good news or to be upfront about what has happened.

There is not a simple solution around presenting any aspect of bad news but perspective and context count for a lot. The market and media can be understanding when facts are presented straightforwardly and not hidden from view. Bad news needs a comprehensive explanation not only around what has happened but what action is being taken to ameliorate circumstances. This action being taken can become the lead in media stories if presented in the context of a company's strategy and corporate story. It is not that this context should swamp and take precedence over the bad news being presented. This has to be outlined at the beginning but it needs a cogent surrounding explanation.

If bad news eventuates, there can be sympathy from the market if there is already an appreciation of sound management and a track record of transparent disclosure and communication. While good management teams are necessarily concerned about the minimization of risk, there is never any guarantee of market conditions remaining perpetually buoyant. Fluctuations are going to have an impact on performance, even if only in the short term. A successful management team and company focused beyond the short term have a context in which bad news can be presented.

Bad news for listed companies can come in many guises – changed market conditions, failed initiatives, executive fallout, scandals, missed targets and deteriorating economic circumstances. Some of these may be obvious to the market already and, as market jargon would say, are factored into the stock price. Some events can be included as part of a regular earnings announcement, while others of a larger nature need immediate acknowledgement. Whatever the timing, an attempt to play down negative events or seek to reduce their real importance can backfire and lead to market disillusionment. While it is hard to generalize about bad news, placing it into a wider corporate and strategic context can improve understanding of the circumstances in which events have occurred. Depending on the news, it can seem to be too much of a public relations exercise if context gets in the way of being up front and frank about what has gone wrong. However, there is a difference between providing valuable surrounding information compared with excuses. Among some examples of seeking to offset bad news with broader considerations could be:

- placing the bad news in the context of the ongoing development of the corporate story;
- researching various aspects of industry conditions and providing economic statistics that add objective information to support the corporate experience;
- wrapping the bad news within a corporate strategy explanation that adds a sense of proportionality to events in the context of other, presumably positive, initiatives and aspects of corporate development;
- providing detail around the events that have actually happened, adding credibility to explanations around the course of action being implemented to counter the bad news;

- bringing in the wider context of developing opportunities for the company and its markets;
- being careful with quantification of the extent of the bad news since it is even worse to underestimate and then have to announce again later that things are worse than first thought.

Often with bad news it can be helpful for companies to be ready to act quickly so that the initiative is on the side of swift disclosure. When bad news is broken by others, such as the media, companies are immediately on the back foot. While the following quote needs to be adjusted for the circumstances around disclosure by stock exchange-listed companies, here is what one journalist had to say about management processes around bad news:

> Journalists love a bad news story. Let's be honest, as a journalist myself I don't mind saying that reporters get a much bigger kick out of investigating and writing up a bad news story than a good news story ... By simply picking up the telephone and telling the journalist what is happening you are retaining control of the story. By doing this the journalist will not feel that it is their story as they haven't found out the information through a tip off and haven't come to you with it ... There is nothing worse ... than [to] allow a journalist to write "the MD was unavailable to comment" in a news story. That simply allows the journalist to speculate about the possible problem and also gives readers the opportunity to make up their own minds and, worse still, post their thoughts in the comments section.[36]

Writing announcements

The media is practised at dealing with announcements written in many differing styles and at discerning news values. However, journalists are on the receiving end of hundreds of items of news in a day and are under time pressure to pick what they deem most newsworthy for publication on a particular day. From the corporate perspective, there are often many hands involved in producing announcements, with procedures involving disclosure committees, legal input, approval processes and protocols about releasing news to the market. The outcome of all this can often be a loss in communication and news values, which may lead to announcements being overlooked by the media, not being covered and losing potential to have an impact on stock price.

While news in itself has an objective rating in the eyes of media editors, companies can give their announcements a better chance of achieving media coverage if they apply a media perspective to the words, language and format of announcements they make. This means applying the values of journalism, which means not only an attention to a headline but also the expression, involving shorter sentences, no adverbs and adjectives and word economy. Additionally, it means not treating an announcement in isolation on the assumption that everyone has been following corporate progress. Giving announcements a news angle means not just making an announcement but saying what it means and putting it into the context of the corporate story to give some proportionality to its importance.

Many companies when they make announcements prefer to include promotional language in them to give them their own expression of importance as a way of encouraging readers to view them the same way. Time pressures in the daily media mean that journalists use more press releases than they reject but when they do use them, they tend to rely on the information, not the language if it involves promotional language, according to one researcher. There is a greater likelihood that special interest or industry media may repeat promotional language but the business sections of the media ignore this sort of language in their reporting. The research also points out that press releases using the language of news reporting and seeking to be more objective have a greater likelihood of being adopted by the media.[37] This does not preclude the use of positive language, which other research has found to be beneficial in the way it can influence market reaction, since there is a difference with language that is strongly and overtly promotional.

Research on the media's role in proxy fights tends to reinforce this view, with the media being equally as important a player in these campaigns. While media coverage tends to be balanced in these fights, the media contributes to framing issues of importance and in the majority of cases, "the side that was more successful in shaping financial media coverage ended up winning the election". In these fights "the news release remains the most effective way to broadly disseminate information to the media", with the research also showing there was a significant correlation between issues emphasized in campaign news releases and those given the most attention in financial media coverage. The implication is that these issues were made clear by being in plain language to make them easier to single out to drive campaigns.[38]

While the mainstream media may not use a lot of the exaggerated language they find in company announcements, they will look at the quotes from the chief executive. Time and news value permitting, journalists will also call and speak to chief executives to have them talk about the news and respond to other questions to add independent journalistic input to reporting from news releases. However, given time pressures, quotes from news releases will be reproduced if they are written with journalistic credibility. Quotes provide a good opportunity to bring in the corporate story because they meet the journalistic criterion of saying what the news means, which is something of a style template for writing quotes. Too often quotes in company announcements are self-congratulatory and stilted, not written in language that reflects how someone would actually speak.

Social media

Social media is being increasingly adopted in investor relations. Its main advantage is instant distribution to people who have indicated in advance they want to be kept up to date by a company. The common forms of social media adopted by companies are Twitter and a corporate Facebook page. Twitter invites followers to register to follow news so they receive a brief message in 140 characters. The advantage of this process is that it begins a conversation, instantly news has been released publicly.

While social media is ultimately an endpoint of corporate communications strategy and its content, there is a groundswell towards using it as the following recent statistics show:

- 79 per cent of the top 100 companies in the Fortune Global 500 use at least one social media platform;[39]
- 62 per cent of Fortune 500 companies have at least one Twitter account;[40]
- 63 per cent of corporate use of Twitter in the US is for investor relations;[41]
- 58 per cent of institutional investors and sell-side analysts in the US and Europe believe new media will become more important in their investment decisions;[42]

- 75 per cent of online news consumers have this news forwarded to them;[43]
- Australia has the highest use in the world of mobile phones for social networking;[44]
- 88 per cent of investor relations officers in the US recognize the importance of mobile communication for their work, although currently only 22 per cent of US companies use mobile for investor relations;[45]
- while nine out of ten US wealth managers prefer face-to-face communication with companies, 82 per cent of their clients prefer electronic communication.[46]

However, social media is more than just a distribution mechanism, with a number of benefits including that it:

- connects with audiences that matter, principally because they have to register an interest to receive communication;
- starts conversations and strengthens existing relationships;
- is a listening post for what others are saying about a corporation;
- provides a direct link to sharing a variety of news instantly;
- can be invaluable in contributing to crisis management;
- increases the extent to which a company's news is found in online search engines.

Perhaps a chief reason for the growing and widespread adoption of social media for business news is that it recognizes the wider connection of a listed company with the world around it. A company does not operate in isolation, it prospers through meaningful connections with its stakeholders. Adopting social media in effect reinforces that companies recognize it has become a stakeholder world and not just a stockholder world.

There are corporate governance risks in utilizing social media, which have led to reticence by some companies. Mistakes in using Twitter by celebrities have been the cause of public embarrassment and it could be disastrous for this to be translated into the corporate sphere. However, if social media operates under the umbrella of corporate governance guidelines then the risk of premature release of information is highly unlikely to happen. In fact, the brevity of a Twitter message enforces an adoption of news values in making the message seem worth exploring further. Recent SEC guidelines about the acceptability of social media as a disclosure channel, provided a company has notified stakeholders of it as one of the vehicles it uses, is going to be a significant factor of more widespread adoption of social media in investor relations.

A connection between being in the mainstream media and social media is that it adds another level of connection with relevant audiences. While company news may only be echoed by specialist followers in the social media sphere, the repetition of company news and commentary on social media can be fairly swift. Many specialist websites reproduce PR Newswire distributions of announcements and one analyst measured that it took an average of 2.5 hours for blog commentary to follow mainstream news.[47] While most news flows from mainstream media to blogs, this research from 2008 found that some 3.5 per cent of stories originated in blogs and then found their way to traditional media.

One attempt to link social media with securities trading produced a successful but short-lived experiment. Derwent Capital Markets established a hedge fund based on analysis of tweets to predict market direction. The strategy earned a return of 1.86 per cent in its first month but was then shut down with the technology sold as a trading tool. Commentators predict there could be more of this type of product emerging, although at the moment it is considered that direct news from trusted sources such as news wires and recognized mastheads is more trustworthy than social media sources.[48]

Media protocols

The direct effect of media coverage on stock prices means that companies need to have rules round how they engage with the media. Most companies have protocols around who can speak to the media on behalf of the company and the timing of this. This is usually an extension of disclosure policy, with the chief executive being the most common spokesperson, with other relevant senior executives sometimes included as part of building a media profile. Protocols do not usually cover how it is that companies should engage with the media, with this having become an area on which corporate communications professionals advise. However, media protocols can specify the format for making announcements and procedures for gaining approval for them before public release. Good management of these protocols should also involve processes for informing spokespersons about media inquiries since unanswered media calls can be damaging to a company's reputation. A company's preparedness to be open with the media and to respond to inquiry should be an underlying fundamental purpose of media protocols given the damage that implied negative media coverage can have on stock price.

If companies are to present themselves as being attractive to investors then having their stories reflected in media coverage is an important part of the communications process. Allied with this is how companies communicate with those who own the corporation, which is the subject of our next chapter.

Notes

1 Soltes (2009)
2 Solomon and Soltes (2011)
3 Bacon, W, et al, "Over Half Your News is Spin", 15 March 2010, www.crikey.com. au/2010/03/15/over-half-your-news-is-spin, and Pearson, M and Brand, J, *Sources of News and Current Affairs* (Australian Broadcasting Authority, Sydney: 2001)
4 Winkler, M, *The Bloomberg Way* (John Wiley & Sons, Hoboken, NJ: 2012), Chapter 4
5 Winkler (2012) p 34
6 Winkler (2012) pp 11–12
7 Winkler (2012) p 58
8 Winkler (2012) pp 95–96
9 Winkler (2012) p 102
10 Winkler (2012) p 113
11 Winkler (2012) p 114
12 Winkler (2012) p 118
13 Winkler (2012) pp 118–119
14 Winkler (2012) p 161
15 Winkler (2012) p 162
16 Winkler (2012) p 164
17 Winkler (2012) p 165
18 Winkler (2012) p 166
19 Winkler (2012) p 166

20 Winkler (2012) p 166–167

21 Winkler (2012) p 167–170

22 Zolotoy, L, "Hiding 'Bad' News on Fridays? Not Such a Good Idea!", 2009, http://works. bepress.com/leon_zolotoy/3/, p 1

23 Tetlock, PC, "Giving Content to Investor Sentiment: The Role of Media in the Stock Market", *The Journal of Finance*, LXII (3), 2007, p 1140

24 Quoted in Sexton, E, "Secrets of the Boardroom", *Sydney Morning Herald*, 25–26 October 2008

25 Sexton (2008)

26 Quoted in Verrender, I, "Hardie Seven Face Moment of Truth", *Sydney Morning Herald*, 5–6 May 2012

27 Verrender, I, "The Shameful Legacy of James Hardie", *Sydney Morning Herald*, 5–6 May 2012

28 Verrender, "Hardie Seven" (2012)

29 Quoted in Ackland, R, "Morality Question as Dust Will Never Settle", *Sydney Morning Herald*, 16 November 2012

30 Verrender, "Hardie Seven" (2012)

31 Lamont, L, "Bitter Taste for Board that Tried to Avoid 'Poison Pill'", *Sydney Morning Herald*, 4 May 2012

32 Lamont (2012)

33 Quoted in Main, A, "ASIC Cheers Hardie Ruling", *The Australian*, 4 May 2012

34 James Hardie website, Investor Relations, Asbestos Compensation, www.ir.jameshardie.com. au/jh/asbestos_compensation.jsp

35 James Hardie website, Investor Relations, About Us, www.ir.jameshardie.com.au/jh/ about_us.jsp

36 Draycott, R, "How to Manage Your Bad News", *The Drum*, 18 June 2012, www.thedrum. co.uk/opinion/2012/06/18/how-manage-bad-news#uYHcoEYugvkXheDr.99

37 Maat, HP, "How Promotional Language in Press Releases is Dealt With by Journalists", *Journal of Business Communication* 44 (1), 2007, pp 60–61

38 Ragas, M, "Words with Muscle", *IR Update*, NIRI, October 2010

39 Burson-Marsteller Blog, "Burson-Marsteller Fortune Global 100 Social Media Study", 23 February 2010, www.burson-marsteller.com/Innovation_and_insights/blogs_and_podcasts/ BM_Blog/Lists/Posts/Post.aspx?ID=160

40 Polchin, R, "Alphabet Soup: SM (Social Media)", 12 February 2013, www.icmi.com/ Blog/2013/February/Alphabet-Soup-SM-Social-Media

41 Joyce, S, "New Q4 Whitepaper: Public Company Use of Social Media for IR – Part 1 Twitter & StockTwits", *Q4 Blog*, 25 June 2012, www.q4blog.com/2012/06/25/new-q4-whitepaper-public-company-use-of-social-media-for-ir-%E2%80%93-part-1-twitter-stocktwits/

42 Market Wired, "Building Strong Stakeholder Relations with Social Media: Tips for Investor Relations Professionals", 2010, http://blog.marketwired.com/2010/04/05/building-strong-stakeholder-relations-with-social-media/

43 Journalism.org, Pew Research Center's Project for Excellence in Journalism, "Understanding the Participatory News Consumer", March 2010, www.journalism.org/analysis_report/ understanding_participatory_news_consumer

44 http://rossdawsonblog.com/weblog/archives/2011/12/fantastic-international-comparative-data-on-media-social-media-and-mobile.html

45 www.reuters.com/article/2013/02/19/theirapp-iros-mobile-idUSnPnNY62231+160+PRN20130219

46 www.seic.com/enUS/about/6527.htm

47 Lohr, S, "Study Measures the Chatter of the News Cycle", *The New York Times*, 13 July 2009

48 Grant, J, "How Useful is Social Media-Based Sentiment Analysis to the Buy Side?", *Advanced Trading*, 4 June 2012, www.advancedtrading.com/infrastructure/how-useful-is-social-media-based-sentime/240001417

11 Communicating with shareholders

Shareholders are an important stakeholder for listed corporations, especially since they are the owners. By definition, owners should have significant power in influencing the direction of companies. However, as listed corporations have grown, there has been a distinct separation of power between ownership and management, with management power mostly dominating. A check on management power is the board of directors but in recent years activist shareholders have been making more frequent headlines, if not some progress in overturning corporate decisions. Activist shareholders have not quite turned the tables in terms of the power structure but there are increasing examples of shareholders asserting their views, and votes, to reflect their perspective. These reminders of shareholder power are an indicator of the importance of communication with shareholders. While some of this communication is mandatory, there are also additional communication initiatives that can be implemented. Shareholders can be influenced to be supporters of a company's strategy and objectives if they come to understand a company's story. In this chapter, we will look at the opportunities and potential for effective communication with shareholders.

In the shareholder power structure, institutions are the most powerful, since they control large blocks of stock and in most corporations are the majority group in terms of percentage shareholding. Retail shareholders can be large in numbers, are not homogeneous and tend to be apathetic when it comes to voting and attending meetings. They can be valuable simply because of their inertia and implied loyalty. Activist shareholders can be institutions, hedge funds or groups of shareholders who agitate for change on particular issues. They might be protest groups who have bought stock to enable a vote at annual meetings to give themselves a voice in a public forum. Employees are also an important shareholder group since they have a spread of interests in relation to a corporation's progress. While generally a company's communication effort towards shareholders covers the same content as for other stakeholders, such as across publications and websites, there can be occasions when communication needs to be aimed at particular groupings of shareholders.

Communications purposes

Statutory requirements in communicating to shareholders are not onerous. They can be met by the bare minimum of providing an annual report and electronic notification of any dividends that have been paid, along with the barest information on a company website. However, most companies recognize the lost opportunity from meeting only minimum requirements. Shareholders, excluding for the moment investors with a short-selling focus, have basically made a positive decision towards a company by buying its stock. They have seen potential for capital growth and income and voted in support of a company's story by buying into a share of its future. With goodwill professed in this way, there is much to be gained by companies seeking to garner that support for the long term by communicating effectively with shareholders. A shared vision for the future establishes a base for raising more capital to implement corporate strategy and this likelihood is increased if there is a fulsome explanation around the soundness of that strategy, how it will be implemented and how financial performance is progressing in achieving goals. Communication is effectively the shared part of the bargain. Shareholders have invested because they have a positive vision of the future and companies have an obligation to explain how they are progressing in delivering what is being expected. While the shareholder/corporation relationship may have begun in a positive way, there is also a mutual understanding that companies exist in markets and economies where conditions can fluctuate and communication therefore becomes the means by which companies explain their successes, and possible disappointments, in negotiating the business landscape. The underlying expectation in this relationship is not only for a positive outcome but also frankness if things do not turn out exactly as expected or if time frames are forced to alter as conditions change. Communication is the medium by which companies can make this relationship a journey in which there is a shared recognition of the need for information and explanation about the facts, numbers and narrative of the evolving corporate story.

Given the opportunity to have a supportive group of shareholders, the main purpose of communication is to establish an understanding of what the corporation is trying to achieve. This involves explaining goals and strategy and an elaboration of the corporate story, in a phrase and longer forms, and bringing the company's facts, numbers and narrative together in the context of its industry and competitive environment. This brings shareholders closer to the perspective management has of how it is taking the company into the future and building returns for shareholders. This sense of having shareholders view the competitive landscape as the company sees it is part of building a relationship between owners and management, with communication seeking to establish a unity of purpose. The company is working to deliver returns to shareholders and shareholders are gaining an appreciation that this effort is being well-executed. Communication cannot expect to take away from shareholders a capacity to be critical of corporate efforts but it can establish a level of confidence that plans are being well-executed in prevailing market conditions. What is at stake for companies in this communication process is the building of shareholder loyalty, which can be a valuable commodity, especially in the case of transactions and voting issues where the company is looking for support. Transactions might include capital-raising, intended to reduce debt, make an acquisition or fund new developments. Companies need to make a case for these events and the value they are contributing. The extent of shareholder understanding and loyalty will determine the success of a company in raising new capital, and its cost. Companies may be under attack from what they consider to be a hostile takeover offer or short-sellers may be promoting negative publicity in the interests of driving the stock price down. Having shareholders supportive of existing management's long-term perspective can contribute significantly to repelling these moves.

Achieving loyalty and longer-term support from shareholders is not an easy proposition in markets where short term views of investors tend to prevail. In fact, this is the conclusion of the *Kay Review of UK Equity Markets and Long-Term Decision-*

Making, released in June 2012. The Review pinpoints the sources of short-term views governing equities investment to the erosion of trust and misalignment of incentives. Increasingly the owners of equities in the UK have a short-term view, partly because of the pressure on asset managers to perform in the short term, which is also tied up with performance incentives, and partly because of the nature of the investor, such as hedge funds and short-sellers, which are structured for short-term trading and returns. The dominant players in UK equities investment are asset managers, with individual share ownership down to 11 per cent,[1] and some 72 per cent of daily market turnover now accounted for by a combination of hedge funds, high frequency traders and proprietary traders.[2] These statistics highlight the short-termism that the Kay Review argues should be turned around by improving trust and confidence in the market.

The Kay Review contends that converting a short-term focus into a longer-term view comes down to improving the quality of engagement between investors and companies. A closer involvement of asset managers with companies would improve corporate performance and companies in turn would benefit from developing investor relationships rather than being focused on stock price and the market in general. Kay highlights two aspects of reporting in particular that would help this process:

> reporting of performance should be clear, relevant, timely, related closely to the needs of users and directed to creation of long-term value in the companies in which savers' funds are invested. Metrics and models used in the equity investment chain should give information directly relevant to creation of long-term value in companies and good risk adjusted long-term returns to savers.[3]

Among its recommendations, the Review argued that "high quality, succinct narrative reporting should be strongly encouraged".[4] This is in contrast to Kay's criticism of reliance on the efficient market hypothesis:

> We question the exaggerated faith which market commentators place in the efficient market hypothesis, arguing that the theory represents a poor basis for either regulation or investment. Regulatory philosophy influenced by the efficient market hypothesis has placed undue reliance on information disclosure as a response to divergences in knowledge and incentives across the equity investment chain. This approach has led to the provision of large quantities of data, much of which is of little value to users. Such copious data provision may drive damaging short-term decisions by investors, aggravated by well-documented cognitive biases such as excessive optimism, loss aversion and anchoring.[5]

The Kay Review effectively provides an endorsement for communicating a succinct corporate story to shareholders. A combination of facts, numbers and narrative – that is easily understood, with a longer-term view and surrounding context – is at the centre of seeking to convert short-termism to longer term support for the corporate perspective.

Communication content

While content of communication with shareholders will vary according to purpose, there are requirements at times for an overview and at other times, accompanying detail. The corporate story needs to have a brief version, in phrases and sentences, and then back-up detail across investment presentations, announcements and reviews of operations. The key information shareholders are seeking is company strategy, how it is being implemented and corporate performance in comparison with objectives. They want to know a company has the management capability to implement its strategy, that it has cash flow or the capacity to generate it, that it has a point of difference in its market and that there is independent confirmation of its prospects. Combining the facts, numbers and narrative around these issues is the story shareholders want to glean as part of making an investment decision, or as information around their investment, that is input to how long they might remain as shareholders. How this information is provided can take various forms. It can be in snapshots on a website, in investment presentation content that has been released to an exchange platform or it can be in a longer format, such as an annual report, which may be historic at the time of examination. These various documents are covered below and their content can include a range of information that shareholders may want to know additionally. Investors expect company websites to give them insights into how a company operates, an explanation of its culture and the way it does things. Shareholders need to gather an understanding of strategy and how this is being applied to markets and a company's products, goods and services that contribute to building growth for the long term. Gaining a sense that a company is well-governed and is part of the wider community is also critical to many investors.

Shareholders need to have confidence that they have appropriate and fair information for decision-making. As companies provide information regarding issues on which shareholders are required to vote in a general meeting, they are expected to be even-handed and informative to allow shareholders to consider objectively how they might cast their votes. This does not prevent companies being more persuasive around the corporate perspective than competing views. In relation to takeovers, boards of directors have a greater legal liability to be objective in assessing value and communicating this to shareholders. They usually call on independent advisers to assess a takeover offer so that advice to shareholders about whether or not to accept the offer has a clear stamp of objectivity.

While not all shareholders have a longer-term perspective, the corporation does and so its communications strategy should reflect this. Information content that captures a longer-term view need not necessarily be based around earnings forecasts but can be persuasively achieved by explaining a bigger picture view of a company and its markets. Linking corporate strategy with a company's products and their market positioning outlines not only the attributes of an effective corporate story but also contains ideas around why a company is a promising long-term investment proposition.

Positioning of shareholders

Whether shareholders are more important than other corporate stakeholders has been the subject of debate in recent years. From a communications perspective, they are a critical stakeholder group as owners of the corporation and there is a regulatory obligation on companies to report to them on progress. Many companies define themselves as being focused on delivering shareholder value, which implies shareholders are the first consideration in all corporate actions. While the widespread adoption of the shareholder value idea was prominent a decade ago, it has been called into question in more recent years. A vocal supporter of shareholder value in his time running GE was then chief executive Jack Welch, but he too has come to question the idea of companies giving prime importance to shareholders. His turnaround – he later described shareholder value as being one of the dumbest ideas in the world[6] – attracted much attention.

Another recent critic of shareholder value, Lynn Stout,[7] uses Welch's statement to highlight her perspective that shareholder value is a myth, especially since it is not enshrined in corporate law and, in her view, putting shareholders first is actually harmful to the interests of the corporation and other stakeholders, especially the wider public. A distinction Stout makes is that corporations are an individual legal entity – they are not actually owned by shareholders since the notion of ownership more accurately relates to the corporation's shares. Additionally, Stout argues, shareholders are not a homogeneous group all thinking in the same way. They have differing time horizons and objectives and so to treat them as a single identity with a primary interest in a corporation could be disadvantageous to other stakeholders, such as customers, employees and creditors. Another outcome of focusing on maximizing shareholder value is that it leads to an overemphasis on the short-term view about stock price and detracts from longer-term objectives. Stout puts this down to top executives being rewarded on performance, which is usually measured by the stock price, leading to a short-term focus at the expense of managers being urged to create longer-term value. Stout also blames the corporate governance movement for seeking this alignment, of pay, performance and stock price, leading to an erosion of the value it was seeking to create. Given this divergence of interests, the best a corporation can do is to seek to balance all these objectives rather than have a misguided view that a shareholder perspective will be harmonious with all other views and the differing time frames of shareholders. Stout's solution is for a return to "managerialism", where executives and directors run companies in the interests of a wider group of stakeholders, unhampered by a diversion to emphasizing shareholder value.[8]

While these varying arguments around the positioning of shareholders in the hierarchy of stakeholders are important, there is a sense that all corporations are different too. Some will emphasize that maximizing returns for shareholders is a priority whereas others will broaden the concept to include other stakeholders. Communication with shareholders becomes the output of the corporate view while, at the same time, this issue need not consume the entire corporate story. If a broader corporate objective is to build growth over the longer term then it is a prospect that can carry along all stakeholders, enabling this to become a primary story element and govern the content of shareholder communication.

Means of communication

It is possible for companies to adhere to the bare minimum of mandatory reporting requirements, just providing accounting numbers and minimal wording to accompany them. While conforming to a regulatory minimum, what is missed is an opportunity to encourage an interest in investing in a company and to outline benefits for other stakeholders from corporate progress. Only a minority of companies do pursue just the minimum route to mandatory reporting since there are so many more productive alternatives. This need not involve going to more extreme ends of glossy publications and audio-visual accompaniments, but within established reporting structures there are many opportunities to tell the corporate story and make it compelling. While an annual report is compulsory there are also other useful documents, like corporate profiles, fact sheets and newsletters. A principal audience for these publications might be shareholders but they also have interest for other stakeholders and are used as documents for analysis by the investment community, and competitors.

Annual report

The most comprehensive information document companies produce is an annual report which, while ostensibly a report to shareholders, also encompasses an explanation of many aspects of operations which have relevance for all stakeholders. These reports usually begin with a summary of highlights, covering financial as well as corporate achievements over the past year. These pages present a chance to tell a company story in pictures as well as words and numbers, with illustrations also including graphs to chart corporate progress and diagrams to explain market connections. Financial summaries can also bring out the key metrics by which a company judges its own performance. Following the summary pages are reports from the Chairman, giving a brief strategic overview, and a longer report from the Chief Executive giving a review of a company's operations. What shareholders want to glean from these pages is a candid assessment of how a company is performing. These reports from the two people leading the company are an opportunity to lay out strategy and provide a considered discussion about meeting short and long term goals. The language and tone count. Shareholders are looking for frankness, a telling of what has gone well and possibly not so well and a sense that if mistakes or misjudgements have been made then action has been taken to recover from them and restore a growth path. In these pages, shareholders want to discern a company's story which goes beyond reporting on the individual company to place it in its market environment, to gain a sense of how management is performing in achieving goals and implementing strategy. Reporting frankly on achievements in relation to goals connects directly with how shareholders rate management in relation to credibility. Annual reports are not just intended to report to shareholders on the year gone by but also to outline a path into the future. Imaginative reporting on the past can be a guide to the extent to which companies can generate ideas, implement innovation and absorb acquisitions so there are signposts to whether these will be elements of what to expect in coming years. If promises were made in previous annual reports or expectations raised, then a reconciliation of them with current performance is another contributing factor to enhancing credibility. An explanation of performance in relation to the criteria a company itself uses to judge performance is most helpful to shareholders since they then have an objective measure which they can also apply to competing companies in which they might be investors.

While annual reports contain the actual accounts, notes and auditor's report that are required by law, they also usually include a five year summary of key financial data and metrics by which to judge performance. Incorporation of this data into a spreadsheet assists with making projections of performance and for establishing an intrinsic value per share. From reading an annual report, shareholders should be able to make a judgement about whether their investment is a good prospect for the longer term and whether it is, from their perspective, a buy or sell. In that sense, an annual report is a critical document for a company. While it is in many senses an historic document, in reporting past financial information and on events that have already taken place, it is an opportunity to give a glimpse into the future.

Reporting on individual business segments is an important part of an annual report. It can give a sense of the proportional importance of these businesses to the larger corporate entity and their own market positioning, business conditions and prospects. Annual reports are also the corporate document in which companies report on topics like corporate social responsibility and environmental, social and corporate governance issues. It is here that shareholders should gain a sense of corporate culture, where employees fit into the picture and the priority a company gives to these issues. Since shareholders can include employees and possibly environmental groups that may want to exert pressure on particular issues, this element of reporting can be critical in presenting corporate policy on industrial relations and the environment.

While all these arguments around the importance of annual reports can be well made, statistics indicate that readership of reports is quite low, around 12 per cent according to one survey and then only for a short time, with it considered by some the least helpful way of gaining investment insights.[9] While this may be true across a large group of shareholders, it is usually the case that readership among institutional shareholders, opinion leaders and journalists researching companies is high. The existence of low overall readership statistics does not devalue the proposition that annual reports are a key vehicle for setting out a substantial version of the corporate story.

One page profile, fact sheets

While the annual report is a lengthy set piece report to shareholders, there is also a place for condensing the entire company story to a brief document which gives a snapshot of what a company is all about. Graphic design of these documents which bring together relevant pictures, charts and an industry overview can make one page profiles, usually covered on two sides of a sheet of paper, a very useful document for shareholders. It is also a vehicle for encapsulating the corporate story succinctly, making it easier for shareholders to absorb and discuss with others exactly what a company does and is trying to achieve. With these documents also included on the corporate website, they offer a simpler document to save or print as well as being kept up to date as circumstances and achievements change.

Newsletter, half year report

Newsletters and half year reports can be a means for communicating more regularly to shareholders than once a year through the annual report. While a half year report might have a level of formality to it in terms of including half year accounts and looking like an abridged annual report, a newsletter has no regulatory structure to it. It allows a company to present in an appealing graphically designed format a range of information about its business and people. It can traverse business, financial and marketing issues, giving some background to contracts won and new developments, at the same time as covering cultural issues and interesting events in which the company has been involved. It can cover product development and marketing and give insights into the practicalities of how a company is implementing its strategy.

Website, electronic communication

Websites have become the most common way shareholders glean information about companies. While they consider financial and non-financial information, surveys have shown that, among the topics shareholders look for on websites to evaluate companies, the primary elements are to make an assessment of a company's reputation, its competitive advantage, positioning in relation to macro-economic trends and its strategy against which they gauge investment prospects.[10] Websites have become the easiest way for companies to communicate with shareholders as well as other stakeholders. Many companies have a section of their websites devoted to investor and shareholder information. This is intended to overcome the most irritating aspect some users of corporate websites nominate, which is that crucial information is too many clicks away.[11] In these sections, shareholders can access announcements made and released to exchange platforms as well as investment presentations. There would be a digital version of the annual report and any documents that have been produced for shareholders, like company profiles or half year reports. There is often a link to the exchange platform which also provides a live update of stock price.

The investor sections of websites are additionally helpful when they include the names of stock analysts and their firms which are following a company and their firms. Some companies also provide copies of analysts' reports on their websites, although arguments against this contend that they are a way of using analysts' reports to endorse a company's strategy which some in investor relations do not see as appropriate. The NIRI practice principles prefer just the names of analysts rather than reports.

These specialized sections of websites can also include a calendar of events relevant for shareholders, such as when earnings releases are to be made, dates of dividend posting and when the annual report is to be released and annual meeting held. There can also be an opportunity for shareholders to register to receive company information electronically. This can include signing up to receive announcements by email and Twitter and also see a link to a company's Facebook page.

Other parts of a company's website reinforce communication with shareholders, with it being essential to gather a succinct version of the corporate story on the home page, backed up by more detail in other tabs. Shareholders want to know who is running a company, from the board to senior management, with photos as well as career descriptions being informative. A company's history reinforces a track record and corporate trajectory, providing an indication of promise being fulfilled. As well as providing information around a company's products and services, the corporate story is rounded out by providing information on the market in which these products are competing, including geographic locations and demographics which relate to the depth of markets a company is targeting. The relevance of all this surrounding information is in providing supporting evidence of the long term prospects for a company's strategy. It does not need to be provided in massive detail that swamps a story but the combination of facts and figures within a narrative add to its authority. The range of tabs will be determined by the extent of a company's operations but an effective website should be able to answer most questions, from key stakeholders, like shareholders. Possible website features that can be useful to shareholders can include video and podcasts of corporate events and also access to an RSS feed (a format for delivering regularly changing website content) of regular announcements which would enable them to be received in formats for easy republishing.

It has become more economical for companies to have an electronic communication process with shareholders, especially as it is a more convenient means for most shareholders to receive information. Having shareholders' email addresses not only makes it easier for communication of essential information but also opens up processes for sending out newsletters and product material if shareholders have consented to this.

It is also a way of providing notification of dividend payments and voting papers for annual meetings.

Investor days

Investor days are not the exclusive domain of shareholders, since attendees usually comprise the wider investment community and exclude retail investors, but they are a popular source of information and input to investment decision-making. Investment presentations are often noted as a leading source of information for the investment community but at investor days they also expect more. They like to hear from a wider representation of a company's management group and they also expect to learn something, since "not hearing anything new" is the most common criticism of investor days.[12]

Investor days can last for a whole day and include tours of operations but they commonly are for a half day and can also be held in city locations to make them more convenient for investors to attend. While institutional investors would usually attend, retail shareholders tend not to be invited to be there in person but encouraged to listen to a webcast if this is part of the event. The value for companies in these events is that, given nearly 90 per cent of attendees view these types of events as a valuable use of their time, they have a powerful forum to which they can convey their corporate story, especially in providing the long term strategic perspective that investors want to hear.[13]

Shareholder meetings

The annual meeting is an opportunity for shareholders to vote on company issues and hear reports directly from the chairman and chief executive, with special meetings called from time to time as shareholder approval is needed on transactions or capital-raising issues. Any meeting of shareholders provides companies with a choice. They can see it as an intrusive formality which can be completed within minutes or an opportunity to communicate the corporate story and provide a view about strategy and direction over the longer term. Larger companies tend to opt for the latter but there are some that take pride in completing an annual meeting in minutes, on the basis that it should be taken for granted that management is doing the best it can.

A common structure for an annual meeting is for the chairman to give an overview of how the company has performed, its strategy and direction while the chief executive reports on how operations are performing, initiatives being taken, current business conditions and factors affecting the outlook. Both these addresses are an opportunity to set out the corporate story and provide insights into the company's competitive position and long term prospects. This can be achieved with or without PowerPoint presentations and can include video. The overall purpose is to reinforce a supportive relationship with the shareholders who have taken the time to attend the meeting. There is also scope to present company products to shareholders, through displays and samples, making shareholders familiar with what the company is producing. Posters and display photos in the room can extend understanding of how and where the company is operating. When the meeting is over, light refreshments are usually provided, enabling shareholders to mingle with company directors and representatives.

Standard resolutions at annual meetings are a presentation of accounts and election of directors. The opportunity for shareholders to ask questions exists and increasingly in the era of shareholder activism, question time presents an opportunity to cover

Case study

Berkshire Hathaway – Buffett's AGM, Woodstock for capitalists*

Berkshire Hathaway is the listed investment vehicle for Warren Buffett, arguably the world's most successful investor. Buffett gained control of Berkshire in 1965 and by 2012, it had become the nineth largest company in the US with a market capitalization of around US$220 billion and A class voting stock selling at $134,000 each,[14] compared with $15 when Buffett first bought in.[15] The annual meeting of Berkshire Hathaway has now become legendary. At its May 2012 meeting, around 35,000 people attended, including Bill Gates, who is also a director of Berkshire Hathaway and friend of Buffett's. Over the past few years, they have shared the rivalry of being the wealthiest people in the world. One of Buffett's nicknames is the "Sage of Omaha", linking his home town with his investing prowess and ability to talk about it with conviction, humour and in plain English. This is why huge crowds attend the company's annual meeting each year and since a movie about the meeting in 2000 was called *Woodstock for Capitalists*, the name has stuck.

For the 2012 annual meeting, Berkshire Hathaway issued shareholders with a 28-page booklet[16] outlining the programme and events, beginning on a Friday evening and going all weekend. Shareholders are welcomed at a reception on Friday evening and the meeting itself lasts all day Saturday at the Century Link auditorium in Omaha, Nebraska, where Berkshire Hathaway is headquartered and Buffett has lived most of his life. Doors to the auditorium open at 7.00 am, with shareholders provided with a continental breakfast and a box of See's butterscotch candy to ready them for the 8.30 am showing of the specially made movie that is a feature of each year's meeting. This year, Buffett starred as a quarterback in the University of Nebraska football team playing a team of robots led by Herman Cain.[16] A previous year's movie had Jamie Lee Curtis pretending to fall in love with Buffett business partner Charlie Munger, aged in his late 80s at the time.[18]

From 9.30 am to 3.30 pm, with a break for lunch, shareholders and visitors fire questions at Buffett and Munger. A variation for the 2012 meeting was to include a panel of three well-known journalists – from *Fortune*, CNBC and *The New York Times* – who received shareholder questions by email in advance of the meeting, allowing them to choose the most interesting. Three financial analysts formed a second panel to be part of the questioning regime.

Chairman Buffett loves the questions and this is what the crowd comes for. In the *Visitors' Guide*, he lays down the guidelines: "Neither Charlie nor I will get so much as a clue about the questions to be asked. We know the journalists and analysts will pick some tough ones and that's the way we like it.

"We will have a drawing at 8.15 at each of the 13 microphones for those shareholders wishing to ask questions themselves. At the meeting I will alternate the questions asked by the journalists and analysts with those from winning shareholders."[19]

Only 15 minutes is allocated for the formal business part of the meeting, which is all over by 4.00 pm, leaving some time for shareholders to visit all the exhibits from companies in which Berkshire Hathaway is invested, before the big BBQ, which goes through till 8.00 pm.

Squeezed into the day's programme is a competition for tossing a newspaper onto a porch, allowing Buffett to return to his boyhood skills and to reflect Berkshire Hathaway's recent foray into newspaper ownership, including the *Omaha Herald*. Buffett and Gates indulged in some friendly rivalry, with Buffett winning although Gates reckoned he had been practising.[20]

Sunday is shopping day in Omaha, especially at Borsheims jewellery store, owned by Berkshire Hathaway, and with Buffett performing his one day of the year role as chief salesperson. Buffett's favourite steakhouses also provide special events for shareholders.

Gates has been on the board of Berkshire Hathaway since 2004 and he thought the 2012 meeting was one of the best. He looks forward each year to the "pilgrimage to Omaha to learn from this remarkable business leader and teacher" and he also catches up with old friends, this year including Bono with whom he discussed their work in Africa.[21]

There is little doubt the Berkshire Hathaway annual meeting would be the biggest in the world and one in which the largest amount of time is allocated to questions and answers. This is certainly democracy in one form although answers from Buffett and Munger are definitely from the perspective that they are running the company and, while shareholders are treated well, they are going along for the ride determined by the Sage. Still, with the sort of returns he has achieved, there is little complaint.

*The material is copyrighted and used with permission of the author.

Table of Contents

CENTURYLINK CENTER
OMAHA
455 N. 10th Street • Omaha, NE 68102
(402) 341-1500

2014 ANNUAL MEETING MAY 3

Mark Your Calendar

controversial issues as well as seeking further information on corporate performance and items in the accounts. Shareholders can also propose resolutions if sufficient notice is given in advance of the meeting. Under Australian and UK law, resolutions can be proposed if they have the support of 100 shareholders or a shareholder with at least five per cent of the stock. In the US, shareholders owning stock worth US$2,000 for more than a year can submit a resolution. Meeting this condition means companies are required to distribute the resolutions and any relevant supporting information to all shareholders as part of the notice of meeting.

While annual meetings demonstrate the power shareholders can exercise they also point up the limitations of this power. Company constitutions define the powers of boards of directors and shareholders, with boards and their management teams having the power, and legal responsibility, to run companies. Companies can reject resolutions from shareholders that seek to exceed the powers of an annual meeting. Shareholders cannot put resolutions to the meeting that tell directors how to run the company but they can express opinions during question time. Members of special interest groups can become shareholders and put resolutions to meetings if they can find the wording that meets the power of the meeting to consider them. Since these are a reflection of a minority group, they do not have a history of being passed at annual meetings but interest groups usually realize this inevitability and gain satisfaction from raising their issue in a public forum and with possible accompanying media attention.[22]

Say on pay

One type of resolution that has now become common for annual meeting agendas is the so called "say on pay" resolution in which shareholders can vote on senior executives' compensation package. It is the aftermath of the GFC and some notable company failures which have highlighted how executive compensation has become disconnected with company performance and resulted in community concerns about executives being overpaid. One way of making companies more accountable for this has been to allow shareholders to vote at annual meetings on senior executive pay and related issues of performance shares. Mostly these votes are non-binding on boards of directors. In Australia there is a two strikes rule under which, if these resolutions receive a "no" vote of 25 per cent or more in two consecutive years, it triggers a spill of the board. The company is required to put a board spill motion to shareholders and if 50 per cent of shareholders vote in favour of this motion, the company is required to call a further general meeting at which all the company's directors, excluding the managing director, will face re-election. Say on pay votes have been in effect since 2011 in the US, with the new Dodd-Frank law requiring companies to put their pay practices to a shareholder vote at least every three years. NIRI reported in July 2012 that 90 per cent of S&P500 companies had implemented voting and that 89 per cent of these had received approval votes in excess of 70 per cent with 30 companies receiving negative votes. Introduction of say on pay voting has resulted in companies providing more information to shareholders to assist voting. Companies have also increased the extent to which they have been engaging with shareholders and proxy advisory firms on pay issues to avoid negative votes.[23]

While these voting figures overall might indicate a majority trend of support for a company's executive compensation arrangements, eliminating insider votes and accounting for absentees can show a different picture. A *New York Times* analysis[24] of voting at one large company's 2012 annual meeting showed that votes cast indicated 82 per cent approved the company's pay and only 3.41 per cent of shares voted opposed it, allowing the resolution to be passed. But by eliminating insider votes and absentees, only 8.9 per cent of independent shareholders supported the pay and almost double that percentage – 17.3 per cent – opposed it. While shareholder democracy is increasing its power, the effectiveness of the system still depends on shareholders actually exercising their votes rather than being apathetic if they want to influence important issues.

One shareholder group that has been active in the US on pay voting has been labor unions and their pension funds. In 2012, 36 per cent of all shareholder proposals coming to a vote at Fortune 200 companies, the 200 largest listed companies in the US, were from this group.[25] The Proxy Monitor report on these voting patterns notes that these union sponsored proposals mostly relate to union campaigns rather than the wider concerns of shareholders. Of the remaining shareholder proposals in the 2012 proxy season, 31 per cent were from three individual investor groups, 22 per cent were from groups with a "socially responsible" purpose, 10 per cent were from individuals with their own specific purpose and 1 per cent were from institutional investors not affiliated with any of the other groups.[26] The report summarizes this activity:

> In 2012, labor unions and associated organizers under the "Occupy" umbrella have been especially active in challenging executives' pay. These activists, along with "socially responsible" investing funds allied with certain academics, nonprofit groups, and Democratic Party activists, have also challenged corporations' political spending – an issue brought to the forefront of public discourse by a presidential election campaign.

However, the report also notes that only 6 per cent of shareholder initiated proposals received majority backing, down from 7 per cent in 2011 and the lowest figure over the 2006–12 period.[27] Proxy Monitor believes its data over this six year period:

> challenges the efficacy of the shareholder-proposal process, at least from the perspective of the ordinary investor. The prominent role being played by a small number of investors, most prominently labor-union pension funds whose actions in this area appear to deviate from concern over share value, suggests that this process may be oriented toward influencing corporate behaviour in a manner that generates private returns to a subset of investors while harming the average diversified investor.[28]

Shareholder activism, proxy access

Shareholders have increasingly been seeking to influence voting on other issues, such as election of directors, governance and some activist issues like the environment or social justice concerns. A stumbling block for exercising this form of democracy is for resolutions to meet the constitutions of companies, to be received sufficiently in advance of the meeting and then to be accepted by the board as valid resolutions to be put before shareholders at a meeting. This process is referred to as proxy access and it is one in which companies tend to hold the power despite the rise of shareholder activism and increasing extent of shareholders putting forward resolutions. When shareholder activism arises it is not often that all shareholders are aligned with each other. Different groups of activists can have conflicting interests and varying views about how to improve shareholder value. Poor handling of institutionalized power by corporations can result in a dent to reputation if the battle over resolutions becomes public and heated.

There can be a number of positive aspects for companies from shareholder activism. It can motivate boards to pay greater attention to issues that are important for all shareholders and can also lead to better returns as companies sell off poorly performing businesses and improve efficiency in the interests of achieving a better valuation. On the negative side, if shareholder activists are focused on short term gain, their proposals may not be in the interests of all shareholders. It can be time consuming and expensive to defend a company against this type of activism, again highlighting the importance of the communication aspects of how companies respond to shareholder activists, especially if they are hedge funds seeking significant change.

While institutional shareholders may be beneficiaries of activism, there is still a reluctance on the part of some to take publicly critical positions and also to invest the considerable amounts of time that being an activist can involve. As one fund manager put it:

> It's a lot of work for you to change something and you only get a small portion of the benefit. So people have started to say 'why should I go to the hassle? The manager might decide not to talk to you again and they're often very influential people. You take all that flak, you can see why it's not a business thing to do. There is an element the person you are dealing with … you are highly likely to deal with them again. … Our experience is that you get more traction if you do things in private. The suggestions made privately are much more listened to than they were 10 to 25 years ago. These days boards generally are receptive to suggestions from shareholders. However, if that doesn't work, then the public approach can work and I believe again these days you have much more chances of success than five years ago. However, to get up at an AGM and publicly decry people can also backfire, so you need to be careful and approach each situation differently.[29]

The world's largest asset manager, Black Rock, also favours behind the scenes engagement but it is increasingly taking more seriously its position in relation to voting proposals. Black Rock has sometimes been accused of siding too often with corporate management but in 2011 it issued a letter to all companies in which it was a shareholder, advising that it could not be taken for granted it would follow proxy advisers but would form an independent view on any shareholder voting proposal.[30] This attitude places the onus squarely on companies to communicate their stories effectively in relation to voting proposals put before shareholders.

Hedge funds

Along with increased shareholder democracy has come greater use of shareholder voting by hedge funds to put pressure on boards to increase stock value. Part of these tactics include seeking board positions and from this platform discussing, often publicly, an agenda that reflects alternatives about company strategy and implementation. Activist shareholders from this perspective are not all hedge funds but could be shareholders seeking alternative means to an acquisition proposal to control a company's agenda. Hedge funds do not usually have a long term agenda but want to agitate for change in the short term to achieve maximum return for their own investors. In this sense, hedge funds represent a stark distinction between pursuing their own interests in contrast to wider objectives of a corporation and its shareholders, with the two viewpoints quite often at odds. The appearance of hedge funds on the register of shareholders can be the start of a torrid period of crisis and the increase of hedge funds seeking shareholder voting to exert influence led NIRI to issue practice guidelines around preparing for and dealing with this eventuality. Successfully managing dealings with hedge funds revolves around communication with all shareholders and in particular the activist hedge funds which have become shareholders. The starting point, according to NIRI[31] is to assess where unlocked value could lie within a company since these aspects can be what makes a company vulnerable to a hedge fund. It might involve under leveraged assets, excess cash, a need for restructuring, excessive overheads, under performing assets, ineffective marketing, untapped merger and acquisition opportunities, poor corporate governance or insufficient expenditure on research and development. Each of these issues provides topics for communication content and strategy.

Hedge funds are looking for this untapped potential within a company, especially reflected in a lagging stock price and underperformance in comparison with peers. Perhaps a company may have succumbed to competitive pressures and yet still have a capability to generate cash. Or maybe there is a market perception that a company has missed opportunities and could have governance weaknesses exhibited by an entrenched board or management. Any of these events can attract hedge funds so there is a necessity on the part of listed companies to maintain vigilance around changes on the share register that might signal the appearance of a hedge fund. This requires an assessment of a hedge fund's track record, since some are quite prepared to work with boards privately to implement change while others prefer the tactic of a high profile aggressive campaign. Regular communication and engagement with existing shareholders should give companies an understanding of whether hedge funds might have a basis for being critical of a board and management. It is also important to initiate a dialogue with a hedge fund to establish the nature of their demands and how they want to go about pursuing them. The most common demands from hedge funds, according to NIRI, are seeking seats on the board, asset sales, sale of the entire company and return of capital through stock repurchases or special dividends. They might also want a change in direction or to break the company up into parts that could yield a higher value than being part of the whole enlisted entity.[32]

NIRI also advises trying to keep discussions with hedge funds out of the public eye since hedge funds relish disputes gaining wider attention since it gives them an opportunity to have the final word, in the media or with the investment community. If the issues do become public, the pressure is on companies to focus on their growth stories and to appear reasonable, in either taking on hedge fund suggestions or being critical of them. Depending on how the communications campaign progresses, it may well lead to the company hiring proxy advisers who can assist in bringing out the vote when it is time for these issues to be aired at a public meeting of shareholders.[33]

Baruch Lev notes that many outcomes of hedge funds appearing on share registers are positive for stock price and so are welcomed by shareholders. He quotes research pointing out that activists gained board representation in 73 per cent of cases in which they demanded it, practically all calls for share buy backs were met and in 50 per cent of cases where hedge funds demanded strategic changes, the target company responded positively.[34] In Lev's view, the worst response a company can have when activists strike is no reaction.[35] He points out that in many cases it is painless for companies to meet many hedge fund demands but where these demands are inconsistent with corporate strategy, they should be vigorously opposed, using a public relations campaign, supported by expert opinion, to shore up management's position and communicate this to institutional shareholders.[36]

Combining company and shareholder interests

There are a number of actions companies can initiate that are in the mutual interests of a corporation and its shareholders. One example of this is dividend reinvestment plans, in which shareholders can opt to have dividends not paid in cash but to be in the form of new stock. These new shares are usually issued at a discount to market price, commonly five per cent, if they want to encourage shareholders to take up this option. The advantage for companies is that it is a form of preserving cash and raising new capital.

Many investors also want to see companies be responsible corporate citizens, giving back to society in some form, such as caring for the environment as a standard part of their operations or becoming involved in some charitable activities. Most companies these days do initiate some form of corporate social responsibility. While this involves corporate expenditure, it is often seen by shareholders as a necessary part of what companies are expected to do and so it rarely becomes the subject of shareholder objection.

As a way of showing their appreciation to new investors, some companies provide welcome shareholder kits following a first investment. This is often in the form of a letter from the chairman and usually includes a brief corporate profile to begin the process of implanting the corporate story with new shareholders.

While investor days and tours of operations have been a way of companies keeping in touch with the buy and sell side they can also be part of how companies can reinforce retail shareholder loyalty. Company annual meetings can be held at headquarters that involve operations and these meetings can also be rotated to differing cities to encourage more personal contact between shareholders and the board and management.

Electronic communication of information to shareholders can also reflect a mutual benefit. It is certainly more economical for companies to reduce printed communication and the advantage of electronic communication is that it can give shareholders instant notice of company announcements and initiatives. Some annual reports can include audio-visual components if they are sent electronically and the use of social media can lead to dialogue with shareholders as part of an ongoing electronic conversation.

Shareholder communication takes on even greater importance when viewed from the perspectives of mergers and acquisitions, an initial listing on a stock exchange and in crisis management, as we shall see in the next chapter.

Notes

1 Kay (2012), p 31
2 Kay (2012), p 38
3 Kay (2012), p 12
4 Kay (2012), p 13

5 Kay (2012), p 10
6 Guerrera, F, "Welsh Condemns Share Price Focus", *The Financial Times*, 12 March 2009, www.ft.com/intl/cms/s/0/294ff1f2-0f27-11de-ba10-0000779fd2ac.html#axzz2LgskvUnS
7 Stout, L, *The Shareholder Value Myth: How Putting Shareholders First Harms Investors, Corporations and the Public* (Berrett Koehler Publishers Inc., San Francisco, CA: 2012)
8 Eisinger, J, "Challenging the Long-Held Belief in 'Shareholder Value'", *The New York Times*, 27 June 2012
9 Jones, D, "More Evidence that Few Read Annual Reports", *IR Web Report*, 13 July 2011, http://irwebreport.com/20110713/few-read-annual-reports
10 Investor Relations Report, "Investors Want Fully Loaded IR Websites", *Investor Relations Guide Bulletin* (Kennedy Information: June 2006)
11 Investor Relations Report (2006)
12 Corbin Perception, "Planning an Effective Investor Day", *Inside the Buy Side*, 2013, p 3, www.corbinperception.com
13 Corbin (2013)
14 Tilson Funds, www.tilsonfunds.com/BRK.pdf
15 History of Berkshire Hathaway, www.buffettsecrets.com/berkshire-hathaway.htm
16 *Visitors Guide*, www.berkshirehathaway.com/meet01/2012BerkshireVisitorsGuide.pdf
17 Kass, D, "Notes From 2012 Berkshire Hathaway Annual Meeting", http://blogs.rhsmith.umd.edu/davidkass/uncategorized/notes-from-2012-berkshire-hathaway-annual-meeting/
18 Richardson, K, "Omaha Notebook: Fat Cats and Desperate Housewives", *The Wall Street Journal*, 7 May 2006, http://online.wsj.com/article/SB114684573302044986.html
19 Visitors Guide (2012)
20 Gates, B, "Woodstock for Capitalists: Berkshire Hathaway Annual Meeting Unlike Any Other", 7 May 2012, www.thegatesnotes.com/Personal/Berkshire-Hathaway-Annual-Meeting-Photo-Gallery
21 Gates (2012)
22 Hunt, N, Semple, C and Friedlander, D, "Shareholders Can't Run Public Companies", *Australian Financial Review*, 15 October 2010
23 IR Advisor, "NIRI Briefing Paper: 2012 US Proxy Season", NIRI, July 2012, pp 1–2
24 Morgenson, G, "When Shareholders Make Their Voices Heard", *The New York Times*, 7 April 2012
25 Copeland, JR, "A Report on Corporate Governance and Shareholder Activism", *Proxy Monitor Report*, Fall 2012, www.proxymonitor.org/Forms/pmr_04.aspx
26 Copeland (2012), p 1
27 Copeland (2012), p 1
28 Copeland (2012), p 1
29 Quoted in Whyte, J, "Agitators Get to Grips with Boards", *Australian Financial Review*, 2 July 2012
30 Craig, S, "The Giant of Shareholders, Quietly Stirring", *The New York Times*, 18 May 2013
31 Kelleher, LY, "Hedge Fund Activism: What You Need to Know and What You Can Do About It", *Executive Alert*, NIRI, 13 April 2007
32 Kelleher (2007)
33 Kelleher (2007)
34 Lev (2012), pp 252–253
35 Lev (2012), p 258
36 Lev (2012), p 259

12 Transactions and issues
M&A, IPO and crisis

As transactions and issues confront a corporation, the corporate story becomes a compass, providing a direction and rationale for events ahead. In mergers and acquisitions (M&A), the statistics for failed transactions are surprisingly high, with the most often cited reason being the breakdown of communication in the integration phase. When companies first list on a stock exchange, in a transaction known as an initial public offering (IPO), the development of an appealing investment proposition is the basis for attracting investors. After listing, it is this proposition that becomes the platform for competing with other companies for attention in the capital markets. At times of crisis, the listed corporation not only needs to protect its reputation in resolving issues but also be mindful of how its management of events affects stock price. Across all these transactions and issues, communication is critical, not just in dealing with an event in itself but in placing around it the corporate context. It is communication that can convey an understanding of the company's business and values to underline why it is taking the action it is. The corporate story is not a static piece of information but the way it embodies a company and its context – the combination of facts, numbers and narrative and its various forms, from phrase to strategic explanation – represents the communications armoury for entering transactions and conveying persuasion to carry participants along on the journey. Adapting the corporate story for action is an important part of its evolution.

Mergers and acquisitions

Among commonly quoted statistics about M&A are that some 70–80 per cent do not create significant value above the annual cost of capital and, over several decades, failure rates for M&A have been 50 per cent or higher.[1] Nevertheless, growth by M&A is a common objective for many corporations and, allowing for a slowdown caused by the global financial crisis, M&A have continued to grow in recent decades and are expected to resume more substantially as business conditions globally improve. While the reasons for failed transactions can be many – from poor planning to unrealistic expectations, too high a price, changed business conditions and cultural clashes – a common ingredient in successful transactions is the existence of a good communications programme and its successful implementation.[2] One survey among senior executives showed they attributed success in M&A to mastering the three stages of the transaction: "conducting due diligence, understanding cultural integration issues, and most critically, planning and executing the integration process."[3] It is the integration process that throws up most of the issues that can derail a successful transaction. Communication plays less of a role in the original due diligence phase but the actual transaction has four phases – preparation for making the transaction public, day one of the actual announcement, input to the transaction to finalization, then using communication to achieve positive outcomes in the integration process.

Transaction preparation

As analysis of a merger or acquisition transaction nears completion and terms are worked out, how to communicate the essence and rationale of it becomes a high priority. How the transaction is received by the market and the media can be a significant determinant of success or failure of the deal. While the transaction is a reflection of the evolution of corporate strategy, communication strategy is governed by combining an explanation of the transaction within the corporate story, directed to key stakeholders who can influence perceptions and outcome of the transaction.

Offence, defence and combined interests

Development of a communications strategy for M&A transactions depends on perspective, varying according to whether a company is an acquirer, is on the receiving end of a takeover offer or whether two companies are merging. An acquirer has the advantage of preparation in advance, as both sides do in an agreed merger, while a company receiving an offer has to respond quickly and develop further communication as the transaction follows its path. In each case, there are three components to communication. One is to develop an argument around the transaction itself, either supporting the reasoning around it and developing ideas around why it is beneficial, or opposing it. The second is to explain the context around these views and how the transaction perspective fits with the corporate story. The third is to have an advice perspective for shareholders, either encouraging them to accept the transaction as being beneficial for them or to heed advice that they should do nothing until directors have had a chance to consider how a company should respond to an unsolicited takeover offer.

The corporate story perspective is critical in M&A transactions because the nature of it connects so directly with corporate strategy that explanation needs to convey compatibility of the transaction with the company's direction and longer-term view. Communication needs to show how the transaction is positive for topics such as market positioning, strategic development and, most importantly, earnings. For companies on the receiving end of an unwanted offer, their story becomes the main defence as they seek to highlight their own management position in progressing well in their markets without any need for outside interruption to these plans. Of course, as the offer is assessed, other factors such as implications of value for shareholders become a weightier argument than a board and management wanting to remain independent to implement a strategy they have developed.

Stakeholders

In the planning stage of an M&A transaction, communication input needs to consider the various stakeholders that will be affected by the transaction. This encompasses not just the company making an offer but also stakeholders in the company that is the subject of an offer. Any transaction like this is going to affect employees and trade union groups, which might represent a significant component of employees. It may also have implications for the industry overall, which could attract the attention of government competition regulators. Political representatives, at local, state and federal levels may have an interest in how the transaction might unfold. Industry or environmental groups may be affected and there could be marketing implications as brands are adjusted to suit a new approach to customers, who will also need special consideration.

Not all these stakeholders are priorities on the first day of an announcement but are part of how a communication plan is unfolded as the transaction progresses.

Shareholders, investment community

Shareholders are the ultimate determinants of success of a transaction, with large institutional shareholders being critical. None of these groups will make up their minds instantly when a transaction is announced but they will be influenced by the calibre of the arguments and consistency with the corporate story. The course of the transaction will allow documents to be mailed and face-to-face meetings to be held with key players and how this develops is an important part of the planning process.

Media

The first opinion leaders on the transaction will be the media. Journalists will report immediate market reaction and, while it may be some months before a transaction is finally completed, initial reactions can set the scene. There will be an instant market view about how well the deal has been priced and also how well it meets the story consistency test. How to engage with the media and opinion leaders is not just important on day one but it needs to be an ongoing relationship as news and information develops during the transaction, particularly in a hostile takeover that involves two sides parrying arguments about the merits of a deal.

What people want to know

Facts, numbers and narrative sum up how transactions such as M&A need to be presented, making it a story within a story as the deal is linked with corporate direction. When these transactions are reported in the media, the size of the deal is a critical piece of information, along with how its pricing compares with market price of a company being acquired and how the merger terms are presented. While the deal itself needs to be explained, the persuasive power is in the bigger picture and the narrative surrounding it as the implications for the future weigh on how the transaction has an effect on the evolving story of transformation. The benefits of the deal, for shareholders and other stakeholders, need to be highlighted. Basic facts need to be made clear so that readers do not have to go searching for percentage shareholdings, market shares and key financial performance numbers. Most transaction announcements usually contain the term "synergies", in which the savings from combining two operations are used as justification for a deal proceeding. The economic nature of these terms may have persuasive financial logic but when the savings also involve people losing their jobs, it emphasizes a sensitive area of communication that needs to be managed with key stakeholder groups in both companies. Synergies are also an estimate around what might be achieved in the future, and when they are not realized, there is a communication issue down the track that will need to be managed. The transaction timetable sets out deadlines for accepting offers and possible shareholder meetings, consequently delineating further concentrations of communication effort. Ultimately the key piece of information any commentator on the transaction needs to know is its basic logic and why it makes common sense for it to be accepted. Perceptions of the common sense of the deal, and whether it might need keener pricing, are part of the tactics to be played out. However, if the fundamental deal logic is made clear from the beginning, then a sound communications story platform has been laid.

Announcement day

With the preparation stage including establishing the story around the deal, how it fits into company strategy and key stakeholder audiences, announcement day becomes based around the logistics of how the messages will be communicated. The initial legal responsibility is to announce the transaction to the market. If this is done early in the day then it leaves the rest of the day for managing communication directly with key stakeholders. The content of the announcement would reflect preparation around the transaction, emphasizing the corporate story through key messages related to the logic of the transaction and its value. Announcement day strategy would involve presenting this information to the investment community and media, through a combination of conference calls, personal presentations, a press conference and probably a webcast.

For large transactions this might involve a presentation to a live audience that would be webcast to a dial-in audience in other locations. The presentation can elaborate on the background and implications for strategy and to make the story around the deal and its pricing appear compelling. The performance involves elements of marketing and persuasion as well as presentation of facts. The objective is to convince a fairly hardened audience that the transaction is worthy of support. The presentation enables direct questioning from the audiences of key spokespersons. This can highlight areas of interest from the investment community as well as providing an opportunity to use questions to bring out anecdotes that emphasize the transaction storyline.

While the media may attend or tune into such an event, having a separate and smaller press conference with key writers, with those in more distant locations on a conference call, provides an opportunity to give direct quotes in response to media questioning. The content cannot stray from the actual tenor of the announcement and main webcast but meeting with journalists in a small group gives the storytelling some immediacy and an opportunity to respond to market reactions that might have arisen since the announcement. This event also enables media photographers and television crews to capture live the company's perspective on the news.

During the remainder of the day, there is an opportunity for a chief executive to be in touch directly with other key stakeholders. This may involve telephone links with people in government and politics who may have an interest in the transaction. Heads of trade unions, industry associations, employee representatives and special interest groups will also be on a call list, recognizing that some of them may well see the transaction as jeopardizing their interests and lead to opposition as it progresses. Telephone contact is part of the diplomatic communications package and would need to be followed up by providing copies of announcements and surrounding logic about the transaction.

Progressing to finalization

As much as announcement day may be excellently implemented as a logistics exercise, it does not guarantee the terms of the transaction will be immediately accepted by all. Where the deal comprises a merger, its terms have been agreed by the two companies in advance, usually allowing the transaction to proceed steadily towards completion. A hostile takeover announcement may well go through many stages as pricing is debated and subjected to independent review by financial advisers. The media enjoys these battles and gives them news prominence so there can be much public debate about deal strategies and the views of major shareholders. Media interest allows both sides in a transaction to bolster the arguments supporting their views and to seek to have media coverage influence how others might see the transaction and decide in their favour. Media engagement heightens the need to be careful with comments about pricing. Journalists will use their best tactics to slip under the guard of a chief executive who may well be contemplating increasing the price of a takeover offer but is not yet prepared to say so publicly.

The other area of focus for companies in the midst of an M&A transaction is the attitudes of major shareholders to the deal. They will need time to consider their positions and since these transactions tend to continue for some months before being finalized, they have the luxury of time before a definite decision has to be made. Institutional shareholders often hold out until the last moment since their large shareholding gives them a position of power to influence success or failure of a bid. Consequently, they will entertain arguments from both sides as the transaction progresses.

Key influences on decision-making in these transactions are how the market as a whole reacts and public perceptions about how the two companies and their management teams are perceived. The judgement people are being asked to make is which management team has the greatest likelihood of achieving superior longer-term growth. In a sense, these perceptions have been laid before the transaction has been announced and so how well a company has communicated its corporate story up to the time a deal was launched can also be influential.

Market reaction is usually a sound guide to how the deal will conclude. In a hostile takeover, the company making the offer will need to make an offer above market to indicate the premium it is prepared to pay to achieve a change of control. While takeover premiums to gain control of a company can vary, an average yardstick is around 30 per cent above stock price 20 days before a bid is made.[4] This reflects what an acquirer might ultimately pay and not the opening bid in a takeover skirmish. The initial offer will depend on the price level of a target company at the time, which may well have been marked down because of poor performance. Market assessments of an offer will account for the multiple of earnings the bid represents and once a takeover offer is announced, the stock price of the target will move closer to the offer price. Market anticipation of a possible increased offer from an acquirer to achieve control can also attract hedge funds that focus on arbitrage opportunities, with the intention of profiting from these transactions as offer prices are calibrated towards achieving a successful resolution. An important aspect of the market's assessment of value of an offer depends on how an acquirer intends to transform the company that is in its sights and the extent of synergies it expects it can realize from bringing two companies together. Market reaction also depends on the type of offer being made, with cash offers being more highly valued than those based on an acquirer issuing more of its stock to achieve control.

While arguments swirl during the transaction about value, as deadlines for accepting an offer approach, an argument that becomes influential is asking shareholders to assess the likely stock price of a target company if the offer lapses or is unsuccessful. When hostile takeovers are announced, the stock price of a target company usually rises to the level of the offer or thereabouts. If the market believes the offer is underpriced, price may go higher and as well as hedge funds moving in to influence the outcome, other bidders might be attracted to make an alternative takeover offer. Sometimes this alternative might be solicited by a target company as it seeks a "white knight" defence by falling into the arms of an acquirer with which the board may see greater compatibility. An intransigent target company may be faced with a significant fall to pre-offer stock prices if it continues to reject an offer. This places pressure on the directors of a target company's board to make sure they get their responses right. A persistent view about a target being undervalued by the offer may well be accurate but it needs to demonstrate how it might achieve this future promise if directors are to be let off the hook for rejecting an offer the market deemed satisfactory.

Other elements to an M&A transaction as it proceeds to finalization are a possible meeting of shareholders to approve the deal. These meetings could be hostile if there are public concerns about pricing or the giving up of independence and company brands. The transaction may involve both companies having shareholder meetings to justify the deal and so criticism may flow from all angles as stakeholders seek to express their views. Winning the day is one aspect of it all, since hostile meetings can pose problems for the next crucial phase of a transaction, which is integration, the ultimate determinant of whether a transaction was well conceived.

Integration

Successfully completing an M&A deal is just the start of a more complex phase of bringing two organizations together. The morale and attitudes of employees is all important, since it is their motivation that determines whether synergies are achieved, especially when job losses are involved. A few years ago *The Financial Times*[5] posed a question raised by Sir Martin Sorrell, chief executive of the WPP group, who referred to the challenges of uniting cultures after a merger or acquisition as bringing together "different tribes" and "warring factions". When four experts from differing disciplines – an executive veteran of 60 acquisitions, a management consultant, an academic and a public relations consultant – were asked how to solve this issue, they each had varying perspectives.

The executive view was to make it clear about what was being bought – whether technology, brand, product or people – since that was the source of being able to implement consistent, honest and well thought-out communication to the employees of both companies as a way of minimizing friction. The leadership of both companies needed to spearhead this communication and since employees easily detect insincerity, communication had to be undertaken by executives dedicated to the success of the new combined entity.[6]

The management consultant suggested four actions to minimize tensions. First was to create quickly a common purpose, such as beating the competition. Next was to take the hard decisions early, especially about which senior executives were staying and which were not. Third was to keep up communication, even when there was not a lot to say since rumours start in a vacuum. Fourth was to form a team from both companies to guide integration, offering rewards for success. The important factor overall was to define one culture for the organization to avoid the damage from unmanaged parallel cultures.[7]

The academic believed it could be a costly waste of time to seek to articulate common cultures. The goal of the transaction was to win business quickly and this had to have priority. In his view, cultural aspects could be overengineered, especially when internal communications teams became bigger than those focused externally and on marketing, since too much of an internal focus was a boon to competitors. The key to successful mergers was leadership, since the intention was not to buy a culture but business and if that were the main message, the troops would follow.[8]

The public relations consultant believed that since cultural fit was what delivered value over the longer term, then the focus had to be on the people whose effort and commitment were needed to deliver this. This begins at the top, requiring an articulation of the new organization's vision and strategy, with communication of this message at the heart of any integration plan. Clear and consistent communication is required for the differing audiences of employees, shareholders and customers.[9]

The common thread across all four responses was the importance of communication in achieving a successful integration phase after a merger or acquisition.

One piece of research that compared the financial and human aspects of mergers was from Harvard professor Rosabeth Moss Kantor.[10] She noted that the post-financial crisis economic environment encouraged some bargain-hunting acquisitions, but studies showed that they only added marginal value in terms of cutting costs at times of a weak economy. She found that the more successful transactions were based less on a bargain basement strategy but rather on integrating and motivating new talent. "The winners do not act like conquerors sending out occupying armies. Instead they act like welcoming hosts and eager learners. Behaving as fixers rather than destroyers, they turn sceptics into fans." As an example of this, she gave: "France-based communications company Publicis Groupe treated its purchase of cash-strapped Saatchi & Saatchi as a reverse acquisition, adopting Saatchi's operating system as well as its management philosophy."[11]

In assessing research around the role of communication in the integration phase of M&A, it is words such as "vision", "strategy" and the diplomacy of integrating talent that recur. They are essentially concepts that are tied up with the notion of the corporate story. Bringing together facts, numbers and narrative around the merged corporation and its market environment sum up how the combined group will move forward and achieve growth. It is the communication effort that will bring together the merged teams to implement strategy. It will also represent the message to be communicated to the media and investment community, who are not only participants in the journey but ready commentators and critics as well should integration not look as though it is succeeding.

IPOs

The basic decisions underlying an IPO are financial. The raising of new capital and consequent listing on a stock exchange could be because a private company with a successful business wants funding for growth, or a promising technology needs finance for development or perhaps original investors need to exit, with an IPO being the mechanism that brings this about. From that beginning of financial motivation comes the essential need for a company story to be explained to enhance the capital-raising process. A company has to sell its story to prospective financial advisers so they might see merit in the company's prospects and have confidence they in turn can convince investors of its value and raise capital from them. So the company story, of facts, numbers and narrative, is present from the early stages of an IPO. It is an essential part of the roadshow around the investment community and with the media to launch the transaction, critical as listing takes place and then a template for explaining unfolding developments as a listed company implements its strategy.

One study of IPOs has highlighted the importance of communication in articulating corporate strategy. It becomes a signal to financial analysts, especially if it is articulated with "clarity, intensity and consistency", and has a positive effect on returns when it is directed to focusing on specific market targets rather than being broadly based and less well-defined.[12]

The lead up

Assuming financial advice has determined a company is ready for the IPO process, it has to have its accounts in shape and audited, enabling an enterprise value to be established. An underwriter will take into account the company's value, its story and potential, the amount of capital required and how it will be used as part of its assessment around how it will approach potential investors to raise this capital. In contemplating listing on a stock exchange, companies have to put in place the corporate governance procedures necessary for the disclosure of information regularly and have the appropriate financial reporting measures in place to make it possible to release financial information in a timely way. The main information document governing the IPO process is a prospectus or offer document. In this a company will disclose its financial position, the amount of new capital it is seeking and how it will be used, its structure and capabilities and most importantly, its business model, story and strategy to take on a new direction with the capital raised. Usually, the prospectus will disclose an earnings forecast for the period ahead, creating a goal that displays an attractiveness to investors but also one that the company believes is achievable, since its reputation will depend on it.

The prospectus includes a lot of information that is required by law and so becomes a lengthy document, including various independent expert reports. However, it is also a communication document, being the main vehicle for reaching out to investors to give them an understanding of how a company works, what it is good at and how it will achieve success and growth in the future.

Since the raising of capital from the public carries with it significant legal responsibility, the prospectus is submitted to regulatory authorities to ensure it meets basic requirements for raising money from the public. Until it has been through this process, a company cannot begin to promote it to investors generally, although underwriters involved in the capital-raising can approach sophisticated investors who are familiar with risk assessment and the judgements required in making investment decisions.

The actual lead up in terms of documentation, due diligence and fulfilling legal requirements is a lengthy process, often distracting from running a business but a necessary requirement of the capital-raising process. While developing the corporate story for the prospectus is part of this, the information a prospectus contains is also anchored down by the legal process, with all statements about a company and its marketplace needing to be verified to remain in the document. The actual marketing of the story becomes the next stage of the IPO process.

Case study

Facebook IPO – investors burned for following, followers burned for investing

The basic idea underlying the Facebook business model, and its corporate story, is that "the best type of advertising is a message from a friend".[13] From beginnings in 2004 when founder Mark Zuckerberg was studying psychology at Harvard, Facebook has become a phenomenally successful social networking site, global in its coverage. By September 2012, Facebook achieved the milestone of 1 billion registered users, or around one-seventh of the world's population. Significant as this achievement was, it came four months after Facebook became the second largest IPO (initial public offer) in the US with its listing on the NASDAQ exchange. The IPO was successful in raising US$16 billion in new capital, with the $38 a share issue price valuing Facebook at $104 billion, making it the 23rd largest stock in the US by market capitalization.[14] However, the IPO was not without several aspects of controversy.

Over the eight years from start-up to listing, Facebook had grown at a rapid rate. From the small gang involved in its beginnings, employee numbers had grown to nearly 4,000 by mid-2012 and in the lead up to listing, they planned an all-night "hackathon", or computer programming session, at Californian headquarters to usher in the listing at 6.30 am San Francisco time.[15] However, it wasn't long before the excitement around stock exchange listing gave way to some market realities. "Nasdaq delayed the opening of trading and botched orders"[16] and the "underwriters bought Facebook stock to keep it from falling below the IPO price".[17] While the stock price remained at US$38 at the end of the first day of trading, it gradually slid backwards over succeeding months to reach a low of $17.55 by September, less than half the value at which it debuted.[18]

The share price slide brought out the critics. One charge was that Facebook had been overvalued. Its value at the time of listing represented 107 times the previous year's earnings and 26 times the previous year's sales, multiples that represented a value more than double that of Google when it listed in 2004.[19] From this perspective, the stock price fall was caused by a spreading concern about overvaluation, with questions creeping in around whether Facebook might be losing out in not having begun earlier to build earnings from mobile use of the site.

Another concern around listing was whether institutions were given the inside running on knowing about weakening earnings of Facebook in advance of the IPO, information that was not shared with other investors. Ultimately the primary underwriter, Morgan Stanley, without admitting or denying the claim, was fined US$5 million by the SEC in relation to the issue.[20]

Another issue was whether Facebook tried too hard to maximize its sale price at the IPO, with one critic castigating the CFO in relation to this, only to cause a significant debate about whether he had done a bad or excellent job in putting the company up for auction and accepting the best price.[21]

Some of the harder challenges for Facebook in the post-IPO price slide were responding to questions around whether it could take the step with its story that the market was expecting, which was to "monetize" its business model. In the lead up to the IPO, CEO Zuckerberg had caused consternation with some analysts by turning up to his first big investor meeting in sneakers and trademark hoodie instead of a suit.[22] Although this may have seemed to indicate a casual approach, more recent announcements have shown Facebook taking monetization very seriously. In October, Facebook for the first time released information that showed it was making progress in generating income from mobile business, with 14 per cent of advertising revenue for the September quarter being from mobile, worth about

US$3 million a day. Earnings for the quarter were slightly ahead of analysts' expectations and, despite reporting an accounting loss for the period, the stock price was at last moving upwards from September lows.[23] More positive news from Facebook came out in November, with the introduction of a gift service, making it easier for Facebook users to buy presents for friends. To begin with, it was just available in the US, and to make it work Facebook rented a warehouse in South Dakota and created its own software to track inventory and shipping. Stock analysts warmed to the news, seeing it as giving Facebook a toehold in the e-commerce market as well as adding more to the personalization of Facebook's data, which in turn could lead to more targeted advertising.[24] Again the market responded positively and by early 2013 stock price had reached US$31.54, with NASDAQ showing that the consensus of analysts' price expectations over the next 12 months was for the stock to reach US$34.50.[25] By August 2013, Facebook had finally returned to its IPO price, reaching $38.54 and with consensus showing it would maintain that price over the next year.

While the prevailing investment view about Facebook at the time of the price fall might have been "connect with your friends on Facebook, stay away from the stock", the acceptance of Facebook as a phenomenon that is here to stay seems to be the way the market is "liking" the story.

The roadshow

Underwriters to an IPO want to be able to take key members of a company's management team to meetings with potential investors. This can mean many meetings a day with a roadshow also covering a number of city locations where prospective investors are located. Preceding these meetings the underwriter will have sounded out the most likely prospects. Usually the sell-side stockbroker, which is the underwriter, will focus on the institutional buy-side, since this group will take the bulk of the stock in an IPO, but retail investors will also be needed to provide a spread of shareholders. The proportion of retail investors will depend on the extent to which the company is known, its size and surrounding circumstances.

Initiation of a roadshow presupposes a company is ready to talk about what it does and why it might be an interesting proposition for investment. While there is little doubt a 100-page prospectus will contain all the essential information to meet the requirements of due diligence, investigating accountants and legal advisers, the essence of a corporate story can be lost in this morass of detail. Without a story, an IPO is lifeless, and it is not made more attractive by a company making promises that may prove too hard to keep. The understanding of a business that needs to be communicated in a roadshow is conveyed in a presentation document that is far briefer than a prospectus. The communication is also oral as well as written. Potential investors make judgements based on how the story is told as well as on the basis of a prospectus. A useful accompanying document is a brief story summary on two sides of an A4 page, enabling it to be left behind as part of an information package and making it easy for investors to repeat the key story messages to others on an investment committee.

A roadshow is a combination of providing information and marketing. Like any presentation, it will work best if sufficient time for preparation is allowed. This enables development not just of key points for emphasis but phrases, one-liners and anecdotes that implant how a company's business model works and its characteristics that will give it an advantage in its marketplace. The Q&A process requires anticipation as well as being able to convey a confidence to the audience that the company has a strategy and the capability to implement it successfully. Having the market understand a company's story is critical and this understanding is anchored in good communication. While the success of IPOs tends to be judged on whether they meet forecasts, the market can be more forgiving if it understands a business and the environment in which it operates. As the roadshow progresses, it becomes a process of refining the art of corporate storytelling, combining written, spoken and non-verbal communication in getting across the facts, numbers and narrative that sum up an interesting investment proposition and goes beyond letting numbers speak for themselves.

When an IPO is ready for public announcement, this element of IPO marketing involves engagement with the media. While the same presentation content can be used with journalists as was done with the buy-side, the news elements need a strong and yet simple presentation so that media reporting will reflect the enthusiasm and competence of management in bringing to the market a company that has appealing prospects. An accompanying news release helps this process, with its value enhanced if its content and quotes recognize principles of journalism. If the IPO has a reasonable size, it will attract journalists to a press conference, enabling a close engagement with a company's chief executive. These relationships can prove to be long-lasting beyond the IPO, providing there is preparation and management around how the story is told and allowance for a company to meet reasonable expectations. Achieving photo stories in the print media and online as well as television coverage can build considerable capital-raising momentum for an IPO. Conversely, mistakes can be magnified and prove to be difficult for the capital-raising process since media coverage will have a significant influence on how investors, especially retail investors, take to the IPO story.

Listing and onwards

When IPOs meet the capital-raising deadline and have a register of investors keen to see their stock listed on an exchange, a company is ready to continue its life as a listed entity. Actual listing usually involves an exchange ceremony, possibly with ringing the bell to begin trading, and then there is a genuine public reaction to IPO pricing. A fact with which many IPOs need to contend is that some investors will sell on the first day on the basis that the opening stock price will rise above issue price. This is an inevitability and can apply to wholesale and retail investors but if a company has presented its story well it should retain the vast majority of original shareholders when it lists.

Being listed is also the start of implementing corporate governance and disclosure procedures that were not part of common practice for private companies but are an essential aspect of communicating with the market. The media and investment community with which a company engaged during the roadshow period are also going to want to see a company live up to its promise and communication about this will be a large part of managing expectations.

The success of an IPO campaign can only be viewed retrospectively and to a large extent is dependent on a company's actual financial performance and its ability to have met the expectations it created during the roadshow. However, if some of the communications elements were established effectively, they guide how a company responsibly explains its performance in relation to market conditions and management input. Substantiating credibility of management is a critical IPO success factor. This in turn is tied up with having developed a campaign theme and strategy to communicate key elements of the business model. It will have implanted a compelling investment story and developed a profile and image for the company that enhances credibility as well as increased understanding of the business and its competitive advantage. A successful campaign will have established a group of journalists and analysts prepared to be followers of the unfolding story as well as a management team comfortable in dealing with the media, having gained a heightened appreciation of news and how to communicate it to the marketplace. Perpetuating these elements is the basis for listed companies successfully communicating their corporate stories.

Crisis

A simple Internet search of the term "crisis management" produces a vast variety of tips and trite advice that seem designed to make management of unexpected events seem routine. There seems to be no shortage of examples of crises that have been poorly managed that tend to fuel the selling pitch that all that is needed is to hire a crisis management adviser to implement a plan to make a crisis go away. A simple set of rules for crisis management can be formulaic, so the rule-makers suggest. While this simplification seems a serious underestimation of the complexity that can be involved in seeking resolution of a crisis, there would be general agreement that the consequences of crisis can be significant, leading to loss of reputation and a plummeting stock price. The most likely reality is that crises of some unpredictable kind will always be with us and that a more responsible route is not to consider how simple they can be to manage but to elevate the seriousness of the potential consequences so that crisis management is dealt with at the highest levels of a corporation, with extensive planning in place to cope with an array of possibilities that might arise.

One crisis management practitioner[26] has found there are three elements of the crisis process that always come as a surprise to companies. It is not so much that crisis is unexpected, since business conditions following the global financial crisis have represented a continuing difficult environment on top of the unexpected. Rather it is how the crisis process works that can cause consternation for those with responsibility at the top of organizations. One element of surprise is how long it can take for those at the top of corporations to realize something serious is going on. A common reason for this is that employees at the front line want to try to handle things themselves before reporting it higher. This reticence might seem natural on a personal level but the delay in those with corporate responsibility for handling a crisis in finding out about its evolution can be critical in how a crisis is handled. If corporations are to be in the race for effectively handling a crisis, they need to instil a cultural mentality that understands the damage a crisis that is badly managed can have on overall corporate wellbeing. The reason for the importance of wider notification within a company of the onset of a crisis is the second surprise related to the nature of crisis. That is how quickly the pressure can build when a crisis becomes public. The advent of social media has contributed further to a speeding up of time within which a company needs to respond. If a crisis has wide repercussions, it does not take long for the media calls to come in demanding an instant response. For listed companies, the market reactions also set in fast. This prompts the third surprise, which is how closely a company's value is linked to whether or not it is able to deal with a crisis quickly and effectively. This value can range from initial seriously negative effects on revenue, share price and reputation, with the speed of recovery depending on how a company responds to the unfolding crisis.

These three elements of surprise point to the measures a company should take in preparing for and dealing with crisis. Most research around crisis points to two fundamental aspects around the better handling of the unexpected. One is that preparation for unforeseen events is a large part of successful handling of them. The other is that effective communication is the critical factor in limiting damage from crisis. Some recent research reported in *IR Magazine* among investor relations managers globally has found that crisis has become more prevalent and at the same time, more companies are showing an awareness that preparation is important. The research showed that a corporate crisis has affected one in three companies over the past five years, ranging across a variety of events such as the global economic downturn, employee disputes, regulatory investigations and hostile takeover attempts. The survey also showed that two-thirds of companies have preparations in place for the next crisis.[27]

Crisis preparation

A lot of literature around crisis management links the process to issues management. It is monitoring issues and being aware of their life cycle that builds in anticipation that some issues might escalate into crisis. A common method companies implement in preparing for crisis is the consideration of possible scenarios, procedures to be followed if anticipated events take place and a setting out of relevant communication messages. While the scenarios help to develop specific messages related to events that might occur, a crisis also relates to the corporation as a whole and so involves it taking place in the context of the corporate story. By applying the corporate story to crisis response, it is possible to bring the bigger picture to bear on particular events, which in turn can reflect an aspect of effective management of crisis.

The *IR Magazine* survey mentioned above showed that while quite a number of companies extend crisis preparation to simulating possible scenarios, the majority opt for a more general consideration of possible scenarios and then put in place a crisis plan. The survey showed that larger companies were more prepared for crisis than smaller companies, with many of them enacting crisis simulation as part of their preparation efforts. Given that acting quickly when crisis strikes is a key to being able to implement a plan effectively, an important aspect of planning is putting in place procedures to make it easy for senior management to be alerted immediately a possible crisis emerges. This planning should extend to having all employees understand the need to report what could turn out to be exceptional circumstances to their managers, who in turn are required to pass this on directly to those in charge of crisis management. Sometimes a crisis may come to the notice initially of people external to the company, resulting in calls to the company that should immediately trigger action under crisis protocols. While chief executives would be prime spokespersons, contingency plans also need to be in place if they are unavailable.

Crisis preparation also involves establishing priorities for action in seeking to manage a crisis. The *IR Magazine* survey showed that investor relations managers give top priority to a company's reputation, with this being nearly twice as important as stock price and shareholder retention. While these three factors are intertwined, the effects on stock price and shareholders are seen more as consequences of damage to reputation rather than as contributing to that damage. As the survey finds:

> In their interdependence, corporate reputation affects share price and shareholder retention more than share price and shareholder retention affect reputation, so the best way to keep and encourage investors as well as maintain a healthy share price in the long term is to focus on corporate reputation during a crisis.[28]

According to research by Accenture,[29] the impact on stock value following a crisis is not only negative but is often pronounced and can persist over a prolonged period regardless of the industry in which a company operates.[30] Effects on stock price can follow a few stages, with negative effects continuing for longer if there is a market perception that a crisis has been handled inadequately. Where there is a faster recovery, Accenture's research attributes this to swift implementation of a public relations plan, involving efforts to get out messages early as a way of preventing crisis escalation. In these cases, communication paralleled an active operational crisis response to the issues themselves

Among the measures Accenture proposes for improving crisis management capability are to challenge a corporation's planning assumptions by considering a range of potential crisis issues and then the resources available to meet these eventualities. This enables preparation for a seamless connection with risk management and crisis management. Management structures should consider internal and external responses. A priority should not be production of a manual that might gather dust waiting for a crisis but to focus on the practical, like actually being prepared to manage an event operationally and make sure that all relevant people are informed as quickly as possible, including senior management and the board. With that part of a plan actioned, a company is then prepared for external communication, with key stakeholder audiences predetermined, such as employees, customers, the investment market and the media.[31] Recognizing widespread views about effective crisis management, Accenture advises: "recognise the crisis as early as possible and take quick, decisive action."[32] Accenture develops the medical analogy about the "golden hour", in which the most important treatment in preventing possible death from a traumatic injury occurs within the first hour after the event has occurred. In corporate circumstances, while initial communication is critical, it also has to be ongoing, especially in today's environment when there is a 24-hour news cycle.

What the media wants to know when crisis occurs is what has happened, what the reason is for it and who is to blame. This line of inquiry points to where the risks can lie in crisis management. A company's preparation has to be around being able to gather facts quickly so that the fist element of communication can be around giving a description of actual events factually. Outlining reasons and blame is rarely possible with accuracy at the moment crises occur, and speculating about them before sufficient evidence is to hand can be an unfortunate mistake in crisis management. Companies that seek to deny that anything is their fault and that inquirers should just leave it to the company to sort out are heading in the direction of alienating the media and objective observers. It is open communication that becomes valued as being effective in crisis management. If companies do not know the reasons immediately they should say so and give a time frame for when they might know so that they can prevent others speculating on what might have happened. It is lack of information being communicated regularly during a crisis that creates a vacuum for the media in particular, forcing journalists to seek outside observations and comments on events that have transpired. If there is misreporting of events, then this also needs vigilance by companies and swift correction, which can be effectively achieved by providing the information the media needs to report responsibly.

When crisis occurs, while companies might prefer that such events had not happened and have a natural reluctance to have to admit openly to events, it is overcoming this reticence that plants the seeds for observers to see effective crisis management. Hiding from the facts or seeking to cover them up, is never an effective course, as so many crisis disaster examples show.

Supporting what have become accepted ways of effective crisis management are two perceptive quotes from investor Warren Buffett. One is: "It takes 20 years to build a reputation and five minutes to ruin it. If you think about that, you'll do things differently."[33] The other is: "No crisis improves with age".[34] Both these aphorisms support the need for swift action, with protecting corporate reputation as the number one priority. Since reputation is intertwined with what a company does and its values, it is the corporate story that must envelop crisis key messages. If a company is to effect a sincere handling of awkward information around events that have arisen, it is the corporate narrative that provides a structure within which it can indicate it is doing its best, not only to communicate about what has and is happening but that it is being operationally effective in dealing with events.

While crisis management teams will involve people from many parts of a corporation, at the centre of the process will be someone who heads up the function of corporate and investor communication who is also the custodian of the evolving corporate story. While crisis is one aspect of this role, it is time to see what the overall aspects of this job entail.

Notes

1 Clayton, BC, "Understanding the Unpredictable Beyond Traditional Research on Mergers and Acquisitions", *E:CO Issue* 12 (3), 2010, p 1
2 Papadakis, VM, "The Role of Broader Context and the Communication Program in Merger and Acquisition Success", *Management Decision* 43 (2), 2005, p 236
3 Herd, T, "M&A Success: Beating the Odds", *Business Week*, 23 June 2010
4 James, B, Gilmour, A and Yates, G, "Control Premium Study", RSM Bird Cameron, 2012
5 "Is Tribal Conflict Inevitable in Mergers and Takeovers?", *The Financial Times*, 16 July 2008
6 Ranninger, R, quoted in "Judgment Call: Is Tribal Conflict Inevitable in Mergers and Takeovers?", *The Financial Times*, 15 July 2008, www.ft.com/intl/cms/s/0/3d106de2-527c-11dd-9ba7-000077b07658.html#axzz2loxbvK5p
7 Coughlin, R, quoted in "Judgment Call: Is Tribal Conflict Inevitable in Mergers and Takeovers?", *The Financial Times*, 15 July 2008, www.ft.com/intl/cms/s/0/3d106de2-527c-11dd-9ba7-000077b07658.html#axzz2loxbvK5p
8 Moeller, S, quoted in "Judgment Call: Is Tribal Conflict Inevitable in Mergers and Takeovers?", *The Financial Times*, 15 July 2008, www.ft.com/intl/cms/s/0/3d106de2-527c-11dd-9ba7-000077b07658.html#axzz2loxbvK5p
9 Hedges, N, quoted in "Judgment Call: Is Tribal Conflict Inevitable in Mergers and Takeovers?", *The Financial Times*, 15 July 2008, www.ft.com/intl/cms/s/0/3d106de2-527c-11dd-9ba7-000077b07658.html#axzz2loxbvK5p
10 Kantor, RM, "Mergers That Stick", *Harvard Business Review*, October 2009
11 Kantor (2009), p 122
12 Gao, H, Darroch, J, Mather, D and MacGregor, A, "Signalling Corporate Strategy in IPO Communication", *Journal of Business Communication* 45 (1), 2008

13 Adams, T, "Why Has Facebook's Stock Market Flotation Been Such a Disaster?", *The Guardian/The Observer*, 21 October 2012, www.guardian.co.uk/technology/2012/oct/21/facebook-mark-zuckerberg-shares-flotation

14 Raice, S, Das, A and Letzing, J, "Facebook Prices IPO at Record Value", *The Wall Street Journal*, 17 May 2012 and Spears, L and Frier, S, "Facebook Stalls in Public Debut After Record $16B in IPO", *Bloomberg*, 18 May 2012

15 Raice et al (2012)

16 Rusli, EM, "Citigroup Assails Nasdaq over Flawed Facebook IPO", *The New York Times*, 22 August 2012

17 Spears and Frier (2012)

18 Nasdaq, Facebook Inc., Price chart, www.nasdaq.com/symbol/fb/stock-chart

19 Spears and Frier (2012) and Spears, L and Womack, B, "Facebook Increases IPO Price Range to $34–$38 a Share", *Bloomberg*, 15 May 2012

20 Levy, A and MacMillan, D, "Morgan Stanley Settles Facebook IPO Case", *San Francisco Chronicle*, 21 December 2012, www.sfgate.com/business/article/Morgan-Stanley-settles-Facebook-IPO-case-4139765.php

21 Sorkin, AR, "Who is to Blame for Facebook's IPO? A Mix of Responses", *The New York Times*, 4 September 2012

22 Hamilton, W and Guynn, J, "Is Mark Zuckerberg in Over his Hoodie as Facebook CEO?", *Los Angeles Times*, 17 August 2012

23 Dembosky, A, "Facebook Fillip from Mobile Growth", *Financial Times*, 23 October 2012

24 Sengupta, S, "With a Billion Birthdays on File, Facebook adds a Gift Store", *New York Times*, 27 November 2012

25 Nasdaq, Facebook Inc., Analyst Research, www.nasdaq.com/symbol/fb/analyst-research

26 Deverell, J, "All Companies Should Expect a Crisis", *IR Magazine*, Crisis Management and Communication Research Report, June 2012, pp 10–11

27 *IR Magazine* (2012), pp 1–9

28 *IR Magazine* (2012), p 9

29 Accenture, *Corporate Crisis Management: Preparing for a Rapid Response to Unexpected Events*, Accenture, 2011, http://www.accenture.com/SiteCollectionDocuments/PDF/Accenture_Corporate_Crisis_Management.pdf

30 Accenture (2011), p 4

31 Accenture (2011), pp 8–9

32 Accenture (2011), p 10

33 Accenture (2011), p 2

34 Quoted in Parkinson, E, "Executives in Crisis Told to Tell Facts Fast", *Australian Financial Review*, 1 May 2012

13 Role and responsibilities of a chief corporate and investor communications officer

The title will vary among listed companies but, within the senior executive team, will be someone who is designated the role of being in charge of corporate communication with key stakeholders. Among the titles could be corporate affairs director, investor relations officer (IRO, as they are commonly known) or media and investor relations director. In line with the responsibilities involved, NIRI introduces another title, chief disclosure officer. In some companies the roles of media relations and investor relations are split between two managers reporting to someone taking a larger view of corporate communication. However these roles are designated, they all have a common factor, which is that these people are custodians of the corporate story. They are the explainers of what a company does and how it is performing financially in implementing its strategy. The primary stakeholders to whom they communicate are the investment community, shareholders and the business media but this group can also expand to government, customers, employees and the wider public, depending on issues or crises that might arise. How this role is organized and implemented is the content of this chapter.

Evolution

While technology has influenced communication in many ways in recent decades, the fundamental importance of developing messages and building relationships in communicating those messages has not altered. Another constant factor is the relevance of information for financial markets, heightened by the speed at which information is now communicated. A little over three decades ago, announcements to a stock exchange platform were made by delivery of letters. This was then superseded by faxing announcements to the exchange and, subsequently, email delivery. Trading then was by an open outcry system on the floor of an exchange, with company news relayed to the trading floor by broadcast announcements. Most media outlets had press boxes overlooking the floor of the exchange for reporting back to their newsrooms, often dictating copy over the phone to copy-takers. Distribution of news to the media was by courier delivery of printed news releases, supported by telex machines delivering printouts to newsrooms. The fax machine was a considerable advance but the fast adoption of computer technology not only led to electronic trading on exchanges but also faster delivery of news to exchanges and on to the media. Today not only is news delivered in a shorter time frame of seconds and minutes but it is also spread more widely, with the advent of social media and a myriad of online news outlets. The news cycle has sped up and is now also a 24-hour process.

In the midst of this information revolution, the role of the investor relations officer has also evolved, with a title that did not even exist some three decades ago. Faster distribution of information has led to increased demands for more information, meaning that companies have had to create roles involving not only management of communication to investment markets but also the assessment of market opinion and the calibration this involves for communication strategy.

Role overview

In enacting the role of head of corporate communication or IRO, technology has certainly had an impact on implementation but there are also several constant components. Among these are developing content for communication, selecting targets and determining how information is to be communicated. These primary activities reflect the definition of investor relations from NIRI, with it involving:

> a strategic management responsibility that integrates finance, communication, marketing and securities law compliance to enable the most effective two-way communication between a company, the financial community and other stakeholders to contribute to a company's securities achieving fair valuation.[1]

The introduction of the term "two-way communication" connects with the most widely understood version of James Grunig's theory of public relations. This describes the most effective form of communication as a corporation accounting for the views of stakeholders in the way in which it communicates with them. Later revisions of the theory by Grunig allowed for aspects of asymmetrical and one-way communication. For IROs, there is also a sense in which the role needs to account for the reality of three-way communication, with the generalized financial market being another participant. Primary stakeholders might be the buy- and sell-sides of the investment community, shareholders and the media, but the stock market is a powerful third force that ultimately delivers a verdict, in the form of stock price, on how well a company is performing and communicating.

The content of financial and investor communication essentially involves preparing the corporate story to produce a good understanding of the company, its attributes, market positioning and business strategy. This story has many voices, in short and long form, as it is delivered conversationally, formally in presentations and in writing. As custodian of the story, the IRO needs to ensure it reflects the changing reality of a company, in line with financial performance and fluctuating market conditions. The IRO is also involved in helping others convey the story to key stakeholders. Disclosing news relating to performance and achievements, or lack of them, falls within IRO responsibilities. In considering stakeholders to whom the IRO should relate, the primary focus tends to be on external stakeholders, since their views can be the main determinants of stock price. However, IROs also have an important internal constituency. As part of the senior management team, internal audiences need to absorb nuances from the chief executive officer and chief financial officer about how the corporation is performing so that changes can be reflected in communication. The numbers and facts as they vary need to be incorporated into a dynamic narrative. The communications role not only needs IROs to take into account these variations in the form of disclosure but also how it affects the story and the way in which the story is told. The IRO, as communicator and marketer needs to develop for the executive team an evolving story to capture what is interesting from the mass of corporate information flow each day. Another key internal audience for an IRO is the board of directors, to whom it is customary to report market opinion and commentary on stock market action in relation to a company's stock.

The head corporate communications role is pivotal in connecting a company with its marketplace and stakeholders. It is partly a weather vane, in reporting within the corporation about the direction of winds from the market and stakeholders, and partly a producer of the information that can influence wind direction in terms of investment views about the company.

Representing the corporate perspective

The multifaceted role of the head of communication is reflected in the management of the many sensitivities surrounding the role of a company spokesperson. Protocols – usually drafted by an IRO for approval by the board of directors – about who can speak publicly on behalf of a corporation, especially on topics that may impinge on stock price, will vary among organizations. In some companies, it is only the chief executive who can be quoted publicly in news releases and speak directly to the media. In other companies this role may extend to the chief financial officer and head of communication. However the protocols may be determined, much of the traffic is directed initially to the head of communications to be handled in accordance with protocols. Even if the CEO is the only official spokesperson, there is still an extensive role to be filled in answering factual inquiries and in shaping the messages the company has disclosed in its market releases. Many calls – from the media, investment community or shareholders – are not necessarily seeking public quotes but for some corporate spokesperson to tell them what a market announcement means in simple terms. Often they just want to hear, in a conversational way, what the latest news means in the context of the corporate story. It is this process of providing context around news that has been announced that describes the support function behind the spokesperson role. It is more than providing background information since it is an interpretative contribution that adds nuances without going beyond the disclosure that has been made. An ability to perform this supportive function authoritatively is what underlines the value of the role of investor relations and gives it credibility in the eyes of key stakeholders. The very nature of the role of chief executives means they can be hard to contact for regular conversations with journalists, key shareholders and analysts. There will be planned events where this can take place but in between those occasions, someone, such as an IRO who is informed about a company and its strategy, needs to be available to answer the most common question, of what an announcement means for the corporation. This information may not be for publication, since an IRO may not be an approved spokesperson, but it is useful background and part of the relationship-building process for these conversations to take place. The answer to many of these questions is the corporate story, the context without new disclosure.

The main sensitivity to master is understanding the strict boundaries of disclosure. This means knowing what can be said and not said in conversations around announcements and company progress. Some questions may want to explore these areas and if it is a widely held concern, may lead to the IRO generating a new official announcement for a company, to be approved within agreed protocols, so that further disclosure can be made. However, in conversations with key stakeholders, no new information can be disclosed without triggering serious legal repercussions or making a public announcement to cover any new disclosure.

In addition to understanding disclosure, another important requirement of the role is mastery of the subject matter. This requires not only a complete understanding of the corporation but also its marketplace and business context. This includes a knowledge of the company's strategy, its financial position, products and services, how they are being marketed and the competitive environment. Overlaid on this is an appreciation of the conditions of the economic environment and how this affects operations as well as the regulatory structure that applies to the business. This knowledge base is extensive and can take some time and effort to absorb.

The task of understanding this subject matter cannot be underestimated, especially since it covers a mass of detail. What is required and what is essentially the main function of the chief communications role is to mould this detail into a story. It is how all the parts come together, the facts and the numbers that make a narrative, that can form an appeal to investors while also being an explanation of a company's purpose and direction for other stakeholders. Creating this narrative and having it guide spokespersons for the company so that it is effective oral communication, is a large part of how the corporate story is conveyed to the investment community, in one-on-one discussion or larger group meetings. This audience is already immersed in a lot of analytical detail around the company and its sector and while it can be impressive to see management equally conversant with the minutiae, it is the overriding narrative that connects the facts and numbers, giving the investment community a story to adopt for their reports and investment recommendations.

Combining these key elements into the supportive role surrounding an official spokesperson – understanding disclosure, mastering the detail and converting detail into story – is a reflection of how the chief communicator's role works in practice. Among the challenges of this position in a corporation are to win the respect of those inside the company, among the board and senior management, and externally, among the investment community and media who seek comment from the company. Often these people will only want to speak to a chief executive and can tend to bypass an IRO, unless they perceive they are achieving a real sense of understanding the corporation by speaking to the person who heads communication. In this way, IROs can fill the position of spokesperson substitute, able to speak with authority on a company's strategy, direction and corporate story, within the bounds of what has been disclosed publicly.

Developing key communication targets

Establishing appropriate targets for communication of the corporate story begins with an internal assessment of a company, in terms of its size, business area, profitability and growth trajectory. These factors help to define external targets for an IRO, with wider corporate communications targets also encompassing government and those that might be relevant in crisis communication planning, such as key customers. From an investment perspective, the key targets are the investment community, media and shareholders but will also encompass the organization's bankers, credit ratings agencies and regulatory authorities.

With each of these key targets, an IRO is seeking to create an awareness and understanding of a company as well as to gain access to capital, achieve liquidity of a company's stock and a fair valuation of it.[2] Prime targets in the investment community that would contribute most to these aims are those whose investing style matches the characteristics a company represents. The sell-side will have analysts focused on particular industry sectors while the buy-side will have investing orientations towards growth or value, short- or long-term. The buy-side will also have preferences about the size of companies in which it invests, views about varying risk tolerances, which would relate to the stage of development a company has reached, and dividend policies. By achieving investment from a number of large, long-only institutions, companies are building in potential support for future rounds of capital-raising.

While it is helpful for IROs to target the most likely institutional investors to buy stock, they also need to spread their storytelling more widely if they are to achieve another aim, that of improving liquidity of a stock. This comes about from increasing the extent to which a stock is traded, which is the result of a wider group of investors taking an interest in the company. Achieving this is a result of ongoing communication with the buy- and sell-sides, which also contributes to another investor relations objective, achieving fair valuation. This is usually an outcome of broadening understanding of a company's strategy and its ability to achieve growth targets based on its track record. By understanding how the market evaluates a stock compared with an internal calculation of intrinsic value developed by an IRO and the company's finance team, an IRO has guidance about what is needed either to boost understanding or tone down expectations around what a company is likely to achieve.

Another prime communications target is the media, with relevant journalists also being influenced by company size and industry sector. Targets will include regular reporters of company news in the metropolitan media and wire services, those who follow a relevant industry sector, investment writers and opinion writers. These journalists may be in a variety of geographic locations. Separately there is the industry media and possibly local media near where a corporation has large operations.

Shareholders, apart from institutional shareholders, usually opt to receive company information electronically and so are kept informed about progress and developments in this way. However, institutional shareholders expect more personal treatment, with a number of face-to-face meetings taking place during a year.

Allied to communicating to these prime targets is establishing a database for regular dissemination of announcements as they are made to the exchange platform. While distribution of material to the mass of shareholders can be managed by a share registry organization, communication to the media and investment community can be made more personal by an IRO crafting a message to accommodate direct distribution of announcements to targets. This target group can go beyond institutional shareholders and include buy-side targets, who could be potential investors, as well as the sell-side and relevant journalists. News coming direct from an IRO, with a message putting news into a context, can be an important contribution to relationship-building.

Monitoring the media and market

For the board and management of corporations, those in charge of communication are the eyes and ears as to what is being said about the company in the media, a conduit for stock market opinion about a company and also a reporter on market action. There are many external services that provide media monitoring, which can include related search terms and cover competitors. Media monitoring can be helpful in picking up reactions from announcements that have been made, especially in assessing coverage of earnings releases, which can include opinion commentary and views from analysts. Assessment would cover who has written the coverage, the extent to which it reflects content and key messages of the company's announcement, aspects that have been emphasized and the way in which chief executive quotes have been incorporated. Media reporting, which is the outcome of engagement with the media on results announcement day, affords an opportunity to assess the effectiveness of this process. Wire service reports, as the first media reactions to announcements, can show how news is being received, with print coverage the next day also reflecting how the news has been absorbed after more time given to it for consideration. The news may have achieved electronic media coverage and been discussed on chat rooms or in social media and covered on various websites. Services are available to monitor all these outlets and may be essential on an ongoing basis, especially in meeting disclosure obligations and monitoring issues that may have potential for evolving into crisis scenarios.

The opinion of the investment community in reaction to major announcements such as financial results is also readily apparent as the market reacts instantly and sell-side reports emerge within 24 hours following the news. These sell-side reports are emailed to institutional and retail investors, with distribution also including the company that is the subject of the report. IROs will pore over the content of these reports and engage with the authors around various aspects of them. Part of the process around important announcements will have involved corporations presenting to the investment community. With earnings announcements, presentations and conference calls are made on the day or a day or two after the announcement to allow a period of reflection on the content. Monitoring reactions and written and verbal content is an important aspect of the role of a chief communications officer since it becomes valuable input to future explaining of the corporate story and progress. The sell-side analysts' reports will make earnings forecasts and it is critical that IROs keep spreadsheets of these market views since they also sum up market expectations of a company's future performance. Since the stock market tends to look forward in its views about earnings, companies need to be aware of market expectations reflected in stock price so that a company's own guidance about earnings, if it is provided, can contribute to managing these expectations as far as it can.

While stock price movements are an indicator of market opinion, often companies want to gather more qualitative views rather than just the direction of market prices and stock turnover. IROs can implement informal surveys themselves from conversations with market participants and they can also commission outside firms to conduct a more formal process, perhaps guaranteeing anonymity to informants to ensure candid opinions are being collected from key market followers among the buy- and sell-sides.

Keeping track of market statistics is also an important aspect of the monitoring role of an IRO. Among these are the extent of turnover each day, the main sell-side brokers trading the stock, whether key shareholders are changing the size of their holdings and keeping track of new entrants to the share register. The type of trading taking place is also relevant, such as trying to discern whether it might be an outcome of high frequency trading, which is more of a trading strategy rather than anything to do particularly with how a company is performing. The extent to which investors might be shorting the company's stock is also critical, along with identities of the funds that may be undertaking this activity. This topic is covered below as well as the reporting function around how this information is conveyed internally within a corporation.

Case study

Brambles – how they develop the corporate story at Brambles

An interview with James Hall, senior director, investor relations and corporate affairs, Brambles Limited (ASX; BXB)

Brambles Limited is one of Australia's top 50 companies, with a market capitalization of A$12.7 billion and employing 17,000 people in its global operations. The media likes to describe Brambles as "the world's biggest pallet supplier". James Hall, who is Brambles senior director, investor relations and corporate affairs, is understanding of this form of shorthand since he used to be a journalist himself, becoming companies editor of the *Australian Financial Review* before moving into investor relations. However, Hall also has a broader agenda. Not only does he want people to understand Brambles' growing footprint in logistics but he also wants communication to form a link between performance metrics and the non-financial components of value at Brambles. Here's how he explains the way they go about communication at Brambles.

Q. There's been some comment recently about whether company annual meetings are a waste of time – what are your thoughts on that?

A. Annual meetings are really important but I would like to see them have less of an emphasis on the administrative side of things, a lot of which can be handled electronically throughout the year, to create more time for a genuine exchange of information about strategy and a proper forum for shareholder engagement. You could really transform the annual meeting. The regulator has a role to play but ultimately it is down to companies themselves to innovate. There is scope to do that within the current regulatory framework.

Q. What do you think about current trends in disclosure?

A. There's some really interesting developments at the moment, initiated by the regulator ASIC, regarding what content should be included in the operational and financial review section of the annual report. Some companies tend to take a defensive view of this – seeing a regulator imposing an additional legal burden – but I think it's positive that, in the wake of the financial crisis, ASIC is trying to develop ways to encourage companies to talk about long-term strategy and value drivers. Of course, the law already says companies should comment on these topics but ASIC is trying to provide more guidance about how it should be done. It presents an opportunity for better communication. This is happening at the same time as international efforts in so-called integrated reporting are developing. Integrated reporting is intended is to bring together a more holistic approach to the disclosure of financial and non-financial value drivers, or "indirect drivers of financial value" as some people call them, such as sustainability issues. To me, it's about communicating the broader proposition of how a company creates and retains value for all stakeholders. This actually represents a cultural change since many companies are used to reporting financial drivers but not necessarily non-financial – and they're used to talking about different stakeholder groups in silos. If you can explain properly how these come together, you are giving a more complete view of company strategy and performance and the way value propositions for different stakeholder groups are inter-linked.

Q. What are some examples at Brambles of how you would connect financial and non-financial issues?

A. A great example for Brambles is asset efficiency. We rent out millions of pallets, crates and containers every day so it's really important – both from a financial perspective and from the perspective of the sustainable use of resources – how efficient those assets are and how often they need to be replenished or replaced. There are various important metrics around loss rate, damage rate and asset turn rate. We don't actually release these statistics externally but the way we're moving is to identify drivers of value and build them into communication so external stakeholders can see what is important and what drives return on capital. Part of the evolving communications task is to have external stakeholders appreciate what it is they should be focusing on when they are looking for value, and internally for a company's people to be able to understand how strategy is devised to create that value and how their actions every day contribute. If you go into any company, a common question is "How well do people really understand the needs of shareholders?" From an investor relations point of view, the job is to understand fully what shareholder needs are and to feed those back into the organization – and also to help employees understand how, for example, the customer value that they drive every day actually creates shareholder value.

Brambles

Q. Can you tell me some of what investor relations involves on a daily basis?

A. A lot of what we do is driven by the annual calendar, such as twice-yearly results announcements, the annual report and annual meeting. These events all involve quite a lot of preparation. Then there are investor roadshows, which require decisions about how long we go on the road for and how many countries we cover. This takes a massive amount of planning – not just logistics but also the preparation that is around who to see and how we are going to tell our story. This also feeds a more challenging part of our planning cycle involving strategy, the budget process and the operations team so that when we get up and talk about the business we are communicating exactly what is happening. So an immense amount of time is spent alongside the strategy and finance teams to ensure we've got exactly the sort of information that shareholders need – and that shareholders needs are being considered in our internal planning processes. It's not just about presenting results. It's also about asking what we need to give shareholders to help them understand the business better. This also involves having an understanding of why people invest in our company in the first place – the investment proposition. There's not much point in a company pursuing generation of cash flow to pay dividends if shareholders are actually pursuing growth and would rather see that cash reinvested in growth opportunities. I categorize all this under the term of "right message". There is a continuum of development of that message, both internally and externally. You need to align "right message" with "right activity", which is the telling of the story. This covers investor days, the extent of roadshows, what's on our website for passive communication, media and getting the story out there. The third component is "right register", which means developing a shareholder base that is aligned to the company's true characteristics. We're basically a company with high return on capital, a solid growth outlook and a strong commercial proposition with a relatively defensive earnings stream – it's a positive growth story but, for example, investors looking for very high dividend yields might not be our main target group.

Q. How important is internal communication to investor relations?

A. What we've realized increasingly is that internal education is very important so that there's an understanding of stakeholder needs. It's hard for us to generate an outcome that shareholders want if key people in the organization don't understand what we are trying to achieve and why. Likewise we need to make sure we are listening to our own people to ensure we are not promising investors something we can't deliver. It's about alignment and balance between the needs of shareholders, employees and customers. This means us doing a lot of work on the platform for getting the messages across to our people. Involved in this is messaging about the values, the vision, the investment proposition, the strategy, why are we structured the way we're structured and the role of our people in delivering for our customers and shareholders.

Q. How do you fit all these tasks into your daily routine?

A. Depending on the time of year – and the structure of investor relations in the company they work for – an investor relations officer can be intensely involved in any number of things. You can actually have the most beautifully planned out day but then the phone starts ringing … if you're operating in a culture of no surprises, then the unexpected shouldn't happen, but it always can. We operate in more than 50 countries and things can happen on an operational basis that can throw your day out completely, and suddenly you're dealing with local media issues. Things like that should not cause problems, but they can blow up if they're not managed properly. On any particular day, the golden rule is that you have to be very responsive to stakeholders, predominantly analysts and shareholders but also, potentially, journalists or other stakeholders. In order to do investor relations well you need to be able to answer these people's questions incredibly quickly. And if you don't know the answer you need to get it, fast. To do this part of the job effectively, you need to have cultivated internal relationships. You can't just be a financial analyst. You need to have an interest in all parts of how a company works because knowing this helps you to earn the trust and respect of the operational people who will support you in getting the information you need. Relationship management is at the centre of investor relations, not just in terms of external stakeholders but also in relation to being connected with people in operations because you need them to be responsive to you when communications issues arise.

Q. You mentioned the "right register" – can you explain how you go about investor targeting?

A. We look at our register closely. The right kinds of investors for us are those that have a long-term view and are interested in a sustainable growth story. We spend a lot of time on investor targeting. In Australia it's relatively easy to get tracing notices of who's on the register and it's rudimentary to know this. Next steps from that are working out who's not on the register and why. It's all about identifying the marginal investor – if you want the company's share price to reflect the investment proposition then you need to know why certain investors aren't on the register because that might represent an opportunity to engage with them. Or maybe there are few investors from, for example, continental Europe or Japan and it's a matter of doing the research to find out why. The answer could be as simple as European investors might not be interested in Australia at the moment or, if they are, it might just be for mining companies, which means for us it's not worth doing a roadshow to these investors. Alternatively, it might be the case that Japanese investors are looking to Australia again because interest rates are so low at home and maybe a Brambles yield of 3 per cent could appear attractive, in which case a roadshow to Japan would seem worthwhile. In order to do this well you need to be spending a lot of time talking to brokers on the international desks, getting to understand what is going on in those markets. It's not worth the investor relations team's time, let alone that of the CEO or CFO, to go and see investors if there's no way they're going to buy the stock.

Q. Does the geographic spread of the business reflect where investors are or is there a disproportionate number of investors in Australia?

A. Yes there are more Australian investors but compared with other Australian companies we have a relatively large international component to our register, which is due to having an international business, to having a unique business and to the fact that we used to be dual-listed in the UK. So our split is about 60 per cent Australian investors, the vast majority of which is institutions. The rest is split between the UK and – to a lesser but still meaningful extent – the USA and Asia. A lot of our bigger shareholders are international.

Q. Does it concern you that the media describes Brambles as one of the world's largest pallet suppliers?

A. No. We certainly don't intend ceasing to be the world's largest supplier of pallets because the business is growing well and is a good business. But within that business we are diversifying and the value proposition is about the service we provide, not the pallet itself. But we're never going to get a journalist describing us as a "supply chain equipment pooling business" because that sounds like industry jargon to them. So what we need to do is work on simplifying how we're described and communicating the value of the business in a simple way. It's important to have a consistent story but you can't expect external audiences to pick up on all the themes if there isn't something meaty behind it. What this comes back to is that you have to be constantly refining, educating and reviewing the messages you're putting out externally and internally to make sure they are authentic and meaningful. Often things are developed for the purposes of communication by the CEO, CFO and head of HR for internal audiences and if there is something really meaningful for external audiences then it becomes our job to interpret this for them. Then you might see these things being reflected in reporting about the company if people can see how they have an impact on how the company performs. If something is not a driver of value then it won't be reported like that.

Q. How does investor relations have a role in the future for Brambles?

A. The really interesting thing is once you've established the basics, then developing the story and communicating it becomes a continuum of value creation and investor relations can be at the centre of this.

This interview was conducted on 31 January 2013 with Ian Westbrook.

There are a number of subscription services that allow the monitoring of market and media information, including chat rooms, blogs and social media comment.

Managing the register

The administrative management of the register of all shareholders of a company is usually outsourced to an organization that implements the physical process of communication, involving distribution of notices and dividends. Shareholders can choose whether they want to receive these communications electronically or by mail. The registry manager will also deal with queries about the technical nature of shareholdings but any aspects of communication are the concern of an IRO. This encompasses crafting messages for shareholder communication, assessing variations in the composition of the share register and working towards an ideal mix of retail and institutional shareholders. There are costs from having large numbers of shareholders, with institutional shareholders being comparatively economical in taking up larger amounts of stock, but retail shareholders can also have more of a longer-term view, which adds a different component to the value of having them as investors in a company.

Knowing relevant statistics around a company's shareholder base is an ingredient of shaping a relevant communications strategy. These statistics include proportions of retail and institutional shareholders and also the costs of registry management since there are a number of competing service providers in this area. Locations, demographics and type of shareholder provide a picture of the make-up of investors that is input to the shareholder-targeting process. This analysis of data around the shareholder base may indicate that particular locations, advisers or sell-side stockbrokers have proven to be supporters of the corporate story and there may be particular institutional investment styles that have found a company appealing. The analysis may also become a guide to targeting new shareholders that have similar characteristics to those who have become investors but may not yet have met management to hear the story around a company's strategy and prospects. From building relationships with institutions that have become shareholders, IROs will have discerned aspects of their decision-making that led them to become investors. Perhaps they may have a value or growth orientation, which establishes an argument IROs can put to other institutions that have a similar investing philosophy. Sell-side supporters can help with introductions to new institutional targets that can also be on the receiving end of company announcement distribution as news is released. The marketing aspects of an IRO's job involve combining the processes of relationship-building with existing shareholders as well as finding new prospects for investment. From time to time, companies may implement campaigns to reach out to new retail investors, with advisers, retail sell-side brokers and investment conferences being useful adjuncts to this marketing effort.

Identifying shareholders

Some investors like to make their identities hard to discover, with their investment being through nominee companies that hold stock on their behalf. The process of researching original identity can be time-consuming and so is often outsourced to service providers who initiate the painstaking search processes and who are also familiar with nominee identities from having provided similar services to other companies. The main reason for wanting to discover identity is that it also helps with discovering motive for investment.

While having anonymity may be the outcome of a straightforward process of just wanting to keep an identity private rather than letting an investment strategy become widely known, it can also be the forerunner of possible acquisition activity. Acquisitions can begin by a shareholder stealthily building a substantial shareholding before it has to be declared publicly. The sooner an IRO becomes aware of this eventuality the better prepared board and management can be in forming a view about how to deal with a potential acquirer creeping up the register to build a larger holding to launch what may become an aggressive assault.

Reporting to board and management

As well as being a conveyor of the corporate story to the market, the head of communication is also the channel of market information and perceptions back to the board of directors and senior management. It is customary for this information to be collated into a report for monthly board meetings. The report would summarize investor relations activity and market reactions to acceptance of the corporate story. It would refer to contact with the buy- and sell-sides and connections with closer followers of the stock. It would also include relevant media coverage and pertinent comments from journalists. Some reports might bring out peer comparisons, from the perspectives of comparative media coverage and also how investment markets view competitors.

Market reports can include excerpts from analysts' reports as well as conversational comments and formal perception studies that might have been commissioned. Changes in shareholding structure are also revealing, as well as commentary on the investment style that key institutional shareholders follow that may explain their reasons for buying, or selling, stock.

A board report might also indicate the extent of investor relations activity over the past month, in terms of engaging with the investment community, participating in roadshows and conferences and common questions that shareholders may have had as they have been in touch with the company. Some of this information could be prepared statistically or graphically.

Senior management will be more closely involved in investor relations activities since most presentations will have been made by the CEO and CFO. They will also want to see and hear market information as it happens so they are aware instantly of media and market reactions to company news and developments.

The process of analysing market developments for board and management also requires an assessment as to whether this necessitates adjustment to how the company is telling its story and any change of emphasis that needs to be introduced to convey how a business is progressing in its marketplace. There may be a call to report in more detail about how new products are achieving acceptance and how competitive position is affected by changing market conditions. These nuances can become part of how an IRO interacts with the market and management in seeking to meet information needs in the light of a company implementing its development strategy.

Benchmarking

As well as keeping tabs on the media and market in relation to their own particular companies, IROs need to be watchful around how peers report, provide information and the market profile they are developing. Companies will have differing styles, often reflecting the personalities of a CEO, but there can also be differences in the extent of disclosure that may create favourable or unfavourable comparisons. Considerable differences in what is disclosed can exist and companies may have genuine views about not wanting to follow exactly what competitors do in how they communicate about their businesses. Benchmarking can also look beyond competitors to see how other companies explain their strategies and corporate stories. Benchmarking can lead to comparative reports across a range of communications issues, such as how websites work, style of annual report and stock exchange announcements and content of investment presentations.

This comparative analysis may lead to an IRO discerning particular aspects of comparative advantage and performance measures that highlight how a company might be gaining shares in particular markets or exhibiting characteristics that may not have been observed by the market. It can lead to generating new information to be included in presentations or on websites. Sector-specific comparative data might provide a new angle around a corporate story that could shine a light on market rankings or demographics where a company has developed an edge. Companies in their markets may well be using differing business models to appeal to market segments, and explaining these models in attractively comparative ways can elevate interest in a business strategy.

Managing the corporate calendar

A company's balance date will determine the timetable flow of key events such as earnings announcements, annual report issue dates and annual meetings dates. It is the role of the head of communications to manage this calendar and plan in advance for all the communications events and activities that flow from these key dates. Each needs advance planning, especially in terms of message development and weaving the facts and numbers into a narrative. Planning includes the approval process, covering the extent of disclosure and vetting by senior management and the board. While production of numbers is the province of the CFO, it is the IRO that needs to produce the story and explanation around those numbers and bind the divisional experiences into a wider corporate narrative. Communications input includes considering how external audiences will view the material to be announced and in anticipating reactions, developing likely questions and then input to how they should be answered. Earnings announcements are usually accompanied by engaging with the media and investment community and scheduling these meetings into the calendar, along with preparation, adds to the calendar detail. Conference calls require notification and scripting and because all these events involve human engagement with a variety of differing points of view and reaction, an IRO will need to rely on relationship skills to gather feedback from the media and market to gain frank opinions of performance from a financial and presentational perspective.

Other additions to the corporate calendar can be investment conferences, which provide an opportunity to market the company story to new audiences, and investor days, when companies invite the buy- and sell-sides to see operations first-hand or set aside several hours for a city-based presentation. Relationship-building meetings, with the investment community, key shareholders and the media, will occur from time to time and then there are the unscheduled events, such as acquisitions, capital-raising and possibly some aspects of crisis that will crop up. A well-developed corporate story is a large part of the advance preparation for all these events.

Strategic aspects of role

A number of the strategic aspects of the role of head of communications or IRO have been covered earlier. These involve connecting corporate strategy with communications strategy and developing the means for conveying the corporate story to key stakeholders. Developing and managing the guidelines of disclosure are a key part of managing the legality and content of communication. Decisions about whether or not to provide earnings guidance will be a key debate involving an IRO and decisions around this shape the types of disclosure companies will make and the timing of them. Procedures developed by an IRO need to govern the announcement process, approvals for announcements and agreed spokespersons. Confidentiality governs a lot of disclosure and procedures need to be established for managing possible policy breaches. Policy should cover dealing with rumours and speculation, blackout periods when those with inside information cannot trade in company stock, when trading halts are necessary in advance of extremely sensitive information being released and the management of wayward chatter on mediums such as chat rooms, blogs and Twitter. Procedures need to be established around the entire interaction process, from announcements to one-on-one meetings with the investment community, dealing with the media and commenting on analyst reports. Common policies on analyst reports are for companies only to be involved in seeking to amend factual errors while leaving it to analysts to make projections about earnings and consequent investment recommendations.

Other strategic elements involve outlining the communication functions and the means of dealing with stakeholders, developing themes and content for the various communications tools.

Role mechanics

The strategic aspects of communication with the investment community, media and shareholders are a pointer to the daily mechanics of the job of IRO. In general terms this relates to developing the content of the corporate story, the discernment of communications targets and determining the means for conveying the story to key stakeholders.

Content

Developing the corporate story from a practical perspective involves prioritizing the facts and numbers to weave into the narrative of corporate strategy. From among the company history and characteristics of a company and its competitive environment there are key points that can contribute to making this mass of information interesting. What is of interest at a particular point of time connects with the marketing component of an IRO's job, since it brings together three differing environments, woven together to make an interesting story for the key three stakeholder groups. The three environments relate to: the company itself, how it is performing and its business model; the competitive environment, highlighting special characteristics a company has in its industry and how its growth strategy is working; and the investment environment, connecting the investing bigger picture and topical trends with the company and its industry sector.

The narrative connection of this three-part structure drives the corporate story and the IRO's job becomes the imposition of a communication discipline around telling this story. This involves the many written formats, from the brevity of phrases to longer descriptions for websites and investment presentations. There are also the spoken formats, involving key messages and anecdotes that tease out the points of interest and connect with marketing the story in a way that makes it stand out and be memorable. In this way, the IRO's job brings together many components, from understanding business and finance to writing, marketing, communication, storytelling and the persuasive arts. A connecting factor that gives colour to each of these disciplines is a selectivity from the vast mass of information surrounding the topics that are relevant so there is a prioritizing of what is important, allowing for differences of emphasis for individual categories across stakeholders, such as analysts, fund managers, journalists and retail investors.

This perspective on content reflects the external focus of the IRO in communicating the corporate story, which reinforces an internal reassessment of communication. From communicating externally, the IRO has an opportunity to discern how messages are being accepted and digested, and relate this back to the internal audience of the board and senior management. This involves gathering feedback, not just from stakeholder recipients but also from the marketplace overall and the trading information the market produces.

A responsible presentation of the corporate story also involves incorporating a consideration of risk factors. This usually comes out in presentations of earnings announcements. While investors need to make their own risk calculations, it is valuable to have a company spell out where risk might lie, from a downside and upside perspective. This also accounts for legal issues that relate to companies making forward-looking statements.

Roadshows

The marketing function of the IRO involves taking the corporate story out on the road to present it face-to-face to existing investors, potential investors, possibly journalists and various groups on the sell-side, such as stockbroking analysts, dealing rooms and sell-side clients. Participation in investment conferences is another part of this marketing effort. The role of the IRO involves the research and management of this roadshow process. Research involves vetting potential meeting targets to establish their interest and enthusiasm for the company and in meeting its management. Since these roadshows usually involve the CEO and CFO being the presenters, participants in the meetings should reflect the senior and serious interest on the part of the chosen targets to increase the potential value of outcomes from the roadshow. The IRO will be involved in the research, scheduling of meetings and also the accompanying flights, accommodation and venues necessary for possible coffee, lunch and dinner meetings to combine social and business aspects of the marketing effort. In larger companies there would be a team that could contribute to accomplishing all these tasks since it can be quite an undertaking if the roadshow is a multiple city effort. There will also be occasions when IROs themselves are presenters of the story.

Conference calls

Organizing a conference call usually relates to earnings or significant event announcements, such as capital-raisings or M&A transactions. A conference call can have a simple notification process of selecting an appropriate day and time a couple of days after announcing earnings or an event, with details provided in the announcement.

Telephone technology providers set up the process that streamlines dial in, making transcripts available and possibly the addition of webcast. In considering timing, especially during a busy earnings announcement season, it is important to be aware of competing events since having key shareholders and analysts being able to join in is a basic ingredient of making the call successful. It is the interaction between these key players and senior management that creates the tension that sees presentation of company information appropriately reflected in stock price.

Organizing the mechanics of the conference call is a basic part of ensuring it goes without a hitch but the crucial ingredient is to manage the communication aspects of the call. Priorities are development of key messages, story and rehearsal of the presentation, involving anticipation of the questions and fine-tuning possible answers. While there can be a routine to structuring a conference call, it is necessary to inject communication values to make it worthwhile for all participants. The downside of strict scripts, which can be necessary from a legal perspective, is that they can be deadening in weighing down how the principal speakers connect with those listening in. Scripts need to be written in spoken language to overcome the effects of reading them out and responses to questions also should not sound like they have been learned by rote. It is the role of the IRO to make the whole process interesting and memorable for all participants, by including meaningful anecdotes to enliven proceedings. Contacting key participants after the call provides a guide to how information has been accepted and picks up on any comments that may lead to refining the process in the future.

The technology surrounding conference calls also allows those managing the call to see who has logged in to hear the call and who has requested to join the queue to ask a question. Since the calls are a public device for the exchange of information, some IROs take the view that they will only allow questions from investors or analysts they know. The technology allows selectivity around who does ask questions while also providing information that enables subsequent contact as part of a future relationship-building process with callers who are not known. A well-briefed CEO capable of applying the corporate story in a question-and-answer setting can convert conference call participants, whether known or unknown, into being closer followers of the story as it develops.

Annual report

For an IRO, annual report productions are a major responsibility each year. Production decisions for glossy reports with photography of operations require considerable advance planning, with reports being several months in the making. They will involve graphic designers and consideration of themes and messages and how these are brought together graphically and photographically. Coordinating copy also needs to begin well in advance, connecting with the report's theme as well as the standard reporting function. If annual reports are for companies with international operations, photographic coordination can involve extensive logistics and possibly capturing directors touring overseas operations. Print run numbers are not as extensive as they used to be as more shareholders now receive reports electronically.

Like any other communications document, beginning each annual report project involves an assessment of objectives and the theme of information that is intended to be presented to key stakeholders. There may be particular aspects of the corporate story requiring emphasis and the annual report can be a vehicle for connecting to higher levels of communications strategy. When the report is finalized and distributed there is also an opportunity to gain feedback on how the report was received by key stakeholders as a way of providing guidance for preparation of next year's report.

Website

Maintaining the investor components of the website is within the role of the IRO. Websites are not static but dynamic communication devices that lend themselves to constant updating and highlighting of recent news that can rejuvenate the corporate story. Being vigilant and creative about this can increase investor traffic as there can be new information that might be useful in highlighting developing aspects of the corporate story. This need not be just corporate news but can include developments in the industry, in relevant technology and markets, since all have an impact on a company and provide news angles that heighten interest and embellish understanding.

Shareholder meetings

Shareholders are invited to gather for an annual meeting and, occasionally, to vote on specific items, such as capital-raising or M&A transaction issues, at extraordinary general meetings. The role of IROs and their teams becomes managing the communications aspects of these meetings. Some of these aspects may be shared with the company secretary function but there are a number of procedural elements that need to be managed, with strict timing and legal issues governing the amount of notice to be given for an annual meeting and, even in advance of that, timing for resolutions to be submitted for consideration at a meeting. Usually a notice of annual meeting is distributed with a company's annual report. This will list resolutions, give an explanation of them and also provide details of date, time and place of the meeting. Date of the meeting determines a record date of who is a shareholder eligible to vote at the meeting. A company's share registry organization would usually manage production of voting papers, assess proxies and count them in advance of the meeting and issue voting cards for the actual meeting. It is often the function of the investor relations team to oversee and manage the proper functioning of this process.

Statistics from NIRI indicate that around half of all company annual meetings in the US are held on company premises, average numbers of attendees are between 11 and 30, the average length of a meeting is 30 minutes and around 30 per cent broadcast proceedings, with most of these being webcast.[3]

The extent to which annual meetings become a marketing event depends a lot on the activities of a company. Where a company is involved in marketing directly to consumers, there can be an orientation to product displays, while others focus purely on the business aspects of the meeting.

Communication aspects of the meeting include crafting addresses for the chairman and chief executive, anticipating Q&A and managing shareholder enquiries in advance of the meeting. There can be a number of indicators of issues that might present communication challenges at the meeting, especially around, for example, pay issues. The investor relations function becomes involved in preparing to respond to these challenges as input to helping the chairman deal with them at the meeting. Annual meetings also allow shareholders to ask random questions, to seek explanations around aspects of the accounts and raise anything from the controversial to the mundane.

Preparing ways of responding to these questions is another communication contribution the IRO makes.

As the meeting is conducted, each resolution for voting is usually prefaced with information around proxy votes cast so an IRO is often involved in gathering and providing this information to the chairman. When meetings conclude, companies are obliged to make an announcement to the exchange platform about the outcomes of voting at the meeting, another procedure in which an IRO might be involved.

Integrated communications

Effective financial and investor communication does not operate in isolation from other corporate activities but is intent on conveying all that a corporation represents to an investing audience. In communicating corporate strategy, there is an indivisibility between investor relations and the strategy itself. In conveying the whole corporation to investors, the investor communication function is integrated into other marketing and public relations activity within the group.

Measurement

Increasingly in recent years there has been a focus on trying to measure the effectiveness of communication efforts. A consideration related to this is that it can be difficult to make definitive claims about cause and effect. While earlier we brought to light a number of examples of academic research that demonstrated a positive link between stock price and communication, it is a different matter to claim that all the output of investor relations can claim to be responsible for all the increase in stock price. There are many factors that influence stock price, not the least of which is earnings. So claims for the contribution that communication might make to this appreciation need to be tempered with a broader market understanding. Nevertheless, there are a number of quantitative and qualitative measures that can be applied to gauge the outcomes from the efforts of financial and investor communication.

A starting point is to consider what objectives were established at the start of an investor relations programme. Assuming these goals were measurable, then differences between the start of a year and its end should indicate a measure of effectiveness of communication. A recent survey of members by NIRI provided findings on measurement. Some 73 per cent indicated they set goals and objectives to measure their IR programmes and companies of larger size were more likely to have done this than smaller companies.[4] Of all the measures indicated, there were five that were considered the most important: individual meetings with top shareholders (93 per cent); feedback from the financial community (93 per cent); relationship with the financial community (92 per cent); qualitative assessment by the CEO/CFO (88 per cent); and responsiveness to investor enquiries (86 per cent).[5]

The survey also indicated the five metrics least frequently used: external recognition and awards (18 per cent); stock liquidity and training (16 per cent); financial news media coverage (14 per cent); change in company stock price (13 per cent); and social media channels (2 per cent).[6]

The survey conclusion from this was that NIRI members tended to place more value on shareholder-facing relationships and interpersonal oriented metrics than third party opinion or financial indicators.[7] Nevertheless, 80 per cent of those surveyed used a combination of quantitative and qualitative measures.

A feature of these survey outcomes is that they do not reflect some of the academic research that shows how communication can have an influence on stock price. A leading researcher in this area, Harvard professor Eugene Soltes, provides an alternative perspective on measurement, which he says should begin by asking two questions:

> What does the IRO control? An IRO can influence the writing quality and effective distribution of a press release that provides information to help investors make sound decisions about purchasing stock. The IRO does not, however, control factors such as the overall economy and company success that contribute to stock price. Ensure that metrics are based on controllable attributes and actions.
> What outcomes do top managers want? For what does management hold you and your IR program accountable? Make sure you know those expected outcomes and ensure that they are outcomes you can control.[8]

Soltes does additionally suggest one quantitative measure to assess the symmetry of communication between a company and investment markets, which is the extent of dispersion among analysts in their estimates of a company's earnings and sales. He says:

> Under Reg FD, all analysts have the same opportunity to receive the same information. Although differences can arise because of variations in analysts' skills, if analysts' numbers are all over the map, this may indicate difficulty in company communication.[9]

Another contribution to the topic of measurement is from the US organization Institute for Public Relations, which considers the outputs and outcomes that can be measured. Among outputs from an investor communications programme could be the number of analyst reports produced, quality of this analyst coverage and the extent of media coverage. Outcomes to be evaluated could include the P/E ratio in comparison to peers, trading volumes and measures of corporate reputation. Outcomes from survey research can also indicate the extent of awareness and knowledge of a company, acknowledgement of specific characteristics and a likely intention to invest. These surveys can point to the need for awareness-building and addressing weaknesses in communication, whether there is a perception of upside for the stock or possibly the opposite.[10]

Some investor relations programmes are implemented to achieve quite narrow and specific purposes that are capable of being measured. An example might be a company wanting to change the nature of its shareholder base away from hedge funds and momentum investors, which have been actively trading a stock, to more investors with a longer-term perspective. A metric to assess progress with this objective could be the average holding period of investors. One company that embarked on a programme such as this was semiconductor business AMD, which began with an 11-month holding period while industry peers had investors showing holding periods of between 15 and 30 months. Turning this around meant finding a new group of institutional investors, with a longer-term perspective, and presenting a corporate story to them that explained strategy in a way that looked beyond the short term. Over a period of five years, the programme achieved a lengthening of the average holding period to 27 months.[11]

Table 13.1 How investor relations could be improved

Buy-side	Sell-side
1. Disclosure	1. Disclosure
2. Transparency	2. Responsiveness
3. Company knowledge	3. Transparency
4. Responsiveness	4. Company knowledge
5. Website	5. Pro activity

Separately to NIRI's research on measurement, another survey, focused more on the outputs that IROs use to measure particular activities, showed that priorities were:[12]

- the number of one-on-one meetings held with top 50 shareholders;
- the extent of contact with potential new shareholders;
- the number of sell-side analyst reports produced;
- the number of participants in operations tours;
- the extent of website traffic;
- the response time to investor questions;
- the number of non-deal roadshows conducted;
- presentations at investor conferences.

While this style of measuring outputs may point to an IRO being very busy, CEOs tend to have a differing perspective in terms of what they expect from investor relations. One research group[13] found CEOs judged effectiveness of investor relations according to:

- feedback from the investment community;
- how well the message is registering;
- valuation and stock price differences;
- ability to develop relationships with the investment community;
- extent and quality of analyst coverage;
- ability to communicate;
- visibility and meeting frequency;
- shareholder retention and make-up of the shareholder base.

Another interesting measure of the effectiveness of investor relations is how it is viewed by stakeholders external to the company. A perception study among the buy- and sell-side in the United States revealed the areas in which these outsiders thought investor relations could do better (see Table 13.1).[14]

The slightly differing responses from these two stakeholder groups reflects not only how they see listed companies, but also highlights how IROs can orient activities and measures of effectiveness to reflect opinions of these stakeholder audiences.

A description of the multifaceted role that confronts those in charge of communicating the corporate story to key stakeholders shows that it does indeed bring together many disciplines. Conducting the role effectively involves having a good grasp of finance, law, communication and marketing. It combines the skills of being literate and numerate as well as being able to mould the words and numbers into a narrative for a strategic purpose. While the theory of public relations and applied finance may not be daily considerations in implementing the role, it can nevertheless provide a framework which explains the value and validity of how communication takes place. Examining the crossover of theory and practice is an alternative contribution to assessing and measuring the effectiveness of financial and investor communication.

Notes

1 NIRI, Adopted by the NIRI Board of Directors, March 2003, www.niri.org/FunctionalMenu/About.aspx
2 London Stock Exchange, "Investor Relations: A Practical Guide", *London Stock Exchange*, March 2010, p 7
3 Walsh, A, "Spotlight on Shareholder Annual Meetings", *IR Update*, NIRI, September 2012, p 13–14
4 Morgan, JD, "Measuring Investor Relations Programs: NIRI Survey Results", *Executive Alert*, NIRI, 10 November 2011, p 1
5 Morgan (2011), p 3
6 Morgan (2011), p 3
7 Morgan (2011), p 3
8 Quoted by Metzker, C, "Measure", *IR Update*, NIRI, June/July 2010, p 10
9 Quoted in Metzker (2010), p 13
10 Michaelson, D and Gilfeather, J, "What You Need to Measure Investor Relations", Institute for Public Relations, January 2003
11 Stewart, N, "Extreme Measures: How to Measure Success in IR", *Inside Investor Relations*, 1 October 2008
12 Stewart (2008)
13 Rivel Research, quoted in Stewart (2008)
14 Stewart (2008)

14 Connecting theory, practice and the corporate story

As investor relations officers and heads of communication of listed companies begin each work day, there is probably one certainty: none of them will be thinking about the theory of communication and applied finance as they plan out their day and go about the many tasks in front of them. Yet, while many of them may not realize it, their priorities are shaped by the signposts of the many aspects of theory that come from those disciplines. The terms they use, the things they see as important and the goals they have – nearly all these have their origins in theory that has developed round conveying messages to a marketplace that has an influence on the future development of their corporations. These communications professionals also would have an innate sense of what works and what contributes to successful outcomes, yet they may wonder whether there could be an objective template that is a guide to effectiveness in financial and investor communication. Experience builds familiarity with tried and true techniques but experiences can be individual and the outcomes of specific trials by fire. It may seem impractical to expect an all-encompassing template might be created from a web of theory and research around the intersecting fields of finance and communication. Nevertheless there is some merit in collecting the primary threads together from theory that substantiates the value that comes from certain actions in the realm of investor relations.

In the course of previous pages we have considered a number of theoretical and research contributions along with the practicalities of the day to day work of investor relations. Here we bring together those threads and forge a connection between theory and practice. The diversity of human experience, even when expressed in the sub-environment of stock exchange listed companies, does not lend itself to a "one size fits all" solution or "how to" guide. Company circumstances vary, CEOs have differing personalities and market situations are constantly fluctuating. From this perspective, the task of having a central reference point for how to implement perfected communication seems daunting. Challenging though it may be, there are a number of important signposts that can be assembled to point in a general direction of a theoretical imprimatur of best practice. Many terms are taken for granted in financial and investor communication. Conversations take up the ideas of story, investment proposition, business model and the need to lower the cost of capital. Just this limited list represents a mixture of actions, ideals, outcomes and an indicator of how communicative action can be measured. There is clearly some benefit in seeking to draw an outline of what could represent a useful combination of theory and practice to delineate a template for effectiveness in financial and investor communication.

Table 14.1 at the end of this chapter collects many threads of theoretical influence, from communication and applied finance, as well as research that relates to listed company communication. The table circumvents the need to repeat this information and allows some larger topics to be considered, such as the primacy of narrative, how it should be presented and the reasoning that supports this approach. The bringing together of theory and practice in the field of financial and investor communication is examined from six differing perspectives. One is the way narrative not only describes a form of communication but how it becomes the mechanism for binding facts and numbers together in a way that improves investor understanding of businesses. Second is the role that rhetoric and persuasion combine in developing the corporate perspective. Third is a reconciliation of disclosure with communication. This accounts for alignment with a company's investment proposition as well as finding a more effective alternative between, on the one hand, meeting minimalist legal definitions of disclosure and, at the other extreme, providing volumes of information without a discernible story. Fourth is that a lot of the practice of investor relations, in not elevating the importance of media relations, does not unleash the whole power of the corporate story. Fifth, the importance of relationships straddles theory, in meeting one definition of describing how corporate communication is described, and practice, in enveloping the highly critical human factor of building support for corporate stories. And sixth, as companies compete for capital, there is a crossover of concepts from theory in communication and economics with primary objectives of investor relations.

The authority of narrative

The use of the word "story" by investor relations practitioners has been common for some time. It has a generally accepted meaning but its pervasive nature is not often considered in this specialist field. The fundamental nature of story, or narrative, as a way of describing communication was put forward in a distinctive way by Walter Fisher in the 1980s, in what he called the "narrative paradigm". Appreciating Fisher's wide-ranging argument is the basis for understanding the importance of the corporate story as being more than just a communications device but a guiding template for communicating with primary stakeholders about corporate progress, direction and performance. The key points of Fisher's view are worth considering in detail and in bringing out from them their relevance to financial and investor communication. This was not Fisher's original intention but creating an applicability of his perspective to the financial sphere adds substance to the work of investor relations practitioners.

Fisher put forward his idea of the narrative paradigm of communication as an alternative to what he described as the rational paradigm. His starting point was that humans are storytelling creatures and that narration is a way of giving sequence and meaning to words and deeds and, in the process, helping with interpretation and understanding. In this sense, narrative combines the argumentative and persuasive strands of rhetoric and, while not denying the relevance of reason and rationality, makes them more easily connected with the way humans actually communicate with each other. In an echo of how financial communication works, Fisher does not see facts or experience as discrete or disconnected pieces of information but rather items that stand in need of a narrative to give them coherence.[1]

The power of the narrative paradigm is seen in contrast with the rational paradigm, which Fisher describes as having been foundational to Western thought. The rational paradigm begins with the idea that the world is a set of logical puzzles that can be resolved through analysis and application of reason, with the main mode of human decision-making and communication being the application of clear-cut argument. In the public sphere, the rational paradigm describes arguments as being carried by qualified people, skilled in the process of putting forward rational arguments and implementing them on behalf of the public. For Fisher, this leaves out the importance of values and recognition of how individuals relate to each other when they communicate. For him, narration is how humans interact and the way they relate the truth of the human condition, with storytelling by individuals in some cases becoming group stories that are taken up as public stories. Stories do not attain this status without good reasons, so Fisher's narrative paradigm does not preclude the rational paradigm, but includes it in what he considers a more descriptive form of what actually happens in communication.[2]

From a psychological perspective, Jerome Bruner arrives at similar conclusions to Fisher. Bruner argues that how we experience reality, interpret it and pass on our version of it to others is through narrative. It is less easy to describe this process from a rational perspective, that knowledge is the result of a logical progression of propositions that are reality, than to accept the narrative perspective that knowledge is never "point-of-viewless".[3] We organize our experiences and our memories in the form of narrative and in this version of reality, stories are expected to achieve a verisimilitude rather than be subjected to empirical verification. Bruner develops ten features of narrative that reflect how our minds construct reality and test the effectiveness of stories. Applying these tests add a layer of analysis that is interesting in itself but perhaps adds complexity beyond Fisher's simpler tests. One supporting concept from Bruner that reinforces the influence of narrative is that of narrative accrual. It is seen in the process of organizations developing ideas about culture, and in the legal profession imposing traditions of case law in which similar cases are decided on precedents from previous legal decisions. Similarly with corporate stories, which gather support as they become accepted constructions of a reality that reflects corporate experiences in industry sectors and with which key stakeholders have a general familiarity.

Narrative rationality

The way humans apply rationality under Fisher's narrative paradigm is that, since narrative is how people communicate, they apply two concepts to test the satisfactory nature of stories. The first test is "narrative probability", in which people judge whether a story is coherent and logical and has consistency of characters and actions. The second test is "narrative fidelity", that is whether a story rings true in comparison with what people know from their own life experience. With these two tests being innate, because that is how we are, we do not need a separate rationalist paradigm guided by elite or expert views since we all have within us the capacity to discern the validity of stories. It is narrative that enables us to understand the actions of others because we live out narratives in our own lives. While the rational paradigm has laws of reason that must apply to argument, the narrative tests of rationality allow people to make judgements based on their own life experience. A feature of the rational paradigm is that it implies a sense of hierarchy, in which some people are better qualified to judge and to lead than others. In contrast, the narrative paradigm does not deny the application of hierarchy in society but it is combined with the concept that people have an innate sense of being able to make judgements about the stories told for and about them and that this also equates with a rational form of decision-making. In politics, and in business, under the narrative paradigm, people who have a general knowledge of an issue are quite capable of making a rational judgement about it based on assessing the arguments they hear and read, applying the narrative tests of probability and fidelity. This is Fisher's form of narrative rationality. We tell stories, reach an understanding of issues by hearing stories and make judgements about them through natural tests of their effectiveness.

Fisher's narrative paradigm not only outlines a way of describing human communication but it also forms a substantiation of what can represent effective financial and investor communication. Sets of accounts, or numbers, on their own are financial information. They are historical and require extrapolation to form a forward-looking picture. Similarly, facts about a business have value in themselves but are static and do not give a guide about how they should be interpreted. Using a narrative to bind together facts and numbers sets up a template to which Fisher's narrative rationality can be applied. Narrative is not only a form of communication we use in our daily lives but it carries meaning that facts and numbers in isolation cannot. It creates a platform for investment decision-making because it also conveys the totality of information investors need. Sound investment decision-making is based on assessing risk and return, both of which are forward-looking concepts, while being guided by past performance. A fully informed information base around these decisions requires an understanding of where a business is heading, that is its strategy, and the competitive forces in its markets that are going to influence that direction and corporate decision-making.

The sources for this information can be varied. It can come from independent research by analysts of industry conditions and company peers. From this and information from companies, analysts write investment reports and reach recommendations about whether investors should buy or sell. The large part of these recommendations is sourced from information supplied by companies, including numbers that reflect financial performance. In assessing the information they receive from companies they apply the tests of narrative rationality. Is the information coherent and does it ring true, they ask, as they assess company accounts, the facts surrounding the business and the company story which elaborates on corporate achievements and progress.

Testing the narrative

In providing the information investment markets want, investor relations officers (IROs) often use terms such as "story", "investment proposition" and "business model". They package this information and convey it in various ways, across oral presentations given by CEOs and in writing, creating market signals intended to manage investor expectations. To test these expectations, IROs conduct conversations and surveys among investors to gauge opinion of a company's performance, management and communication around its progress. These are the tools of their trade in investor relations and if IROs wanted to establish a broad test of the effectiveness of their work, they have a ready template in the narrative paradigm. The end point of their work is in creating the corporate narrative from a combination of facts, figures and industry information. This story becomes the basis of communication with key stakeholders, the investment community, media and shareholders. The tests for the effectiveness of this communication are those of narrative rationality – has it been coherent and did it ring true?

While these tests are at the base of a bigger picture assessment of effectiveness, there are other influences on how stakeholders apply these tests. The tests are not binding conclusions nor are they permanently set in stone. They are subject to external influences such as market forces, even though investor interpretation of this can be shaped by information companies provide around how market conditions affect them individually. Investors are also influenced by how well companies convey their stories, since that also has an effect on conclusions about coherence and truth. Providing information openly is one thing but companies do this in varying ways, which implies gradations of quality of this effort, raising new concepts for consideration in framing and testing acceptance of the corporate narrative.

Rhetoric, persuasion and the corporate perspective

The way arguments and stories are conveyed, and their content, are important influences on narrative rationality. While the narrative overall is subjected to tests of coherence and truth, stakeholders cannot help but be influenced by how well that narrative is presented and how it is reshaped as conditions change. The quality and persuasiveness of a narrative influences coherence and, although truth is a fundamental concept, it also carries with it the idea of a story corresponding with experience as stakeholders know it, enabling a well-prepared corporate story to reinforce an understanding of reality from the corporate perspective. As IROs prepare corporate stories and narrative around financial performance they are focused on the information at hand and seek to use it to form a bridge with key stakeholder audiences. They feel they know what it is that investors want and so they try to prepare information accordingly. A broader view of this process accounts for the many influences on investment decisions. Facts and numbers are core components of any investment analysis. Without basic numbers and a capability to make estimates of future cash flows, investors are unable to discount those cash flows back to a present value to establish intrinsic value per share to be compared with market value. As much research effort has shown, this financial process is not the full explanation of what determines stock price. Non-financial factors are increasingly seen to be more influential in determining value. These non-financial factors have many components, ranging across varying aspects of information investors find relevant, enabling them to form judgements about risk and return. Separately, they also develop perceptions about the quality of management and how well they think the team is performing and may be capable of delivering future growth.

Influences on investors

As companies issue the information key stakeholders want, and make market announcements, the process does not entirely separate out financial and non-financial information. It is the packaging of these components in a corporate story, combining facts, numbers and narrative that provides the bulk of information that influences narrative rationality. Those that have the responsibility of bringing this information together are unlikely to be thinking about principles of persuasion and rhetoric in this process. Yet these underlying concepts are not only influential on outcomes of how stakeholders assess narratives but they are ever present, often in a way not realized by perpetrators and presenters of financial and investment information. Perceptions of management, often cited by research as an influential factor in investment decision-making, are not only the outcome of investors assessing track record but also forming opinions of other aspects of performance by chief executives. The investment community and media have many opportunities to see an executive team give physical presentations, in webcasts, conference calls and in more casual conversations. Aligning this with announcements companies make and how companies react to external events influences perceptions of capability, ethics, readiness to adapt to changing environments and the likelihood a management team is going to be innovative. A common factor of these judgements is that they are separate from whatever outcomes are achieved from spreadsheets about cost of capital and intrinsic value per share. Yet the combination of all these components is the way stakeholders see coherence and truth within narrative rationality. Consequently, communication with these stakeholders needs to account for what is appropriate rhetoric and persuasion when dealing with people who are well-informed about economic, financial and market issues.

Informed stakeholders, like investors and the media, are not easily persuaded by oratory, gimmicks and spin. Their own professional backgrounds and experiences enable them to see through these attempts at communication. Investors in the past may have fallen victim to corporate stories that offered a promise that was not delivered, leaving them to watch a stock price not achieving its potential. Consequently, rhetoric in its dismissive form of "mere rhetoric" is not going to inspire investors but rather increase their cynicism about companies where management seems more focused on "selling" a story than on implementing a strategy that reflects a more powerful corporate narrative. It is this latter approach that is more an example of the implementation of classical rhetoric, which is made more powerful by insights about the psychological principles of persuasion likely to influence well-informed stakeholders such as investors.

Applying rhetoric

The three components of classical rhetoric that described the essence of effective argument were reason (logos), the emotional effect this had on audiences (pathos) and the character of the speaker (ethos). In corporate communication, these terms can be described as content of the argument, the style of presenting likely to achieve a desired effect on stakeholders and the reputation of both the speaker and corporation. As IROs prepare investment presentation content they are highly unlikely to be calling to mind any rhetorical influence from ancient Greece and yet these are the time-honoured principles that come to bear on investors when they assess the quality of arguments being presented to them as they make investment decisions. The principles of rhetoric, like the narrative paradigm, relate to how people communicate with each other on a daily basis and how they make judgements about what they hear, see and read. The world of financial and investor communication, while it includes facts and numbers, is not immune from these human processes. The facts and numbers may be fundamental truths but they cannot walk on their own legs. It is the combination of these truths within a context of argument and presentation, given by people for an audience of people, that lends them influence. Contained within rhetoric are concepts that are fundamental to effective corporate communication. Content is critical. It needs to meet what an audience is expecting to hear, which is one aspect of influence, but it can also have other characteristics. It can guide views about the future, it can have within it information that might inspire investment decision-making and can explain how a company might have dealt with difficult circumstances. The aspect of style within rhetoric has several connotations in the world of financial and investor communication. It can relate to the physical style of presentation, such as how a CEO and CFO tell their story in front of people, conveying a presence and body language. It relates to the language companies use in oral and written communication and the way in which presenters are capable at telling the corporate story and enlivening it with sub-stories and anecdotes that reinforce a narrative strength. Style also brings in visual elements such as the way PowerPoint slides are presented, layouts of reports and announcements and the strength of graphic corporate identity. The structure of arguments is also reflective of style. If presenters are to carry along investor audiences with arguments around the corporate perspective on performance, industry conditions and strategy implementation, then it will not be achieved through generalization or bluster but requires informative laying out of an argument that carries the force of logic, with facts and figures to back up assertions.

To reinforce the applicability of rhetoric to financial and investor communication, it is helpful to bring in two terms from Aristotle, the ancient Greek philosopher to whom description of the art of persuasion is attributed. For Aristotle, persuasion was all the more effective if it contained proof and the term he used to describe the essence of persuasion was the "enthymeme", which is a truncated syllogism. The proof involved in these concepts is establishing premises that prompt a conclusion. The process is also described by the term "deductive reasoning". An enthymeme would have one premise and a syllogism two in leading to a conclusion. With the abbreviated enthymeme, one of the premises is assumed without being stated.

For Aristotle, a syllogism worked this way:

- Socrates is a man.
- All men are mortal.
- Socrates is mortal.

An example of applying this form of deductive reasoning to persuasion in financial and investor communication could be:

- We have three drivers of profit.
- Each of these drivers has been affected by tough economic conditions.
- In the circumstances, keeping profit steady is a significant achievement.

This example obviously manipulates Aristotle's formula a little. To add further to the manipulation, and using the enthymeme idea of an unexpressed premise, an unexpressed intent in the profit explanation is that stock price should not be discounted because profit has not increased. Two aspects of persuasion are intended in this example. One is to provide a proof as reinforcement for an explanation. The other is to hint at a stock market conclusion without expressing an explicit view. Two principles of investor communication are highlighted in this way. Understanding of financial performance is greater if there is sound reasoning to support it. Second, one of the rules around investor relations is not to talk about the stock price and yet, according to the NIRI definition of investor relations, the whole communications process is aimed at achieving a fair valuation. The means available to achieve this is that of deductive reasoning. That is, providing the information and persuasive arguments that point to a desired conclusion.

The concept of reputation also has several rhetorical implications. The corporate communications perspective on reputation is that it is earned and bestowed by others, not claimed by a corporation. It is a reflection of past actions, ethical behaviour and a track record of achievements having reflected expectations. In this sense, it is not a characteristic that becomes the content of corporate communication but it becomes a reflection of the extent to which narrative rationality is exercised by audiences. It is a yardstick by which investors exercise their belief in what companies say as an indication of what companies might actually do and achieve. Reputation for some in corporate communication is the platform of what becomes the corporate story but in the investment arena, it is more an outcome of corporate performance rather than being the content of a corporate story investors expect to hear. Reputation also incorporates the values a company displays in the way it operates. Investors are increasingly paying attention to the way companies adhere to concerns about the environment, their social responsibilities and corporate governance. Investors want to see companies doing the right thing, as well as them doing it right, in terms of delivering investment returns. While corporate reputation is paramount, the concept also carries over, in a rhetorical sense, to the character of the chief spokespersons, such as the CEO and CFO, and the calibre of the board of directors. Blemishes on personal reputations, or perceptions of how directly CEOs respond to investor questioning in conference calls, have a rhetorical influence on how corporate arguments are carried to stakeholders.

These components of corporate rhetoric – content, style and reputation – may not be the obvious reference points for IROs in preparing for the telling of corporate stories. Yet they are important markers for not only expressing how to implement financial and investor communication but also sum up a critical element of interaction between corporate spokespersons and key audiences. Rhetoric has been a permanent influence on how speakers and audiences relate to each other, with many examples in daily life. It is not only present in casual conversation but also in music and other aspects of our daily lives. A number of writers have referred over the years to the presence of rhetoric in music. JS Bach and Brahms are examples. The music and words of the Bach Passions were well known to original audiences and the influence of their rhetoric has been ongoing over the centuries. The voices of the dramatic characters and the instruments that reflect the sense of journey, pain and deliverance represent a transcendent characteristic above the purely obvious sense of enjoying the music. Adapting this analogy to corporate communication, investor audiences are there to absorb corporate content but they are also influenced by the way it is presented, since that adds an overriding power to the story being communicated.

Reassessing symmetry

While style, content and reputation represent a current-day form of rhetorical persuasion in corporate communication, there are also times when companies need to be psychologically persuasive in the way they communicate with key stakeholders. The concept of persuasion is controversial in theory around public relations and communication. On one construction, it can convey a sense of not telling the whole story and presenting information in a biased way to achieve agreement under a subtle form of duress. This collection of negative aspects of persuasion sums up why it has been seen as contrary to the more open forms of communication expressed in the concept of two-way symmetrical communication, often described as the ideal way a corporation should communicate with stakeholders. In the investment arena and in business, this concept of fundamental equality between key stakeholders and corporations requires closer examination.

It is companies which operate in markets where competitive forces influence the development of strategies to sell goods and services. Companies seek to develop a competitive advantage and grow their businesses, with rewards of this growth shared with stakeholders such as investors and employees. These experiences in an industry sector are direct, with corporations also needing to communicate to investment markets about how business conditions have influenced their own financial performance. Communication of corporate experiences means stakeholders, such as the investment community, media and shareholders, only have a secondary experience of influences on performance. They know about drivers of profit and business models from what companies tell them. Of course, they can observe peers and make comparisons but not all companies are identical in the way they react to industry conditions and make plans for the future. Similarly with analysts making forecasts, they make their best estimates of future cash flows but companies themselves are in a better position to make these forecasts, which they do internally, with only some of them making public the likely influences on earnings.

The way investment markets are structured builds in a fundamental inequality between corporations and key stakeholders. This is effectively by definition, since it is corporations having the experiences of running businesses and, after the event, reporting on them. There is an educational aspect to this as well. Companies need to communicate their direct market experiences to stakeholders so they have an understanding of what it is like to develop and implement strategies in the face of diverse competitive forces. This difference does not prevent investors from making judgements about performance and then investment decisions, such as buying and selling stocks. For some activist shareholders and analysts, there are occasions when they feel no compunction in telling corporations they should be performing better or implementing alternative strategies. While these groups form these opinions from assessments of management teams and peer performance, they also know what they do about a company from the corporate perspective that has been communicated.

While there is this input from investors and, when companies communicate by taking into account what investor audiences want to know, in a form of "joint authorship" of corporate communication, the primacy of the corporate account of events is more dominant than stakeholder contributions. In communication theory terms, what takes place is more of a one-way or, at best, two-way asymmetrical communication. Stakeholders play an influential role but it is the corporate perspective that dominates the information base to be assessed in making investment judgements. Even when analysts go about the objective process of discounting future cash flows, the growth and discount rates they use are influenced by company-derived information. Nevertheless, the use by companies of asymmetrical communication is not totally pervasive. There are many circumstances where they negotiate a shared view with stakeholders, exemplifying two-way symmetrical communication, but with financial and investor communication there is a built in bias towards the corporate perspective.

For some contemporary theorists of public relations, the idea of symmetry to describe communication between corporations and stakeholders is outmoded, principally because it does not recognize various aspects of imbalance in the relationships that exist.[4] One aspect of this imbalance, which connects with narrative rationality, is that between perception and reality. Bridging this gap, from the corporate perspective, is less about symmetrical negotiation towards a shared view than it is about companies putting forward their experiences in the reality of the marketplace, based on open disclosure, and using rhetoric, persuasion and narrative, in a reasonable way, to influence perceptions.

Principles of persuasion

While recognizing this bias towards the corporate perspective, there are times when companies hover between asymmetrical and symmetrical communication. This is when they seek to apply persuasion that, with investor audiences and the media, has many gradations of subtlety. In a general sense, persuasion is taking place when companies are asking key stakeholders to see, from a narrative rationality perspective, coherence and truth in their corporate stories. These stories reflect a history, track record and strategies for the future and achieve strong levels of adoption by key stakeholders when companies are performing well. In the process labelled "financialization", these strategies are aligned with business metrics, developed by companies and analysts, which are intended to reflect corporate achievements meeting financial expectations. Meeting these expectations reflects low levels of persuasion but there is an escalation of persuasion when financial performance, for whatever reason, does not achieve what the company and markets were factoring in to stock price.

What begins then is a company trying to have the market adjust expectations, a process that may have varying degrees of difficulty. A company has to set about altering its corporate perspective, possibly with communication about changed market conditions or variations to strategy that might affect earnings in the short term, and try to persuade stakeholders to remain investors while these adjustments take place. If adjustments are significant, or the corporate perspective was not strongly adopted by stakeholders, then the task of persuasion would be difficult. Whatever the circumstances, certain underlying principles of persuasion can contribute positively to the task. These principles again would not be part of the daily thinking of IROs but they operate nevertheless and are often adopted without a realization of their influence. Two terms that apply from the psychological study of persuasion are "coactive persuasion", which takes place when both sides are aware of each other's standpoints and are open to persuasion, and "cognitive shorthands", which relate to some of the psychological subtleties that are taking place.

Investor stakeholders are more open to persuasion if they have been close and supportive followers of a stock and where communication has been regular. Corporate persuasiveness is also more likely to be successful if it adheres to some basic psychological principles. Companies need to be sympathetic to information needs of their stakeholders, respond to changing circumstances in a timely manner with the detail required and build in a high degree of explanation around why circumstances have changed in a way that will affect financial performance. Providing information like this is an important part of the persuasion process. While companies may not be immune from criticism and a loss of confidence in their stock prices, there is room for them to adopt a "yes, but" approach in their dialogues with stakeholders. This involves recognizing shared premises between companies and stakeholders, based on companies having met expectations in the past, but seeking to have stakeholders see the bigger picture of an industry perspective which envelops a company. If companies outline the influences on their own decisions, then through a cognitive shorthand approach, they are asking investors to see the world from their perspective to understand the logic of a need for a change to strategy and to deal with short-term disruption to financial performance. If companies can persuade investors to adopt more of a long-term understanding of the corporate story, they improve the likelihood of shifting focus from the short term, to limit short-term damage to the stock price and lift the extent of shareholder retention.

A contributing factor to stakeholders being open to persuasion to the corporate perspective, and to be receptive to corporate rhetoric, is the practices of companies towards disclosure. The more closely aligned disclosure is to the values of effective persuasion and communication, the greater the influence it can have on narrative rationality.

Reconciling disclosure and communication

Disclosure has become something of a watchword in financial and investor communication. Disclosure is good, according to conventional wisdom, and not saying enough is bad. This formulation, however, implies any amount of information is helpful to investors but this proposition, and its opposite of just meeting statutory disclosure minimums, requires further examination.

Meeting statutory minimums of disclosure is effectively adopting a view of letting the numbers speak for themselves. The bare minimum of disclosure means providing audited accounts and having directors express confidence in a company's state of affairs. Of course there are notes to the accounts and other corporate governance requirements to be met, which can be achieved in a formulaic way. The management discussion and analysis component of annual reports can be quite brief, and historic, in meeting minimal requirements. This minimalist outcome is quite satisfactory to some investors, since all they want is to be able to absorb the accounting information as an input to their investment decision-making. Increasingly, however, this is an extreme position. Companies are realizing there is a market demand for them to disclose more information, especially as most investors are recognizing that stock price accounts for larger amounts of value than balance sheets would indicate, meaning more non-financial information is necessary to create a full investment picture.

Moving to the other extreme, of providing volumes of information to investment markets, runs the risk of quantity outweighing quality when it comes to disclosure. When large amounts of information are released, it raises the issue of risk in several ways. One area of risk is that the key messages of the corporate story can be lost in a morass of detail. Another is that readers of this disclosure include competitors, so some discretion has to be exercised in determining just how much information investors need to understand competitive positioning. A further perspective of risk is that, given the propensity of analysts to absorb every piece of information companies release, then large amounts of disclosure may set up financial expectations companies had not anticipated, leading to slanted views that may be tangential to a more central corporate purpose.

There is a middle course between these extremes, involving companies meeting the evolution of requirements around disclosure while also being judicious about what they release. Regulatory authorities, quite correctly, are seeking to move companies away from minimalist disclosure. The current trend, across many jurisdictions, is towards providing information that investors would reasonably expect to be made available. In general terms, the move is towards having companies explain the drivers of performance and how they make money, involving an elaboration of their business models. Essentially, they want companies to lay out their corporate stories, combining facts, numbers and narrative. They want companies to go beyond self-evident basics – not just to say profit was up but to explain why. Allied to this is bringing in the topic of risk to explanation of performance and also being prepared to be more forward looking in discussing the future, without there being any obligation to provide financial forecasts.

Aligning story, the investment proposition and disclosure

This is not new territory for many companies that are involved in this process without needing a nudge from regulators. Nevertheless there is still a gap between conforming to regulatory guidelines and communicating. Communication strategy implies objectives and an intent to increase understanding with stakeholders. From this there are many ramifications. The greater understanding that can be developed from communication, the more companies are contributing to building reputation and developing the messages for others to pass on about them in investment markets. In a sense the regulators are raising the bar of what they would like to see as disclosure but there are other topics and areas of information companies can provide if they are looking to build supporters for the corporate story. A strategic view of the narrative process is that companies want to achieve a sense of having investors see the world as they do. They want them to realize the competitive pressures and industry forces that impinge on their decision-making. From this perspective, drivers of profit are part of the picture but they are also an historic window into performance. If a narrative is to meet tests of coherence and truth in every respect, it will also be a pointer to strategy assessment and how effective this might be in the future.

Along with the notions of strategy are several issues of alignment. One view of investor and financial and communication is that it is focused on improving understanding of corporate strategy. This in effect represents communication strategy but there are also several questions this raises. For example, does what a company tells the market about its strategy actually reflect what it is that investors think they are investing in when they buy the company's stock? Similarly, is there an alignment, with what managers within an organization see as their priorities, and how the company communicates about its purpose and what it discloses to investment markets? Companies provide incentives to managers based on certain internal criteria, which may be expressed in performance metrics. If this is how the company wants its managers to perform, then how closely is this related to overall corporate performance metrics and is this expressed in terms of the corporate narrative, which is the investment proposition being presented to investment markets? It is also possible that investment community perceptions may be quite different, with investment decisions based on alternative premises. This challenge is significant but conceptually another version of narrative rationality. Only effective financial and investor communication is going to achieve an alignment with story, the investment proposition and disclosure.

Two other issues influencing disclosure and communication are those from the research and integrated reporting perspectives. Research is highlighting, from two differing angles, that non-financial information is a critical driver of stock price. One angle is that, with earnings and book values only accounting for about 30–40 per cent of market capitalizations,[5] the market is consistently valuing stocks for factors other than what is on their balance sheets. They are valuing reputation, brands and pipelines of potential in addition to net assets and earnings. Other research is showing that non-financial information is a prime influence on investment decision-making. The clear message from investors, based on this research, is that in many cases there is a misalignment between disclosure and the investment proposition. Investors are buying stocks, not so much on the basis of information being disclosed by companies in a reporting sense but from other information they are gleaning to round out the corporate story from their perspective.

The other trend, towards integrated reporting internationally, is well on the way to becoming generally accepted but not without reluctance by some companies and jurisdictions. The intention is to bring together, in the one document of an annual report, financial reporting and sustainability reporting, along with commentary on the business model and how it affects both these aspects of information. The International Integrated Reporting Council describes it this way:

> An integrated report is a concise communication about how an organisation's strategy, governance, performance and prospects lead to the creation of value over the short, medium and long term.[6]

While many companies favour this trend, there are some that quake at the thought of 300-page annual reports, allied with the concern that more information is really for the benefit of competitors, who analyse these reports in differing ways to investors. While these fears may be real, they also outline the challenge for financial and investor communication, which is to align communication and disclosure in a succinct way that saves a story from being swamped by the detail.

If disclosure and communication are to be fully reconciled, there is a need to have a broader picture of the stakeholders in the process. A feature of a lot of investor relations is that it is focused on the investment community and shareholders. These are certainly crucial influencers of stock price and communications effort often recognizes that it is wholesale investors, which own around 80 per cent or more of most listed entities, that warrant, and demand, the most amount of attention. Another critical stakeholder in this process, which is not often given appropriate weight of recognition in the area of investor relations, is the media.

Bringing investor relations and media relations closer together

Two propositions outline how investor relations could have a different view on media relations. One is taking account of what the media wants and how it reports business news, the other is research which highlights the positive effects of media coverage on stock price. As investor relations has evolved, there has been a closer connection with the financial and communication aspects of the role. In practice, the communication orientation is more towards financial stakeholders, such as the investment community and shareholders. Increasingly IROs are recognizing the importance of internal communication to achieve alignment with external formulations of the investment proposition. Customers are also part of this communication effort to ensure that what companies are saying about how they relate to major customers is also borne out in how things actually work. There is no doubt these are important priorities of the communication task but what seems to have been downplayed in the process is media relations. Much of the literature produced by investor relations associations focuses on disclosure and how to relate to investors. Only occasionally is the issue of the media addressed.

There are perhaps some reasonable grounds for this caution. Having too high a media profile carries risk. It may lead investors to think a company is placing too much emphasis on promotion or that there is not a lot of benefit from seeing the CEO's photo in the media too often. Media coverage can be prone to mistakes and creating an emphasis in stories that does not always reflect corporate priorities. Sometimes inexperienced journalists may be allocated to reporting on companies when they are not fully conversant with company and industry views and performance. While many of these risks are real, they are not beyond being able to be managed by experienced communication professionals. Applying the same disciplines around message development that take place in preparing to meet investors works similarly with journalists, although there are several differences to take into account.

The outcome of a number of pieces of academic research highlights that being in the media has value for stock price. Disseminating company announcements to the media and achieving media coverage principally lets more people know what a company does and how it is performing. Media coverage lowers the information gap, which is reflected in bid-ask spreads, lowers volatility and, consequently, contributes to a lower cost of capital. A factor that applies is that familiarity breeds investment. The more people know about a company, the more likely they are to buy stock. A common piece of advice, made famous by Warren Buffet, is that people should only invest in companies they understand and that are run by people they can trust. The media can be a conduit for achieving wider understanding and building trust with media readers, investors and potential investors. Other research has found that media coverage does not only influence retail investors but is a common way that institutions find out about companies that represent investment potential.

The investment value from being in the media ought to be an incentive to IROs to lift the importance of media relations to a higher level of priority but there is still the risk factor to be managed. The best pointer towards managing this is to take heed of what the media says it wants to achieve in reporting business news. If companies are providing what the media wants, then their management processes achieve a better alignment of what it is they are trying to communicate with what is likely to be reported. By leaving less to chance, they are building risk management into media relations.

It is a misconception to think the media exists to reproduce company news releases. Journalists are required, if time permits, to research more widely and possibly seek comment from beyond company sources for the stories they write. For companies of a smaller size, there is a challenge in the first place to produce news that might warrant the attention of the media. There is one area of common ground where all these competing objectives meet and that is in the quality of writing. The work of journalists is focused on words. They need facts and context around them and in their own writing output leave out adjectives and adverbs. Their stories often include quotes from company CEOs, with a preference for speaking to these people directly if they can. Being quick with the news is another factor bearing on the output of journalists. If they are to put some background and context around their stories, they need to be able to do it quickly. Having access to this information is important since they are reporting not only what the news is but also the "so what?" element of it, which is to say what it means, in the bigger picture of what a company, industry and economy is doing. Given these priorities journalists face, it is not hard for companies to help them with many of these requirements but an assessment of many company announcements shows they contain poor expression, too many adverbs and adjectives, jargon, self-serving headlines that often do not reflect the facts and quotes that have neither the language or content that enable them to be reproduced by the media.

There are three simple things companies can do to bring investor relations and media relations closer together. One is to reassess the quality and content of written material for the media, the second is to improve the mechanics of news distribution and the third is to build personal relationships with key journalists likely to write news about their companies.

The starting point for reassessing writing quality is often just a change of mindset. Too often company announcements are focused on an isolated item of news. It may be earnings or an achievement that means something if an outside reader has an understanding of the story so far but this singular corporate focus does not equate with how a journalist has to report this news. Journalists have to say what this news means, in the context of a company's history and outlook and its relevance for the wider world around it. Companies can help with this in several ways. They can include the bigger picture perspective and background in their announcements, they can accompany them with backgrounders or institute a news dissemination system that includes a "what it means" note in distributing news to the media and market. This does not mean adding another layer of disclosure since it would be using previously known information in a summary form. Attention to language, quotes and headlines is another change to corporate reporting that is easily achieved if the mindset is adjusted to how media reporting takes place. Formatting and presenting news attractively, with dot points and subheadings, can also make information more accessible and readable for busy media reporters.

The mechanics of news distribution is another easy adjustment companies can make, with a lot of this involving a simple attuning of systems to what makes a journalist's job easier. News going out earlier in the day rather than late afternoon leaves more time for considered analysis. Having spokespersons available to talk to journalists improves reporting quality. Introducing a personally addressed news distribution system rather than mass news posting connects directly with reporters likely to be interested in company news.

Personal engagement with journalists is also a step towards improving the quality and extent of media coverage. This contact process can help journalists towards a better understanding of companies and it is also encouraged by media editors. While there is continuity of the same corporate story being told to journalists as there is with the investment community, journalists also want to know anecdotes around the business and people angles that add elements of interest to future reporting. Since informed media reporting means knowing about the larger strategy of companies, being prepared to talk to journalists about these aspects of corporate development on occasions separate from news announcements helps significantly with the quality of reporting.

As long as companies have a fundamental understanding of the role of the media – which is that it is an independent estate in society, with its function not being to reproduce corporate news releases – strong and beneficial relationships can be established with the media. The benefits for stock price have been established and this lays the groundwork for the investor relations function considering media relations in a different light. The concept of relationships, across a range of key stakeholders also represents another area of crossover between theory and practice.

Relationships and investor relations

When investor relations people talk about their work and how they go about it, they often talk about the importance of key relationships with stakeholders. This aspect of their jobs is not part of the definition of investor relations promulgated by the National Investor Relations Institute in the US and yet it plays an important part of self-described roles. Relationship management is also a strand of public relations theory developed in 2000 by John Ledingham. He argued there should be a shift away from a focus on messages being developed for stakeholders, towards more emphasis on the quality of relationships with them, which would also lead to a better definition of how public relations roles are actually implemented. This crossover of theory and practice not only substantiates a reason investor relations practitioners give relationships a priority but it also provides a template for measuring the effectiveness of relationship building in the practice of communication. Separately to the development of theory in relationship management is research that establishes that the quality of investor relationships is actually a component of value and a market based asset for listed corporations.

The basis of Ledingham's view is that, by accepting that managing relationships with stakeholders is the driving force of communication, it implies that effective relationships are those that are mutually beneficial and the extent to which this is achieved sets up a system for measuring effectiveness. Ledingham established five dimensions for measuring the quality of relationships between an organization and stakeholders and they are a useful template for expressing what IROs would see as effective relationships. The first dimension is trust, or the extent to which an organization does what it says it will do. The second dimension is openness, or how prepared a company is to share its plans for the future. Third is involvement, indicating how engaged an organization is with its community of stakeholders. Fourth is investment, pointing to the resources a company devotes to considering the welfare of stakeholders. Fifth is commitment, outlining the extent to which an organization wants to perpetuate relationships with stakeholders.[7]

The first two dimensions, trust and openness, sum up a lot of what investor relations strives towards in practice. The other dimensions describe how investor relations works as it follows through a corporate calendar of events, seeking to build bridges with its key stakeholders of the investment community, shareholders and the media. The annual report, conference calls and investor days can all be seen from the perspective of relationship-building and investing in the welfare of stakeholders by giving access to information and meeting the management team. Sometimes this connection is through the written word or certain actions, at other times through a physical presentation. Without IROs actually realizing the relevance of a theory of public relations, the way they go about their jobs enacts the dimensions of relationship management. What investing stakeholders want is to develop an understanding of corporate stories and feel they have a sense of companies being frank with them about how well strategies are being implemented. Stakeholders are prepared to extend trust if they have a sense that there is a strong connection with communication, disclosure and the investment proposition. In this way, relationships span communication values and the content of the corporate story, providing a measure for how well the process is being implemented.

Research has also been done on the connection between relationships and value, from the perspective of thinking about investors and the investment community as customers. In a sense this brings in the marketing aspect of NIRI's definition of investor relations. The research covered similar characteristics to those Ledingham used and also emphasized the extent to which relationships were reciprocal. The conclusion was that where relationships were seen to be working well, there were positive investor relations outcomes, such as lowering the cost of capital and improving stock liquidity and analyst coverage. The research did not imply relationships that might breach disclosure or insider trading guidelines but simply introducing a human and service dimension to connections with the investment community achieved positive outcomes. Successful relationships were built simply from companies nurturing trust, meeting regularly and meeting the information needs of the investment community. These processes were also valuable in building new relationships with potential investors.[8]

Similar relationship principles apply to companies and the media. The greater the strength of human connection, the more trust there is between organizations and journalists, while recognizing that daily objectives can differ. Firmer relationships enable journalists to call regarding background to other stories they are writing and this in turn builds in reciprocity to the relationship.

As companies build and strengthen relationships, they create opportunities to tell their corporate stories and establish a firmer basis for the tests of narrative rationality. The combination of a human dimension with those of trust and openness in relationships achieves a greater inclination for stakeholder audiences to assign coherence and truth to the information companies disclose. Relationships with analysts, shareholders, the wider investment community and journalists have different structures as the numbers in these groups vary. It is easier to have close, personal relationships with a few key analysts, institutional shareholders and journalists who know the story than it is with a large band of retail shareholders. Seen from a marketing perspective, the intensity of effort on closer connections is a standard characteristic of relationship-building. Nevertheless, the starting point for all relationships is similar. If companies set out with a communication intention based on trust and openness, they are well advanced in the process of building relationships that add value.

Competing for capital in competitive markets

Some common phrases that relate to the work and objectives of investor relations are that its purpose is aimed at helping companies be more competitive in raising capital and that its enactment, through communication, contributes to achieving a lower cost of capital. These terms also highlight several aspects of theory, from the perspectives of economics and communication.

It was the economist Joseph Schumpeter, in the 1930s, who highlighted the importance of channelling capital to its best use to promote economic growth. Over many decades in economics there has been a longstanding argument about what causes economic growth. Some argue that finance follows growth and so assume away the role of financial markets. Others, following Schumpeter's original influence, see finance and financial intermediaries as being the primary cause of growth. While the debate cannot be resolved here, following Schumpeter's path intersects with the role of financial and investor communication. Schumpeter's influence has several implications. One element of Schumpeter's view was that channelling capital to entrepreneurs leads to innovation, creating new products and new markets, sometimes replacing older technologies in a process Schumpeter described as "creative destruction". Another concept from Schumpeter is that it is financial intermediaries, such as banks and funds, which channel capital from investors towards projects and companies to create innovation and economic growth. In this way, financial intermediaries diversify risk, by pooling investors' funds in portfolios across a number of investments. This process also bridges the term of investing horizons, by giving investors, who might only have short-term options, a chance to participate in longer-term opportunities with possibly higher returns. In this way, financial intermediaries are playing an important role in the economic allocation of capital and increasing the efficiency of investment. They reallocate funds, from investors with excess capital, to firms which have a shortage of capital but provide investment opportunities which show attractive investment returns.[9]

Competition for this best use of capital takes place among companies as they launch appeals to investors, whether they are individuals, institutions or financial intermediaries, to share in potential growth. This competitive process is not just restricted to numbers governing capital allocation but brings in the wider communications process of companies demonstrating they have the strategies and management potential to deliver on the investment promise they are putting forward. In this sense, financial and investor communication helps explain how an organization provides an attractive vehicle for the investment of capital. It also demonstrates how that capital will be invested in the strategies of a business. In fulfilling these functions, investor relations is also playing a role in the wider capital allocation process of an economy. In Schumpeterian terms, investor relations, by steering capital towards its best use, is contributing directly to economic growth.

The concept of capital as it relates to organizations was also broadened by the French sociologist Pierre Bourdieu, who noted that as well as using economic capital, companies create cultural capital, through building the knowledge and skills of employees, and also social capital from their wider role in society. The contribution of communication to sharpening competitive positions in relation to all these aspects of capital has been developed by public relations scholar Ihlen. Applying this to investor and financial communication establishes not only a strong functional connection but also a substantiation from a differing perspective of the wider economic value of this type of communication. For Bourdieu, the competition for capital was a battlefield and language a weapon in improving understanding and creating a more competitive position for attracting and creating capital. Since capital is scarce, in demand and creates differences, there is justification in competing for it, with communication a tool for doing this effectively.

Research has noted the many ways in which communication contributes to lowering cost of capital. A common conclusion is that effective communication with the investment community and the media reduces information asymmetry. Lack of information and poor understanding of corporate stories are the enemies in this equation, since they lead to wider bid-ask spreads and higher volatility of stocks. Whether or not one adopts the efficient market hypothesis, information is the life blood of markets and the more effectively it is expressed and communicated, the greater the influence it will have on the cost of capital equation. The mathematical version of the cost of capital equation involves a weighted combination of the cost of debt, with interest rate the outcome of credit rating, and the cost of the equity component essentially being the outcome of a combination of expected return and risk premium. These concepts, while obviously having a mathematical objectivity, also have subjective components. Credit rating and risk are the outcome of assessments by stakeholders who are on the receiving end of the corporate narrative. They are being asked to respond to narrative rationality as they absorb corporate facts, figures and story from companies that present to them.

Whether companies are competing for capital, applying capital or seeking to lower the cost of capital, there is a case on a theoretical and practical level that financial and investor communication plays an important role in the overall process.

Conclusion

The crossover of theory and the practice in financial and investor communication has six dimensions. First is the importance of developing a corporate narrative, since this is a reflection of how communication takes place among all of us. Second is the value, in competitive and stock price terms, that comes from putting forward that narrative persuasively, adopting rhetoric and the psychological aspects of persuasion in conveying the corporate perspective. Third, communication of the corporate story is a vital link in reconciling disclosure with the investment proposition, which in turn supports investor confidence. Fourth, effective media relations, which research shows adds value to stock price, warrants it having a higher priority in the practice of investor relations. Fifth, relationships not only have value in themselves in building trust but provide a way of measuring effectiveness in investor relations. And sixth, communication has economic and corporate value in making companies more competitive in raising capital and lowering its cost.

It is possible to use these concepts in a formulation that combines theory and practice in financial and investor communication. The application of narrative (N), presented rhetorically and persuasively (R+P) and in a way that reconciles disclosure with communication values (D+C), to the media (M) as well as other key stakeholders, with whom building relationships (R) adds value and makes corporations more competitive in the race for capital (K), in combination make a positive contribution to stock price.

Presented arithmetically, we have:

$$N + (R+P) + (D+C) + M + R + K = \text{financial and investor communication} = \text{stock price}$$

A magic formula? Perhaps that is going too far but at least it substantiates the proposition that stock price is more of a story than a number.

Table 14.1 A template for combining theory and practice in financial and investor communication

Theorist/research area	Contribution	Crossover	Practical elements
Rhetoric	Reason, emotion, character.	Content, style, reputation.	Informative and open disclosure, presented by people of character.
James Grunig	Excellence is in two-way symmetrical communication.	Adopted in NIRI definition of investor relations but one-way communication and persuasion, also relevant.	Disclosure accounts for investor needs but also includes a one-way corporate perspective and story.
John Ledingham	Effective public relations based on building mutually beneficial relationships, which also sets up an alternative way of measuring effectiveness.	Achieved through trust, openness and commitment, with relationship quality being the measure of effectiveness.	Relationships internally build content of the corporate story, with mutually beneficial relationships with the investment community determining successful communication.

Table 14.1 (cont.)

Theorist/research area	Contribution	Crossover	Practical elements
Ihlen/Bourdieu	Building capital – economic, social and cultural – defines competitive position, with communication the tool for competing.	Communication and language help corporations build economic capital, which is used to employ people and make a social contribution.	Communication a factor in raising capital, explaining returns from it and the value from shared returns with investors and society.
Michael Porter	Five competitive forces define corporate strategy.	Information on industry structure improves understanding of competitive advantage and barriers to entry.	Industry positioning moves stories away from being company-centric and adds objective support for strategy.
Peter Drucker	The central purpose of business is to create a customer, giving business two functions – marketing and innovation.	Marketing is a component of NIRI's definition of investor relations.	Creating a corporate story and communicating it are central to marketing a company's investment proposition.
Joseph Schumpeter	Financial markets are central to economic growth by channelling capital to entrepreneurs.	Successful businesses compete to raise capital and debt at the lowest price.	A prime objective of any investor relations programme is lowering the cost of capital.
Markowitz/ Sharpe	The basis of modern portfolio theory is maximizing return while minimizing risk.	While return is critical, portfolio managers also assess risk and correlations of returns in portfolios.	An important element of narrative around financial performance is risk management.
Eugene Fama	The basis of the efficient market hypothesis is that stock prices reflect all information known to the market.	Information provided to markets combines facts, numbers and narrative.	Information, and how it is communicated, moves markets.
Robert Shiller	Stock markets fluctuate on the basis of emotion, not rationality.	Even at times of "irrational exuberance", information influences stock pricing.	NIRI's definition of investor relations advises providing information to achieve fair value for stocks.
Andrew Lo	"Survival of the richest" typifies the adaptive markets hypothesis.	Focused on survival, investment managers have to adapt to changing conditions around risk and reward.	Marketing an investment story requires an amalgamation of a company story with market conditions.
Alfred Rappaport	The primary goal for companies is to improve the wealth of shareholders, with shareholder value a different concept to increasing profit.	The fundamental purpose of investor communication is to give investors the information to forecast drivers of value.	Shareholders are one of a number of stakeholders for the modern corporation, but value drivers remain an important story component.

Table 14.1 (cont.)

Theorist/research area	Contribution	Crossover	Practical elements
Milton Friedman	The social responsibility of business is to increase profits.	Earnings are still critical, even in the current era of "environment, social and governance" criteria for investment.	Communicating around the wider benefits of increasing profits creates a story that straddles the interests of investors and the wider community.
Simon Schama	In history, landscape only becomes familiar through explanation of man's contact with it.	Companies and their industry environments are inseparable.	Since analysts rely on peer comparisons, corporate stories add value by including their industry sector and surrounding conditions.
Walter Fisher	The "narrative paradigm" is a way of describing human communication – we tell stories and hearers test their likelihood of being true.	Investors want to hear corporate stories and are well-qualified in testing their validity, on the basis of whether stories makes sense, and ring true.	Facts, numbers and narrative in corporate stories establish a basis for education and building credibility.
Marshall Ganz	In social movements, stories build shared identity and motivate people to action.	Sharing business challenges with investors helps them see management qualities in implementing strategy.	Corporate stories emanate from sharing a history of progress and meeting challenges, creating a sense of narrative for investors to pass on.
Daphne Jameson	Narrative discourse drives management action, helping to make sense of the past, cope with the present and plan for the future.	Use of corporate stories in business makes them more memorable and helps numbers explain cause and effect.	Extending management stories into the investment sphere broadens understanding of how businesses work.
Froud, Sukhdev, Leaver and Williams	"Financialization" requires companies to align strategies with numerical performance and explain strategy outcomes.	"Financialization" in changing markets can lead to a gap between narrative and actual performance.	Communication around management initiatives reconciles promise and performance in this context.
Warren Buffett	People should invest in companies they understand, run by people they trust.	For easily understood businesses that will survive for the long term, Buffett's favourite holding period is "forever".	Open communication about how businesses work and perform builds understanding and trust.
Benita Steyn	Corporate strategy can only be successful from communicating about it, recognizing a need to educate stakeholders.	Strategic communication with stakeholders necessarily involves one-way as well as two-way communication.	Stakeholder engagement is important in investor relations, involving building a community of understanding of the corporate perspective.

Table 14.1 (cont.)

Theorist/research area	Contribution	Crossover	Practical elements
Paul Argenti	Strategic communication has three drivers – meeting regulatory guidelines, explaining corporate complexity and building credibility.	Strategic communication must be integrated, linking investor relations to the brand, values and a single corporate message.	Investor relations cannot be isolated but to be effective must communicate a total corporate picture, integrated with all corporate communication.
Cees van Riel and Charles Fombrun	A corporate story is a framework for guiding interpretations of a company and conveying its essence.	A successful corporate story accounts for a competitive market and combines positioning, reputation and examples of achievements as proof.	A corporate story adds value by being relevant, realistic and responsive in encouraging open dialogue.
Janis Forman	An effective corporate story has four tiers – authenticity, fluency in the way it engages audiences, a capability to build trust and communication of corporate strategy.	Facts and numbers on their own do not build trust or achieve motivation.	Narrative that binds numbers and facts together can engage the imaginations of stakeholders and be a factor in investment decision-making.
Sabrina Helm	A company's reputation has a positive effect on investor loyalty, which reduces volatility and cost of capital.	Research shows good reputation builds confidence in financial performance and a preparedness to pay higher prices for it.	Reputation and trust are built over time, from performance and values, as well as communication about these things which in turn adds to wider appreciation.
Eugene Soltes	Corporate news dissemination to the business press has a positive effect on the markers of stock price.	Distribution of news to the media reaches investors through media coverage.	Distribution of news directly to journalists increases likelihood of coverage and adds positively to stock price.
Lily Fang and Joel Peress	Media coverage builds awareness of companies and, by generating investor interest, reduces cost of capital.	Achieving media coverage for corporate news has positive investor relations outcomes.	The positive effects of achieving media coverage are enhanced by building media relationships and improving news values in disclosure.
David Solomon and Eugene Soltes	Investor returns are improved by investors participating in one-on-one meetings with companies, confirming the value from maintaining this type of investor contact.	These meetings cannot go beyond public disclosure but benefit investors by adding to their information mosaic which informs decision-making.	Within regulated disclosure regimes, one-on-one meetings with investors are a practice that is beneficial to investors and companies.

Table 14.1 (cont.)

Theorist/research area	Contribution	Crossover	Practical elements
Ben Graham and David Dodd	Management may properly take some interest in the market price of the shares.	The responsibility of management, in the interests of shareholders, includes establishing a fair value for, and marketability of, stock.	Investor relations is necessarily of primary concern to senior management of corporations, since it links strategy, communication and investment.
Herbert Simons and Jean Jones	"Coactive persuasion" comes about when both sides are aware of each other's standpoints but are open to persuasion taking place.	Persuasion in investor relations involves building from shared premises, providing credible information around strategy and industry.	When performance does not meet expectations, persuasion comes from openness and broad explanation rather than minimizing information made publicly available.
Robert Cialdini	"Cognitive shorthands" are psychological principles that influence people to decide in a suggested way.	Outlining less palatable alternative strategies influences people to agree with strategies management has chosen.	Giving insights into corporate decision-making influences people to see management quality.
Michael Pfau and Hua-Hsin Wan	Stakeholders are not equal nor have compatible goals so persuasion plays a critical role in negotiation.	Credible information, in the form of facts, numbers and narrative can be persuasive in changing perceptions.	Providing information stakeholders want can gain their support and build credibility.
Arvid Hoffmann, Joost Pennings and Simone Wies	In integrating finance, marketing and communication, investor relations build customer relationships with investors.	Investor relationship marketing has a positive influence on the markers of stock price and builds competitive advantage.	Building collaborative relationships with the investment community nurtures trust and commitment.
Marc Epstein and Krishna Palepu	Fuller disclosure in financial reports gives analysts the information they need and affects stock prices positively.	Corporate communication strategies benefit from being based around giving analysts information they find helpful.	Communicating an insider's perspective on strategy establishes a value proposition in the way analysts are seeking.
Christian Hoffmann and Chrisitan Fieseler	Non-financial information, in implying future performance, is equally as important for investors as financial information, which explains historic performance.	While non-financial information, such as strategy, governance, brand and reputation, is valuable, quality of communication ranks as most important.	Communication capability of a company and CEO rank highly with investors.

Table 14.1 (cont.)

Theorist/research area	Contribution	Crossover	Practical elements
Baruch Lev	Information not on balance sheets is what the stock market values so, to win investors over, this is what companies should communicate.	Improved disclosure, beyond statutory minimums, has a positive effect on the markers of stock price.	In addition to written information, the tone of frank communication also matters.
Elaine Henry	Framing financial performance in positive language creates a favourable impression on investors, with longer releases a turn off.	While needing to match the circumstances of performance, language influences interpretation.	How information is communicated, as well as content, influences investors.
Sheri Erickson, Marsha Weber and Joann Segovia	When performance does not meet expectation, companies resort to "image restoration", with corrective action the most effective strategy.	Denial and blame are less effective strategies than fixing problems and explaining actions taken.	Image can be restored, in the face of things not going according to plan, by taking corrective action and communicating about it.
Randolph Barker and Kim Gower	Corporate stories, in being memorable and easy to understand, reduce organizational complexity and create vision.	Corporate stories are a basis for sharing knowledge and showing cause and effect.	While needing to be authentic in connecting events to corporate information, tone and content of corporate stories are persuasive.
Daphne Jameson	The way a story is told, as well as what it says, matters.	In accounting for what investors want, these stakeholders become co-creators with companies in shaping corporate stories.	Corporate stories, in converting information into narrative, accompanied by numbers and visual material, influence understanding.
John Kay	Converting a short-term focus into a longer-term view comes down to improving the quality of engagement between investors and companies.	"High quality, succinct narrative reporting should be strongly encouraged."	Instead of large quantities of data, companies benefit from providing information directed to creating long-term value. ·
Lynn Stout	Single-mindedly pursuing shareholder value is harmful to the interests of a corporation, its shareholders and the public.	Companies should be run in the interests of a wide group of stakeholders, unhampered by shareholder value.	Shareholders not only have varying time horizons but also want to see corporations well governed as participants in society.

Table 14.1 (cont.)

Theorist/research area	Contribution	Crossover	Practical elements
Vassilis Papadakis	While M&A deals may fail for many differing reasons, good communication is a common ingredient in successful transactions.	Communication is influential in the progress of M&A transactions but critical in the implementation phase, which determines ultimate value.	In M&A, communication outlines the deal logic, brings together the warring factions and creates a vision for the new combined entity.
Hongzhi Gao, Jenny Darroch, Damien Mather and Alan MacGregor	Articulating corporate strategy in IPOs with clarity and consistency is a signal to analysts of potential positive returns.	Communicating strategy focused on specific market targets is more effective than when broad-based.	Strategy articulation is a thread through the IPO roadshow and beyond to stock exchange listing.
John Deverell	Crisis involves three elements of surprise – time taken to realize its seriousness, how quickly pressure builds and the close connection between stock price and handling a crisis well.	Effective crisis communication, and preparation for it, are critical factors in handling them successfully and limiting the damage.	Issue monitoring and scenario anticipation set up crisis preparation and management.

Notes

1 Fisher, WR, "Narration as a Human Communication Paradigm: The Case of Public Moral Argument", *Communication Monographs* 51, 1984, pp 1–6
2 Fisher (1984), pp 6–7
3 Bruner, J, "The Narrative Construction of Reality", *Critical Inquiry*, 18, 1991
4 Brown, RE, "Epistemological Modesty: Critical Reflections on Public Relations", *Public Relations Inquiry* 1 (1), 2011, pp 89–105
5 Lev (2012), p 147
6 www.theiirc.org
7 Ledingham, JA, "Relationship Management: A General Theory of Public Relations", in Botan and Hazleton (2006), p 471
8 Hoffmann, AOI, Pennings, JME and Wies, S, "Relationship marketing's role in managing the firm-investor dyad", *Journal of Business Research* 64 (2011), pp 896–903
9 Sinha, T, "The Role of Financial Intermediation in Economic Growth: Schumpeter Revisited", in SB Dahiya and V Orati (eds) *Economic Theory in the Light of Schumpeter's Heritage* (Spellbound Publishers, Rohtak, India: 2001)

Index

Printed in Great Britain
by Amazon